THE TECHNOLOGICAL INTROJECT

THE TECHNOLOGICAL INTROJECT

Friedrich Kittler between Implementation and the Incalcuable

JEFFREY CHAMPLIN AND
ANTJE PFANNKUCHEN, EDITORS

Fordham University Press: New York 2018

Fordham University Press has no responsibility for the persistence or accuracy of URLs for external or third-party Internet websites referred to in this publication and does not guarantee that any content on such websites is, or will remain, accurate or appropriate.

Fordham University Press also publishes its books in a variety of electronic formats. Some content that appears in print may not be available in electronic books.

Visit us online at www.fordhampress.com.

Library of Congress Cataloging-in-Publication Data available online at https://catalog.loc.gov.

Printed in the United States of America

20 19 18   5 4 3 2 1

First edition

CONTENTS

THE TECHNOLOGICAL INTROJECT

INTRODUCTION

Jeffrey Champlin and Antje Pfannkuchen

Born on June 12, 1943, Friedrich Kittler left us on October 18, 2011. He had been living and teaching in Berlin. At once a renegade and an outstanding scholar with foundational tendencies, he has left his mark on American discursive practices. An extreme advocate of critical innovation, Kittler opens fields of inquiry that surpass in aim and range the boundaries of academic disciplines and scientific discourse. Addressing the arts and sciences responsibly—if with skeptical acumen—Kittler enjoins us to review and revise what we think we know about the premises that continue to make established perspectives viable. His ability to capture the essence of technology and its poetic counterparts casts a wide net, building on a unique understanding of network vitality. A world class techno-scientific theorist, he also speaks to our *need* for poetic utterance, especially when it comes to gauging the flex of scientific muscle.

Kittler's adherence to poetic claims and aspirations gave him a keen and consistent sense of what counts as well as that which is *discounted* in terms of the cultural and scientific life-forms that bind us. He was unafraid of visiting with the abysses known to a select aggregate of seers: the far-sighted poets, philosophical purveyors of truth or contestation, and intuitive scientific minds of our era whose relentless probes populated his oeuvre. A highly refined troubleshooter, Kittler, for his part, has consistently demonstrated a flair for ferreting out the snags and catastrophic urges of modernity. In many respects, the most contemporary and timely of thinkers—he could skip with joyful assertion from random access memory to optical media and engineering formalism, from Pynchon to Pink Floyd—he always had strong recourse to tradition, even if his intention was to break with recognizable types of knowledge in edgy and determined ways. As with those exemplary critical minds that have grappled in the twentieth century with effects of the scientific will to power, Kittler, too, reserves a special place for Goethe, the unbeatable poet-scientist and statesman of the eighteenth century. As monument and access code to many of our current obsessions regarding the scientific incursion and poetic positing powers, Goethe gave the modern German language its starting point.

For the purposes of this volume, we are tempted to view and transpose the Kittler phenomenon through the lens of those who have made radical inroads into the meaning and force of media technology, but also in light of the genuinely innovative contributions made by younger scholars, coming up in the yet undecided aftermath of Kittlerian thought and praxeology. What are the practices and syntax of inventiveness to which we can attach Kittler's far-reaching influence? What is the nature of the specific institutional disorders and insurrections for which his name has already agitated and will become known in the future of our ever-intersecting disciplines? How do the kinship networks that Kittler set up, and also unquestionably destroyed, continue to impose meaning on the way we approach our tasks and orient research today? For, despite his reputation as renegade, Kittler also formed a significant swath of contemporary research habits and institutional values—most emphatically in the German university system, mother of all higher learning facilities, as Kant justly insisted. What happens in Germany does not stay in Germany, but infiltrates, shakes up, consternates, and builds in the United States in ways that we have yet to discern and negotiate.

Just as fabled New School philosopher Reiner Schürmann refused to write in German, his mother tongue, and went on to propose a politically radical (left) reading of Heidegger in English and French, some of the contributors in this volume have also struggled with the formidable challenges presented by mutations in German thought and caesural histories. In many respects, determined and overdetermined, Friedrich Kittler has forced one's hand, compelling even the most delicate scholar to approach the pockmarked landscape of disaster that Kittler does not hesitate to address in his outspoken work. Some contributors take a U-turn when it comes to some of the controversial outlets, but others encounter the work's exigencies with dare and creativity, consternation and rigor. One often finds embedded in these writings a resistance to the very culture that sponsors unavoidable thinking blocs. We would like to keep some focus on the way things, following Kittler's lead, have inflected a newly minted German-American vocabulary of technological inquiry and theoretical insight.

The shaping of media studies, a field of transdisciplinary intensity and commitment, originates with several crossovers into American resumptions of German forms of questioning. Of course, by now, these entities have been sufficiently hybridized so that what may appear as "German" may be a graft of what is tagged as "American." These cultures have become so acutely intertwined and reciprocally occupied that one cannot always tell with convincing acuity what belongs in one or the other of the categoremes—what we are abbreviating as "German" and "American." To the extent that our histories contaminate and illuminate, appeal and question in ways that remain provocative and essential, we are in the place where reading the other implicates at all times reading something like an assembled self, a historicized and hermeneutically engaged self. Many of our contributors have codetermined the fate of letters and historical correspondence by staying in touch with Kittler or taking up residency in flagged sectors of his work. Bernhard Siegert and Bernhard Dotzler, highly influential exegetes of media theory and leaders in the areas of institution-building, continue to make their marks both in Germany and the United States. Avital Ronell has taken media technology on an American road of political and ethical contestation, while Sam Weber and Laurence Rickels have made their own dazzling contributions to the thinking and practice of technology mandated by the works of Sigmund Freud and Martin Heidegger.

Friedrich Kittler was the doubled and divided disciple of Freud and Heidegger, whose influence he never wished nor was fully able to shake. He eventually closed ranks with Michel Foucault, but this does not represent an evolutionary contradiction to the extent that Foucault himself claims this double provenance. In the United States, his work continues to urge innovation and polemics regarding the role of technology in the spirited history of American politics. For Heidegger, America was the site of a particularly ghostless appropriation of technology. As Rickels argues in *The Case of California*, the continued exchanges between America and Germany remain active and richly problematic. Ronell of course has been very frank, if not Francophile, about her weighted ambivalence toward certain areas of the German unthought. Her friendship with Kittler is therefore all the more illuminating as concerns the continued probe and divergence that these cultures claim and, in many cases, disavow. One of the subthemes of the volume involves the friendship—and aversion—that define the neighboring texts that the contributions set in motion. The struggle that Kittler joyfully promoted continues to serve as a crucial source of inventive writing and its satellite phenomena. We would like to underscore the complicities and bridges as well as the abysses that have had to be cleared by the contributors to the volume. Not everyone can endorse some of his more controversial stances. Yet, the unquestionable ebullience of his work, its freshness and provocation, require us to abide with its steely edges.

The book's title, *The Technological Introject*, indicates a struggle with the unconscious drives that humanity externalizes in its processing machines. Kittler taught us that technology refuses to hold out beyond the subject, and instead crosses it—both traversing it and blacking out its pretensions. In Ferenczi, Freud, and Abraham, introjection speaks to the ego in its endeavor to maintain itself. For Torok, it more specifically provides a mechanism that processes trauma. In Kittler's analyses, though, technology works over the subject, which it dissolves, or otherwise submits, to inscription.

The promise and challenge of Kittler's work persists in its profound, though still not wholly unleashed, academic reception. These texts probe territories that open dossiers left for us by Kittler and that will help to constitute his legacy in a rigorous and lasting way. The essays in this volume respond to the restless wealth of Kittler's thinking with resplendent linkages, framings, and synthesizing insights that testify to its unsettled, and unsettling, power. Although they resist simple paraphrase, some indication of the volume's four headings will allow the reader to provisionally map the circuits at issue. The collection opens with essays that invite contemporary readers to engage with Kittler through new tropic gestures. Part I, "The Kittlerian Turn," leads off with Rüdiger Campe, who codes "implementation" as Kittler's operative reformulation of the humanities. Casting an arc from Vico's institutional "human things" to Hegel's "objective spirit," he positions Kittler's technology on the leading edge of self-exteriorizing culture rather than as a projection of the subject. Hans Ulrich Gumbrecht likewise envisions a broad historical sweep to Kittler's work, linking it to Heidegger's history of being but explicating a shift in emphasis through the planned third volume of *Musik und Mathematik* on the Middle Ages. Exploring Kittler's relation to manias and delusions, Bernhard Dotzler casts media as a play with the promise of interconnection that at the same time increases the loneliness of the subject. From this seemingly barren ground, he takes a political twist on Kittler's polarity between revolutionary new ideas and assured conservatism. Elizabeth Weber traces the mourning of love in Kittler's near-obsession with the darker sides of the world—be this tangled in the wars that use and produce media technologies, or the black holes and boxes that seem to swallow an arcane knowledge but on another level call to be decrypted and hacked free. From his early reading of Bettina von Arnim onward, Weber honors Kittler's almost melancholic desire to free love from a determined fate in scientific-technological discourse.

Part II, "The Romantic Temptation," moves back to the authors that drew Kittler's early attention. Samuel Weber situates Kittler's project as a critique of the metaphysical assumptions of the humanities in favor of a material conception of media that works through commands, data, and addresses. Against the danger of reification in the media model, Weber reads Hölderlin to find a concern for the incalculable in Kittler. Antje Pfannkuchen revisits Kittler's reading of romantic writing, which had assigned codified roles to those who write and those who make others write along largely gendered lines. By showing nature as an active force in the writing ordeal, Pfannkuchen detects a disruption in the confluence of nature/woman. Writing the book of nature, woman, in the sense accorded by Nietzsche, reanimates Eve as the first scientist. Jeffrey Champlin follows Kittler's "decentering" of "The Sandman" to a perplexingly stable moment of self-accused stupidity in the story. Expanding Kittler's logic of the double (*Doppelgänger*) through Hoffmann, Champlin brings back the text's marginalized siblings, challenging the prevalent Oedipal regime while elucidating Kittler's provocative naming of the historical "mutation" of the nuclear family.

Part III, "Live Transference," begins with Mert Bahadır Reisoğlu reading of Kittler's "Auto Bahnen / Free Ways" with Saussure's structural bar between signifier and signified as modeled in the separation between the two opposite lanes of the highway. With reliance on Lacan's speedups, he also takes us on a twisting journey from Heidegger's wooden paths (*Holzwege*) to the "furious pace" of automotive circulation. Dominik Zechner analyzes *Toward an Ontology of Media* as articulating a technological reading of ontology in *Being and Time* that Kittler then extends (against Heidegger's stated intent) into the late work after the "turn." In a linguistic-ontological swerve, Kittler famously once said, *"Es gibt Medien."* Working with the challenges of this richly layered appropriative phrase, Zechner explores the problematically posed juncture of acts of giving (*geben*) and media. Kittler could love Heidegger only through his own techno-materialist revision. This section continues with a compelling piece on "Man as a Drunken Town-Musician," where Chadwick Truscott Smith argues for bones as a remnant of human subjectivity in Kittler's generalized media network. In the process, he develops two ways of going back in time, through a system of media recursion that contrasts with literary recursion. With characteristic style and acumen, Laurence Rickels then pursues the juncture of technology and mourning in the post–World War II period through Kittler's 1988 essay "Media and Drugs in Pynchon's Second World War." He takes up the V-2 rocket in *Gravity's Rainbow* through the work of George Orwell, science fiction writing, and psychoanalysis to push questions of collective mourning to the limits of historical failure.

Part IV, "The Genealogy of Media," offers global interrogations of Kittler's work. Nimrod Reitman traces technologies of the voice through circuits of gender enabled by Kittler and Nietzsche. Developing a contrast to McLuhan and Lyotard, Hans-Christian von Herrmann proposes a reading of *Discourse Networks 1800/1900* geared toward educational reform. In his view, Kittler's goal was to recall the passing of the system that emerged around 1800 and emphasize a new awareness of media. Geoffrey Winthrop-Young traces Kittler's role in simultaneously creating and disturbing the tenets of the new discipline of media studies. He points out that Kittler refuses merely to define some of his most central terms, such as media. Instead of pursuing traditional means of exegesis and elaboration, he follows a recursive feedback loop between theorizing media and mediality that is timed eventually to self-destruct. In German theoretical developments, this dissolution coincides with the move from concepts of media to cultural techniques. Ute Holl conducts a reading of *Musik und Mathematik* that focuses on Kittler's relationship to music from the Greek songs of the sirens to digitally generated sounds. Cutting from *Soundgeschichte* to *Seinsgeschichte*, Kittler sees being "on music" as a mediated version of absorbing drugs when sounds take possession of the body. Bernhard Siegert concludes this part with a probing and forward-looking study of sound in the film *The Fly* that brings Kittler's technological analysis to animal studies and the posthuman fall of species hierarchy.

In an epilogue both celebratory and traversed by the spirits of mourning, Avital Ronell's performance piece follows a musical rhythm and the disclosure of an intricate history. She takes us on a trip—both highly personal and theoretically grounded—exploring zones of friendship, conjuring ghosts, tracing the parallel tracks that Kittler and she have traveled, and continue to visit.

On March 16, 2013, at the memorial conference *The Sirens Go Silent: Remembering Friedrich Kittler* at the Deutsches Haus at New York University, co-organized by Avital Ronell and Arne Höcker, we were honored by the presence and acute attunement of Helen Tartar. A friend to all intellectuals, Helen initiated the making of this book.

PART I

THE KITTLERIAN TURN

1

KITTLER'S HUMANITIES

On Implementation

Rüdiger Campe

Friedrich Kittler's media history has made its impact on the humanities less through theoretical statements than through the operative terms it has put to use. Its transformative qualities manifest not so much in the formal structure of argumentation as in the thorough processes of connecting theories, factual observations, and anecdotes. *Implementation* is such an operative term, and it stands for a specific procedure of tracing the human being in history, particularly its involvement with techniques and technology. The word takes hold in Kittler's vocabulary when he ceases to perform the critical judgment of the literary scholar, and it withdraws when he finally reveals the stakes of an underlying philosophy of being. No other word in Kittler's media history, however, bears witness as tenaciously to the traces of critical judgment within media history and to the conceptual claims of philosophy that had never been absent from it.[1]

IMPLEMENTATION: AN OPERATIVE CONCEPT

I'll start with a random example. After giving one of his signature analyses of information storage in computer architecture, Kittler continues: "If now, on the basis of this model, we return to the European history, it seems that the technologies of storage which are available at any given moment can be determined, with some plausibility, according to these parameters: static versus dynamic, solid state versus mechanical, RAM versus ROM. We should, however, not presuppose without further scrutiny that the storage systems of every possible culture have always been implemented as such."[2] What then follows is a rapid survey of this "European history." First, Kittler lists various phenomena from the physiology, anthropology, and cultural history of the human senses: literary and visual effects, details from the history of the book, episodes from the development of the printing press and the postal service, and examples from administration, education, and what has been called the experimentalization of man and nature in the nineteenth century. Regardless of whether such phenomena use technical processes or instruments, they are, in Kittler's (Heideggerian) use of the word, pretechnological. In contradistinction to the instrument or the tool that is used for a given purpose, the technology of the machine is its own point of departure for any possible use or application; and this is most radically so with the machine of all machines, the Turing machine. The phenomena Kittler mentions as indicative for "European history," are, for him, pretechnological practices and institutions. As such they "can be determined, with some plausibility, according to these functions (i.e., the essential functions of information storage) in the PC." In other words, pretechnological practices and devices become transparent as what they are in the media history of the human being when expressed in terms of technology.[3] Kittler adds that we should "not assume without questioning that the storage systems of every possible culture have always been implemented as such." All cultural phenomena reveal themselves as what they are in terms of the Turing machine; and all history—European history as well as the ethnography of "every possible culture"[4]—unfolds, vice versa, through the variety of solutions provided for those functions that technology and the computer have defined. This encapsulates what "to implement" means in Kittler's media history: applying and putting to work a solution relative to the technological function, and it thus makes it possible to connect the most diverse phenomena as instances of such function and application. The defining implementation is that of the most comprehensive technological system or the system that effectuates technology in its most comprehensive way at any given moment in history. Other pretechnological or technological solutions can be brought into connection with the defining implementation to the extent that they relate to the function it determines.

The verb *to implement* quoted above thus engenders and maintains the enormous stakes of a media-based account of "European history" and "every possible culture." Insofar as Kittler's project has been rightly termed "discourse networks" in the translation of his first book on media history,[5] implementation can be seen as that which organizes the net of the network. We use the word *implementation* in three domains. In the case of a law or an agreement, implementation occurs through some agency different from the legislative bodies, an institution charged specifically with the implementation. In economics and the social theory of organization, implementing refers to theoretical models, often from game theory, and their enactment. Finally, implementation is a term in computer technology. In Kittler, all three domains are at play.[6] There is no doubt, however, that the computer technology has the lead among the three domains. It might even be argued that the configuration of the three fields and the dominance of technology among them precisely express Kittler's purpose in using the term. The computer technology adds a different note to the legal and organizational meaning of implementation. When we speak of the implementing of law or procedure, the designated mechanism is putting something into effect that has previously been planned, formulated, and laid down. Different from hermeneutic application, the implementation presupposes that what has been planned, formulated, and laid down goes into effect as such. Hermeneutic application emphasizes instead the dialectic processes of mutual adaptation between the laws or rules on the one hand and the cases or instances to which they are applied on the other. In implementation, the law or the organizational strategy redefines the situation into which it is introduced. Computer technology gives the particular shade of application that is implementation an even further meaning. Computer technicians sometimes speak of implementation in a broad and unspecific sense. It then designates the installation of a specifically configured complex of hardware and software in industry, for military purposes, or according to some bureaucratic need. In this case, the technology of the computer is implemented in a nontechnological environment, the world. To implement an algorithm or code means, however, inserting a new element into an already existing technological system. The implemented algorithm does not impose the technological solution on a pretechnological world but it rather restructures an existing technological system from within itself, with the older system becoming the environment of the newly implemented system. Technological implementation does not only render effective what has been text (the law) or plan (the strategy) before. It makes a systemic complex operable within its environment (which may itself already have been a systemic complex of a lower order).

Finally, the technological meaning of *implementation* allows a further twist possible in using the word, a twist Kittler employs deliberately and frequently. Whereas the common way of using the term is to express the idea of making a given technological solution operative or effective, it also means by extension that the environment into which it is introduced can adapt to such a technological solution. In this case, it is not the code or algorithm that is implemented (i.e., inserted in an environment) but it is the environment into which the algorithm is inserted that is said to be implemented (i.e., rendered capable of adapting to a technological solution.) It is this extended meaning of implementation that lingers most visibly on the surface of Kittler's media history, turning it into a narrative of the increasing technologization of the world humans experience in history. Although highly visible in Kittler's narrative, this second meaning remains dependent on the first one: in the standard version of media history, the technological function introduces implementability into the world. Self-preparation of the world for implementation is an event of an altogether different order. We will return to it only with the final section of this essay.

To further elucidate how media history in its ordinary Kittlerian understanding proceeds through analyzing modes of implementation, two more questions are to be pursued. First, how does implementation structure the account of the histories it engenders and renders possible? This is a question that is addressed in the following section on the temporality of implementation. Second, what is the type of analysis that can be performed by an analysis of various modes of implementation? This question will be broached in the third section, a brief history of fundamental approaches in the humanities as we have known them up to Friedrich Kittler.

THE REVERSE TIME OF IMPLEMENTATION

How does implementation perform the function of structuring the human being's existence, in particular her physiology and senses, in media history? "Memories Are Made of You," the essay from which I quoted above, offers one of many versions of the story Friedrich Kittler has told in the last two decades of the previous century. It is the story that connects computer architecture intimately and methodically with Europe's history. The two decades of intense rewriting and retelling are often reminiscent of the way certain phenomenologists repeatedly described the perception of time, the structure of intersubjectivity, or the disclosure of the world through the human mind and our senses. Edmund Husserl, whom Kittler didn't particularly like, has been the first and maybe most persistent among them, followed by Maurice Merleau-Ponty. In their works, the same formula, the same description and analysis is resumed time and again; with a new word here and an added fact there, with a slight variation in this respect and a cautious step in another.[7] With Kittler, the one narrative that underlies the many stories he has been telling is, importantly, the narrative of implementation. In this context, it helps to look more closely at what defines the technological function of the operation in its double meaning of implementing a technological solution and rendering an area of the world implementable.

These are the first moves and turns in the storyline of "Memories Are Made of You": At the beginning, Kittler mentions briefly the mnemotechnics of ancient rhapsodists and orators. These *technai* of Old Europe's art of poetry and rhetoric, however, are excluded from the implementation-defined account of Western cultures and European history. What makes Kittler leave them aside is, obviously, that mnemotechniques does not result in duration and expansion beyond the reach of the individuals who have implanted the storage within themselves. Remaining within the realm of *technai*, poetical and rhetorical memorization devices offer no handhold for a takeover by technology, and hence no prospect of implementation in the Kittlerian use. Only when Egyptian, Greek, or Roman epigraphical inscriptions as well as the holy books of Jews and Christian have come into existence does a technology of memory become graspable. Only then storage reaches the level of implementation. This is so, more precisely, because only with the coexistence of these two modes of encoding and storage—and because of their difference in securing duration and spatial expansion—does the structural quality of implemented storage emerge: the opposition between static versus dynamic storage, rest and movement. For storage to be implemented (i.e., to be technological), it must be organized beyond a merely physical level in a pairing of two different states of a system. Only with this additional step can storage become the object of computation and switching. Being made computable and switchable is, in a word, what renders storing information a matter of implementation.

Taking the step Zero of implementation history (mnemotechnics) and its step One (static inscription versus movable holy books) into account already suffices in order to recognize the fundamental nature of the process. The essential nature, or rather counter-nature, is its temporal structure. This is what should be highlighted as the second point in reconstructing Kittler's use of the term *implementation*. In a reversal of what we usually call historical development, the history of implementation always necessarily jumps ahead of itself. More precisely, implementation in the secondary meaning of "rendering a moment of human existence implementable" can be read as the surface meaning of an ordinary historical development from an earlier to a later moment in time. But such historical development in the usual sense is possible only because of the reverse structure on the deeper, categorical, level. "Rendering this or that implementable" can only be understood from the point of view of the technological function to be implemented; and this function is the more advanced technological solution, and hence comes later in time. This is implementation's intrinsic definition and the intrinsic mechanism through which it engenders Kittler's standard media history. Implementation in its deeper meaning refers to what at each time in history is the most (or at least more) complete mode of an existing program or algorithm. This then determines not just the solution but the function for which solutions can be found.

Computer architecture thus has been the measure of the most complete existing state of implementation for Friedrich Kittler and his moment in time, and hence as the point of view from which he set out to tell the history of implementation. And this time, I assume, is still our time. In the story of implementation, Greek inscriptions and the epistles of Saint Paul emerge as articulated by a function that is ahead of them: in the case mentioned, the dichotomy of the static versus the dynamic state of storage systems. Implementation stories are stories reversed in time. It is always the algorithm or program, and the function as defined by them, that is effectuated by whatever counts as implementation. The nature of things, the nature of man— the lifeworld which Kittler for a long time would never mention without calling it "the so-called life world"—are sites of implementation to come. At the same time, implementation is nonteleological: technology is not another candidate for nature. Technology is implementability, and hence the genesis of the reversal of time and development into its own, cultural, form of history.

FROM VICO TO KITTLER: RECONCEPTUALIZING THE HUMANITIES

What kind of an enterprise is it to develop such a storyline with such a reversed temporal structure? The answer suggested in what follows reads Friedrich Kittler's work on the history of technology and its place in human existence as the latest version of the humanities as they have existed since Giambattista Vico.

Speaking of Kittler's humanities may seem to be in blatant violation of everything the humanities stand for; and in the eyes of other, Kittlerian, readers doing so may seem a fundamental misunderstanding of or even anathema to his work. In both cases, Kittler's professed antihumanism makes it indeed counterintuitive to think of Kittlerian media history as the further development of what has been called humanities in the Anglophone tradition, *sciences humaines* in France, and *Geisteswissenschaften* in German. The point here is indeed not to reclaim Kittler for any concept of humanism, given his professed antihumanistic stance at least in his media-historical work. Nor is the intention to reestablish a sense of idealism, however new, for this work. But this is not what the humanities—*les sciences humaines* or *die Geisteswissenschaften*—necessarily have been or what they are when properly understood in their meaning and purpose. From the beginning on, they have been a response to hard science—experimentation, calculation, and technology—on the part of what has not participated in the new science's formation since the sixteenth and seventeenth centuries. The humanities have always been responsive in nature, a reconceptualization of knowledge within their own domain, but also in the domain of the hard sciences. In the traces of this enterprise, Kittler's media history is the most advanced to date.

Thinking of Kittler's writings as contributions to the humanities and their permanent revision is in accordance with Kittler's own development. At two important junctures of his work, he inscribed his project into the humanities or rather, in German terms, the sciences of the Hegelian spirit, the *Geisteswissenschaften*. First, in the years while he was working on his first truly Kittlerian book-length study, *Discourse Networks*, he organized a lecture series (1978) under the decisively German title *Austreibung des Geistes aus den Geisteswissenschaften* (literally, driving the spirit out of the sciences of the spirit).[8] As the title indicates, Kittler mounts an attack on the humanities or *Geisteswissenschaften*, but he has also the intention of taking them over. Whether the takeover was meant to be hostile is irrelevant as long as we keep the revisionist character of the humanities in mind. At this point in his own thinking, Kittler was just on the brink of juxtaposing the reconstruction of romantic literature as an effect of hermeneutics around 1800—his older project from literary history—with his new, 1900 project. This new project concerned the emergence of electric media and their destructive impact on romantic accomplishments such as authorship, spiritual education through the voice of the mother, and Schleiermacher's general hermeneutics. In accordance with the envisaged two-part structure of *Discourse Networks*, Kittler announced his quest for a new form of humanities as the dispersal of the romantic concept. This concept had been, according to Kittler, emphatically one (the spirit, the mother, the author), and as such it had been pursued in German academia since Wilhelm Dilthey. Kittler's first attack on the traditional humanities, in double alliance with Foucault and Derrida, was the deconstruction of their monolithic understanding. In an elegant move, he argued that ethnography, psychoanalysis, and Saussurian linguistics share in the heritage of the one spirit in the sciences of the spirit following the end of romanticism, and he maintains that no philosophical master discourse could ever unite these three heirs again. The new humanities, according to Kittler in 1978, are not one.[9] In 1998, after developing the story of implementation for twenty years, Kittler gave a lecture series under the title "A cultural history of the analysis of culture."[10] This was the second juncture of his inscribing himself in the enterprise of the humanities or *Geisteswissenschaften*. The lecture series from 1998 aimed at proposing media history as the final and indeed reunited form of all possible theories of cultures, the very ground in which to anchor the history of all attempts to cope with human existence in history in a scholarly and, indeed, scientific form. But it accomplished the work of reunification through a diligently controlled storyline rather than any new, philosophical, theory. The story of implementation unfolded and repeated itself in Kittler's work incessantly and methodically between his early and his later statement on the tasks and failures of the humanities. It had a prehistory in literary criticism which motivated the first part of *Discourse Networks* on the formation of romantic literature; and it found a philosophical commentary beyond itself in his late work on the Heideggerian disclosure of truth in the *Odyssey* and in the school of Pythagoras and the Pythagoreans.[11]

Implementation can be understood as specifically reformulating the basic operation that occurs in the humanities in one way or another. Put differently, it is the latest reassessment of the humanities' theoretical procedure to date, rather than the ultimate theory of its procedures. In order to establish the point, one would have to begin, as Kittler did in *Cultural History of the Theory of Culture*, with Giambattista Vico. In this context, I can only offer an abbreviated version: For Vico, we may paraphrase the operation in question as a "creation out of ignorance." Creation out of ignorance, alias poetic creation, is Vico's human counterpart to the model of creation by the Jewish-Christian Creator God which, although it was also creation out of nothing, had full self-awareness of its own doing.[12] Creation out of nothing accompanied by the self-awareness of the creator belongs to a history that, as such, neither allows nor requires a theory of poetical or cultural invention. It is the Pentateuch's history of creation and redemption. On the other hand, all cultural history is, for Vico, distinctively pagan. From the smallest units—the *picciole favolette* of myth and metaphor—to the three fundamental cultural forms of establishing human culture—divination, burial, and marriage—all such acts of inventing (pagan) culture are destined to secure duration in time and expansion in space. They organize time itself in divination, the realm of the living in marriage, and the time-space of the dead in burial. In each of the three cases, these acts of cultural invention proceed tentatively, out of ignorance and under the latent supervision of the Creator-God and his embracing authorship. The three core elements of spatiotemporal duration, divination, burial, and marriage Vico calls the principal *cose humane*. Human things or human matters are the elements of the *nuova scienza* or humanities in the material and the metahistorical sense. They are "cultural things" insofar as they organize space and time in proto-historical forms.

The operation which fulfills the equivalent function in Wilhelm Dilthey's *Geisteswissenschaften* is more familiar to us. It comes as no surprise that Kittler, the editor and spiritus rector of *Austreibung des Geistes aus den Geisteswissenschaften*, gives no place to the godfather of German *Geisteswissenschaften*, Wilhelm Dilthey, in the *Cultural History of Cultural Theory*. But Dilthey is present in the guise of the heavily discussed Hegel's *Phenomenology of the Spirit*.[13] The defining operation in Dilthey's *Sciences of the Spirit* is in fact a generalized theorem from Hegel's *Phenomenology*, the theorem of objective spirit. In Hegel, the relevant forms of objective spirit emerge in the field of what he calls the ethical and the normative rules of family, law, and nation state.[14] While these are still restricted instances of what we may call institutions, in Dilthey whatever results from human creative production can be seen under the aspect of objective spirit: a poem and a novel, the furniture in our homes, and certainly also the law, the arts, the constitution, systems of education, forms of socialization, ways of practicing scientific knowledge and so on.[15] Again, all of these forms of objective spirit, or institutions, are material elements of culture as well as seminal patterns for providing duration in space and time. In contradistinction to Vico, however, the elements of culture in Dilthey's version of Hegel exhibit essentially a character of externalization and alienation in their production. Under its objective form, spirit no longer recognizes its own agency. Such externalization may be more obvious in Hegel than in Dilthey. But Dilthey's heirs in later decades, from Simmel to Lukács and Heidegger, more than make up for this lack in a broadly conceived type of humanities along the lines of Dilthey.[16]

With Vico's *cose humane* the inventiveness of people, the moment of poetic creation, is always transparent (even if it is, unlike God's creation, a creation out of ignorance of its own grounds and purposes). In contradistinction, the institutional forms of the objective spirit juxtapose interiority and exteriority in an emphatic manner. Kittler's operation of implementing technological solutions can be read as the third generation of the same type of operation—after Vico's invention as creating *cose humane* and Hegel and Dilthey's institution-building objective spirit. Kittlerian implementation—the implementation of technology whose sites of intervention are the human and the natural world—appears to reverse "invention out of ignorance." Implementation operates in a field where invention itself is organized beyond the alternative of creativity or ignorance, the field of technology. Further on, such invention beyond creativity or ignorance has learned from the emphasis on exteriority in Hegel and Dilthey, as well as Heidegger's *Being and Time*. However, technology is not an institution and, hence, not the product of objectifying something that had been subjective before. The exteriority of technology in implementation does not result from alienation or anything else except itself. Implementation collapses the Dilthey-Hegelian operation again into something as transparent and quasi self-identical as had been Vico's *cose humane*. It is only that *cose humane* and implementation are the exact opposite of each other. Technologically implemented programs are quasi self-identical and no longer subject to the difference between subjective intention and the institutional. Put succinctly, Kittler's implementation is another *nuova scienza*, a new science, however, with reversed sides. The nearly self-identical form of procedure in Vico's poetic invention of *cose humane* returns, upside down, in the self-identical processes of implementation. In them, practices and institutions appear as cultural elements to the extent that a technological function imposes its marks on them.

If this is so, implementation is not only the third generation of the basic operation of culture, human existence in history. It also lays bare the structure of the humanities in unprecedented clarity. All humanities projects have been undertaken according to the model of what historically seems to emerge after them. They mirror science and technology as that which is always still to come. Vico responds in the name of old erudition, law, poesy, and human history, to Descartes's geometry. Dilthey reads theology and literature following the model of the pyschophysiology of Hermann von Helmholtz and Gustav Fechner.[17] Kittler's implementation reveals the structure of the humanities project as what it is: the humanities are the response to and the inverted mirror of what comes after them. The humanities explore sites of implementation.

THE LIMITS OF IMPLEMENTATION, BEYOND IMPLEMENTATION

A full description of the Kittlerian analysis of technology in the history of human being—the more formal expression for what media history means with him—would have to explore implementation's relation to other key terms from the basic vocabulary, including "plain text" (*Klartext*), "to express something in algorithmic terms" (*anschreiben*), "situation" (*Lage*), and "system of inscription" (*Aufschreibesystem*, translated in English as "discourse network"). These expressions are related to each other in what they do for Kittler's analytic procedure, and all of them refer either to specific practices ("plain text" refers to cryptography, "to express algorithmically" to mathematics, "situation" to the military) or are literary quotations ("system of inscription" refers to Daniel Paul Schreber's *Memoirs of My Nervous Illness*). Like "implementation" with its reference to computational technology—and, additionally, to law and organizational sociology—none of those terms are invented for theoretical use, they rather relate to practices and procedures existing in the world. They are operational activities and concepts in the Kittlerian humanities.[18]

But how can a work that is historical and theoretical in nature be restricted to operational concepts? The answer to this question leads us back to Kittler the literary critic before he became a media theorist, and it points toward the philosopher of the later work who took Heidegger's history of being as his guiding thread. To develop these two directions in reading Kittler is beyond the scope of this essay. However, I'll add two qualifications to the reconstruction of "implementation" that might provide some points of orientation.

The discussion of implementation provided so far suggests the level on which it is operating and the type of problem it is supposed to tackle. It is a different task, however, to observe the functioning of the term in its contexts, and to inquire into its theoretical scope. Asking these two questions means to qualify implementation even within the domain of media history proper.

First, a remark on contexts in which implementation occurs. It might be argued that Friedrich Kittler develops the operative concept of implementation within two historical projects of different scales, a small-scale history and a large-scale history. Depending on which of the two types of history we are facing, the ways in which implementation works are different. Even if we assume that only his later books, the two volumes from the series *Musik und Mathematik* (Music and Mathematics), actively undertake what I call the large-scale history, the large scale has been there as a possibility and a final horizon since the beginning of Kittler's media history.

Discourse Networks 1800/1900 can be called small-scale history, even if, under any usual circumstances, two centuries are not a small span of time to cover in a scholarly work. The book is structured in two parts, "1800" and "1900." Implementation, in this case, is presupposed as the very basis of the book's design. It is the implicit meaning in the configuration of the two parts of the book. This is perhaps why the term is not and cannot be made explicit in the book. For the readers, this lack of the term's discussion presents a certain difficulty. They face two parts of an argument that are supposed to echo each other but offer in fact very disparate materials and divergent ways in giving account of them. The first part, "1800," discusses romantic literature as the emblematic moment of inventing the individual persona behind the text, the mother's voice for the male reader and the author's face for the female reader. This, according to the first part of *Discourse Networks*, is the realm of the romantic production of meaning. The basis on which the romanticism effect is achieved is pedagogical and educational. From the infant's alphabetization to the introduction of interpretive assignments in the *Gymnasium* (the traditional German high school) to the celebration of the individual author in higher literary education after 1800, romantic literature relies on the pedagogical "formation" ("*dispositif*" in Foucault's parlance) of the self and its ability to produce meaning. "1900," the second part of *Discourse Networks*, then responds to the first part by reconstructing the emergence of film, gramophone, and typewriter at the end of the nineteenth century. This is the moment of the great reversal of such pedagogical effects and, importantly, of all pedagogy in principle. Partly, the technological devices substitute for the hermeneutic operations of sense-production: seen in this vein, technological devices contribute, as media in the usual sense of the word, to sense-production without implying human intentionality. Partly, however, technological devices are developed as devices for the experimental exploration of the humans' operations of making sense. Configuring these two parts, *Discourse Networks* is neither a history of media technologies in their development from romanticism to modernism; nor is it an account of how training in literacy changes from the romantics to the modernists in such a way as to transform authorship-based reading into modernist interplay between literature and the new media. Instead, the implicit argument of the book and its two parts is that the substitution of technology for the production of meaning by humans circa 1900, along with subjecting physiological and psychological functions to experimentation, reverses the installation of hermeneutics in the human self through socialization and pedagogy circa 1800. The argument, in a word, is neither a history of pedagogy nor a history of media technology but a history of the substitution of the one by the other.

At the moment when the Foucauldian discipline of the reading body is overturned by and retroactively reconceived through technologies that test and address physiological functions while foregoing intentionality, implementation emerges in Kittler's work for the first time and in its basic form. It is the complex and implicit case of it. At first sight, it seems to give technology and implementation less of a defining role; the discipline of the reading body plays an active, self-driven part in *Discourse Networks*. And yet, if there is anything in Kittler resembling a proto-technology, a technology before technology implemented, it is, unexpectedly, romantic literature, the literature of the authorial voice and the reader's training in interpretation. In this self-refashioning of the literary work, technology appears as anticipated and even prepared for by what is to become the site of future implementation. For Kittler, this happens through the self-technologization of literature when it retropes all traditional, rhetorical, and poetic devices by the one figure of acousma and visualization or, as Kittler has it, acoustic and visual hallucination—the acousmatic presence of the mother's voice and the visualization of the author's face.

In an essay in which he gives a first account of *Discourse Networks*, "Authorship and Love," Kittler speaks in fact of the "self-fulfilling power" of romantic literature in this respect.[19] Self-fulfilling prophecy then is one, very specific, variant of the process. Implementation finds the possibility of its application in the existing structures of the site where it is to take hold. Modern literature, with its applications of alphabetization and hermeneutic skills, amounts to the self-technologization of old European poetical and rhetorical *techné*. *Discourse Networks* thus prepares for the operative concept of implementation, without using the word, in its two-part structure.

The large-scale project comes fully into view only in Kittler's latest work, the two completed volumes of *Musik und Mathematik*. But it is present from

the onset, and it has been a substratum of his writings. This fact may be illustrated by the opening passages of an essay entitled "Rock Music: A Misuse
of Army Equipment," which Kittler revised for republication in 2002.[20] Although Kittler, in the essay, argues that rock music relies on acoustic technology whose origins lie in World War II—and that rock says as much in its own
lyrics—the introduction makes an even more sweeping statement. It connects
the rock music of the twentieth century to Nietzsche's view of Greek metrics
and poetry. In Nietzsche's account, this had meant the development of rhythmic speech for the sake of securing repeatability in time, expansion of spatial
reach, and, first and foremost, the physiological innervation of stimuli without the implication of intentionality. Kittler comments as follows: "Regarding
Greek poetry, Nietzsche . . . describes a procedure of storage and a procedure
of transmission of information—first a mnemotechnics which renders poetry
less forgettable than prose, and second a channeling of discourse which carries the information over long distances. . . . Storing messages and transmitting them without relying on such dubious entities as the human mind or the
human soul—this is exactly what defines media. In the 'rhythmic tic-tac' of
the Greeks—following Nietzsche's analysis—it was upon men or even upon
gods to supplement, with their ears, their memory, and their feet, those apparatuses whose invention was still to come."[21] The verb *to supplement* should be
underlined: in the German original (*supplementieren*). The word is as much
borrowed from the French of Jacques Derrida, as implementation in German is
borrowed from computer science English. This, obviously, marks large-scale
history: Dionysian innervation meets the possible installation of technological media, the emergence of electronic music; rock or modern experimental
music alike, turns out to be another advent of Dionysus and the pagan gods.
The possibility of such a moment brackets all small-scale histories which play
out between forms of literary *technai* and technological media. With such
a moment, all the stories that negotiate between literature and the media
appear just as so many historical episodes within the fundamental return of
Greek supplementation in technology's implementation. Still within the logic
of implementation, the supplementation of Greek ears, feet, and memory for
the apparatuses to come is diametrically opposed to self-fulfilling prophecy.
Supplementation, as a large-scale process, coincides with what Nietzsche, and
a Nietzschean Kittler with him, highlight in their empathy with Greek ears,
feet, and memory. They provide or just leave open the site for the epiphany
of an implementation that is not the advent of God for one single reason: Dionysus is one of many pagan gods, and gods are themselves forms of supplementation, that is, sites for implementation to come.[22] In his announcement of
the *"Kehre,"* a lecture given at Tate Modern in 2008 under the title "Preparing

the Arrival of the Gods," Kittler repeats the reference and the thought.[23] This time, he makes unmistakably clear that in this Nietzschean moment of rock music he has identified Heidegger's coincidence of truth disclosing itself primordially and its return through modern technology. Large-scale history is to assume openly its grand name—history of being. In this moment, it may be added, finally a self-preparation of the world for implementation becomes thinkable, the secondary meaning of implementation becomes its first and primary one.[24]

A fuller explication of implementation in Kittler would have to take this final revelation into account, a final appearance that in the standard media-historical work had always been there, even if in latency. Without it, the operative concept would lack any account of its theoretical scope. At this point, we may be reminded of a theological resonance in implementation which probably never occurred to Kittler but helps elucidate its far-reaching implications. In Saint Augustine's commentaries on the John gospel, Christ is called *impletor prophetarum*, the prophets' fulfiller: being another prophet himself who speaks the word of God, Christ also transcends prophecy as such by becoming the living word.[25] By being extended to the Holy Spirit, implementation can take on further meanings: filling in (setting human mouths and ears up for speaking and understanding all languages and language as such) and enacting (renewing the old law by providing the living practice of the new one). Certainly, such a reading of implementation could hold for Kittler only with further conditions. Through Hölderlin, whom he invokes often in *Musik und Mathematik*, Christ and the Holy Spirit would have to be reinterpreted as another Dionysus; and with Heidegger, the coming of Hölderlin's God would have to be taken as coinciding with the disclosure of truth and with the renewed epiphany of the Gods from the midst of the technological world.

For the time being, we may return to a more modest redescription of implementation, a redescription in terms of small- and large-scale histories. Implementation, one might thus argue, requires the combination of two tasks for the clarification of its theoretical scope. One task is to perform small-scale histories, the histories of many single and singular historical a prioris (which in fact are a prioris ex posteriori). Media are thereby shown to implement their technological functions in a pretechnological world or environment. The other task is to bracket all the small-scale histories in a systematic account of the role of *technai* and technology for human being in history. Only such a systematic account could hold off the dogmatic reading of small-scale histories of implementation that would render computer technology the telos of history. The small-scale histories, and only they, help us recognize at any point in history our "situation" as that which it is, according to Kittler. And yet, being content with them would be the ultimate misrecognition of what "situation" means in the first place. There is no ultimate form of implementation. Implementation belongs always to the latest but never the last state of technology. The "situation" is the one we are in at any given moment. Only large-scale history can make us realize this principal insight into the limits of implementation.

On the one hand, this means that implementation is the fundamental operation that has no outside. It is and organizes its own, total, history. On the other hand, implementation is bound in Kittler's account specifically to the principle of the Turing machine, the machine of machines. But it is improbable, as Kittler asserts, that the binarism of the Turing machine exhausts—to paraphrase Kittler—the possibilities of what has been called nature.[26] At least for now, the time of Friedrich Kittler's *nuova scienza* which is our time, implementation is, by its own standards, provisional. There is an outside of implementation history, even if it is only the history of another implementation.

ΠOTES

1. A detailed survey of Kittler's work is offered in Geoffrey Winthrop-Young, *Kittler and the Media* (Cambridge, UK: Polity Press, 2011); for an excellent succinct survey on Kittler's themes and methods see Stephen Sale and Laura Salisbury, "Editors' Introduction," in *Kittler Now: Current Perspectives in Kittler Studies*, ed. Sale and Salisbury (Cambridge, UK: Polity Press, 2015). For Kittler's final statement on his intellectual journey from literary criticism to media history and "back" to philosophy see the introduction to Friedrich Kittler, *Philosophien der Literatur: Berliner Vorlesung 2002* (Berlin: Merve, 2013), 9.

2. Friedrich Kittler, "Memories Are Made of You" (1997), in *Short Cuts* (Frankfurt am Main: Zweitausendeins, 2001), 47; my translation. The volume offers a good collection of the work which is here called Kittler's standard account of media history.

3. The phrase "can be determined" is Hegelian diction and means "is to be understood conceptually as such and such." The technology of media history occupies, in Kittler, the place of Hegel's concept.

4. The Eurocentric view applies to epistemology and technology in Kittler in the same way as it has been the case from Hegel to Heidegger. "Every possible culture" (*jede beliebige Kultur*) is a cursory reference to the ethnographic strand in Kittler's earlier work on family structures and its roots in Claude Levy-Strauss and Jacques Lacan. See Kittler, "Poet, Mother, Child. On the Romantic Invention of Sexuality," in Kittler, *The Truth of the Technological World*, trans. Eric Butler, afterword by Hans-Ulrich Gumbrecht (Stanford, CA: Stanford University Press, 2013), 1–16. The relativism of cultural analysis and the normativity of the epistemological-technological argument need not necessarily conflict with each other, and they never have for Kittler. In this respect, he does hardly differ from Edmund Husserl, *Crisis of the European Sciences and Transcendental Phenomenology*, trans. David Carr (Evanston, IL: Northwestern University

Press, 1970), 14–16 and throughout. For Kittler as for Husserl, it is philosophy as the normative discourse on understanding and technology that is uniquely European. See Kittler, *Philosophien der Literatur*, 9–10.

5. Kittler's first book, his dissertation, is a magisterial study in psychoanalytic structuralist criticism: Kittler, *Der Traum und die Rede: Eine Analyse der Kommunikationssituation Conrad Ferdinand Meyers* [Dream and discourse. An analysis of the communicative situation of Conrad Ferdinand Meyer] (Bern and Munich: Francke, 1977).

6. As examples for the use of the term in legal studies, see Mark Tushnet, "How Courts Implement Social Policy," *Tulsa Law Review*, no. 45 (2010): 855–62, or Tushnet, *The New Constitutional Order* (Princeton, NJ: Princeton University Press, 2003), 8–32; for economics and game theory, see Luis C. Corchon, *The Theory of Implementation of Socially Optimal Decisions in Economics* (Basingstoke, UK: Palgrave Macmillan, 1996); for computer science see Allen B. Tucker, *Computer Science Handbook*, 2nd ed. (Boca Raton, FL: Chapman and Hall / CRC, 2004), in particular section 44, "The Organizational Contexts of Development and Use" by Jonathan Grudin and M. Lynne Markus, and section 17, "Digital Computer Architecture" by David R. Kaeli.

7. The process of almost infinitesimal approximation to what the phenomenologists, following Franz von Brentano, called the adequate or full "description" of the phenomenon is documented in the volumes of drafts and sketches in the Husserl work edition even more than in his published writings; see, for example, Edmund Husserl, *Zur Phänomenologie der Intersubjektivität*, 1–3, in *Husserliana: Gesammelte Werke*, vols. 13–15 (The Hague, Netherlands: Martinus Nijhoff, 1955–2008). In Merleau-Ponty the work on perception is probably the best example; see Merleau-Ponty, *Phenomenology of Perception*, trans. Colin Smith (London: Routledge and Paul, 1962). Kittler does not describe phenomena; instead, with the many repetitions and overlapping passages, he appears to be zeroing in on the perfect montage of the story, the story of implementation.

8. Friedrich Kittler, ed., *Austreibung des Geistes aus den Geisteswissenschaften: Programme des Poststrukturalismus* (Paderborn, Germany: Schöningh, 1980).

9. See Kittler, "Einleitung" [Introduction], in *Austreibung des Geistes*, 7–14.

10. Friedrich Kittler, *Eine Kulturgeschichte der Kulturwissenschaft* (Munich: Fink, 2000).

11. See Friedrich Kittler, *Aufschreibesysteme 1800/1900* (Munich: Fink, 1985), translated by Michael Metteer, with Chris Cullen, as *Discourse Networks, 1800/1900* (Stanford, CA: Stanford University Press, 1990), part 1, "1800;" and Friedrich Kittler, *Musik und Mathematik*, Bd. 1, *Hellas*, Tl. 1, *Aphrodite* (Munich: Fink, 2006).

12. Giambattista Vico, *New Science*, 3rd ed. (1744), trans. David Marsh, introduction Anthony Grafton (London: Penguin Books, 1999), 75–85, 119–49.

13. Kittler, *Kulturgeschichte der Kulturwissenschaft*, 87–127.

14. Georg Wilhelm Friedrich Hegel, *Phenomenology of Spirit*, trans. A. V. Miller (Oxford: Oxford University Press, 1977), 266–363.

15. For relevant excerpts, see Wilhelm Dilthey, *Selected Writings*, trans. and introduction H. P. Rickman (Cambridge: Cambridge University Press, 1976), 159–245.

16. Georg Simmel, "The Conflict in Modern Culture" (1918/1921), in *The Conflict in Modern Culture and Other Essays*, trans. K. Peter Etzkorn (New York: Teachers' College

Press, 1968), 11–26; György Lukács, *Theory of the Novel* (1916), trans. Anna Bostock (London: Merlin Press, 1971) and Lukács, "Reification and the Consciousness of the Proletariat," in *History and Class Consciousness: Studies in Marxist Dialectics* (1923), trans. Rodney Livingstone (Cambridge, MA: MIT Press, 1971), 83–22; Martin Heidegger, *Being and Time* (1927), trans. John Mcquarrie, Edward Robinson (New York: HarperOne, 1962), 169–224.

17. Cf. Wilhelm Dilthey, *Introduction to the Human Sciences: An Attempt to Lay a Foundation for the Study of Society and History*, trans. Ramon J. Betanzos (Detroit, MI: Wayne State University Press, 1988), 92–96.

18. I have proposed *Verfahren*—operational activities and concepts—as a basic term for the humanities; see: Rüdiger Campe, "Verfahren: Kleists Allmähliche Verfertigung der Gedanken beim Reden," *Sprache und Literatur*, no. 110 (2012): 2–21.

19. Friedrich Kittler, "Authorship and Love" (1980), trans. Matthew J. Fraser, *Theory, Culture and Society* 32, no. 2 (2015): 35.

20. Friedrich Kittler, "Rock Music: A Misuse of Military Equipment" (1988/1991), in *Truth of the Technological World*, 152–64.

21. Kittler, "Rock Music," 153. (The English translation has "ears, memories, and feet had to supplement . . . for other apparatuses," instead of "for apparatuses." Ears, memories and feet are, importantly, no apparatuses for Kittler.)

22. In *Aphrodite*—the account of the Greek unconcealment of truth in being and thinking, which is the first installment of *Musik und Mathematik*—Kittler, inversely, ascribes the emergence of technology ("the machine") to the Pythagorean philosopher Archytas. Such emergence still belongs to the soft manner of genesis which is unconcealment, and it applies also to this "ancestor of all engineers" (325). The word *implementieren* does, however, not occur in this late, Heideggerian, context (with its characteristic and dubious avoidance of words gleaned from the Latin).

23. The lecture is sweepingly programmatic: Friedrich Kittler, "Preparing the Arrival of the Gods" (2008/2011), in Sale and Salisburg, *Kittler Now*, 95–112.

24. Hans-Ulrich Gumbrecht has underlined Kittler's alliance with Heidegger's history of being in his afterword to Kittler, *Truth of the Technological World*, 307–29.

25. "He was the lord of the prophets, the fulfiller [impletor] of the prophets," quoted in Saint Augustine, Tractate 24.7, in *Tractates on the Gospel of John 11-27*, vol. 79 of *The Fathers of the Church* (Washington, DC: Catholic University of America Press, 2010), 237.

26. "When clouds rain or waves are formed, it is hardly a digital computer that dwells in them—a machine which through computation would make today's and tomorrow's weather. The laws of the equations by which segments of the future have by and by become predictable rather describe an illiterate nonreader. This is why there is what in former times has been called beauty and the sublime. If, however, Turing's discrete machine is not universal, the old question of the limits of its powers reemerges. First mathematical steps have been taken to demonstrate that the rapid multiplication of transistors per chip surface—which seemed the panacea for two decades—is not able to compete with the complexity of nature's feedback operations in

principle. The digital approach defines limits which do not apply to analog computers—computers whose architecture is however still entirely hypothetical. Potentially, the computer alphabet is not the end of history as such, as media prophets indulge in professing, but it may rather be a stage in computing what remains noncomputable in Turing terms." Friedrich Kittler, "Computeranalphabetismus," in *Short Cuts*, 132–33; my translation.

2

TRISTAN'S FOOLISHNESS AS A TRUTH EVENT

On Two of Friedrich Kittler's Late Texts
That Expose the History of Being

Hans Ulrich Gumbrecht

Long before his death, Friedrich Kittler had already assumed a distinguished place in the academy: he is considered the visionary and founder—by way of several important books—of media studies, a field that emerged from the border shifts and internal structural changes that have reformed the humanities, particularly in Germany. Kittler's thought, however, has an appeal, a charisma even, that surpasses this institutional role. Through the translation of his texts, Kittler's name appears in many academic circles that in no way share the German fascination for media phenomena. This doubtlessly has to do with Kittler's premonition of a coming intellectual sensibility that no one had foreseen until the last quarter of the twentieth century—that is, at least at first glance, a passion for literature and philosophy inclusive of mathematical and technological forms of thought and directed toward "driving the spirit [*Geist*] out of the humanities [*Geisteswissenschaften*]." Kittler is the only professor of German literature and, later, of aesthetics whose bequest to the *Deutsches Literaturarchiv* in Marbach includes a synthesizer, and he is likely to remain the only such German academic for some time.

Whoever has read or was able to meet Kittler knows that these two predicates—"founder of media studies" and "inventor of a new intellectual sensibility"—fail to bring into perspective the important, incomparable, and perhaps most central of Kittler's dimensions. It does not occur to most of his enthusiastic readers to seek continuity between the media theorist Kittler, author of the long ago canonized *Discourse Networks 1800/1900 (Aufschreibesysteme)*, and the Kittler whose last two posthumously published books take on ancient Greek culture and the relationship between music and mathematics (*Musik und Mathematik*). Following studies on Greece and Rome, Kittler intended to write a third volume dedicated to the Middle Ages, which would have taken as its central figure the siren Isolde, a work that remains incomplete. The volumes on Ancient Greece that Kittler published in his lifetime disappointed those readers who were exclusively interested in media theory, and those disappointed readers went on to discourage others who might have been open to the work's new ideas. For this reason, Kittler's reception history resembles that of Martin Heidegger, the modern philosopher whom he most admired. Today, there are few among the philosophically minded who would deny the historical significance of the publication of Heidegger's *Being and Time* (*Sein und Zeit*) in 1927. However, whenever the oft-invoked "turn" in Heidegger's work may have occurred, many consider the texts from the final decades of his life to be enigmatic, pseudo-religious—even "intellectual charlatanry."

In his late work, Heidegger develops the concept of the "history of being" (*Seinsgeschichte*) in various ways; in Kittler's late work, particularly in the two books on Greece, it becomes clear that his work was invested in the history of being from its inception. This common interest accounts for the parallelity in the reception histories of Heidegger's and Kittler's late texts. The concept of the history of being uncompromisingly deepened the rupture within the tradition of Western philosophy that had begun with the general acceptance of the import of *Being and Time*. In this book, Heidegger reacts to the apprehension about the growing divide between "subject" and "object," between human self-referentiality and the surrounding world, by describing existence as "being-in-the-world" (*in-der-Welt-sein*), wherein the objects and institutions of everyday life are "always already" familiar and "ready-to-hand." Following the mid-1930s—and even more so after the 1947 publication of his "Letter on Humanism"—Heidegger's thought gravitated toward the motif of delivering man from his eccentric posturing toward the world and from the constant desire to confirm his understanding. Heidegger's late phase has never garnered the wide acceptance that his existentialogical beginnings received.

When seen according to the history of being, "truth" (*Wahrheit*) is no longer the truth of ideas, the conceptual truth lying open to the subject "under" the surface or "behind" the foreground of the material world. Truth, according to Heidegger's decisive intuition, reveals itself as the "coming forth" of things in their absolute substantiality. In the "truth event" (*Wahrheitsereignis*), wherein being emerges, the individual objects of the world show themselves free of perspective or interpretation. The role, the duty—or, as Heidegger put it, the "debt" or "guilt" (*Schuld*)—of human existence, or *Dasein*, is to be present in the world in a state of emotional calm or "releasement" (*Gelassenheit*). Without such releasement, neither would being reveal itself to itself, nor would thought be there to apprehend being in this self-revelation. Heidegger seems to have thought the temporality of this self-revelation to be epiphanic. For only mere moments does being become experiential—only for moments that cannot be controlled, even though *Dasein* is responsible for and dependent on what becomes of this being. In the conception of the history of being, history only has significance insofar as it refers to the fact that in different epochs the evaluability, the probability of the occurrence of truth events differs. Heidegger always saw ancient Greece as the authentic time of truth in this sense, but he also thought the mid-twentieth century, with its great technological advances, to be such a time. By means of technology, his own age had the potential to become a time in which being is revealed as itself.

The Friedrich Kittler of the late 1970s and early 1980s—this is clearer today than it was back then—who published such unprecedented and innovative books, began his work with the Heideggerian history of being. The late Friedrich Kittler, the Kittler of the unfinished work on mathematics and love, developed an enthusiasm for Greece motivated by the history of being that took up Heidegger's own lifelong enthusiasm for the Hellenes. As is clearer today than at the time when Kittler's books on Greece first appeared, the history of being lends continuity to Kittler's entire corpus. With this in mind, we can assure the many baffled readers of Kittler's late works that the selfsame Heideggerian thinking found in these works also provides the philosophical basis for his early texts.

Despite the peculiar chiasmus that binds Kittler to Heidegger, their thinking differs when it comes to history, and it is this difference that the book at the heart of this paper demonstrates. Kittler, not Heidegger, saw in the Middle Ages—at least in medieval courtly literature—a moment in the history of being, a moment of possibility for the revelation of being as being. This was to be the theme of the third part of *Musik und Mathematik*, and in preparation Kittler translated the Oxford version of the Old French text "La folie Tristan" from circa 1200 into German free verse and wrote a still unpublished essay on its potential for the history of being for a romance studies conference in Kiel.

I cannot claim that these connections occurred to me when I first read Kittler's *Discourse Networks* with several students at Ruhr-Universität Bochum in the early 1980s. What impressed us, like so many others, was its fresh perspective on the history of media. I also felt the excitement that the book's intellectual power unleashed, which made it my great wish to meet Friedrich Kittler as soon as possible. The first opportunity arose when, after moving to the Universität-Gesamthochschule Siegen, I organized a colloquium on the transition from late-medieval to early-modern literature on the Iberian Peninsula. I had in fact expected the *"new Germanist"* Kittler, whose name was on every academic's tongue and who had just become a private lecturer in Freiburg, to decline our invitation—or perhaps to accept it, but with the caveat that he would not be at the three-day conference because of his expertise in romance or medieval studies. Friedrich, however, simply accepted his invitation in one of the polite, formal letters that academics wrote in those days. At the conference, he seemed at ease among the medieval specialists—and not only because ashtrays still awaited intellectual smokers in seminar rooms at that time. He understood the content of fourteenth- and fifteenth-century Castilian texts well, and he read Old French and Old Occitan as fluently as only few Romanists. After this, I never again saw Friedrich participate as intensively in a discussion, which likely had to do with the fact that, at this colloquium, he was unburdened from his usual duties as a lecturer. This was one of my discoveries: Friedrich Kittler's love for medieval literatures. My other discovery took the form of a surprise that I did not fully register at the time. When we "triumphant medievalists" reacted with the impatience and ferocity of hunting dogs to every textual feature in which we found the "symptoms of modernity," Kittler would look at us and furrow his brow, as if he saw in us the early warning signs of decadence. He, who told us in the coffee breaks that he played electric guitar and understood programming, he alone seemed to want to delay the arrival of the Middle Ages until his later years.

All of this is meant to indicate, as I suspect today, that Friedrich Kittler already sensed something of the potential for the history of being in the courtly texts of the High Middle Ages. Though a former medievalist, I myself had never seen this literature in such a way until I read Kittler's essay "Isolde als Sirene" (Isolde as a siren). Its intuitions are as plausible as can be for a literary account of the history of being, a perspective that is, as Kittler emphasizes, largely incompatible with the history of being. Of course, such strong argumentation requires substantiation, especially when it is positive, and this is to be found in the new literary-historical view of the emergence of medieval courtly literature that arose two decades ago and whose argument has since grown more prominent and more convincing.

In the earliest Occitan troubadour songs, which date from the years around 1100, there are clear "countercultural" traces to be discovered. These songs were dedicated to aristocratic audiences, to whom every gesture of presumptive disobedience or revolt against the restrictions imposed on everyday life by the clergy would have been a cause for joy—particularly in a world where humans were exposed to nature and violence in a way that is unimaginable today. William IX, Duke of Aquitaine—whom literary historians used to call the "first troubadour" because the oldest surviving linguistic corpus in this genre is connected to his name—stood at odds with the authority of the church for much of his life. The provocative gestures in "his" songs mostly concern situations of sexual desire and the rush of male gratification. There is, for instance, a song directed against the religiously motivated duty only to write down—on expensive parchment—what could be considered edifying. In the most literal sense imaginable, the following is a song "about nothing":

> Farai un vers de dreyt nien:
> non er de mi ni d'autra gen,
> non er d'amor ni de joven,
> ni de ren au,
> qu'enans fo trobatz en durmen
> sobre chevau.
>
> No sai qual hora.m fuy natz:
> no suy alegres ni iratz,
> no suy estrayns ni sui privatz,
> ni no.n puesc au,
> qu'enaissi fuy de nueitz fadatz,
> sobr'un pueg au.
>
> I will write a song about nothing at all:
> neither about me nor anyone else,
> neither about love nor about youth,
> nor any other thing,
> I first heard it while sleeping
> on my horse.
>
> I do not know the hour of my birth:
> I am neither joyful nor angry,
> I am neither foreign nor native,
> and I cannot do a thing about it,
> one night I was enchanted
> on a high mountain.

Kittler's reading of "La folie Tristan" fixates on what could be seen as an act of resistance against restrictions on media and morality. Here we are dealing with an ontic, not ontological, dimension of nothingness and everything, of sleep and dreams that turn into reality. This is a dimension of enchantment, not of development or education: the song comes to the singer in his sleep, and he is enchanted on a mountain.

Fifty years later, in the romances of the great Crétien de Troyes and in the courtly culture that produced them, the varnish of the discursive order already seems to have set on such direct outpourings of desire. Crétien's knightly heroes, particularly Erec and Yvain, are sent on adventures to follow a double path that will teach them to bring courtly love (*Minne*) and Christian marriage into harmony. Even Andreas Cappelanus's Latin "rules of love"—which Friedrich quotes more than once and which originated in Friedrich's own cultural-historical milieu around the court of Marie de Champagne—conduct countercultural energy into clearly paradoxical expressions while nonetheless providing a basic order of "rules" and "laws"—no matter how "ironically" these structures are understood.

If we take the number of extant manuscript copies as our measure, then the most popular of Chrétien's romances was "Lancelot," a text that does not allow for the reconciliation of courtly love and marriage and that Chrétien never finished, perhaps for this very reason. Because Lancelot loves Guinevere, the wife of his king and feudal lord Artus, there can be no conciliation. The constellation of courtly love and marriage found in "Lancelot" also has a place in the Tristan and Isolde material, which inspired an incomparable variety of short and long stories in the French and German vernaculars around 1200, including the Oxford "folie Tristan." "La folie Tristan" constitutes a complete textual composition, not a fragment, as is so common among extant medieval vernacular manuscripts, even those in the Tristan corpus. It is moving today to see in the text to what great extent the narrator's voice assumes that the audience is acquainted with other stories about the two lovers, cares about these lovers, and even wants to relive well-known stories about them. It is not any less moving to see Kittler's certainty about the potential for the history of being in this text and the patience (and enthusiastic impatience) with which he reveals that potential. As Friedrich emphasizes at the start of the essay, we are not speaking about "interpretation," but instead about a process of "exposure" or "uncovering" (*Freilegen*). Against all cultural, discursive and generic structures and conventions—all of which Heidegger would have subsumed under the concept of "being" (*das Seiende*)—Kittler points to what is concealed in the text about being. However, in saying that I find it moving to observe Friedrich (after his death) exploring this potential, I by no means intend to deemphasize the sense of wonderment I experience for his translation and his essay.

His translation is already involved in this process of exposure, and it therefore belongs to the tradition following Hölderlin—as well as Baudelaire and Walter Benjamin's "Task of the Translator"—in which the translator seeks equivalency with the tone of the original, instead of philological exactitude. The tone of Kittler's free verse shies away neither from archaism, nor from surprisingly modern or colloquial expressions. The simultaneously distanced and extremely direct experience of reading this verse lends it something of the feel of medieval courtly texts, which so often speak as if from across a great divide, but with a touching directness. The semantic and syntactical freedoms taken by such translation themselves belong to the task of Kittlerian uncovering. To take an example: in verse 786 of the Old French text, Tristan says to Isolde, *"quant me plaiseit venir a vous,"* which can be translated literally and unproblematically as, "when it pleased me to come to you." Kittler, however, renders this line, "when the desire for you overtook me" (*wenn mich die Lust auf euch ankam*) and exposes something more of desire than would have been spoken eight centuries ago.

I do not know when or for what occasion Friedrich wrote the essay "Isolde as Siren." It seems to have been a lecture, and I am certain that he produced it late in his life because the essay has an attractive abruptness that reminds me of the second volume of his work on Greece. The author shows the reader what he himself sees, while seeming to indicate that he is unable to help those who fail to discover what is so evident to him. In other words: late Kittler perfects the stylistic figure already found in Kittler's early work as the "hyperbole of the factical." From the outset, there was for him no doubt or discussion, no system or argument, but rather the certainty of the factical as revealed by epiphany. But while the factical is on display with equally exuberant documentation in his early books, Kittler's hyperbole of the factical eventually developed into an abbreviated gesture. "Whoever does not immediately see (or hear) I cannot (and will not) help," I constantly read between the lines in his late work—although Friedrich of course would have insisted on the completeness of his composition.

The steps of his abbreviated exposition follow one another in quick succession. In Kittler's translation, Tristan, who introduces himself as a fool, answers King Mark's questions about his identity and heritage by stating, "mother was, for me, a whale— / she roamed as siren in the sea" (*mutter war mir eine walfrau— / die schweifte als siren' im meer*). However, Tristan's dissimulation is itself a dissimulation, and this second-order dissimulation allows him to speak the truth without the truth being understood as such. Friedrich exposes how, on a fundamental level, the "literary" narrative of "Tristan's foolishness" is only the discursive domestication of a song, and for this reason he heaves a sigh of relief that we have inherited this work without the author's name. The song originated in desire's enchantment, and ultimately desire—as Jacques Lacan insisted—is to be identified not only with pleasure and the drive for its fulfillment, but also with death and the being of death. "Above all," Kittler writes, "only women can complete the 'work' of opening their legs for the secret beloved."

The findings of Kittler's history of being do not speak to the politically correct, nor do they constitute "literary history." But they are exactly what Friedrich Kittler sought and found in "literature," including that of the Middle Ages.

Translated by Alexander Lambrow

Originally published as "Tristans Narrheit als Wahrheitsereignis," in Friedrich Kittler, *Isolde als Sirene: Tristans Narrheit als Wahrheitsereignis* (Munich: Wilhelm Fink Verlag, 2012).

3

IDIOCY, FORGETTING, AND OUTDATEDNESS

Friedrich Kittler's Avant-Gardism
and the "Time for Other Stories"

Bernhard J. Dotzler

Let us say, as the enlightened people we are, that there is no enlightened understanding of the world as truth, but rather only systems of conviction, or, more pointedly, of delusion.

Friedrich A. Kittler also had his delusions, or at least insistent moments of madness. To affirm this about him, however, diminishes neither his person nor his work. On the contrary: more than once he recognized that "in madness is the truth and vice versa,"[1] and it is no coincidence that the term he made famous (and that made him famous), *Aufschreibesysteme (discourse networks)*,[2] emerges from Daniel Paul Schreber's influential *Denkwürdigkeiten eines Nervenkranken (Memoirs of My Nervous Illness)*. Perhaps it is precisely because to "program in machine code" implies the danger of madness that Kittler cherished programming in ways both practical and theoretical.[3]

Ad personam or *in memoriam hominis* only this: Friedrich Kittler's death affected me deeply. We had only sporadic contact over the years, but with the news of his death an instantaneous shock nevertheless cut through me; from now on, there would be a void in the world. As I read James Fenimore Cooper for a different occasion—and yet fortuitously, because I received the invitation to the Commemorative Colloquium for Friedrich Kittler at the same time— his enlightened lines touched me, as they reminded me of Friedrich's death: "it is unphilosophical to grieve; but for thee I must weep, in bitterness of heart."[4]

The following text, however, will concern "Friedrich" no further—it will be not about the person, but rather about "Kittler" and several of his writings. This is not an obituary, in which both "Friedrich" and "Kittler" would have arguably merged. Though requested by a newspaper in October 2011, I did not write one, because I would have needed more time than the requesting publication would grant me. Had I written it, however, it would have become a digression on loneliness, and on idiocy as a concept that unites the two names (Friedrich and Kittler), and which now allows me to come to my point.

The ἰδιώτης (idiot) is a human being in isolation, outside the community. Marshall McLuhan invoked the Greek meaning of the word early in his career: "Idiot: Greek for a private person."[5] Likewise, Vilém Flusser took recourse to this meaning and, in some ways, based his entire media theory on it. For Flusser, the human being communicates not because he or she is a social creature, but rather because he or she is a solitary one, and both the foundations and heights of his solitude are to be found in the bare fact of mortality. The human being is essentially an idiot. He or she strives to fight against this, to be instead a ζῷον πολιτικόν (political animal)—this is precisely the purpose of his entire communicative activity, and thereby of the entire realm of that which constitutes "media."[6]

Media might be an antidote to idiocy, were they not themselves instruments for creating isolation. In contrast to previous gatherings on the ἀγορά (agora) of a πόλις (city), the masses who follow political events on their television screens are nothing but discrete individuals and not a single mass. This was once Flusser's example,[7] although Kittler takes his cue from literary history: The Sorrows of Young Werther—the first true paperback success in German literature. This novel by Goethe concerns that which he (or the book itself) invokes: the intimate reader who remains, while reading, as alone and focused on himself in his passion.[8] Jacques Lacan spoke of masturbation as being literally the "jouissance de l'idiot," and Kittler identifies this idiocy as the manifest (because once revealed by Goethe himself) secret of Werther, who loves Lotte with his entire soul, yet only emotionally, because he doesn't wish for the fulfillment of his physical-erotic desires in any way.[9] On the one hand, this is a historical observation that gives rise to a historiographical question: from where comes the idiocy of love? How does our celebration of (unfulfilled) sexuality define itself to date? Kittler writes, "There are other bodies with other gestures, other organs and other adventures that come together at various times."[10] On the other hand, this same observation implies a question that is posed to the present but oriented toward the future, a question as to the possibility for yet another adventure—it is, for Kittler, the opportunity to formulate a programmatic position, a mission statement. "Writing today," he claims, "can only mean to write in opposition to the fact that sexual intercourse does not cease not to write itself."[11]

It is not difficult to recognize in this statement a program running through Kittler's oeuvre—from the celebration of passion at the end of Discourse Networks

1800/1900 right up to the eroto-mania of his unfinished history in *Musik und Mathematik* (Music and mathematics). The latter, an almost posthumous re-invention of what is now fashionably called *sound studies*, in turn refers to the young Kittler who established himself as an avant-gardist in literary and media studies by presenting the world of text, sound, and noise in Pink Floyd's "Brain Damage" as both the oldest and newest instance of European poetry.[12] In that early essay, he was already occupied with the Greeks and their "God who dwelled in the acoustic realm." Pink Floyd's electronic sound-arts provide the "announcement" of the immortality and eternal return of the Nietzschean-antichristian and anti-media-theoretical truth of the "fucking gods" (to use Roger Waters's expression).[13]

Sound and the *rapport sexuelle* have an unmediated quality in common, one that is beyond writing. As the ears are (again according to Lacan) "in the field of the unconscious, . . . the only orifice that cannot be closed"—sound is pure relentlessness. Thus, according to Kittler, passing through ears "that cannot defend themselves," sound implodes every distinction "between outside and inside." Sound falls upon one "immediately and without distance the center of perception itself." Sound is ultimately "beyond writing"; sound is music's "immediate technical implementation."[14] Here, sound and sex correspond to one another—because writing to oppose "the fact that sexual intercourse does not cease to not write itself" simply opposes it but does not institute change. The question thus is what, precisely, the program might have been, or possibly still is.

An answer to this question can perhaps be found among Kittler's many stylistic exercises in the manifesto-style. One could, either along this trajectory or in addition to it, follow his many explicit and implicit references to Heidegger's existentialism of "de-distancing" (*Ent-fernung*),[15] which serves as the signet of *Dasein*'s idiocy and idiocization by media. One can then see how an analysis of *Dasein*'s modes of existence and nonexistence in technological times could take shape, that is, as a lesson in how to perceive (*vernehmen*) Being (*Sein*) as φύσις (physis) as well as τέχνη (techné) under pretechnological and high-technological conditions. Likewise, one could and must take into consideration a legacy that is not, according to Kittler, his own, but rather Dracula's: the legacy of *Technische Schriften* that try to describe, in the medium of writing, that which is beyond writing[16]—who knows whether in an opposing or affirming way. In any case, for all which never writes itself, what "does not cease not to write itself" there is the counterpart of that which conversely perpetually writes itself: what "never stops transmitting"[17] (*sich [ein]zuschreiben*) discourses that "never cease not to cease."[18] To keep this fact in mind would thus be the task at hand (again used programmatically), in order to then deploy it as a counter-foil for that which governs us in place of our own intentions, strivings, and volition—not to mention our wishes.

However, as Kittler wrote amid the raging methodological debates of 1970s and 1980s: "It's time for other stories."[19] This, too, can be read as a mission statement. "To write for opposing . . ." would then be a program of terminating that creates space and generates openness for the new, no matter whether of a foreseeable kind or not. One may detect this in Kittler's reading of Nietzsche: "How One Eliminates that of which One Speaks";[20] or again in his recourse to Heidegger and his mission of "destruction" and "not just deconstruction" of metaphysics;[21] or in the legendary and in fact programmatic proclamation of the *Austreibung des Geistes aus den Geisteswissenschaften*; or in Kittler's obituary for Foucault: "we've lost a *dépeupleur*, a depopulator. One who sorts out where others still multiply;"[22] or, finally, in the simplest of all Kittlerian essay titles: "Forgetting," in which he writes in a footnote: "What is meant by a critique of discourse can't be specified: how can discourses criticize discourse? Abandon some discourses, take up others—less than that can't be done."[23]

Minimal, yes, but still—the program would in this way be to defend freedom. This program, however, also demands that one must realize its genuine antiprogrammatic implications. "It's time for other stories," Kittler claims in that very essay "Forgetting," and he does this within the outer frame of a frame narrative in which an "I"—just writing to oppose the fact that sexual intercourse does not cease to not write itself—tells its love story. On the other hand, one can and should therefore accept the mission also, if not from the beginning, as an incitement to track the peculiarity of the "I" in Kittler's writings. Both the programmatic aspects of his work and his efforts to liberate himself from any program have their origin here.

The "I" that most clearly refers to the person of Friedrich Kittler may be the one that begins an autobiographical note entitled "Bio-geography" (*Biogeographie*). It sketches out what others might call their "media socialization": to be raised in a devastated landscape and to stumble upon once-futuristic technologies from World War II that in the meantime have become the "strategic present."[24] This also would deserve to be read programmatically. But this is beside the point. The point is that he asserts that he has never published this word, the "I" at the beginning of Kittler's text (its first word), before: "I, who has never published this letter—."[25]

Nothing could be more wrong than this claim, regardless of whether this falsity results from a conscious lie or from the manic second it took to write down the letter I. In reality, "I" appears often in Kittler's writings, and indeed already in the young Kittler, as in, for instance, the aforementioned essay on Nietzsche. This essay is concerned with the "I = Saying-I" (*Ich = Ich-Sagen*) of

Ecce Homo, and it opens with an anecdote: how "I sat in the airplane headed south" and then saw, "under the sun, vertical in the sky, the book in the sand," before coming to a conclusion: The other Friedrich's "narcissistic-ecstatic 'I' = saying-I" (*narziβtisch-rauschhafte Ich = Ich-Sagen*) shut down the hermeneutic category of "the human" and in its place installed the empirical narrative of "how one becomes the accident one is."[26]

Or, considering the example of Werther's idiotic sorrows and joy at the "adventures of our sexualized bodies," there is also an "I" that reports empirically on the act of composing the study at hand: "I pick up documents."[27] The same "I" then appears in "Forgetting": "I reread *The Order of Discourse* in order to write these pages." This "I" appears in the same manner as the "I" of the frame narrative, in which the promise of the essay's title finally materializes. "Black out. It's time for other stories. I got your postcard without words,"[28] read the last lines of this text, one which begins with the negation of readability and writability, namely with darkness and sound:

> One night—the music was loud—you said as you were leaving; don't forget. I did not forget and told you. But you had forgotten the don't forget. And since then I no longer know what I heard, whether you said don't forget or forget me.
>
> What's the difference. It's all the same—here where I and Me and Not play no role. The rest [*das andere*] is words.[29]

Which "others" (*andere*) can be addressed here? Precisely those basic words ("I" and "Me" and "Not") that play no role where there is immediacy: pure positivity, if "not" is just pointless too, if it's simply the night, the music, the forgetting, and the forgetting about the forgetting. To say it again—as a short love story, this frame narrative enlists writing to oppose "the fact that sexual intercourse does not cease to not write itself."

At the same time, it emerges *with*, and thereby *from*, the presence of (at least) three different "I"s that may be distinguished in Kittler's "*Ich-Sagen*." Alongside the "I" that claims to never have said "I" in print, we have to imagine one that declares the "I-word" irrelevant, and both of these in turn have to be seen alongside a third "I" in which each is reflected in the other (on one side, its insignificance, and on the other the claimed "never" of its being-said): the "I" as the basic example.

> I reread *The Order of Discourse* in order to write these pages. But no order and no discourse can protect us from the beautiful accidents and voices that make us forget even what we have reread. And so a little apparatus comes into being. Marks next to quotable sentences (in pencil, so they can

be erased again); cross-references from one marking to the next; copied passages . . . , marginal comments—all these are tools for inscribing a few foolish associations into a corpus of books, storage devices so I will not forget what I wanted to write about forgetting.[30]

In short, what this example of the "I" represents is nothing else than a "system of notation" (*Aufschreibesystem*)[31]—a term not coincidentally brought into play (not for the first time though) by precisely this "I."

"The phrase discourse network," as the eponymous book has asserted since its second edition, "can also describe the network of techniques and institutions that allows for the addressing, storage, and processing of the relevant data for a given culture."[32] Accordingly, in "Forgetting," which is a study of forgetting's opposite, namely "books, mnemo-techniques, and memory machines,"[33] we read:

> Archives themselves provide plenty of material to archive. Only imperial myths propagate the belief that sentences are eternal once they have been hewn into stone, once they have become lapidary. No storage device operates in isolation. Archives are hooked up with other archives directly or via interfaces, and are themselves archivized in other archives. Archives require input and output stations (even if these be just sense organs and brains). Archives contain mechanisms that bring about and/or prevent the erasure of their data. The development of electronic computers has merely provided precise terms and circuit diagrams for factors which come into play in all cases of archivizing.[34]

The avant-gardist who dedicated his undertakings to Pink Floyd (and thereby already the computer, in the form of the synthesizer, as well) thus updated the initial paranoiac concept of discourse networks by fitting it to the technological state of the art. As a foil for grammatology, the discourse network is clearly a Foucauldian concept. At the same time, however, it directs discourse analysis methodologically "beyond Foucault," toward a "diagnosis of the present state of data storage, transmission, and calculation in technical media."[35] Foucault's world, illuminated by discourse analysis, is the world of the library in which Nietzsche, in his furor over the "*Ich-Sagen*" in *Ecce Homo*, had already done away with "the human." Kittler's exemplary "*Ich-Sagen*" tracks the transposition of this world of books into the new world order of electronic data processing:

> I go to a reserve library. First I put together a bibliography from the latest bibliographies, then go through the relevant review, find this book recommended, that one panned, look up a highly praised book in the card catalogue—but this time it is for naught: the volume is missing from its place. I

imagine the cunning, self-serving reader who got there before me. Probably he/she did not steal the book at all, just placed it elsewhere.

From here a basic transcription arises:

The card catalogue is a RAM (Random Access Memory), which can record new data (purchased books) and erase obsolete data (stolen or lost books). The Bibliography and the review journal are PROM's (Programmable Read Only Memories), which take up less space but on the other hand do not allow for erasures. The call numbers are interfacing Switches between two RAMs, the catalogue and the shelf system. And the so as not to is an address cunning reader, forget him/her, selector of the sort that is hooked up to the latest generations of IBM computers. To keep programmers from getting at the data (no longer just harmless books, but corporate earnings or fingerprints), the address selector equipped with a randomness generator sends the incoming data to free positions, the exact address of which does not appear at any of the many output stations. This is how electronic memories forget the "human being."[36]

There are no tears to be shed for this "human being." Already for Nietzsche, there were none. Just as when Foucault—himself sufficiently poetic—proclaimed this same "human" to have vanished like a face in the sand at the shore. And thus, it is in Kittler.

Nevertheless, it is the observation of a disappearance, one of systematic and thus programmatic value—like the mode of the "Saying-I," in which the same programmatic aspect is presented as a specific, and thereby relativized, momentum.

So, to finish for now with the systematic-programmatic concerns: The "Time for other stories" that "Forgetting" already saw coming finds its echo—linguistically as well as with respect to the subject—in the afterword to the third edition of *Discourse Networks 1800/1900* (though this text is certainly free of "I"); there, its continuation to "Discourse Networks 2000" is also called "another story." Not only, but especially by being called "another story," the "Discourse Networks 2000," as the impossibility of an archaeology of the present, are moved into the queue for both pending analysis *and* the postponement of such an analysis into the *FILO stack* of media studies (to say it in appropriate terms): *first in (FI), last out (LO).* This is the future-orientation of the insight that "all libraries are discourse networks, but discourse networks have ceased to consist necessarily of books for a long time," and thus the forward-facing gaze is the one that opens the eyes to a gaze aimed back to that which "stores, and transmits data, and that such operations in the age-old medium of the alphabet have the same technical positivity as they do in computers" whereas "laments over the death of Man or the subject," taking into account this positivity, "always arrive too late."[37]

Yet if there are then no more dirges to be sung (on the contrary, abolishment, exorcisms, and the joy of forgetting are indeed the watchwords here), the corresponding observations [*Feststellungen*] (notices of loss or negative reports, if one wishes) still belong systematically to the theoretical concerns of discourse analysis. It always deals with "forgetting" and "disappearance," with "disintegration" and "erosion."[38] As a result, there is in Kittler's work a Nietzschean affirmation and the continued avant-gardism of the *Il faut être absolument moderne*, perhaps in the form of a strike against Foucault who remained the "old-fashioned archivist of old-fashioned things"[39] because he didn't get "Shannon's kind of discourse analysis."[40] Or, as we see in the then following outlook:

> The Cabbala predicts a terrible day when words will lose their meaning and become simply words, dead stones which fall from our mouths. That day need not be terrible and no longer has to be predicted. Somewhere in catalogues and discourse analyses words have been discarded and forgotten, personal information and fingerprints have been left in data banks, the latest historical events in television stations. People no longer need memory.[41]

On the other hand, however, there is also the tacit knowledge that Rimbaud's popular lyrics (*Il faut être absolument moderne*) took on a life of their own out of his (amply delirious) *A Season in Hell* (*Une saison en enfer*). There is the clear negative balance here, in the same manner of the essay on Pink Floyd when Kittler writes: "*Brain Damage* needs no further description. The damage has already been done."[42] And there is, eventually, the concession that the sort-out work of all discourse network analysis are themselves old-fashioned, outdated, or even "archaic." As "archaic as inevitable,"[43] writes Kittler pointedly, thereby declaring the conceded outdatedness to be part of his program too. For it also finds expression when he suddenly vaunts the course of his own education in the foreword to his *Technische Schriften*. The "freedom to begin a literary criticism of technical media," he writes, is owed to American universities and French theory, that is to say, to the avant-garde on the one hand, and to the "intellectual freedom of or from the codes in German *Bildungsanstalten*" on the other,[44] meaning the good old, very specific German universities which had, as Kittler writes, already successfully begun to commence with their own demise.

Further examples of this same outdatedness could be offered, but it should be enough here to rather question their function. When "freedom" gets to be part of the argument, to what extent is it—perhaps itself a piece of the old-fashioned—still once more at stake?

There is a simple reason why it's not only about celebrating the contemporary *state of the art*, but also about contrasting it with the swan song of downfall, of decay, or simply with the evanescence [*Vergänglichkeit*] of what is going to pass: if Walter Benjamin's "Now of recognizability"[45] is the result of the renunciation of the perspective of decline and progress, the recognizability of the now appears only as a reflection of progress that has been achieved and all that has been lost on the other.[46] Only then one can notice the *facticity* of what *was*, what *is*, and what—heralding the next future—presently *occurs*; only in this way does the look back lead to an "assessment of the effects" of ongoing transformations, rather than being mere nostalgia (or a simple concurrent chronicle);[47] only in this way do things appear in their authentic-fundamental *variability*.

And it is about this variability when Kittler not only points to things that have vanished but also selectively retains them (as is the case of, for example, the concept of the "*Semesterferien*"),[48] that is to say, when he switches *Zukunft* to *Herkunft*. The point is not to suspend the course of things, but to think the possibilities of other options. If today is different from yesterday, yesterday evidences that today needs not inevitably be as it is. The "I" of Kittler's "*Ich-Sagen*" might also, and not least, be grasped this way: as going through the options as in a game, where it is not just one of those options in itself. It signifies the fact that this science is "a gay science and not theory."[49] It puts itself into play so that, for its part, that which it says is simply brought "into play" instead of being presented (*referierbar*).[50] It is the moment—or *momentum*—of a programmicity which is at the same time demonstrated and annihilated—or, in short, the moment and *momentum* of exemplarity.

Black out. I understood his postcard without words. To each the time for his or her own other stories.

Translated by Chadwick Truscott Smith

NOTES

1. Friedrich Kittler, "The God of Ears," in *The Truth of the Technological World* (Stanford, CA: Stanford University Press, 2013), 51.

2. The standard English translation of Kittler's title, discourse networks, does not precisely align with the German *Aufschreibesysteme*, which is more literally rendered as "notation systems." The German phrase has the advantage of focusing on the material substrate of discourse (notations) as the precondition for a more abstract understanding of "discourse."

3. Cf. Friedrich Kittler, "Protected Mode," in *Draculas Vermächtnis: Technische Schriften* (Leipzig: Reclam, 1993), 210.

4. James Fenimore Cooper, *The Spy: A Tale of the Neutral Ground* (Boston, MA: Houghton Mifflin, 1911), www.bartleby.com/1007/, ch. 33, para. 41.

5. Marshall McLuhan, *Verbi-Voco-Visual Explorations* (New York: Something Else Press, 1967), item 2.

6. Cf. Vilém Flusser, "What is Communication," in *Writings* (Minneapolis: University of Minnesota Press, 2002).

7. Vilém Flusser, "Fernsehbild und politische Sphäre im Lichte der rumänischen Revolution," in *Von der Bürokratie zur Telekratie*, ed. Peter Weibel (Berlin: Merve, 1990), 109.

8. Cf. Marshall McLuhan and Quentin Fiore, *The Medium Is the Massage: An Inventory of Effects* (New York: Penguin Books, 1967), 50: "the portable book, which men could read in privacy and in isolation from others," as complete idiots.

9. Friedrich A. Kittler, "Autorschaft und Liebe," in *Austreibung des Geistes aus den Geisteswissenschaften. Programme des Poststrukturalismus* (Paderborn, Germany: Schöningh, 1980), 145–48; translated by Matthew J. Fraser as "Authorship and Love," *Theory, Culture and Society* 32, no. 2 (2015), 15–47.

10. Kittler, "Autorschaft und Liebe," 145.

11. Ibid., 168.

12. Friedrich A. Kittler, "Pink Floyd: Brain Damage," in *Europalyrik 1775—heute: Gedichte und Interpretationen*, ed. Klaus Lindemann (Paderborn: Schöningh, 1982), 467–77; Expanded Version: "Der Gott der Ohren," in *Das Schwinden der Sinne*, ed. Dietmar Kamper and Christoph Wulf (Frankfurt am Main: Suhrkamp, 1984), 140–55.

13. Kittler, "God of Ears," 45 and 47.

14. Ibid., 49. The citation from Lacan is from *The Four Fundamental Concepts of Psychoanalysis*, trans. A. Sheridan (New York: State University of New York Press, 1977).

15. Cf. "God of Ears," 43. See also, Friedrich Kittler, "Martin Heidegger, Medien und die Götter Griechenlands. Entfernen heißt die Götter nähern," in *Philosophie in der Medientheorie*, ed. Alexander Roesler and Bernd Stiegler (Munich: Wilhelm Fink, 2008), 133–43.

16. Cf. Kittler, *Draculas Vermächtnis*, 8.

17. Kittler, "God of Ears," 54. The phrase already appears in Friedrich A. Kittler, "Forgetting," *Discourse*, no. 3 (Spring 1981): 92.

18. Friedrich Kittler, "Ein Verwaiser," in *Anschlüsse: Versuche nach Michel Foucault*, ed. Gesa Dane et al. (Tübingen: Brandes and Apsel, 1985), 142.

19. Kittler, "Forgetting," 116.

20. See Friedrich Kittler, "Wie man abschafft, wovon man spricht: Der Autor von *Ecce homo*," *Literaturmagazin*, no. 12 (1980): 153–78.

21. Kittler, "Martin Heidegger," 134.

22. Kittler, "Ein Verwaiser," 142.

23. Kittler, "Forgetting," 117n4.

24. Friedrich Kittler, "Biogeographie," in *Mediengenerationen*, ed. Jochen Hörisch (Frankfurt am Main: Suhrkamp, 1997), 91.

25. Ibid., 90.

26. Kittler, "Wie man abschafft, wovon man spricht," 164, 153, and 170.

27. Kittler, "Autorschaft und Liebe," 143.

28. Kittler, "Forgetting," 116.

29. Ibid., 88.

30. Ibid., 93.

31. Cf. Kittler, "Forgetting," 92. For a history of the concept of *Aufschreibesysteme*, see *Grundbegriffe der Medientheorie*, ed. Alexander Roesler and Bernd Stiegler (Paderborn: Wilhelm Fink, 2005), 28–31.

32. Kittler, *Aufschreibesysteme 1800/1900*, 3rd rev. ed. (Munich: Wilhelm Fink, 1995), 519; afterword to the 2nd exp. ed. (1987). See also (the virtually identical) "Über Aufschreibesysteme," in *Mitteilungen des Deutschen Germanistenverbandes*, no. 3 (1986): 3.

33. Kittler, "Forgetting," 90.

34. Ibid., 93.

35. On "Discourse Networks," 3rd. ed., see the (virtually identical) *Aufschreibesysteme 1800/1900*, 519. On this critique of Foucault, especially where the computer is embraced in his observation, see also Friedrich Kittler, "Heidegger und die Medien- und Technikgeschichte: Oder: Heidegger vor uns," in *Heidegger-Handbuch: Leben—Werk—Wirkung*, ed. Dieter Thomä (Stuttgart: J. B. Metzler, 2003), 502.

36. Kittler, "Forgetting," 94.

37. Kittler, *Aufschreibesysteme*, 524, 519, and 520.

38. Kittler, "Forgetting," 91.

39. Ibid., 115.

40. Kittler, "Verwaiser," 146.

41. Kittler, "Forgetting," 115.

42. "The God of Ears," 46.

43. Kittler, *Aufschreibesysteme*, 522.

44. Kittler, introduction to *Draculas Vermächtnis: Technische Schriften*, 10.

45. Cf. Walter Benjamin, *Das Passagen-Werk: Gesammelte Schriften* (Frankfurt/M.: Suhrkamp, 1991), 5.1:578. For a contrast between Benjamin's philosophy of history and Foucault's effective history (and thus Kittler), see Bernhard J. Dotzler, "Frühneuzeit der Kybernetik: Urgeschichte oder Archäologie?" in *Spuren der Avantgarde: Theatrum Machinarum—Frühe Neuzeit und Moderne im Kulturvergleich*, ed. Helmar Schramm et al. (Berlin, New York: de Gruyter, 2008), 10–27 (*Arcades Projects*, Convolute N3,1).

46. Cf. Kittler, "Forgetting," 91: "It is only against the backdrop of disappearance . . ."

47. Kittler, *Aufschreibesysteme*, 523.

48. Cf. Friedrich Kittler, *Eine Kulturgeschichte der Kulturwissenschaft* (Munich: Wilhelm Fink 2000), 249.

49. Horst Turk and Friedrich A. Kittler, "Einleitung," in *Urszenen: Literaturwissenschaft als Diskursanalyse und Diskurskritik* (Frankfurt am Main: Suhrkamp, 1977), 43.

50. Kittler, *Austreibung*, 12.

4

NIGHTBLACK

Formatting Love

Elisabeth Weber

In recent years, Friedrich Kittler's work has repeatedly been associated with the project of Heideggerian *Seinsgeschichte*. Most prominently, in a text published in 2012, Hans Ulrich Gumbrecht argues that in light of Kittler's posthumous texts and his two volumes on Greece, *Musik und Mathematik* (published in 2006 and 2009), the project of *"Seinsgeschichte* constitutes the continuity of Friedrich Kittler's entire oeuvre," thereby lending "an explicitly philosophical ground to the early texts" as well.[1]

The term *Seinsgeschichte* is both easy and hard to translate: literally, it is "the history of being." What is meant is, to quote a rough definition by the philosopher John McCumber, "the uncovering of epochal transformations in Being which . . . lie wholly beyond, yet govern, everything else that happens."[2] According to Gumbrecht, Kittler's text on "La folie Tristan" dis-covers the latter's potential to unveil *Seinsgeschichte*, that is, its actual occurrence as "truth event" (*Wahrheitsereignis*).[3]

In this reading, Friedrich Kittler—the great theoretician of media, who often quoted philosophers only to deride them and to resolutely distance himself from them—would be not just a philosopher, but, to use Heidegger's language, a thinker of nothing less than *Seinsgeschichte*, in the sense, to quote Heidegger again, that *"the destiny of beyng devolves upon the thinkers."*[4] Not only would the two volumes *Musik und Mathematik* embody this ambition (and indeed, they do to a considerable extent);[5] according to Gumbrecht, it would equally apply to Kittler's early oeuvre. Already Geoffrey Winthrop-Young, in his excellent book on Kittler's work, had remarked that Kittler's concluding word on Foucault could be read as a self-description *in nuce*: "What remains is his lifelong circumscription or paraphrase of a word by Heidegger (*Umschreibung eines Heideggerwortes*): *Seinsgeschichte*."[6]

Indeed, Friedrich Kittler himself claimed the term for his work, explicitly so in *Musik und Mathematik*. Asked in an interview published in January 2009 to sum up what he was doing when he was "carrying out media-science" *(wenn Sie Medienwissenschaft betreiben)*, he replied: "Eine Seinsgeschichte, die *up to date* ist, sozusagen [a *Seinsgeschichte* that is, as it were, up to date]." He attributed the leading edge (even "leading world-wide") that the work of scholars inspired by his methods had to "precise historical research" on the one hand, and to the "connection with philosophy" and the awareness of the "philosophical heritage" on the other.[7]

In 1989, David Wellbery advanced an argument that seems perhaps no less startling than the assertion of Kittlerian *Seinsgeschichte*, although of course very differently so. In his remarkable foreword to the English translation of Kittler's *Discourse Networks*, Wellbery writes:

> The point at which discourse networks reveal most sharply their specific impress is in the pathologies they produce. Just as post-hermeneutic criticism [which is how Wellbery defines Friedrich Kittler's work] focuses on the difference between information and noise, sense and nonsense, that defines every medium, so too it attends to the difference between normal behavior and aberrance (including madness) that lends every cultural formation its identity. The victims who people Kittler's book—the Bettinas, the Günderodes, the Nietzsches, the Schrebers—speak the truth of the culture they suffer. Whoever would look for the bonds of solidarity that orient Kittler's investigation will find them here: in its unmistakable compassion for the pathos of the body in pain. Hermeneutics would appropriate this corporeal singularity in the construction of a meaning. Post-hermeneutic criticism, however, draws its responsibility precisely from the unassimilable otherness of the singular and mortal body. This is the ethical reason it stops making sense.[8]

Friedrich Kittler, the scholar who once said that he only wrote for those who understood higher mathematics,[9] thus echoing "Lacan's refusal to discuss the subject of language with anybody not versed in cybernetics";[10] Friedrich Kittler, the scholar who asserted that "given the strong influence of technical constraints and challenges, [one should] learn at least one or two formal languages in order to overcome the dominance of and hence dependency on large computer companies such as Microsoft" and be able "to command [one's own] PC rather than be commanded by the machine";[11] Friedrich Kittler who, accordingly, "wanted to establish a real *computer literacy*" and consequently offered not only courses on literature but also graduate seminars on computer programming languages[12]—when did this scholar "morph into Elaine Scarry?," as Winthrop-Young ironically asked in response to Wellbery. "He has repeatedly trounced theory's sentimental fetish of the body, and now we are to believe that he is ruled by compassion for 'the sufferance of the body, its essential pathos'"?[13] But dismissing Wellbery's argument all too quickly, Winthrop-Young cautions, "misses out on [his] underlying point that some of the more subtle and crucial aspects of *Discourse Networks* which remained unappreciated in Germany could receive a more informed welcome in North America" because of American academics' greater familiarity (in 1990) with issues such as the discursive construction of gender and the "medial blurring of body/technology boundaries."[14]

From the broad philosophical pursuit of *Seinsgeschichte* to an attentiveness to the body in pain, the continuum in Friedrich Kittler's work can be found, I maintain, in his never-abandoned reflection on love. I will focus on two facets of this reflection. First, not surprisingly, for Kittler, love is formatted by media: those media that are openly and generally acknowledged as dominant, and, even more powerfully, those that are de facto already dominant but not yet known or perceived as such. Second, on some occasions in Kittler's work, love is described as what one could call a "truth-event." In the sense this concept is given by Alain Badiou who, like Kittler, has solid knowledge of higher mathematics and who, like him, knows the work of both Martin Heidegger and Jacques Lacan inside out, it might prove to be productive for Kittler's work as well.

If one sets out to understand his media analyses of discourse networks around 1800 and 1900 as uncovering "epochal transformations in Being," then, on the one hand, "love," and in some instances sexuality, functions as a seismograph for such "epochal transformations," but on the other hand, "love" occurs as a "truth event" only in the disruption of its media-dictated formatting; in those moments, as Wellbery puts it, when the "unassimilable otherness of the singular and mortal body" speaks "the truth of the culture [it] suffers." Kittler's latest texts speak about love as a rebellion against the truth of the pervasive culture singular and mortal bodies suffer. The truth of this culture, of its all-programming, all-formatting, and all-surveilling networks, is nothing but war. Contrary to what an adept of the media-historic, antihermeneutic Kittler might assume, Kittler's later texts do not invite the reader to "mentally open the drone as a system of war" to discover a "beautifully fragile system" that might align more with (presumably Greek) polytheism than with monotheism.[15] Rather, those texts advocate a form of resistance through noncooperation: neither ignorance nor forgetting, but boycott in discourse and practice.

AN ARCH OF MOURNING

When Kittler described his magnum opus, *Discourse Networks*, as "written in black in every sense," this was understood to allude to "the black academic market (that is, outside established schools and trends)" for which it was written, but also "to the German political color coding that associates black with conservatism."[16] Kittler himself described his book as a melancholical book.[17] In that sense, "black in every regard" includes at least one more dimension: *Discourse Networks* was written in mourning.

It is love as both rebellion and punctuating "truth event" that his writing often mourns. The two volumes *Musik und Mathematik* celebrate and mourn "love" openly and with great pathos: Greek, or rather, the sirens' love as freely flowing, unconcealed truth of being, long-lost, but discoverable for the free. Without doubt, Kittler wrote those books in order to show the rediscoverability of that love.[18] Kittler's early works have a very different tone: they do mourn love, but discretely and irreverently. One of the earlier texts, "Writing into the wind, Bettine," spells out love as a truth event in the sense of a rebellious, joyous, bold, if fragile disruption.[19]

There are other reasons why most of Kittler's oeuvre, not just *Discourse Networks*, is "written in black." Even though Kittler describes in an interview *Gramophone, Film, Typewriter* in contradistinction to *Discourse Networks* as a "joyful" book *(ein fröhliches Buch)*,[20] whoever wants to read it first has to pass through two massive arches of mourning: the preface and the introduction, dated 1985.

Four quotes will help to substantiate the view that Kittler's writing "in black" is a writing in mourning. After three decades, these quotes have not lost one bit of their sharpness in assessing the situation in which they were written, and in which we read them today:

From the introduction: "All the orders and judgments, announcements and prescriptions (military and legal, religious and medical) that produced mountains of corpses were communicated along the very same channel that monopolized the descriptions of those mountains of corpses."[21]

From the first page of the preface: "Increasingly, data flows once confined to books and later to records and films are disppapearing into black holes and boxes that, as artificial intelligences, are bidding us farewell on their way to nameless high commands."[22]

From the second page of the preface: At the turn of the nineteenth century into the twentieth, the "terror" of the "novelty" of technological media was "registered more acutely than in today's alleged media pluralism, in which anything goes provided it does not disturb the assumption of global dominance by Silicon Valley."[23]

In 1985, the introduction draws "a ghostly photograph of our own present as future" *(ein Geisterphoto unserer Gegenwart als Zukunft)*—of the present in 1985, but also of our present in 2017:

People will be hooked to an information channel that can be used for any medium – for the first time in history, or for its end. Once movies and music, phone calls and texts reach households via optical fiber cables, the formerly distinct media of television, radio, telephone, and mail converge, standardized by transmission frequencies and bit format. The optoelectronic channel in particular will be immune to disturbances that might randomize the pretty bit patterns behind the images and sounds. Immune, that is, to the bomb. As is well known, nuclear blasts send an electromagnetic pulse (EMP) through the usual copper cables, which would infect all connected computers. The Pentagon is engaged in farsighted planning: only the substitution of optical fibers for metal cables can accommodate the enormous rates and volumes of bits required, spent, and celebrated by electronic warfare. All early warning systems, radar installations, missile bases, and army staffs in Europe . . . finally will be connected to computers safe from EMP and thus will remain operational in wartime. In the meantime, pleasure is produced as a by-product: people are free to channel-surf among entertainment media. After all, fiber optics transmit all messages imaginable save for the one that counts—the bomb.

These are the premises of Kittler's work. Everything else is placed in that light, or rather, in that blackness: "Mountains of corpses" in the past of the monopoly of writing, and "the bomb" looming in the future.[24] What Kittler writes about love is never unaware of this arch of mourning.[25]

While the night-sight technology for machine guns, tanks, submarines and the cockpits of fighter jets that pierced the "nightblack" in World War II was not decisive for the outcome of the war, it provided the "sensor-technology whose raw data are used today in digital signal processing."[26] From the medium of writing via analog technology to digital media, the history of communication technologies is a "series of strategic escalations: . . . techniques of data processing surpass and outperform each other reciprocally by means of their own dynamic."[27] Kittler assesses the escalatory destructiveness of techniques of data processing as so thoroughly pervasive that in his later texts, he turns to the earliest phases of pretechnological media, in particular the Greek alphabet, in what could be described as a boycott of war machines in favor of what he portrays as the medium of love.

FORMATTED LOVE

Kittler's description of love as constitutive of the discourse network around 1800 is well-known. He contrasts two codifications of love, the medieval clan

(*Sippe*) on the one hand, and the invention of educated bourgeoisie in the seventeenth and eighteenth centuries with its "nuclear" or "conjugal family" on the other. Winthrop-Young succinctly summarizes the argument:

[Drawing a] sharp contrast between two very different body-medium links that represent two very different ways that writers evoked and readers experienced love, [Kittler first] presents Paolo and Francesca, Dante's infernal couple, whose doomed love drastically short-circuits texts and bodies, leading them to physically (re)enact the adulterous love story they had been reading out loud. (Their narrative, in turn, manages to physically knock out their spellbound listener.) Against this Kittler sets the equally ill-fated love recorded by Goethe of Werther and Lotte, who celebrate a far less physical but no less delirious communion by allowing their souls to share the spirit of Klopstock's beloved poetry. [Paolo and Francesca's] [i]mpassioned bodies cede to [Werther and Lotte's] yearning souls, nameless desires communicated by an anonymous text make way for the spirit of authorship, and manuscripts to be read aloud in the company of others are replaced by printed books to be devoured in solitary silence.[28]

In his essay "Authorship and Love," Kittler sums up the stakes of these two scenes, separated by four and a half centuries:

Nothing . . . has remained the same. The single word *love*, which we hear so timelessly, can neither bridge the opposition nor conceal it. . . . [If in Dante's time, desire was governed by] a law of quite literal—which is to say corporeal—incisions and dissections, which regulated not life and daily routine but rather modes of death . . . the inverse holds for modernity: the law has been displaced by the norm which, as in Foucault's formulation makes live and lets die. Instead of the neatly-calibrated death penalties, which follow and result from the act, what await us are the countless norms that precede every action and make it into a "socially relevant" one. In the place of sovereign power, which had only political-juridical effects, a power emerges without names and signifiers, one which for the first time in human history takes control of daily life – and this "in the name of the people," which is to say, in the name of no one at all. With bio- and psychotechniques, it directs [*steuert*] and explores the conditions of life themselves.[29]

This is why Kittler's patient text analyses "emphasize" that "power stands over the entire relation. The discursive net called understanding has to be knotted." Around 1800, this happens through the enforcement of a new pedagogy, a new way of learning how to read and its corresponding "selection and control of discourse . . . even if hermeneutics owes its victory to having initially masqueraded as the opposite of that control."[30] Quoting Nietzsche's "On the Future of Our Educational Institution," Kittler identifies the "new idol" that exercises its power in every act of hermeneutic understanding: the state which, first and foremost in each lecture given under the assumption of academic freedom by professors at public institutions of higher learning, stands "at a modest distance" behind both the professor and the listening students.

> There is such a thing as understanding and being understood only once a new type of discourse control has learned to practice its "modest distance" in order merely to point out from time to time that the state is the "purpose, goal, and essence of this odd speaking and listening procedure." Over the free space of hermeneutics there stands, as above every language game, an "order word." This command is the unique knot that itself will not and cannot be understood. The state remains closed off to every hermeneutic. Because understanding, despite its claim to universality, is one speech act among others, it cannot get behind the speech act that instituted it. Texts that are part of the hermeneutic net allow the power that governs them to come to light only in a masked fashion.[31]

To put it in a nutshell then, the by now famous argument of *Dichter-Mutter-Kind* and of *Discourse Networks* is that "love" in 1800 is coded as mother-love, through which authors (*Autoren*) and public servants (*Staatsbeamte*) of the Prussian state are equally produced, Goethe being the prime example of both. Together, the coding of the new pedagogy of mother-love and the institution of the "new human sciences," or humanities, program and format sexualities. The new disciplines of the humanities—in German, tellingly, *Geisteswissenschaften*, "sciences of the spirit"—were "invented in the eighteenth century to invent individuals and souls," whose "correlative," in all logic, is "hermeneutics."[32] At the same time, the "familiarization of the erotic" provides "one of the most effective steering mechanisms [*Steuerungsmaschinen*]."[33] Thus, the family and the school serve as "the production sites" of the individual, the latter being the "real correlate of the new techniques of power that save its data and produce its discourses."[34] However, in the discourse network of 1800, data and discourses are entirely based on writing and the book. Contrary to the appearance mirrored back by countless literary and scholarly texts, in letter-based media that "capture and produce the symbolic,"[35] the "I" does not reside "as king in the innermost regions of the soul . . . instead, it commands there as a lieutenant, read *lieu tenant* [place-holder, deputy], where Others have commanded it to go—from far outside, on the battlefields of discourse." On this battlefield, "'I' must only be able to confirm, in the case of occasional monitoring inquiries on the behalf of power, having received my orders."[36]

Moreover, contrary to the praxis still prevailing in many, if not most literature departments, the discourse networks of 1900 and of 2000 have irrevocably dispersed the "cloud of meaning" that surrounded the discourse network of 1800, giving literature the "nebulous legitimation" of hermeneutical intelligibility instead of identifying it as "a matter of what has been programmed and programs in turn."[37]

The discourse network of 1900 reflects the break of the monopoly that writing and the book held on "processes of storing and processing." As Sybille Krämer observes, "as soon as other types of discourse networks emerge with technological, analog media, . . . an archeology of present forms of knowledge can no longer be practiced by discourse analysis but must rather be taken over by technological media analysis."[38] This is the thrust of Kittler's *Gramophone, Film, Typewriter*, whose "historical approach transforms discourse analysis into the reflex and symptom of a specific—and since ended—media epoch." Krämer identifies the "crux of this story of the metamorphosis of the discourse-analytical approach" in the "technological transformation of the notion of media itself: media are no longer directly linked to signs, to communication, or, for that matter, even to information, but rather to data, in other words to the material 'carriers' of information. The operations of media structure the terrain of data processing: they select, store, and produce signals."[39] What Kittler calls "the adventures of our sexed bodies" is deeply affected by this development.[40]

How, then, is "love" produced in the discourse-networks of the twentieth and the twenty-first centuries? In a short 2001 article entitled "The programmed eros: Love in the age of technical media," Kittler outlined his response to this question.[41] Reading Thomas Pynchon's *Gravity's Rainbow*, Kittler shows how, with the advent of new media of transmission and storage, sexuality (which he explicitly differentiates here from love) is transformed into a "function of a scientific-technological discourse, which reduces subjects [*Subjekte*] to test subjects [*Versuchspersonen*]. Whereas in Racine or Goethe the combinatory labyrinths of love served in the end the purpose of committing individuals behind their backs to the reproduction of the species," in *Gravity's Rainbow*, by contrast, the eerily matching Poisson distributions of the hero's sexual adventures in London during World War II and of the impact of German V2 rockets "peg the test subjects to the production and reproduction of technologies which, like vampires, as it is said explicitly, suck blood and life."[42] In other words, as Kittler continues,

There is not first a Bergsonian man who would subsequently expand his life to include discrete media hacking up time [*diskrete Medien der Zeitzerhackung*];

rather, there is first a firearm which centuries later calls forth its own mathematics and again centuries later the measuring instruments for the latter. This technology as *"Gestell"* or "enframing" (to use Heidegger's term) enframes also man. In any case, the requirements of rocket technology exacted well-nigh the miniaturization of all of today's information media. . . . "In the future," a famous soft-ware billionaire instructed his programmer slaves in internal memos, "in the future, we will treat end-users just like computers: both are programmable."[43]

Similar to Heidegger's observation that whether we use it or not, all of us are thrown into the age of the typewriter,[44] all of us are thrown into the age of the computer, where the end user is not the agency governing the machine. The computer age is the last phase of a military and media history that "can be told, at least partly, as the story of a series of steps of escalation where one innovation in technology really does triumph over its forerunner."[45] As one of the prime examples and "heavily influenced" by Paul Virilio's *War and Cinema*, Kittler traces in *Gramophone, Film, Typewriter* the history of the movie camera as coinciding "with the history of automatic weapons" and concludes: "The transport of pictures only repeats the transport of bullets. . . . In the principle of cinema resides mechanized death as it was invented in the nineteenth century: the death no longer of one's immediate opponent but of serial nonhumans [*serieller Unmenschen*]."[46]

Taking seriously the observation of "escalation," one of the questions that begs to be asked today is how media such as short-circuit video cameras, video games, and automatic weapon systems yielding unmanned drones and killer robots, not only program the so-called end users to kill, but also in which ways they program the love-making and loving of those "end users." In the age of warfare carried out by "unmanned aerial vehicles" and its extrajudicial killings, in an age, in which, in the words of the Palestinian writer Atef Abu Saif, "the drone eats with me,"[47] Avital Ronell's remarks on the first Gulf War are as pertinent today as they were in 1994: "We do not know how to think war as something we should wage, which is why we think we can conduct warfare as if it were extraneous, momentary, simulated, and not engaging the very core of our being."[48] But "engage the very core of our being" it does, even if there is hardly a public reflection or debate about it. To paraphrase again Kittler's comment on Heidegger, all of us are thrown into the age of drones, whether we like it or not.[49] The often invoked "global war on terror" has through its weapon of choice indeed become, as Derek Gregory puts it, "the everywhere war." On the ground, this means concretely that this "'war' is more like a vast campaign of extrajudicial executions: a strategy of targeted assassinations" that obeys no longer the "geocentric interpretation of the laws of warfare," but rather, in Grégoire Chamayou's succinct formulation, the "manhunt doctrine."[50] The latter's apparent paradox resides in the fact that in spite of its global expansion, its actual "conflict zone appears as a space fragmented into a provisional multitude of kill boxes that can be activated in a manner both flexible and bureaucratic," but that also entirely unhinge the laws of armed conflict.[51]

During an interview, Kittler specified that the discourse network of 2000 would only materialize as "the content of all the servers of the world. No human being can write that any more. That would be . . . *ach!*"—the German *ach* expressing here, most likely, resignation or despair.[52] The link between love and war technology is alluded to in another interview, conducted in 2003:

> When I speak about love in Europe, *I really mean it*. It is something that I put into action, something I have written papers on and spoken about at conferences. . . . To give you an example, at present, one of my preoccupations is the fight against all monotheistic Gods which, until recently, were represented in the world by three male warriors: Saddam Hussein, George W. Bush, and Ariel Sharon. I fight against these warriors because all three believe not simply in one God but in one *male* God. Thus, they refuse to have a female Goddess at their side. . . . [I]t is for me very important to argue that Aphrodite, the Goddess of love and beauty, is a Goddess for *all* animals, inclusive of men and women.[53]

Seinsgeschichte is short-circuited here with the suffering bodies of all animals, lovers in particular being first and foremost animals.[54] In other words, the question of love in the discourse network of 2000 needs to be answered by first acknowledging that within the latter, *love* is all but impossible. Therefore, Kittler declared in the same interview that "the single most important thing to do at the present time is to tell the story of how love has been forbidden from the time of ancient Greece to this very day"[55]—a story that is one of the major motivations for *Musik und Mathematik*.

Coming from a different angle, Alain Badiou presents a reflection on love that resonates with Kittler's observations about the principle of cinema. Badiou diagnoses a correspondance between the propaganda of so-called surgical warfare that promises "zero deaths," and the propaganda of Internet dating sites which promise love with "zero risks." Of course, as Badiou points out, in reality, the risk factor is never eliminated; rather, the publicity of no-risk Internet dating sites, "like the propaganda for imperial armies, says that the risks will be everyone else's!" He continues:

If you have been well trained for love, following the canons of modern safety, you won't find it difficult to dispatch the other if he doesn't conform to your comfort. If he suffers, that's his problem, right? He's not part of modernity. In the same way that "zero deaths" apply only to the Western military. The bombs they drop kill a lot of people who are to be blamed for living underneath. But these casualties are Afghans, Palestinians. . . . They don't belong to modernity either. Safety-first love, like everything governed by the norm of safety, implies the absence of risks for people who have a good insurance policy, a good army, a good police force, a good psychological take on personal hedonism, and all risks for those on the opposite side.[56]

Accepting this asymmetry is possible only at the condition, as Jacques Derrida observed, that "one doesn't count the dead in the same way from one corner of the globe to the other."[57]

LOVE AS TRUTH EVENT

Does it then make sense to speak about love as truth event?

If there is, in Kittler's earlier work, one figure for whom love occurs as a truth event, it would be Bettina Brentano. Polemicizing against the secondary literature on her which tends to focus on the social issues close to her heart (nineteenth-century anti-Semitism, social injustice, and the misery of the working class), Kittler argues that politics actually start much earlier: in Bettina Brentano's writing, which through its very form is incompatible with nationalism and the state, and rebellious against the discourse network around 1800. Bettina Brentano, thus, is an example for the very possibility of differences *within* a discourse network. Analogously, according to Kittler, Isolde in the twelfth-century poem "La folie Tristan" gambles, "in the game of games, with the God of the Christians" (*setzt den Gott der Christen . . . aufs Spiel der Spiele*) to subvert the social order by publicly making love with Tristan.[58]

The difference between Bettina and Isolde, though, is significant: Whereas with Tristan and Isolde, what remains is, to quote Badiou, "the meltdown concept of love," in Bettina's "*écriture automatique*," as Kittler calls it,[59] love disseminates unpredictably and irresistibly.

In Alain Badiou's summary of Tristan and Isolde's story, "the two lovers met and something like a heroic act for One was enacted against the world. . . . [L]ove is consumed in the ineffable, exceptional moment of the encounter, after which it is impossible to go back to a world that remains external to the relationship." Bettina Brentano, on the other hand, challenges this "powerful artistic myth" as "existentially seriously lacking."[60] Kittler's reading shows again and again that Bettina Brentano is never a "heroic act for One" and thus never enacts her love "against the world"—too infinite is the world, and too boundless her passion:

> Surely, melodies are God-created beings that go on living in themselves, every thought brought forth from the soul alive, man doesn't generate thoughts, they generate man. Oh! Oh! Oh!—A little linden flower just fell on my nose—and now it's raining a bit; what am I writing rubbish here, and can hardly read it anymore, it's getting quite dark—how beautifully though nature spreads her veil—so luminous, so transparent—now the souls of the plants are starting to roam about, and the oranges in the shrub. And the fragrance of the linden—it comes flowing over, wave after wave—It's already getting dark—
>
> . . .
>
> How indeed can a person [*der Mensch*] not refrain from wishing to be anything other than a lover?[61]

As Kittler underlines, in the age of the invention of the "author," Bettina Brentano doesn't "provide her discourse with any basis of ownership or unifying principle,"[62] too many are her stories which overflow in her letters, defying any unity and, thus, any oeuvre,[63] and any *Seinsgeschichte* too: "In an age whose romantic men seek a New Mythology to reconcile all the traditions of Europe, Bettina prefers to found a new religion. Rule one: no education allowed. Rule two: expunge the error of friends of wisdom and church fathers that God is wisdom; *for God is passion.*"[64]

Kittler's later texts, such as the two volumes *Musik und Mathematik*,[65] introduce a significant turn insofar as they shun a direct engagement with the all-pervasive contemporary media and offer to think "love" without any relation to the latter, even though Kittler asserts a recursive continuity in *Seinsgeschichte* via the alphabet and its numerical values up to today's signal processing. To think "love" in the "digital now" would require, with *Musik und Mathematik*, to recognize that *Seinsgeschichte* at different epochal turns, rewrites writing and "plays" recursively, and to recognize that only with the "patience of a different beginning" a "recursive convocation of alphabet-writing" will yield the deep connection between love and the alphabetic knowledge of music, numbers, and cosmic elements.[66]

An engagement with today's media would necessarily divert from this *seinsgeschichtliche* approach, especially since a deep misunderstanding permeates media's omnipresence: Kittler remarked in an interview in 2003, that he found it "terrible" that people "continue to imagine that the Internet is the means by which they themselves are linked to others worldwide. For the fact is that it is their computers that are globally linked to other computers. Hence the real connection is not between people but between machines. . . . I do not believe that human beings are becoming cyborgs. Indeed, for me, the development of the Internet has much more to do with human beings becoming a reflection of their technolgies, of reacting or responding to the demands of the machine."[67] In the age of drone warfare, the demands of the machine are tantamount to dismantling notions that Grégoire Chamayou qualifies as "elementary" and that include the most elementary relation in love as Kittler understood it: reciprocity.[68] Unmanned drones render established categories obsolete, since they create, as Chamayou writes, "intense confusion . . . around notions as elementary as zones or places (geographical and ontological categories), virtue or bravery (ethical categories), warfare or conflict (categories at once strategic and legal-political)." Chamayou examines what he considers to lie "at the root" of this "crisis of intelligibility," namely, the "elimination, already rampant but here absolutely radicalized, of any immediate relation of reciprocity." [69]

Reciprocity is indispensable in Kittler's discourse on love, which is why it cannot live in or with a discourse on today's high-tech media and their culmination in highly sophisticated technologies of warfare:

> I must confess that I cannot stand on American soil with much pleasure. In fact, my antipathy to America is one of the main reasons why I often avoid talking about the military-industrial complex since for me to talk about the devil is to talk with the devil. As a good friend of mine said to me lately, we in Germany should not say a word about America's war on Iraq or speak any longer of the seemingly endless necessity of reforming Germany. We should not so much forget all this as not talk about it. Instead, we should focus on changing ourselves and speak about other things. So I asked him what we should discuss as an alternative and he answered that we should talk about love in Europe.[70]

In lieu of a conclusion, let me add some rapid observations on *Musik und Mathematik*, two books on Greece that arguably start and end with the sirens.[71] Love coincides here with music in the truth event of the sirens whose name Kittler translates as muses and as incarnations of Aphrodite, thus as lovers. Because Circe wanted to deceive Ulysses, she portrayed the sirens as lying and deadly dangerous.[72] Through this portrayal of truly *seinsgeschichtliche* consequence, the trinity (if I may) of women (in the plural), music and love was violated and concealed, resulting in a repression of all three, cemented with Platonic philosophy and monotheism, ever since. The West believed Circe instead of reading Homer closely. In the Roman and all subsequent empires and their cities, "the sirens go silent."[73]

Nonetheless, perhaps similar to Heidegger's thinking, where the city is shunned in favor of forest paths, in *Musik und Mathematik*, the sirens continue to sing in the countryside and on remote Greek islands in languages that have not experienced modern media of transmission.

Geoffrey Winthrop-Young described the "ethnocentrism" characteristic of Kittler's late insistence on Greece's position as "unique world-historical exception."[74] *Musik und Mathematik* indeed postulates a watershed of, again, *seinsgeschichtliche* dimensions between Semitic languages, built on a system of consonantal radicals in which vowels are not written, and Greek that has vowels and thus can sing.[75]

The sirens' free love and their song called forth an alphabet that included vowels. Free love and song, freely flowing through a vowel-infused and thus liberated alphabet that for Kittler is inseparable from political freedom, form the antipode of oriental despotisms, their mute-sounded alphabets and their implacable tyranny regarding the strict observance of their writing.[76] With Plato and the monotheistic religions, Greece's many-facetted freedom was forced to conceal itself. And "Europe's universities," Kittler writes in mourning and not without bitterness, "caved in from the beginning," suppressing the sensuality of the original link between writing, singing, and loving in favor of the assertion that writing was invented to record trade, transactions and travel, all under the aegis of the state.[77] But Greece's freedom still manifests itself in privileged moments: Isolde's free love is one,[78] and from the vantage point of *Musik und Mathematik*, Bettina would be speaking Greek too.

"We certainly won't cave in," Kittler writes, "because we are standing in an open field battle (*in offener Feldschlacht*). So mercilessly rules writing, in which nobody may delete or add a single letter, whereas the *Iliad* and the *Odyssey* are transmitted in thousands of free variants. Despots lust after bolting down their own signs, so that even Christian love, even though it promises to abolish the law, paradoxically remains law; only, fortunately, in vain."[79] Our urgent task today would be to remove the thick layers of Platonic and monotheistic deception that structure our world through and through and have led us to the brink of a third world war, in which, in fact, Christianity, Judaism, and Islam are already engaged.[80] Our task would be to prepare the return of Aphrodite whose free love is available to us, if we open our eyes and ears, and if we learn how to think and speak according to the alphabetical holism of pre-Platonic Greek.

The implications of this later turn in Friedrich Kittler's thinking are numerous and some of them are troubling. After all, arguments asserting the tyranny of the letter in Judaism and the lovelessness of the Jews, the original Semites, have been fundamental for German, and indeed, European anti-Judaism and anti-Semitism throughout several centuries. These troubling implications are also preprogrammed, I would argue, with the project of *Seinsgeschichte* and end up heavily overshadowing what Kittler had set out to celebrate: That with the Greek alphabet, for the first time, *relations* between numbers and sounds were thought.

Ulrike Bergermann offers a refreshing critique of the roles women play in *Musik und Mathematik*, and Michaela Ott offers an eloquent and succinct critique of Kittler's presentation of the Greek alphabet and of his reinterpretation of *Seinsgeschichte* as "history of voice-writing and of poetry and music" (*in Stimm-Schrift-Geschichte, in Poesie- und Musikgeschichte*).[81] I can only add a very brief response to the above-mentioned implications and their asserted mediatic foundation. I would start with recalling that not writing vowels does not mean not speaking or singing them. It allows speaking and singing to resonate in versions whose vividness should not and cannot be standardized or archived. Not writing vowels is not equivalent, as Kittler writes, to "arbitrary possibilities of re-interpretation."[82] Rather, it honors, to adapt David Wellbery's already quoted formulation, the "unassimilable otherness of the singular and mortal [voice]." Not writing vowels implies that in speaking, relations are fragile, just as in singing and, should I add, loving. Bettina Brentano knew this. The author of texts such as "Writing into the wind, Bettina," my teacher Friedrich Kittler whom I mourn, knew it too.

NOTES

1. Hans Ulrich Gumbrecht: "Tristans Narrheit als Wahrheitsereignis. Über zwei späte Texte von Friedrich Kittler, die Seinsgeschichte freilegen wollen," in *Isolde als Sirene: Tristans Narrheit als Wahrheitsereignis*, by Friedrich Kittler and Hans Ulrich Gumbrecht (Munich: Fink 2012), 11; my translation.

2. John McCumber, *Metaphysics and Oppression: Heidegger's Challenge to Western Philosophy* (Bloomington: Indiana University Press, 2013), 264n12.

3. Gumbrecht, "Tristans Narrheit," 17.

4. Martin Heidegger, *The Event*, trans. Richard Rojcewicz (Bloomington: Indiana University Press, 2013), xxiii. In his effort to distance himself from ontology, Heidegger introduced a different spelling of the word *Sein*: "Seyn," translated as "being."

5. Friedrich Kittler, *Musik und Mathematik, Bd. 1, Hellas, Tl. 1, Aphrodite* (Munich: Wilhelm Fink, 2005), *Musik und Mathematik, Bd. 1, Hellas, Tl. 2, Eros* (Munich: Wilhelm Fink, 2009). Indeed, the frequent use of Heideggerian terminology such as *Entbergung* (unconcealment), *Sterbliche* (mortals), *verwinden*, and *Seinsgeschichte* in these books indicates that one of the goals is to follow in Heidegger's footsteps.

6. Geoffrey Winthrop-Young, *Friedrich Kittler zur Einführung* (Hamburg: Junius, 2005), 163. The quote is from Friedrich Kittler, *Short Cuts* (Leipzig: Zweitausendeins, 2002), 39; my translation.

7. "Friedrich Kittler im Interview mit Christoph Weinberger: Das kalte Modell von Struktur," *Zeitschrift für Medienwissenschaften*, no. 1 (2009): 102.

8. David Wellbery, foreword to Friedrich A. Kittler, *Discourse Networks 1800/1900*, trans. Michael Metteer with Chris Cullens (Stanford, CA: Stanford University Press, 1992), xv–xvi.

9. Kittler in conversation with the author. See Geoffrey Winthrop-Young and Michael Wutz, "Translators' Introduction: Friedrich Kittler and Media Discourse Analysis," in Friedrich Kittler, *Gramophone, Film, Typewriter*, trans. with an introduction by Geoffrey Winthrop-Young and Michael Wutz (Stanford, CA: Stanford University Press, 1999), xviii: "The same impatience underlies Friedrich Kittler's comment that 'media science' [*Medienwissenschaft*] will remain mere 'media history' as long as the practitioners of cultural studies 'know higher mathematics only from hearsay.' Just as the formalist study of literature should be the study of 'literariness,' the study of media should concern itself primarily with mediality and not resort to the usual suspects—history, sociology, philosophy, anthropology, and literary and cultural studies—to explain how and why media do what they do. It is necessary to rethink media with a new and uncompromising degree of scientific rigor, focusing on the intrinsic technological logic, the changing links between body and medium, the procedures for data processing, rather than evaluate them from the point of view of their social usage."

10. Winthrop-Young and Wutz, "Translators' Introduction," xviii–xix: "By emphasizing Lacan's frequent references to circuits and feedback (not to mention Lacan's refusal to discuss the subject of language with anybody not versed in cybernetics), Kittler moved Lacan out of the hermeneutically soiled realism of old-style psychoanalysis, philosophy, and literary scholarship."

11. Markus Krajewski, "On Kittler Applied: A Technical Memoir of a Specific Configuration of the 1990s," *Thesis Eleven* 107, no. 1 (2011): 35. See also John Armitage, "From Discourse Networks to Cultural Mathematics: An Interview with Friedrich A. Kittler," *Theory, Culture and Society* 23, nos. 7–8 (2006): 26.

12. Krajewski, "On Kittler Applied," 35.

13. Geoffrey Winthrop-Young, "Krautrock, Heidegger, Bogeyman: Kittler in the Anglosphere," *Thesis Eleven* 107, no. 1 (2011): 13. Wellbery's sentence is from his foreword to Kittler, *Discourse Networks*, xv.

14. Winthrop-Young, "Krautrock, Heidegger, Bogeyman," 13.

15. See the intervention during the conference dedicated to Friedrich Kittler, *The Sirens Go Silent*, www.youtube.com/watch?v=QK9cGjF1uGo (72nd minute).

16. Winthrop-Young and Wutz, "Translators' introduction," xvii.

17. "Friedrich Kittler im Interview mit Christoph Weinberger," 100. See also Eva Horn, "Maschine und Labyrinth: Friedrich Kittlers 'Aufschreibesysteme 1800/1900,'" in *Friedrich Kittler. Kunst und Technik, Tumult: Schriften zur Verkehrswissenschaft*, ed. Michaela Ott and Walter Seitter (Wetzlar: Büchse der Pandora Verlag, 2012), 16. According to Horn, *Discourse Networks* could only be written as a "Untergangsgeschichte," a "history of downfall" or "doom", since "rules appear as addressable and describable only once they are no longer valid."

18. Kittler, *Musik und Mathematik*, Bd. 1 and 2.

19. Friedrich Kittler, "Writing into the Wind, Bettina," *Glyph: Textual Studies*, vol. 7, ed. Samuel Weber (Baltimore, MD: Johns Hopkins University Press, 1980), 32–69.

20. "Friedrich Kittler im Interview mit Christoph Weinberger," 100.

21. Kittler, *Gramophone, Film, Typewriter*, 4.

22. Ibid., xxxix.

23. Ibid., xl. Describing the project of *Gramophone, Film, Typewriter*, Kittler explains why the information technology whose monopoly was "coming to an end" around 1900 was able to "register" this very information through the employment of "an aesthetics of terror" whose writings offer "a ghostly image" (more literally "a ghostly photograph") of our own "present as future" (*ein Geisterphoto unserer Gegenwart als Zukunft*).

24. Kittler spoke of a "technological quantum leap" with regard to the Iraq war of 2003: "Technisch ist der Krieg ein Quantensprung," interview with Markus Albers, *Welt am Sonntag*, March 2, 2003.

25. To quote Ingeborg Bachmann, who is the first person after an unnamed "you" to whom Kittler expresses his gratitude at the end of the first volume of *Musik und Mathematik* and whose poem "Erklär mir Liebe" Kittler studied with his students in spring 2007.

26. Friedrich Kittler, "Die Nacht der Substanz," in *Kursbuch Medienkultur: Die maßgeblichen Theorien von Brecht bis Baudrillard*, ed. Claus Pias et al. (Stuttgart: Deutsche Verlags-Anstalt, 2000), 508. Of course, my title refers to this essay.

27. Friedrich Kittler, "Geschichte der Kommunikationsmedien," in *Raum und Verfahren: Interventionen 2*, ed. Jörg Huber and Alois Martin Müller (Basel: Stroemfeld-Roter Stern, 1993), 188, and Sybille Krämer, "The Cultural Techniques of Time Axis Manipulation: On Friedrich Kittler's Conception of Media," *Theory, Culture and Society*, 23, nos. 7–8 (2006): 104.

28. Winthrop-Young and Wutz, "Translators' Introduction," xxiii. See also the beginning of the book *Dichter-Mutter-Kind* (Munich: Fink, 1991), whose argument was already presented in the essay "Autorschaft und Liebe," in *Austreibung des Geistes aus den Geisteswissenschaften: Programme des Poststrukturalismus*, ed. Friedrich Kittler (Paderborn: Schöningh, 1980), 142–73, translated by Matthew Fraser as "Authorship and Love," *Theory, Culture and Society* 32, no. 3 (2015): 15–47.

29. Kittler "Authorship and Love," 18–20.

30. Friedrich Kittler, *Discourse Networks 1800/1900*, trans. Michael Metteer with Chris Cullens, foreword by David E. Wellbery (Stanford, CA: Stanford University Press 1992), 20 and 21.

31. Kittler, *Discourse Networks 1800/1900*, 21. The concept of "order word" is quoted from Gilles Deleuze and Félix Guattari's *A Thousand Plateaux*.

32. Kittler, "Authorship and Love," 26, and *Discourse Networks*, 21.

33. Kittler, *Discourse Networks*, 20.

34. Kittler, "Authorship and Love," 28.

35. Krämer, "Cultural Techniques of Time Axis Manipulation," 94.

36. Kittler, "Authorship and Love," 31.

37. Kittler, "Authorship and Love," 31, and *Discourse Networks*, 22.

38. Krämer, "Cultural Techniques of Time Axis Manipulation," 97.

39. Ibid.

40. Kittler, "Authorship and Love," 17.

41. Friedrich Kittler, "Der programmierte Eros: Die Liebe im Zeitalter technischer Medien," *Neue Zürcher Zeitung*, June 23, 2001, www.nzz.ch/aktuell/startseite/article6my6p -1.512324; my translation.

42. Ibid.

43. Ibid. Part of the text omitted from the quote reads: "Since that time, computers rely on tiny integrate circuits [whose] empire grows and grows precisely with the unbearable promise of erecting the instantaneous web-democracy."

44. Armitage, "From Discourse Networks to Cultural Mathematics: An Interview with Friedrich A. Kittler," 29: "What is important is that all of us are thrown into the age of typewriting, whether we like it or not."

45. Ibid., 28.

46. Ibid., 26, and Kittler, *Gramophone, Film, Typewriter*, 124. See also Kittler, "Media and Drugs in Pynchon's Second World War," in Friedrich Kittler, *Literature, Media, Information Systems*, ed. with an introduction by John Johnston (Amsterdam: Overseas Publishers Association, 1997), 103.

47. Atef Abu Saif, *The Drone Eats with Me: Diaries from a City under Fire* (Manchester: Comma Press, 2015).

48. Avital Ronell, "Supplement: Papers on the Gulf War," in *Finitude's Score. Essays for the End of the Millenium* (Lincoln: University of Nebraska Press, 1994), 297–98.

49. Armitage, "From Discourse Networks to Cultural Mathematics," 29.

50. Derek Gregory, "The Everywhere War," *Geographical Journal* 177, no. 3 (September 2011): 238; Grégoire Chamayou, *A Theory of the Drone* (New York: New Press, 2015), 57; Grégoire Chamayou, "The Manhunt Doctrine," *Radical Philosophy*, no. 169 (September–October 2011): 1.

51. Chamayou, *Theory of the Drone*, 55 and 57–58. See also Elisabeth Weber, *Kill Boxes. Facing the Legacy of US-Sponsored Torture, Indefinite Detention, and Drone Warfare* (Brooklyn, NY: Punctum Books, 2017), especially chs. 5 and 6.

52. "Friedrich Kittler im Interview mit Christoph Weinberger," 101.

53. Armitage, "From Discourse Networks to Cultural Mathematics," 30.

54. See, for example, Kittler, *Musik und Mathematik*, 1.2:171 and 173.

55. Armitage, "From Discourse Networks to Cultural Mathematics," 37.

56. Alain Badiou with Nicolas Truong, *In Praise of Love*, trans. Peter Bush (New York: New Press, 2012), 8–9, translation modified.

57. Jacques Derrida, "Autoimmunity: Real and Symbolic Suicides," in *Philosophy in a Time of Terror*, ed. Giovanna Borradori (Chicago: University of Chicago Press, 2003), 92.

58. Kittler, *Isolde als Sirene*, 37–38.

59. Kittler, *Discourse Networks*, 127.

60. Badiou, *In Praise of Love*, 30–31.

61. "Gewiß, Melodien sind gottgeschaffene Wesen, die in sich fortleben, jeder Gedanke aus der Seele hervor lebendig, der Mensch erzeugt die Gedanken nicht, sie erzeugen den Menschen.—Ach! Ach! Ach!—Da fällt mir ein Lindenblütchen auf die Nas—und da regnet's ein bißchen; was schreib ich doch hier dumm Zeug hin, und kann's kaum mehr lesen, jetzt dämmert's schon stark—wie schön doch die Natur ihren Schleier ausbreitet—so licht, so durchsichtig—jetzt fangen die Pflanzenseelen an umherzuschweifen, und die Orangen im Boskett. Und der Lindenduft—der kommt Well auf Well herübergeströmt—es wird schon dunkel— . . . Wie kann sich doch der Mensch nicht enthalten, irgendwas anders sein zu wollen als ein Liebender?" Bettina Brentano, *Die Günderode*, quoted in Kittler, "Writing into the Wind," 35–36, 59; translation modified.

62. Kittler, *Discourse Networks*, 127.

63. Kittler, "Writing into the Wind," 50.

64. Ibid.

65. See also Friedrich Kittler, "Number and Numeral," *Theory, Culture and Society* 23, nos. 7–8 (2006):51–61.

66. Kittler, *Musik und Mathematik*, 1.2:80–81. On the "name" "recursion": "For this new way to write history [*Geschichte erschreiben*], there is only one way, one name: Recursion. We are attentive to the return of the same—and this in the same measure as it transforms itself *seinsgeschichtlich*. We 'run backwards' in time, from today to the Greeks, simultaneously however also forward in time, from the first beginning to its repeating overcoming [bis zu seiner wiederholenden Verwindung]." The term *Verwindung* stems from Heidegger. For a more detailed discussion of "recursion," see Wolfgang Ernst, "Kittler-Zeit: Unter Mithilfe technologischer Medien um andere Zeitverhältnisse wissen," in *Friedrich Kittler. Kunst und Technik, Tumult: Schriften zur Verkehrswissenschaft*, ed. Michaela Ott and Walter Seitter (Wetzlar, Germany: Büchse der Pandora Verlag, 2012), 100–107.

67. Armitage, "From Discourse Networks to Cultural Mathematics," 35–36.

68. See *Musik und Mathematik*, 1.2:77–78.

69. Chamayou, *Theory of the Drone*, 14.

70. Armitage, "From Discourse Networks to Cultural Mathematics," 28.

71. See Kittler, *Musik und Mathematik*, 1.1:36 and 1.2:266. Book 1 begins with the muses that make music, and thereby, the sirens are related to them. Book 2 ends with nymphs, which is, according to Kittler, another name for sirens. Translations my own.

72. Kittler, *Musik und Mathematik*, 1.1:45.

73. The title of the conference dedicated to Friedrich Kittler's work, New York University, March 2013.

74. Winthrop-Young, *Friedrich Kittler zur Einführung*, 156. Kittler himself spoke about his "Eurocentrism," for example, in a seminar session in summer 2010: Friedrich Kittler, "Götter und Schriften rund ums Mittelmeer: Transskript einer Seminarsitzung Sommersemester 2010," in Ott and Seitter, *Friedrich Kittler*, 131.

75. In a breath-taking short-circuit, this corresponds to the distinction between veiled and fully clothed Persian warriors and Greek warriors who are represented as

fighting naked (*Musik und Mathematik*, 1.2, plate 15). In "Number and Numeral," the disdain for Solomon and his "hindered" thinking caused by undifferentiated mathematical thinking, and the disdain for a God who doesn't have mathematical concepts, as well as for "bureaucratic scribes of Egypt and Babylon" who are sharply contrasted with the "free Greeks," is blatant (53–54).

76. See Kittler, *Musik und Mathematik*, 1.1:105–14.

77. Ibid., 1.1:112–13.

78. One may ask though how the potion that made Tristan and Isolde's love affair a rather compulsive matter would fit here.

79. Kittler, *Musik und Mathematik*, 1.1:113.

80. See, for example, the last words of "Isolde as Sirene"; Kitter, *Isolde als Sirene*, 38.

81. Ulrike Bergermann, "Kittler und Gender: Zum Asyndeton," in Ott and Seitter, *Friedrich Kittler*, 83–90, and Michaela Ott, "Philebos' Erbe," ibid., 91–99; my translation.

82. "Worte in Konsonantenschriften sind fast beliebig umzudeuten." Kittler, *Musik und Mathematik*, 1.1:107.

PART II

THE ROMANTIC TEMPTATION

5

THE CALCULABLE AND THE INCALCULABLE

Hölderlin after Kittler

Samuel Weber

Allow me to begin with a recollection, which takes me back to the years around 1980, when Friedrich Kittler and I saw each other regularly and during which time we collaborated on several projects. Friedrich was still an assistant professor at the University of Freiburg, preparing his *Habilitation* (postdoctoral thesis), which would be published in 1985 as *Aufschreibesysteme*, and which in 1990 would be translated into English under the significantly different title of *Discourse Networks*. In the early 1980s, I was spending part of each year in Strasbourg, and so Friedrich and I were able to visit each other fairly often and discuss common concerns, of which there were many. For both of us had been invigorated by the emergence of French poststructuralism, in particular by Lacan, Derrida, and Foucault, whose writings at the time seemed to pose a serious challenge to traditional ways of thinking as well as to the institutions that perpetuated them.

A few years earlier, in 1977, Kittler had coedited with Horst Turk a collection of essays that was to be quite influential at the time, entitled *Urszenen*.[1] In it, Friedrich published a text entitled "Das Phantom unseres Ichs und die Literaturpsychologie" (The phantom of the I and the psychology of literature) dealing with E. T. A. Hoffmann's story "The Sandman" in the light of Freud's reading of it in his essay on "The Uncanny," and of Lacan's subsequent discussion of both.

But as the Hoffmann story and the psychoanalytic theory of the Uncanny might have suggested, this "phantom of the I" was not to be as easily exorcised as many of us at the time expected. Kittler's next major publication—another essay collection which he edited on his own—stated in bare terms the program that he was to follow in the coming years. Its title, roughly translated, was

"Exorcising spirit from the humanities: Programs of poststructuralism."[2] The main title is not easily rendered in English. But since the problem of translation here touches on certain aspects of Kittler's later work, let me dwell on it for a moment.

The original title is *"Austreibung des Geistes aus den Geisteswissenschaften: Programme des Poststrukturalismus."* One of the untranslatable words is of course *Geist*: spirit, mind, or intellect. But none of these words even begin to render the multiple connotations of the German word. Languages, which are singular systems, are often incommensurable in their most neuralgic moments. There is no "adequate" English correspondence for *Geist*, and even less, for the disciplines that study them: *Geisteswissenschaften*. "Humanities" is surely related to *Geist* but by no means identical with it. The German rendition of "humanities" or *"sciences humaines"* is *Humanwissenschaften*. It sounds as artificial as "sciences of the spirit" would in English.

All of this is not merely a linguistic accident, nor is it trivial in its implications and consequences. I dwell on this issue for the following reason: I am convinced that writers in general—and in this case, the writings of Kittler— gain enormously when they are read as *responses* to determinate situations, to distinct and not necessarily universal traditions and conventions, which can vary enormously from one linguistic area to another. Academic discourse traditionally—at least in the three languages with which I am familiar, but presumably in others as well—lives and thrives on the axiom of its *universality*. Given however the vastly different, incommensurable intellectual and institutional histories of the German- and English-speaking countries—areas that already are highly diverse *within* themselves—the assumption of such universality, which is the precondition of the expectation of perfect translatability, results frequently in an extreme parochialism, insofar as the universality that is presupposed turns out to be nothing but the projection of a very particular set of experiences and structures upon very different situations.

This situation is something of which Kittler was acutely aware, even if he did not always address it explicitly. Here however is one striking and exemplary exception: "A medium is a medium is a medium. Therefore it cannot be translated. To transfer messages from one medium to another always involves reshaping them to conform to new standards and materials. In a discourse network, which requires an 'awareness of the abysses that divide the one order of sense experience from the other,' transportation necessarily takes the place of translation. Whereas translation excludes all particularities in favor of a general equivalent, the transposition of media is accomplished serially, at discrete points."[3] One of those "discrete points" of what, in translation, Kittler refers to as "transportation"—but which in German involves a word that is much larger in its connotations—is *Übertragung*, the literal German equivalent of the Greek "metaphor." The word in both Greek and in German, strongly connotes not just a change of place, as it does in English, but rather a change in what is changing place. In this sense, a better translation in English would be *transfer*, or even *rendition*, rather than *transportation*; or even *transport*. To be sure, Kittler is characteristically referring to the transition from "one order of sense experience" to another one—but the word he uses suggests that the "abyss" mentioned separates not merely "*one* order of sense experience from the *other*" but moreover and primordially *each* individual "sense experience" from itself, which is to say, from its conventionally determined form.

As a result, it can be argued that "translation," impossible in the sense of identical reproduction, not only occurs all the time—not just between different languages and media, but *within* them—but that it also tends to obscure and conceal the transformative nature of the process. In doing this, it avails itself of several traditional devices, not the least of which is the belief that so-called proper names—for instance, that of "Friedrich Kittler,"—necessarily guarantee the self-identity and constancy that the process of transfer, translation, and transport constantly belie. Another related device, closely linked to the notion of the proper name—especially where persons, subjects, or authors are concerned—is precisely that "The phantom of the I" apostrophized in the subtitle of Kittler's first essay collection, *Urszenen*. The belief in a unified medium or in the unity of a particular "sense experience" is thus closely tied to the belief in the unity of that I or ego that the *Urszenen*, whether Freud's or Kittler's, sought to call into question.

This belief or expectation of a unity of sense-experience or of the medium associated with it is related to another phantom, against which Kittler argued from the start: that of self-identical, universal, and unchanging *meanings*, as the object or product of what Kittler addressed as *Geist. Geist*, as the title of his second essay collection proclaimed, was to be "exorcised" or, more literally, "driven out"—expelled—from the institution that perpetuated it, namely the *Geisteswissenschaften*, which, once they had been purged of this *Geist*, could then return in a substantially altered, more materialistic form, namely, as *Medienwissenschaften*.

At the time—and indeed ever since—I was and remain troubled by the second word that is difficult to translate, but that is decisive for a major part of Kittler's writing, the word: *Austreibung*. The word is not innocent, and its English renditions—exorcising, exclusion, or expulsion—hardly do justice to its historical resonances. In German, it is difficult to separate the term from one of the many trauma that haunted German society in the postwar period, namely that of the German populations that were "expelled"—the German word used was (and is) *vertrieben* rather than *ausgetrieben* (exorcised)—from areas in which they in part had lived for centuries, as the political map of Central Europe was redrawn following World War II. In short, there was a theological, even spiritistic violence in the notion of *Austreibung* that concerned me then as now, but that I also felt corresponded to the violence of recent German and European history.

Not that I felt that the allusion to violence in academic or intellectual matters was something to be avoided on principle. Such avoidance, it was and is clear to me, often serves as a means of restricting the notion of violence to acts that are less firmly institutionalized—of individuals, for instance—and to legitimate, by implication, forms of institutionalized violence. One of these—and here I was certainly of the same opinion as Kittler—was surely associated with the notion and word *Spirit*, for reasons subsequently discussed by Derrida in his book *Of Spirit*, whose subtitle reads: "Heidegger and the Question."[4]

Rather, what worried me at the time and what continues to concern me is the suspicion that exorcism itself could constitute a form of avoidance. For although I had no illusions about the dangers involved in a culture that placed a universalizing concept of *Geist* at the summit of its values, I was no less concerned with the project of "driving (it) out." For it was clear that this title announced not an accomplished fact but a future project and program. It did this by forming the substantive out of the infinitive, using the form *Austreiben* rather than *Austreibung*. To me at least this underscored the *unfinished*, ongoing nature of the process and defined itself as a call to action, an appeal. This was to emerge as a constant characteristic of Kittler's prose: behind its many declarations, often decried as apodictic, stood an appeal to action: here, the action of driving-out a "spirit" that had outlived its usefulness. Or at least, of exposing its institutionalized cover in the academy.

However, it was not this call to action that concerned me, then as now, but rather its efficacy. For I was reminded of a remark by Adorno in an essay on Kafka that I had translated some years earlier—from his book, *Prisms*: "No sooner has the surveyor expelled (*vertrieben*) the annoying apprentices from his room in the country inn, then they return through the window, without the novel bothering to dwell on this apart from simply reporting the fact; the hero is too tired to expel them again."[5] In contrast to Kafka's antiheroes, Kittler never grew too tired to renew his effort to exorcise—*auszutreiben*—what he felt had outlived its usefulness. And that began, but did not end, with the dominant academic conventions that dominated the institutions in which he had to function, the German university. It is here that I feel it indispensable that readers of his work recall or are informed of the situation of the German university against which Kittler was reacting. If he began by seeking to limit if not deprive the *Geisteswissenschaften* of their indispensable object, *Geist*, it was also because he had had to endure the power of the academy to limit critical thinking that called its basic principles into question. The desire to make a clean break with the past—felt to be an impediment to the future—drew him to Lacan and Derrida, but especially to Foucault, who at the time had popularized the notion of the *"coupure épistémologique"* derived from Gaston Bachelard to emphasize the fundamental discontinuity between historically distinct discourses and systems. This in turn would encourage the kind of periodization that informed Kittler's first two major books: *Aufschreibesysteme 1800/1900* (1985; *Discourse Networks 1800/1900*) and *Grammophon, Film, Typewriter* (1986; *Gramophone, Film, Typewriter*). The latter title, designating a pure sequence without any sense of completion—no "and"—thereby suggested the technical devices that would supplant the notion of a "spirit" guiding the development of history according to a more or less transparent teleological pattern. As a result, the academic *Geisteswissenschaften* would be reorganized as sciences of technical media. But in turn, such media techniques would be defined in part at least through the way in which they would exclude and transform a long tradition dominated by discursive semantics claiming to draw their authority from the universality of meaning.

From Kittler's many pronouncements on the subject of media, the following has the virtue of being both short, and sweet; from an essay originally published in German in 1988 entitled "The City as Medium": "Media exist to process, record, and transmit numbers."[6] And a little further on in the same essay:

Media record, transmit and process information—this is the most elementary definition of media. Media can include old-fashioned things like books, familiar things like the city and newer inventions like the computer. It was von Neumann's computer architecture that technically implemented this definition for the first time in history (or as its end). . . . This network of processing, transmission and recording, or restated: of commands, addresses, and data, can calculate everything (based on Turing's famous proof from 1936) that is calculable. . . . And this is reason enough, moreover, to decipher past media and the historical function of what we refer to as "man," as the play between commands, addresses and data.[7]

Thus, on the one hand, the "break" between new and older "media" was presented as a clear and distinct discontinuity, while on the other, it was to provide a basis for seeing the development of history as a continuum whose structure only the newer media allow us to comprehend fully; or as Kittler puts it in the passage just quoted, to "decipher" ("this is reason enough . . . to decipher past media . . . as the play between commands, addresses and data").

It is in thus deploying as a key to historical understanding this notion of "deciphering" that a point is attained where those "annoying apprentices," to whom Adorno refers in his Kafka essay, return massively, through the rear window—or rather, to use Kittler's vocabulary, return transported by the "bus" of the circuit board, through the "gates" or "ports" of Boolean algebra, "gates and ports" which, as he notes, can be considered to constitute "simplest elements" of the computer insofar as they "have no memory" and are therefore dependent on the "built-in memory" of the "bus" in order to be operational.[8]

In what consists then this "return"? I suggest that it consists in the unquestioned epistemological authority of the writing subject that signs his texts "Friedrich Kittler" or sometimes, more simply, "FAK," which in part at least seems to me based on the distinction of functions that are only functional insofar as they are interdependent: that of storage, processing and transmission of something called "data." I am reminded a bit of Saussure's famous attempt to justify the priority and independence of the synchronic over the diachronic state, by referring to the game of chess. What Saussure omitted—and his own notes to his lectures show that he was fully aware of this—was that the so-called synchronic state is structurally divided by the "move"—by the fact that one of the two players has the move and the other does not. In short, a certain diachrony intrudes on the apparently self-contained chessboard precisely insofar as it is a "game." What I want to suggest is that a certain diachronic overlapping of functions breaks down the clear-cut distinctions into processing, storage, and transmission, since each is implied and involved in the others, which limits their distinct self-identity. Thus, in a lecture on "Universities: Wet, Hard, Soft and Harder," Kittler seeks to interpret the functions of the medieval institution according to his triadic model, as "the data-processing lecture, the data-storing university library, and the data-transmitting mail."[9] But a lecture or seminar can be considered as much "data-transmitting" as "data-storing," and mail and the library also can be considered to "process" the date by the ways they store and transmit it.

Similarly, the notion of "address" is not simply an aspect of "storage" but can also designate a form of transmission or at least of movement: it applies both to the library and to mail, for instance. It can be a factor orienting or directing the flow of such information as much as designating its more or less fixed location and retrievability.

I want to suggest that despite the unquestionable global dimensions of the technicity with which Kittler was concerned, that his "addressing" of it was very

much a response to the specific traditions of German humanistic scholarship—
and that his thought is therefore not entirely separable from the notions em-
bodied in words such as *Geist* and even *Geisteswissenschaft*. Kittler was initially
trained as a literary scholar, and the field of literary studies was—and to a certain extent still is—dominated in Germany by what is called the "hermeneutic
tradition," which portrays literary texts as the articulation of meaning, generally fulfilling the intentions of the writing subject qua "author." This ultimately
theological tradition, going back to the biblical account of the creation of the
universe through the words of a single deity, became sedimented in the rules
of biblical textual *Auslegung*—explication or unfolding of meanings that are
held to have been contained in or symbolized by the sacred text. As the direct
authority of the Church weakened, first through the Reformation and then
through the Enlightenment, the explication of texts—and of artistic works
more generally—took up the slack as it were, becoming the exemplary instances through which an initial, authorial and creative meaning was to be re-
cuperated and reappropriated by world-bound finite and mortal "spirits." The
cult of authority, imposing itself through intentional meaning and action, thus
found one of its strongest defenses in this hermeneutic tradition, whether in
its Hegelian form of an Absolute Spirit qua Knowledge, or in its more cautious
Diltheyian form distinguishing between scientific—causal—"explanation" and
humanistic "interpretation."

This then constituted one of the first, negative "addresses" of Friedrich
Kittler's writing, understandably, since it dominated the institutional context
in which he had to work, and which would constitute the condition of further
research. Recent revelations about the opposition to his postdoctoral *Habilitation* on the part of certain senior faculty members only underscores the reality
of the power relations in and against which he (and his peers) had to work.

Kittler's fascination with war as the medium both of historical and of
technological-medial development can be seen therefore as in part at least a response both to the more immediate reality of recent German history—which
in his case as in so many others had directly affected his family and his childhood—and to the hostile power relations that pervaded the academic context
of his writing, and which threatened to put an early end to his career—as it
had done a half century earlier to the academic career of Walter Benjamin.[10]

Thus, although Kittler from the start was intent on driving the *Geist* out of
the *Geisteswissenschaften* and thereby opening the way for their transformation
into *Medientechnik* and also *Kulturwissenschaften* (media-technical and cultural
studies), his reliance on a paradigm borrowed from contemporary media—as
the storage, processing and transmission of information—threatened at times
to introduce a new dogma into the soon-to-be-established sciences of media,

and one which, somewhat but not entirely paradoxically, would wind up rein-
stating the epistemic authority of the scholar as founder of a cult or school. For
the process of *Austreibung* implies or entails an exorciser, with priestly powers,
but also as what Lacan once called the *sujet supposé savoir*, the subject supposed
to know. The spirit as absolute knowledge thus returned to haunt the extraor-
dinarily erudite and remarkable stylist that was Friedrich Kittler, establishing
yet another, if highly innovative "school" after the many "schools" and "circles"
that marked German cultural, intellectual, and artistic life since at least 1800:
another continuity that the advent of the digital age apparently has not disturbed. The existence of such schools, and above all the demand to which
they respond, appear to transcend the undeniable alterations brought about
by the rise of new, electronic media—a fact that I am not certain the triad of
data storage, processing, and transmission alone can satisfactorily "address,"
which does not mean that this triad cannot be helpful in contributing to an
interpretation of the persistence of this phenomenon.

This "reactionary" dimension marking the return of an authority that
in many ways was no less absolute than those of the *Geisteswissenschaftler* it
was supposed to supplant, was neither peculiar to Kittler nor by any means
the only aspect of his prodigious writing. But it does pose a problem that demands attention in evaluating the scope and ramifications of his work—work
that has no doubt profoundly and durably altered our understanding of what
E. P. Snow many years ago called the "two cultures" and what today is designated as the "digital divide."

It must be added, however, that alongside a certain totalizing tendency in
his presentation of the historical significance of technical media, his writing
often expresses a sense of necessary limitation about what can be thought and
said of their impact. Of this an interesting instance can be found in Kittler's
essay, already quoted, "The City as Medium," in a sentence that refers to von
Neumann's "computer architecture" that leads to the microprocessor: "This
network of processing, transmission, and recording, or restated, of commands,
addresses and data, can calculate everything . . . that is calculable."[11] The question that remains unasked, although implied, is: Are there limits to the calculable? And if so, then can we think or experience what is incalculable and if so,
how does this relate to what can be calculated?

In the literature that Kittler surveyed in his first book, there is a highly
significant attempt to introduce a certain calculus into the writing and theorization of poetry and in particular of the literary genre of tragedy. I am thinking
of the famous opening comments of Hölderlin's "Remarks on Oedipus." Given
the relevance to this discussion, and given the density of the passage, I take the
liberty of quoting it at length:

It will be good—in order to assure the poets, including ours, a decent existence [*eine bürgerliche Existenz*]—if poetry, including ours, subtracting [*abgerechnet*] the difference of times and constitutions, can be elevated to the μηχανή [*mēkhanē*] of the ancients.

Also, other works of art, compared with those of the Greeks, are lacking in reliability [*Zuverlässigkeit*]: at least they have until now been judged more for the impressions they make than for their lawful calculus and other procedural modes through which the beautiful is brought forth. Modern poetry however is particularly lacking in schooling and handwork [*an der Schule und am Handwerksmäßigen*], so that their procedural modes can be calculated [*berechnet*] and taught, and once learned, reliably repeated in their exercise. One has, among humans, with each thing, above all to attend to (the fact) that it is something [*daß es Etwas ist*], i.e. that in the means [*moyen*] of its manifestation it is recognizable [*erkennbar*], that the way in which it is conditioned [*bedingt*] can be determined and taught. Therefore, and out of higher grounds, poetry requires particularly certain and characteristic principles and limits.

That is where that lawful calculus belongs.

Then one must be attentive to how the content distinguishes itself, through which procedures and in the infinite but thoroughly determined context particular contents relate to the universal calculus, and the goings-on [*Gang*] and that which is to be set in place [*das Vestzusetzende*], the living sense [*der lebendige Sinn*] that cannot be calculated, is brought into relation to the calculable law.[12]

Hölderlin—a schoolmate and friend of Hegel and Schelling who was formed through an intensive confrontation with the German idealistic philosophy of Kant and Fichte—here does what according to Kittler all of metaphysics, from Plato to Hegel and beyond, refused to do, namely, to introduce technics and calculus into the determination of poetry as something other than as the act of a subject. In so doing, Hölderlin is also well on his way to overcoming the polarity of "form and matter" that Kittler, following Heidegger, sees as one of the hallmarks of traditional metaphysics. This gesture of Hölderlin's seems to me profoundly related to Kittler's demand to include knowledge of "the technical state of the art" in any effective "ontology of media." Such knowledge would concern the "technical state of the art," which Kittler associates with the "blueprints, layouts, mainboard designs, industrial roadmaps and so on . . . namely, the hardware of high tech,"[13] and in particular with its numerical dimension, "a mathematical medium" that, as "the early modern invention of real numbers and general exponents, brought forth an acoustic medium."[14] When Hölderlin in the passage cited makes the production and understanding of tragedy dependent on the knowledge of certain general laws and their application, which he interprets as a "calculus," he construes "tragedy" as inseparable from rules that can be taught and transmitted, which in turn make the writing of tragedies in part at least into something like a "handwork" and not just the result of genial "inspiration" or "creation." Compare this to the following general assessment to be found in Kittler's essay, "Number and Numeral":

> The principal difficulty resides in not submitting *our world made up of mathematical calculus, epistemic things and technological media* to a supreme being, be it God, Meaning, or Man—something the early modern age was incapable of doing. From Leibniz to Kronecker, the simplest of numbers (binary or natural) (were said to be a gift of God; and from Descartes and Hegel to Dilthey the 'meaning' imposed by subjects on objectivities or media was a covert resistance against thinking about technology. Evidently numbers had to leave humans behind and become part of machines that run on their own in order for technology to appear as a frame that conjoins being and thought. This turn was completed by Alan Turing.[15]

The "turn . . . completed by . . . Turing" was not one that Hölderlin sought to take—not at least in his *Remarks on Oedipus and Antigone*, written after having translated both plays. Indeed, he warned against taking certain turns that sought entirely to overturn existing systems of values, however much he wished to have them altered and transformed; and this was because his "world" was not that described by Kittler in the previous excerpt, and attributed to all of us: "The principal difficulty resides in not submitting *our world made up of mathematical calculus, epistemic things and technological media* to a supreme being." However much Hölderlin argued for a revalorization of technique, general principles, and "lawful calculus" in their application, he also was aware that his world did not consist exclusively of "mathematical calculus, epistemic things and technical media" for the simple reason that not all things could be considered strictly from the perspective of the *episteme*. And this is also where his notion of the medium—for which he invokes the French word *moyen*—certainly diverges from the one invoked by Kittler: namely, in reserving an irreducible place to their *singularity*. For if he demanded that in the practice of poetry "each thing" be seen as a "something"—which is to say, recognized with reference to the general conditions of its singular emergence—he also insisted on the irreducible gap separating those general principles, and all calculability, from what he called "the living sense"—not to be confused with the notion of a universally valid "meaning," which Kittler justifiably identifies as constituting the major obstacle to a rethinking of technology and media, one which would no longer be dependent on the paradigm of a supreme Being, God, Creator, or autonomous subject. No, the "living sense" of which Hölderlin writes is that which precisely is set off by and against the general calculation as that which resists resolution in an equation even while presupposing equations and algorithms in order *at the same time* to comply with them.

The singularity of this "living sense" thus involves a movement that is neither linear nor circular, neither strictly sequential nor strictly parallel. Kittler concludes his essay "Towards an Ontology of Media" by recounting the "dream most dear to solid state physicians," namely, one of "computers based on parallel and tiny quantum states instead of on big and serial silicon connections," and notes that if this "rosy dawn" should ever really arise, "I, or rather my successors, shall withdraw this paper."[16] Without claiming to fully understand the implications of this dream or the likelihood of it "dawning" sometime soon, rosy or not, I would like to believe that the shift—not turn—from sequential to parallel (quantum) thinking, although not computing, is already at work in the poetry, translations, and remarks of Hölderlin. At the close of his *Remarks on Antigone*, Hölderlin seeks to confirm his theory that tragic presentation (*Darstellung*) is designed to preserve a certain "equilibrium"—*Gleichgewicht* is the German word he uses, which in *Antigone* means a certain balance between Antigone and Creon. But it is a balance that is preserved only through imbalance. This is summed up in Hölderlin's use of the German word *gleich*, which is rather "like" the English word *like*, stressing similarity but retaining difference. What is *like* is never simply equal or identical. The implications of this equivocal *like* are unfolded when Hölderlin, toward the end of his *Remarks on Antigone*, comes to articulate the *political* import of the tragedy. But before citing this passage, it may be useful to point out that Hölderlin also employs a tripartite structure somewhat "like" what Kittler, in "Towards an Ontology of Media" designates as a "new trinity" destined to replace the old polarity of "form and matter," namely, the triad "made up of commands, addresses, and data"—whereby the question remains whether Kittler's "new trinity," however ironic the use of the term, does not carry some of the implications of the "old" trinity, by *likening* the notion of "medium" to that "Supreme Being" he also wishes it to replace. Hölderlin, for his part, seeking to analyze "tragic presentation," acknowledges that some sort of relationship of bodies to the "godlike" is constitutive while insisting that this relation is hardly one of "submission" as Kittler puts it: rather it entails striving, conflict, and tension. It is this tension that results in the triadic structure that I want to set against Kittler's "new trinity." Here then is the relevant passage, quoted *in medias res* as it were: "Preeminently however tragic presentation [*Darstellung*] consists in the factical word that, more context than [actually] enunciated, destined [*Schicksalsweise*] to go from beginning to end; in the mode of provenance [*Hergang*], in the grouping of persons against each other [*gegeneinander*], and in the form of reason that constitutes itself in the terrible muse of a tragic time."[17]

Hölderlin's "new trinity" here clearly takes its distance from both the traditional polarity of form and matter (or content) and the no less traditional trinity: it begins not with an origin or creator, but with a *Hergang*; which is to say, with the question of *provenance,* the "where-from," and hence with the trajectory that has been followed in arriving "here" (*her*); if this can be compared to the process of "storing" data, in the case of the tragic "medium"—and more specifically of *Antigone*—such "storage" is shown to be highly unstable and inconstant, since it consists in what Hölderlin goes on to designate as an "upheaval" (*Aufruhr*), which in turn is the result of an "infinite overturning" (*unendliche Umkehr*). Unlike the "turn" that Turing is said to have "completed," for Hölderlin such a turn can never be consummated, not at least for man as a "cognizant being": "A complete overturning in this is however—like complete overturning generally, without anything to hold on to (*ohne allen Halt*) is not permitted for humans as cognizant beings."[18] In such situations, "where the entire figure of things changes" and where "nature and necessity, which always remain, incline toward another figure, whether to savagery or a new figure" what is possible for man is the feeling of being profoundly *shattered* (*Erschütterung*) and this in turn impels the shattered persons to redefine themselves, or as Hölderlin puts it, to "formalize themselves"—for instance, as "persons of rank" (*Standespersonen*).

In short, the experience of a shattering turnover of all values and realities drives those whom it affects to transform their self-understanding from that of individual persons to that of members of a class—and hence, as dependent variables. In this sense, the second category of Hölderlin's triad emerges out of this initial experience of being both shattered and of belonging to a larger group, a *Stand* or "estate." Hölderlin calls it a "grouping." But here again, the "grouping" can be "likened" to (although not identified with) what Kittler "addresses" insofar as it designates the way in which individual elements or "data" are localized—namely, in interdependent but discrete relation to one another. Hölderlin describes this relation of dependent variables as agonistic, and more particularly, with respect to *Antigone*, as a "contest of runners" in which "the one who first gasps for breath and jostles the opponent *has lost.*"[19] Hölderlin does not tell us how such a race is *won*, but only how it is *lost*, as if in this kind of (tragic) race there are no winners, but only losers—which of course is a pretty good description of *Antigone*. This losing race in which it is not permitted to touch the opponent or to breathe heavily could be likened to the processing of discrete data that has been collected through its "*Hergang*."

But to see how strained and excessive these "likenesses" are, and how their discrepancies serve to bring out what is *un-like* in the two "trinities," we need only proceed to the third branch of Hölderlin's triad, namely, what he calls the "form of reason" (*Vernunftform*), which for Socrates in *Antigone* he considers to be "political and namely republican." Here, as with Kittler, it is necessary to keep in mind that to which and against which Hölderlin is responding and reacting, namely, the prevalent monarchical form of government that prevailed in most of Germany at the time. Republican, as non-monarchical, requires a certain plurality or diversity in governance. In the play *Antigone*, this takes the form of the conflict "between Creon and Antigone," which Hölderlin also describes, chiastically, as that between the "formal (Creon) and antiformal (Antigone)." And now comes the decisive phrase, which I will translate as literally as possible, and hence awkwardly—"the equilibrium [*das Gleichgewicht*, the aim of the tragic caesura] is held *too like* [*zu gleich gehalten ist*]." Normally, the two words ("too like") used by Hölderlin are commonly written as one word in German (*zugleich*), which signifies "at once" or "at the same time." However, by introducing a space between the two words, *zu* and *gleich*, Hölderlin has them say—process or transmit—a supplementary meaning, which although less common is also more literal. The republican form of "reason"—a political reason—is indicated "by the fact that at the end, Creon is practically mistreated by his servants."[20] In other words, by the fact that his social and political form is degraded, just as that of Antigone has been through his punishment of her. In this separation of mortal living being, whether Antigone or Creon, from its formalized social rank, the balance or equilibrium (*das Gleichgewicht*) is upheld, but precisely through a certain excess. By becoming "too (a)like" in their destinies, the two figures maintain a tense balance between singularity and generality, between mortality and endurance, a tension that derives from an excess of likeness rather than from a simple equation.

This, then, seems to be that "living sense" that Hölderlin demands from tragic presentation and that presupposes the laws of its calculus—through which a certain equilibrium is first imposed by the caesura on what could be called the death-drive of the "tragic transport"—but only in order to set off what remains incalculable (*unberechenbar*), since it is inseparable from the singular dimension of the living—which is to say, from its mortality. This singular dimension cannot be equated with an "epistemic object," because, like the uproar and overturning that is its medium, it can only be "felt" but never cognized, only experienced as an overwhelming shock, but never entirely calculated or programmed.

It is this self-limitation of cognitive experience and authority in the name of the incalculable and of a certain feeling that, I submit, fascinated Friedrich Kittler who also reacts to it through his effort to replace the dominion of a

Supreme Being with the reign of computers, numbers, and of a recursivity that defies all sense. "A medium is a medium is a medium" he wrote famously in his magnum opus, *Discourse Networks*; I would like to suggest that this insistence on the untranslatability of the medium in relation to other media, upon which each nevertheless depends, calls for another, equally gnomic statement to be fully operable, this time from Jacques Derrida. That statement is truly untranslatable, so I will have to quote it first in French, and then try to paraphrase it in English: "Tout autre est tout autre"—"Every other is utterly other."[21]

Media theory and analysis *after* Kittler may thus call for a rereading of texts that ostensibly belong to a period that have long since passed. But such rereadings may also turn out to coexist "at once"—*zugleich*—with the extension of calculability that is one of the hallmarks of the digital age. They coexist with it by raising the question of whether that *zugleich* may not *at the same time* be: *zu gleich*, *too alike* and therefore singularly *unlike*. Perhaps this is the subtext, or at least the question, haunting the "rosy dream" of "parallel" computing, which Kittler acknowledges ironically, but perhaps did not entirely share.

In the film *The Codebreaker*, Alan Turing is depicted shortly before his death confiding the following to his therapist and friend, Dr. Franz Greenbaum: "Mathematicians talk of the beauty of numbers. But I know, because I was one, that what they mean is the beauty of what can be resolved. But what about the rest? The greater infinity? What's not computable lies beyond the infinitesimal sliver of knowledge we've managed to subdue in our fragile, trembling consciousness, a consciousness which is in fact decaying within us from the moment we're born." To maintain a *Gleichgewicht*, which acknowledges such decay without seeking to neutralize it through faith in a Supreme Being or even through the kind of negative teleology that the lack of such faith can easily trigger, is perhaps what is required to think not just Hölderlin after Kittler, but Kittler after Hölderlin—and both after Alan Turing.

NOTES

1. Horst Turk and Friedrich Kittler, eds., *Urszenen* [Primal Scenes] (Frankfurt am Main: Suhrkamp, 1977).

2. Friedrich Kittler, ed., *Austreibung des Geistes aus den Geisteswissenschaften: Programme des Poststrukturalismus* (Paderborn, Germany: Schöningh, 1980).

3. Friedrich Kittler, *Discourse Networks 1800/1900* (Stanford, CA: Stanford University Press, 1990), 265.

4. Jacques Derrida, *De l'esprit: Heidegger et la question* (Paris: Galilée, 1987).

5. Theodor W. Adorno, "Auszeichnungen zu Kafka" [Notes on Kafka], in *Gesammelte Schriften*, Bd. 10.1, *Prismen* (Frankfurt am Main: Suhrkamp, 1997), 258; my translation.

6. Friedrich Kittler, "The City as Medium," trans. Matthew Griffin, *New Literary History* 27, no. 4 (Autumn, 1996): 720.

7. Ibid., 722.

8. Ibid., 720.

9. Friedrich Kittler, "Universities: Wet, Hard, Soft and Harder," *Critical Inquiry* 31, no.1 (Autumn 2004): 245.

10. For a journalistic account of the controversy surrounding Kittler's postdoctoral process, see Jürgen Kaube, "Spucken hilft nicht, Herr Kollege!," *Frankfurter Allgemeine Zeitung*, April 23, 2012, www.faz.net/aktuell/feuilleton/friedrich-kittlers-habilitationsverfahren-spucken-hilft-nicht-herr-kollege-11727699.html.

11. Kittler, "City as Medium," 722.

12. Friedrich Hölderlin, "Anmerkungen zum Oedipus" [Remarks on Oedipus], *Sämtliche Werke und Briefe*, ed. Michael Knaupp (Munich: Carl Hanser Verlag, 1992), 2:309; my translation.

13. Friedrich Kittler, "Towards an Ontology of Media," *Theory, Culture and Society* 26, nos. 2–3 (2009): 29–30.

14. Ibid.

15. Friedrich Kittler, "Numbers and Numeral," in *Theory, Culture and Society* 23, nos. 7–8 (2006): 58; emphasis added.

16. Kittler, "Towards an Ontology of Media," 30.

17. Hölderlin, "Anmerkungen zum Oedipus," 374–75; my translation.

18. Ibid., 375.

19. Ibid., 376.

20. Ibid.

21. Kas Saghafi lists eight different translations of this untranslatable phrase in *Apparitions—Of Derrida's Other* (New York: Fordham University Press, 2010), 172–73.

6

A SCIENCE OF HIEROGLYPHS, OR THE TEST OF *BILDUNG*

Antje Pfannkuchen

With his *Aufschreibesysteme 1800/1900*, translated as *Discourse Networks 1800/1900*, Friedrich Kittler stirred up the German academic scene of the 1980s. The manuscript was written to be his *Habilitation* (the highly formalized second book, or postdoctoral thesis, in the German academic system), produced to ensure a degree-like professorial certification, to entice the endorsement of the scholarly community, the willingness to accept the author in their midst—and Kittler nearly failed to reach this approval. The first affront was the obscure title *Aufschreibesysteme*[1]—literally: systems of writing down, of notation, or possibly inscription—a borrowed neologism from civil servant/psychotic Daniel Paul Schreber who used it in his own *Rehabilitation*, thereby producing one of the most famous self-descriptions of a mental disease. In the late nineteenth century, Judge Schreber had reached the highest public standing as senate president of Saxony's supreme court before turning delusional. He was able to reverse his legal incapacitation and to reinstate his own lawful status with the publication of *Denkwürdigkeiten eines Nervenkranken* (*Memoirs of my Nervous Illness*),[2] a feat that, in hindsight, might seem as surprising to observers today as *Aufschreibesysteme* appeared suitable to some critical readers to serve the purpose of achieving institutional acceptance for their writer.

In several of Kittler's obituaries, writers summoned the memory of thirteen (instead of the usual three) academic evaluations (*Gutachten*) that it took in the summer of 1983 to have the study finally approved.[3] A fundamental objection of the most critical reviewer concerned the missing "gravitas." Kittler's script was accused of repudiating "the seriousness of scholarly rationality" and did not appear academic enough to the scholarly reader who in his defense of German *Bildung* claimed that the work "misses in principle the scholarly discourse, in part, in fairly large part, it is not even rational discourse."⁴ The critic does admit, however, that it is not so much a falling short of the discourse—as this would have implied an aiming at it—but a fundamental refusal to partake in it. Even without knowing what Kittler shared in one of his last interviews—that the first part on Goethe's Faust was written "under the influence" as prudent Americans would call it, "*bekifft*" (stoned) as he put it⁵—most readers would agree that "rational scholarly discourse" is not a hallmark of *Aufschreibesysteme 1800/1900*. Instead, Kittler took the reader to a dance performing the double life of poet/civil servant that he described as a central theme for the *Aufschreibesystem*, or culture of writing and education, around 1800 and it remains a kind of coup that he was able to mix the two to the extent he did and still eventually get the approval he sought—to become a civil servant (*Beamter*) himself, with this postdoctoral thesis subverting so many established standards of German academia. As he had diagnosed himself: "States demand a commitment from their servants that forbids poetizing and fictionalizing."⁶ Poetizing and fictionalizing (*Literarisierung*) are precisely the accusations made. Stylistic poetizing, "against which nothing or little could be objected," would have been tolerable but the critical evaluator is outraged about "fictionalization in the substance itself."⁷ Only in poetry and fiction, he charged, is it permissible to stage and suggest in place of the restrained reasoning, which is required from a serious participant in the German *Bildungssystem*.

Where Plato had excluded the poets from the republic entirely, the *Aufschreibesystem* around 1800 (under which the type of public German university developed that required a postdoctoral thesis from their future professors) tolerated them if they kept their poetry clearly separated from their professional commitment as civil servants (*DN*, 103). Now Kittler in his own *Aufschreibesystem* 2000 was permeating this separation by allowing his academic writing to flirt with fiction and poetry, instead of soberly analyzing them. The choice of the title *Aufschreibesysteme 1800/1900* declared in a different form Kittler's aversion to a hermeneutic tradition that the title of a volume he had previously edited stated more bluntly: the goal was to expel the spirit that had turned into a dusty ghost from the humanities.⁸ Instead of recapitulating the same old scholarly discourse once again, *Aufschreibesysteme 1800/1900* disrupted this discourse at its core. Turning away from grand German toward subversive French-influenced ideas, Kittler declared his title "a good word to conduct literary history on an elementary level, as history of the practices whose interactions created a culture of writing."⁹ Following in his footsteps of subversion and attention to detail, a rereading of *Aufschreibesystem 1800* reveals yet another elementary level with the power to shake up even some of Kittler's basic assumptions.

Kittler's fundamental claim based the writing culture around 1800 on clearly and binarily divided gender roles: "The difference between the sexes . . . coincided in a mathematically exact way with the dichotomy between writing and authorhood on the one hand, and with that between the voice and motherhood on the other. The difference allowed the Woman as the Mother's Mouth every right to be a Voice but no right to have one" (*DN*, 66). Zooming in on this picture with Kittler-trained eyes, the polar opposites begin to dissolve in their exactitude and become more permeable in areas that mathematics cannot quite reach. Instead of a digital order of zeros and ones, writing around 1800 turns out to not always follow this "natural" gender division. With Kittler, the function of Nature, which is The Woman "consists in getting people—that is men—to speak" (*DN*, 25). His Lacanian muted Woman/Nature produces discourses without ever saying a word by seducing men into speaking and writing. Kittler's trope to describe this constellation is the *Muttermund*, only half-appropriately translated as "Mother's Mouth."[10] But nature around 1800 also had other ways to make men write—by writing herself and thereby breaking the gendered assignments.

In his reading of E. T. A. Hoffmann's "Der Goldene Topf" ("The Golden Pot"), a "fairy tale from the new time," Kittler delivered what he thought of as one of his *Musterinterpretationen*,[11] an exemplary reading that also meant he saw no need to ever return to it, defying even the remotest appearance of allegiance to hermeneutical practices. This leaves it to us to keep reading not only Kittler but also the works he had found to be exemplary. In the beginning of Hoffmann's fantastic tale of the student Anselmus and his dealings with Privy Archivist Lindhorst we find Anselmus under an elder tree at the banks of the Elbe river in Dresden railing against his own awkwardness that seems to determine his fate. The gloomy soliloquy is interrupted by three little snakes materializing out of a complex soundscape of "rustling and whisking, . . . the evening wind . . . shaking the leaves, as if little birds were twittering among the branches, moving their little wings in capricious flutter to and fro."[12] The little snakes turn out to be the three daughters of Lindhorst, who is not only a famous archivist in town, and therefore a member of bureaucracy whose double-life in a poetic fairy tale world Kittler riffs on; Lindhorst also has an interest in all manner of "secret sciences" that he purportedly practices, notably experimental chemistry (*GP*, 12). Anselmus gets a taste of these experiments in his first encounter with the snake-daughters. When one of them holds out her little head to Anselmus he feels the effect immediately and physically: "An electric shock seemed to penetrate his entire body, he trembled inwardly; he stared upwards and saw a pair of magnificent dark-blue eyes looking at him with inexpressible yearning" (*GP*, 5). This electric shock came not only through romantic-blue-flower-like eyes, but also through a science *en vogue* in Hoff-mann's time: galvanism was part of a new kind of chemistry concerned with the study of animal electricity that Luigi Galvani had first detected in frogs' legs. The subversive spark conducted through snake eyes catapults Anselmus into an oscillating state between two poles of the highest and lowest feelings, between poetry and science, between the father's and the mother's voices.

In Kittler's new education model of the *Aufschreibesystem* around 1800, children followed their erotically charged Mother's Mouth with as rapt an at-tention as Anselmus submitted himself to the insinuations of the three little snakes that met him in the elder bush. In the thoroughly motherless story of "The Golden Pot" (only one evil nurse gets a role in this tale of fathers and daughters) the little snakes and daughters take over as the Mother's Mouth and the voice of nature. Following their aural/oral initiation, Anselmus, on his way to becoming a romantic poet, need only "learn how the voice that was originally Nature can be made into a book, without having the vision collapse into mere letters" (*DN*, 80). To conduct this learning process, he apprentices himself to *Archivarius* Lindhorst and encounters in his library different ver-sions of books of nature. Anselmus eventually learns to make his own, guided not so much by a voice but by writings that seem to spring up directly from nature, magically translated through the little female snake *Serpentina*. After Lindhorst assesses Anselmus's skills in copying a number of difficult manu-scripts, he leads his student to the final test, to "the chamber where the masters of Bhagavadgita are awaiting" them to "copy, or rather paint certain works, written in special characters" (*GP*, 50, 51). Pulling a leaf from a palm tree that turns out to be a roll of parchment, Lindhorst spreads it out before Anselmus who "was astonished by the strangely intertwined characters." Studying "the many dots, strokes, dashes, and curlicues, which seemed by turns to represent plants, or mosses, or animal shapes, his courage almost failed him" (*GP*, 52). But Serpentina's presence makes it clear how much this test is also a temptation,[13] as she will remain at Anselmus's side throughout. The final mysterious tran-scription project presents, to Kittler, "originary script, the mythic beginning of all writing," which "can be identified because it is not (*yet*) written. No one could write or read this text, this 'writing without alphabet, in which signs, sig-nifiers, and signifieds are identical'" (*DN*, 85). The originary script written by no one appears as an unreadable text because it is an image that does not con-tain the code for its decipherment.[14] Kittler reminds the reader how Lindhorst calls "the plant- and animal hieroglyphics that he placed before his despairing secretary . . . the work of the masters of Bhagavadgita," which suggests, in Kittler's reading, that the text was written in Sanskrit. He concludes that this gives the parchment "the same status as the handwritten text of Nostradamus in *Faust*, which is a foreign-language text *and* a revelation of Nature" (*DN*, 85). What Kittler ignored in this comparison is that Nostradamus wrote in Latin letters. So, while his writings might not have been easily comprehensible, every European copyist could have transcribed them without much difficulty. Anselmus's test piece, on the other hand contained "twisted strokes of . . . foreign characters"—presumably Sanskrit—that remained hieroglyphic to all but the most advanced readers.[15] The oscillation between "a foreign culture and a foreign nature" connects the Sanskrit characters less to Nostradamus than to Egyptian hieroglyphs that were not to be deciphered until 1822, but also to another kind of hieroglyph, or cipher that captivated Hoffmann's contemporaries.

The poet and mining engineer Friedrich von Hardenberg, better known as Novalis, described a hieroglyphic code in the opening passage of his *Die Lehrlinge zu Sais* (*The Novices of Sais*): "Various are the roads of man. He who follows and compares them will see strange figures emerge, figures which seem to belong to that great cipher which we discern written everywhere, in wings, eggshells, clouds and snow, in crystals . . . beasts and men, . . . on scored discs of pitch or glass or in iron filings round a magnet, and in strange conjunctures of chance."[16] Novalis found the magic figures that seemed to belong to a great secret language everywhere in nature and also on "berührten und gestrichenen Scheiben von Pech und Glas" which are, of course, not sufficiently translated as "scored discs." Some were *berührt* (affected) by a conducting material to cause an electric discharge; others were stroked or bowed with a violin bow to make a layer of sand vibrate. And whereas many readers recognized bowed Chladni glass plates in this passage, many fewer shared Novalis's familiarity with the "berührten Scheiben von Pech" (*affected discs of pitch or resin*) that Georg Christoph Lichtenberg first described in his experiments with an electrophorus, a state of the art electrical device. The ciphers Novalis enumerated subvert the educational structures of the *Aufschreibesystem* 1800. Woman/ Nature did not seduce a human author into writing, she wrote herself. These hieroglyphs resemble pure writing in a Derridian sense, no "linguistic sign before writing" exists.[17] They ask to be read while not disclosing their key.

This type of nature writing was found and recognized in a laboratory in Göttingen where Lichtenberg became witness to a new *Bildung*, a formation, that the romantics would seamlessly merge with the other *Bildung* of education. Nature herself was here educating through formation. In dust configurations that Lichtenberg discovered in the 1770s on the surface of his electrophorus, the natural force electricity began to reveal itself in a novel way. *Lichtenberg figures* brought a new visual dimension to the field of electrical research and thereby started electricity's transformation from a curiosity into a technology.

The figures conserved an image of a spark. Something perceived as largely invisible and extremely fleeting—electricity—suddenly left a permanent trace, a moment inscribing itself to be observed and studied over time. This kind of *Bildung* caused Lichtenberg to break into romantic poetry when describing his scientific find:

> In the beginning of Spring 1777 the construction of my electrophorus had just been completed. The room was still full of resin-dust that had accumulated when the cake was being polished. It covered all the walls and books and with every little whiff of air it was stirred and then, to my great dismay, often collected on the cover of the electrophorus. Once, after I had started to pull up the cover toward the ceiling, the dust fell onto the cake. Suddenly it did not cover the surface evenly anymore but, to my great joy, formed little starlets in certain places. In the beginning, these were faint and hardly visible but when I deliberately sprinkled more dust on the surface they became clearer and beautiful and appeared embossed. At times countless stars, milky ways and larger suns became visible. The arcs on their concave side were plain, on their convex side they were adorned with manifold spouts. Exquisite little branches developed, like those on frosted windows.[18]

Lichtenberg's awe in contemplating his dust stars was not unlike that of Anselmus before Lindhorst's manuscript. Nature performed as The Woman seducing men into speaking and writing poetically by writing herself. Man's task became to recognize her writing as writing, and not just discard it as irritating dust.

Despite his momentary poetic self-indulgence, Lichtenberg declared the study of the properties of electricity to be the most important aspect of these figures. But it did not take long for the beautiful stars to become popular beyond the immediate scientific community. A few years later, Ernst Florens Friedrich Chladni introduced sound figures (*Klangfiguren*) that he declared to be inspired by Lichtenberg's experiments. From a purely physical point of view this did not make any sense. His technique was completely different from anything Lichtenberg ever practiced. The only connection between the two figures was the one fact that soon fascinated the romantics: nature seemed to "write" information about itself that was otherwise inaccessible: Chladni and Lichtenberg were interested in physical forces—sound and electricity, respectively—that resisted mathematical investigation. Chladni's inventive method was to draw a violin bow over the edge of a plate of glass or metal that he had previously sprinkled with sand. Once the plate began to vibrate the sand was thrown off the parts that were in motion and formations or images manifested themselves. The illustrations Chladni published with his text appear schematized and the first collections of patterns look like they are trying to resemble Lichtenberg's starry sun and moon galaxies even though such patterns materialize rarely through sound.[19] The romantics quickly recognized just how much these new types of images differed from any previous scientific illustration. Visual representation used to require a human draughtsman, painter, or writer. For Lichtenberg's and Chladni's figures the (human) observer "only" had to build the set or stage on which nature could then perform and inscribe itself. In the romantic imagination nature wrote these figures entirely of her own accord. Johann Wilhelm Ritter, Novalis, E. T. A. Hoffmann, and a few others then read the figures as hieroglyphs that simultaneously (re-)presented and hid a secret knowledge. In parallel to the Egyptian hieroglyphs that were thought to contain the secret wisdom of the ancient cultures, Chladni's and Lichtenberg's figures seemed to hold the secrets written by nature. The figures became as mysterious and meaningful as the leaves in Lindhorst's magic palm tree library where Anselmus, guided by Serpentina, effortlessly transcribed the scripts from Mother Nature, in full accordance with Schelling's view that "Nature for us is an ancient author who wrote in hieroglyphs, and whose leaves are immense."[20] In that sense Lindhorst's declaration to show Anselmus the "Masters of Bhagavadgita" could also be read as showing him the work authored by an ancient nature that is master even to the author(s) of the Bhagavadgita.

Ritter and Novalis took this claim of nature as oldest author one step further by declaring Lichtenberg's electrical and Chaldni's sound figures to be actual prefigurations of the characters of our alphabet, a kind of original letter. In Novalis, under the entry "Physik und Grammatik" (Physics and Grammar), we read, "Figurelike sound movements like/as letters. (Should the letters have originally been acoustical figures. A priori letters?)."[21] This nature-writing, staged and suggested by romantic scientists in its confluence of woman and nature creates a writing that precedes and subverts male authorship once it is no longer excluded from the "culture of writing." Romantic authors received nature's writing as shibboleth, having registered and forgotten again the technology that inscribed their bodies, recording only the attraction of the secret hieroglyphic language.

These secret hieroglyphs simultaneously attracted Kittler's investigative drive to conduct "literary history on an elementary level" and mirrored his desire to perform a sort of hieroglyphic secrecy in his own writing. Disapproved, as we saw by some academic readers he produced at times a romantic murmuring laced with innuendo, always alluding, never explaining but making his work as fascinating as it is vexing. At times, he seemed to return to the romantically charged pedagogic impetus he had archeologically described for the *Aufschreibesystem* of 1800: the seducing Mother's Mouth had lost its temptation when it was institutionalized in German basic and higher education. Kittler's intellectual seduction made up for that. His lectures were cultural events; his arrival as maverick professor in Berlin attracted journalists as much as young impressionable students who flocked to his auditorium in great numbers. "It shocked people, but, strangely enough, most of them ran over."[22] He was a tinkerer of *Denkmodelle*,[23] thought models, prototypes. Hard facts ("pitiless use of dates"), hardware, and mathematics became the currency, usability the test. With pride did Kittler observe toward the end of his life that *Aufschreibesysteme* is one of the few postdoctoral theses still being read and translated twenty and more years after its complicated birth.[24] His writings, having passed the test of time, remain hieroglyphic in the romantic sense and will continue to challenge the breadth and depth of their readers' *Bildung*.

NOTES

1. The title, in typical Kittler style, was not explained until recently, in a previously unpublished introduction he had been forced to write to help solve the controversy over the acceptance of *Aufschreibesysteme* as the "scholarly" work it claimed to be. See *Zeitschrift für Medienwissenschaft* 6, no. 1 (2012): 117–26.

2. Daniel Paul Schreber, *Denkwürdigkeiten eines Nervenkranken, nebst Nachträgen und einem Anhang über die Frage: "Unter welchen Voraussetzungen darf eine für geisteskrank erachtete Person gegen ihren erklärten Willen in einer Heilanstalt festgehalten werden?"* (Leipzig: Mutze, 1903; new edition with an introduction by Wolfgang Hagen, Berlin: Kulturverlag Kadmos, 2003).

3. Although there were not quite thirteen, they were significantly more than the usual three and thanks to Ute Holl and Claus Pias one can now consult them directly: "Aufschreibesysteme—1980/2010. In memoriam Friedrich Kittler." Insert in *Zeitschrift für Medienwissenschaft* 6, no. 1 (2012): 114–92.

4. Hans-Martin Gauger, "Gutachten zur Arbeit 'Aufschreibesysteme 1800/1900' von Herrn Dr. F. A. Kittler," *Zeitschrift für Medienwissenschaft* 6, no. 1 (2012): 137; my translation.

5. "'Wir haben nur uns selber, um daraus zu schöpfen'—Friedrich Kittler im Gespräch mit Andreas Rosenfelder," Welt am Sonntag, January 30, 2011, accessed April 9, 2016, www.welt.de/print/wams/kultur/article12385926/Wir-haben-nur-uns-selber-um-daraus-zu-schoepfen.html.

6. Friedrich Kittler, *Discourse Networks 1800/1900*, trans. Michael Metteer, with Chris Cullen, foreword by David E. Wellbery (Stanford, CA: Stanford University Press, 1990), 104. Hereafter cited in text as *DN* and page number.

7. Hans-Martin Gauger, "Stellungnahme (Sondervotum) zur Arbeit von F. A. Kittler 'Aufschreibesysteme 1800/1900,'" *Zeitschrift für Medienwissenschaft* 6, no. 1 (2012): 185–86; my translation.

8. Friedrich Kittler, ed., *Austreibung des Geistes aus den Geisteswissenschaften: Programme des Poststrukturalismus* (Paderborn: Schöningh, 1980). The German word play based on *Geist* which translates as spirit or ghost and is also part of *Geisteswissenschaften* (humanities) is lost in every possible English translation of this title.

9. Friedrich Kittler, "Aufschreibesysteme 1800/1900 Vorwort," *Zeitschrift für Medienwissenschaft* 6, no. 1 (2012): 114; my translation.

10. Literally, in German the *Muttermund* is the anatomical term for *Ostium uteri*, the uterine orifice. This choice of metaphor implies and causes an erotically charged birthing process that in this case produces children as readers. The *Muttermund*/Mother's Mouth becomes the partial object that turns learning how to read into an erotic experience.

11. Friedrich Kittler, "Das kalte Modell von Struktur," interview with C. Weinberger, *Zeitschrift für Medienwissenschaft*, no. 1 (2009): 96.

12. E. T. A. Hoffmann, "The Golden Pot," in *The Golden Pot and Other Tales: A New Translation by Ritchie Robertson* (Oxford: Oxford University Press, 2009), 5. Hereafter cited in text as *GP* and page number.

13. Cf. Avital Ronell, *The Test Drive* (Urbana: University of Illinois Press, 2005), 133.

14. Unreadability implies attempts at decoding this open secret, which is "at once . . . exposed and hidden" (Ronell, *Test Drive*, 85).

15. *Bhagavadgita* was first translated into a European language in 1785 by the English Orientalist Charles Wilkins. The earliest translations into German were provided by the Schlegel brothers, in part after "The Golden Pot" had been written.

16. Novalis, *The Novices of Sais*, with illustrations by Paul Klee, trans. Ralph Manheim (Brooklyn, NY: Archipelago 2005), 3.

17. Jacques Derrida, *Of Grammatology*, trans. Gayatri Chakravorty Spivak (Baltimore, MD: Johns Hopkins University Press, 1976), 14.

18. Georg Christoph Lichtenberg, *Observationes: Die lateinischen Schriften*, ed. Dag Nikolaus Hasse (Göttingen, Germany: Wallstein, 1997), 151; my translation. The "cake" refers to the insulating filling set in a metal dish that formed the base of the electrophorus. It could be made of resin, pitch, wax, or a mixture of these.

19. As can be seen on a wide variety of examples on YouTube.

20. Friedrich Wilhelm Joseph von Schelling, *Vorlesungen über die Methode (Lehrart) des Akademischen Studiums: Auf der Grundlage des Textes der Ausgabe von Otto Weiss*, ed. Melchior Meyr (Hamburg: Meiner, 1990), 40; my translation.

21. "Figurierte Schallbewegungen wie Buchstaben. (Sollten die Buchstaben ursprünglich akustische Figuren gewesen sein? Buchstaben a priori?)" Novalis, *Schriften: Die Werke Friedrich von Hardenbergs*, ed. Paul Kluckhohn, R. H. Samuel, and Hans Joachim Mähl (Stuttgart: W. Kohlhammer, 1960), 1:1277; my translation.

22. "Es hat die Leute geschockt, aber die meisten sind übergelaufen, komischerweise." Friedrich Kittler, "Das kalte Modell von Struktur," 96.

23. Ibid., 98.

24. Ibid., 98 and 102.

7

THE CLARA COMPLEX

Kittler on "The Sandman"

Jeffrey Champlin

Clara, Clara, *ach, ach*. Kittler's early article on "The Sandman" embraces the doppelgänger both at the thematic level of psychic disturbance and at the logical level of the text's own paired step. Kittler sets the stakes of his inquiry very high, arguing for a programmatic overhaul of the relation between psychology and literature. He enacts what he calls a "decentering" of the story in the direction of psychoanalysis, but in the process reinscribes Clara as a model of interpretive illumination. Restoring the hermeneutic import of Clara's effacing self-accusation of stupidity with the work of Avital Ronell reveals a larger dissemblance: the dispersion of the siblings who may challenge the Oedipal structure that has ruled Hoffmann's text since Freud. In this way, expanding Kittler's logic of the double through Hoffmann answers questions Kittler himself leaves open related to the historical "mutation" of the nuclear family.

Published in 1816, E. T. A. Hoffmann's story "The Sandman" tells of the student Nathaniel's continued battles with monstrous doubles that figure a childhood trauma. Kittler draws the title of his essay from the first of the story's three sections, in which, through a misdirected letter, Clara tries to talk her beloved Nathaniel out of his struggle with "the phantom of our ego" that shows up in a shadowy barometer salesman. A century later, Freud's article "The Uncanny" (1919) elevated "The Sandman" to the status of a privileged text for literary study and at the same time imposed a powerful deciphering that appears to reduce the story to master psychoanalytic signifiers. Specifically, Freud sees the threat to the eyes that runs through the story as indicating anxiety around the "castration complex."

Kittler allies himself with Freud in order to challenge a simpler psychologically oriented literary criticism that faces becoming superfluous when modern literature explicitly privileges psychological themes. In his words, the psychological interpretation of modern literature operates as "empty doubling" (*leere Verdopplung*), merely repeating what literature already said first.[1] The critic circles the text in a dance that adds nothing to it. Rather than denying the power of the double though, Kittler proposes a "decentering" of psychology. He will show that psychoanalysis allows us to see the "soul as a phantom" (*Seele als ein Phantom*) that cannot be interpreted away as a misapplication of reason but rather points to a broad structuring power of the unconscious (139). "The Sandman" for Kittler, as for Freud, offers a prime case study because it thematically engages the question of diagnosing madness. Through literature, as with dreams, we not only glimpse the powers that produce insanity and sanity, but question the opposition between these two psychic determinations.

Despite these programmatic statements, Kittler's practice of "decentering" poses a question of displacement rather than offering a confident shift of conceptual terrain. In comparison to rational psychology, psychoanalysis moves from a focus on the subject to an attunement to structure. However, this can only be a heuristic simplification, since Kittler also recognizes the Freudian tendency to circle again around the father. Staying with the phantom raises the stakes of a critical approach to the structure of mediation: this spirit indicates a power of positioning but also slinks away, haunts from the corner, and possesses the living.

A unique ghostly eccentricity emerges when Kittler engages both Freud and Hoffmann, and then adds Lacan and Foucault to the mix. As a matter of method, I acknowledge the risk of narcissistic dissolution that Kittler names at the start of his text but also assert the honor of the fading art of commentary. Philology loves the double, it embraces words through words. As hermeneutic scholar, it may be that Clara barely says anything new, but she may also—in a new combinational complex, another *plex* as the twine of the twin—point to a mutant future.

ROMANTICISM'S FATE, CLARA'S FATE

Kittler repeatedly returns to Hoffmann in the years leading to the 1985 publication of *Discourse Networks 1800/1900*. Indeed, when looked at from a certain perspective, Hoffmann becomes Kittler's privileged writer, playing an analogous role to that of Hölderlin to Heidegger, or Goethe to Freud. His choice may surprise literature scholars, who generally do not grant Hoffmann the metaphysical gravitas of Hölderlin, or the world historical insight of Goethe. Even within the contours of the romantic movement, Hoffmann clocks in late, well after the theoretical innovations of Friedrich Schlegel, and modifying, rather than originating, the return to the fairy tale genre initiated by the Brothers Grimm.

Hoffmann may seem to merely illustrate the interiorizing pull of romantic discourse, but Kittler works out a theory of romantic mediation through Hoffmann in terms of aesthetics, epistemology, and metaphysics. According to the framework of *Discourse Networks 1800/1900*, interiority and self-presence constitute the romantic subject, while the incomplete modern subject looks outside itself. However, the very elements of Hoffmann's work that seem to be "too much"—such as comical automatons, nostalgic scenes of education, and hyper-repetition of motifs—are the elements that highlight the mediated nature of romantic subjectivity. From this point of view, Kittler's very description of successive subjectivities consolidates one of his well-known theses: that the conception of the subject changes over time due to the media system of that period. A case study of his reading of "The Sandman," however, opens a view of a dynamic struggle between media and the subject it creates—a struggle discounted in the broader reception of Kittler's work that too often accuses it of determinism. In particular, using the organic term *mutation*, Kittler takes Foucault to Lacan with a distinctive critical twist irreducible to either of these thinkers.

Perhaps in response to Freud's own lengthy repetition, Kittler claims that the plot of "The Sandman" can be "quickly told" (*rasch erzält*; 140). I will note the danger of wanting to speed up as one provides an orienting compass since such velocities often attempt to smuggle in unexamined interpretive assertions. Nonetheless, we cannot really get started without a minimum of schematic paraphrase. The story falls into three sections. In the first part, Nathaniel writes a letter to his friend Lothario that recounts a story of childhood trauma in order to explain a disturbing recent encounter with a barometer salesman. Clara, Nathaniel's love interest, intercepts the letter and replies with an apparently therapeutic message. With a reflective gesture of romantic irony, the narrator interrupts his story in the second section. He raises doubts with regard to its poetic efficacy to which he responds with a deceptively clear principle. In the remainder of the text, Nathaniel encounters the scientist Coppola and his daughter Olympia. Mirroring Nathaniel with the *"ach, ach"* of narcissistic echo, she turns out to be a kind of better Clara—and also, as a wind-up doll, one of literature's first robots. (This is the part most familiar to the wider public from ballet and opera adaptations by Léo Delibes and Jacques Offenbach.) Finally driven to madness by Coppola and Coppelius, Nathaniel throws himself to his death from a tower.

Kittler reads Hoffmann through Freud from the start to contrast a psychological with a psychoanalytic approach to literature. He first defends his sense of psychoanalysis against simplistic accusations that reduce it to gestures of phallic mastery. Kittler, drawing on Freud's reading of Jensen's *Gradiva*, instead emphasizes the free play of the literary text. Psychoanalysis, in contrast to rational psychology, works through the "methodical bracketing out of reference" that unleashes an "endless play" (144). It does not seek to distinguish true from false but instead aims at the laws of the unconscious that this play reveals. Thus, psychoanalysis shifts from the classical epistemological concern with knowing the outside world to an inner truth of understanding the drives of subjects, what they want and where they are going.

Zooming in on how Kittler builds his argument around Clara will allow a need for a further decentering to emerge from the text itself. Within the specifics of his reading, Kittler attributes the clarifying impulse to Clara. In this regard, he joins a long line of critics who perhaps fall prey to the seductions of metonymy. Even those later scholars who tune in specifically to the gender dynamic of the story tend to take this route. For example, Gwen Bergen and Nicole Plette deploy a vocabulary of transparency and say that "Clara sees through Nathaniel's fantastic fears."[2] Shifting up in register, Caroline Rooney writes that "Clara tries to reassure [Nathaniel], indicating to him that he paranoiacally exaggerates the virilising role of the shadowy father figures."[3] Rooney thus expands Clara's supposed pedagogical goal to disabling patriarchal powers.[4]

Following his own paraphrase of the story, Kittler sums it up as "an argument over madness" (141). Nathaniel's beloved Clara takes on the role of trying to clear up the nightmarish vision he has had of the barometer salesman that reminds him of a hated associate of his father. In Kittler's words, Clara "explains the identity of Coppelius and Coppola as a product of an imagination that alienates free will in an unavoidable fate" (142). In these terms, Clara thus intends to restore the autonomy of Nathaniel. Kittler then expands on Clara's role in the broader debate over Nathaniel's madness: "Clara neutralizes the discourse of madness when she distinguishes real and imagined events, true and false" (144).[5] As the psychologist, Clara would offer a rational deciphering of irrational episodes. When Clara identifies the "dark power" in Nathaniel's mind, she also exposes it to the light of rational thought that would bring health.

Kittler thus describes Clara as the representative of the simplistic psychological reading of Nathaniel's delusion. Clara's psychological mode of interpretation rationally decodes the figure of the sandman. In contrast, the sandman himself stands as the figure for psychoanalysis (143).

THE PHANTOM OF OUR STUPIDITY

Kittler lays a great deal of interpretive weight on the phrase "phantom of our ego." The phrase, though, appears in a strange and errant course of citation and distance. Clara intercepts Nathaniel's letter to Lothario and she responds partially of her own accord, but also partially in her brother's name. Moreover, she not only closes her interpretation, but also introduces it with a gesture of self-effacement.[6] Examining the envelope that delivers her interpretation will allow us to see that pinning the crime of the single interpretation on the minoritized other reduces the eccentric effect that this figure may have on the Oedipal house.

As Clara builds up to the key passage on the phantom of the ego, she tempers her message with the following qualifying words: "I perhaps do not find the right words at the end and you laugh at me, not because I mean something dumb [*weil ich was Dummes meine*], but because I am so clumsy in saying it."[7] This phrase breaks in at least two directions. On the one hand, putting an accusation in Nathaniel's mouth could cause him to lower his guard and inoculate her from the charge of an overbearing interpretation. The text primarily lulls its interpreters in this direction. On the other hand, though, it could be that Clara demotes herself to an object of laughter in such a way that it negates her stated message. Since we cannot simply situate the stupidity that Clara names, we are left with a double bind. By emphasizing linguistic form as she tries to convey her meaning, Clara inserts a moment of hermeneutic disability within the heart of the interpretation she proffers.

The work of Avital Ronell allows us to negotiate this apparent roadblock by opening a path along the fault line of philosophical and literary modes of dealing with stupidity. In her explication, philosophers have a kind of half-witted relation to *Dummheit*, an inkling but not much more. They *start* their inquiry "in the mood of stupefication" (68), but claim to have left it behind by the end of their works. Ronell offers, for example, the obvious stupidity of spirit simply reflecting on itself at the end of Hegel's *Phenomenology of Spirit*. In a resonance of Kittler's complaint against psychological criticism, we are left again with empty doubling.

Philosophy has not been able to name a stupidity which does not let knowledge go. Ronell employs particularly provocative phrasing at this point in her argument: "Fundamental stupidity has not really been upgraded to the level of a problem" (68). Etymologically, *fundamental* comes from the Latin *fundare*, meaning "to found." From this perspective, we might ask how can there be a "founding" stupidity, not of politics (which we think we can understand) but thinking? Later, in her chapter on Paul de Man, Ronell gestures to a conceptual answer in the experience of linguistic misfire. For de Man, language repeatedly takes aim at meaning but never hits its mark. In this sense, we might speak of a founding stupidity that creates effects from a well-intentioned but deluded base.

Stupidity does not want to admit this errancy though and tends to target the minority, children or women. Ronell offers three instructive cases: the illiterate but divinely inspired Joan of Arc in Schiller's Jungfrau von Orleans; the loquacious "woman writer" that annoys Musil; and Eve's mere "curiosity" that obscures a deeper drive for knowledge in *Genesis*. Ronell's emphasis on the "woman as a figure for stupidity" shows us that fundamental stupidity cannot be named by philosophy but reveals itself through the collateral damage of its figuration.

Reading Ronell with "The Sandman" compels us to open the window on Clara's citation and think again about who stupidity targets. Following her equivocation above, Clara continues: "It is also certain, Lothario added, that the dark psychic power" converts external encounters into figures of its own such that "it is the phantom of our own ego, whose inner relations and deep effect on our sensibility throws us into hell, or charms us into heaven" (23). The passage goes on to reveal that Clara relays the diagnosis of her brother. From this point of view, she just passes along a reading from the masculine source. At the same time though, she potentially ties the *challenge* of linguistic formulation to her brother.

Just when we might think the siblings are all on the same page, Clara loops back to the noncomprehension with which she introduced the diagnosis: "I do not completely understand [*verstehe ich nicht ganz*] Lothario's last words, I just feel like I know what he means and yet it is to me as if all were very true [*als sei alles sehr wahr*]" (23). Once again, we cannot say if Clara intends to demote herself or to empower her interpretation by phrasing it in a less confrontational way. In either case, her last words are not those of knowledge but of a figurative certainty, truth "as if" it were truth. And not just *as if* it were truth, but as if it were *very* true, with the intensifying adjective further destabilizing what should be a binary alternative. Through these hesitations and envelopments, Clara passes along the material of language as distinct from its understood referent.[8] She admits she does not understand the essence of the phantom and in doing so introduces a rhetorical distance to the critic's attempt to clear up the figure of the sandman.

Nathaniel becomes a model for literary critics to come when he clears all of this up. According to his response, Clara writes an exemplary philosophical interpretation of stupidity in Ronell's sense. He paraphrases the letter when he writes back to Lothario, saying that Clara "has written me a very moving philosophical letter in which she thoroughly proves that Coppelius and Coppula only exist inside of me and are phantoms of my ego" (24). When Nathaniel takes Clara's words as a "philosophical letter" he ignores the way she thematizes nonknowledge and lets stupidity, the phantom, and even the *stupidity of the phantom*, roam.

MUTANT HISTORY AND SIBLING INSCRIPTION

Our revised view of Clara's "psychological" approach requires that we now reconsider its relation to Kittler's contrasting psychoanalytic position. Clara does not exactly bracket out reference, but her moments of acknowledged incomprehension do extend in principle to what Kittler calls the "endless play" of signification (144). For him, when psychoanalysis allows self-reference to emerge, it positively outlines the phantom of our ego "as the symbolic truth of the production of the human (*Hominization*)" (149).[9] In this way, Kittler, through Freud, emphasizes the process of doubling rather than the identification of the double.[10]

Does recovering linguistic errancy through Clara just repeat Kittler's point regarding the emergence of psychoanalytic structures at another level? If so, my commentary would add just one sheen of insight to Hoffmann's text. This would be an appropriately modest reward of philological attention. Yet succumbing to the story's tendency to push its readers into ever further splits, I will conclude with another suggestion. While speculative in nature, it responds to a further puzzle. Why, in the final section, does Kittler, apparently without reflection, deploy another term of troubled genesis: *mutation*?

Kittler branches off the Freudian register just as he opens the question of the discourse of the subject over time with his own key term *Aufschreibesystem*: "Before subjects . . . seek a unique and secret meaning of their life in childhood, the nuclear family must become a privileged 'Aufschreibesystem.' The fact that literature speaks of heroes that become detectives and victims of family discourses is in itself a discursive event and to be located in the mutation of rules of communication" (162). Following Foucault's use of the term in *The Order of Things*, which Kittler cites in this section of the article (though not directly in this connection), a "mutation" means something like "historical instantiation." After a long study of literature that narrates not-finding-oneself, a specific mode of reflection apparently emerges that enables and delimits psychoanalytic coding. In other words, even if literature escapes the doubling of psychology and psychoanalysis, it appears to meet its match in history.

Within the limited context of the quote above, Kittler appears to use the term *Aufschreibesystem* to refer to a historically determined set of rules that provide meaning. The nuclear family, rather than the extended clan, becomes the structure that decides at a certain moment how identity will appear. David Wellbery's foreword to *Discourse Networks 1800/1900* justifies the translation of *Aufschreibesystem* as "discourse network" in structural terms that situate Kittler primarily in the protective realm of Foucault. As Wellbery also notes though, the term could more literally be translated as "systems of writing down."[11] In the context of my reading of Kittler's article on "The Sandman," I prefer this translation because it recalls the phrase's origin as the strategy that the schizophrenic Schreber employed to protect himself from the rays of God. By emphasizing *writing*, this translation suggests the possibility that the system may not just instantiate itself but also change. In this sense, we can also hear in Kittler's term the alternate translation "system of inscription," or even, risking a French hybrid, *écriture-system*. (Both of these suggestions, of course, recall another one of Kittler's eminent influences, Derrida.)

Insisting on the potential miswriting of the system carries Kittler's stated emphasis on decentering through to the completion of the article. Accepting Kittler's troubled imperative of doubling commentary summons not only Clara but Nathaniel's other siblings from the long shadow cast by the army of father figures including the Sandman, Coppelius, and Coppola. In this respect, sisters and brothers reopen the question of the mutant historical context of psychoanalysis. Kittler moves from psychology to psychoanalysis, but even as a symbolic structure, indeed particularly as symbolic structure, psychoanalysis enforces an orbit around the position of the father. Following Kittler to Clara has let her to emerge not so much *from* the shadows as *with* the shadows of stupidity. In doing so, she suggests a counter-writing, or at least a possible displacement, of the Oedipal system through sibling inscription. As Stefani Engelstein phrases it, psychoanalysis privileges "vertical lineages."[12] Working with *Antigone*, she argues that the sibling "allows us to move beyond both self-other dualisms and the mother-child dyad as the only grounds for intersubjectivity, and recognizes the subject as instead embedded in a network of *partial others*" (40). While it would be hasty to admit "intersubjectivity" in Hoffmann's story since it continually challenges the subject as such, I do see an interpretive potency in extending Engelstein's reference to *"partial others"* to "The Sandman."

From this point of view, the siblings suggest that when Kittler goes from Lacan to Foucault at the end of his essay he points to questions of displacement of kinship.[13] In at least two points, the siblings of "The Sandman" seems to scurry away from the paternal regime. First, when recounting the original story of the sandman from his childhood, Nathaniel refers to siblings (*Geschwister*) in the plural (12). They are anonymous in the strict sense from the start. Without names, they hover as an indistinct brood. Indeed, the original command that so scared Nathaniel has a plural referent, with his mother yelling "Now Children!" (*Nun Kinder!*; 12). In this respect, the approaching sandman has the power to hurt not just Nathaniel but everyone who does not obey. Nathaniel also later refers to the nurse of his "youngest sister" (*jüngste Schwester*; 13) which implies that he has other sisters as well, but does not identify precisely how many.

We also know that when Nathaniel was ten, his mother removed him from the "children's room" (*Kinderstube*; 14). Left alone, he succumbs to the traumatic encounter with Coppelius and his father. From that point on, we never hear of the siblings again. Within the narrative logic, Lothario and Clara take their place, described by the narrator as "children of a distant relative who had also died" (*Kinder eines weitläufigen Verwandten*), as had Nathaniel's father (27). Even following this substitution, Lothario remains a spectral (non)presence, never getting in a word of his own, even when he challenges Nathaniel to a duel over the treatment of his sister.

Clara thus becomes the carrier of the siblings, even though, at the end of the story, she joins another nuclear family. While Clara settles down, "The Sandman" ends with an undecidable moment. Granted, the Oedipal grid can assign a place for all newcomers, such that, for example, Clara would stand in for the mother who originally tried to put Nathaniel in his place. In their very dispersion, though, the siblings may slip away from the power of the father. From that point of view, they could point to a challenge to the symbolic law that emerges through its literary instantiation. Siblings rustle in Nathaniel's narrative, if not with the dignity of the phantom then perhaps with *frission* of minor spirits.

Kittler reminds us that Hoffmann's story begins "with an epistemolary first person discourse of the hero that according to the hero no one adequately answers" (162). The lost siblings of the text echo this noncorrespondence and perhaps resist its interiorizing pull. In their shadow network, the partial other indicates a relay that would continually postpone the destined identification through the father. This system, another kind of *Aufschreibesystem*, cannot exclude the possibility of expressing itself clumsily, to appeal again to the way that Clara describes her own interpretive work. In the sense of an interruption of sending (*schicken*), the sibling system affirms epistemological and psychic bumbling, constitutively *ungeschickt*.

NOTES

1. Friedrich Kittler, "'Das Phantom unseres Ichs' und die Literaturpsychologie: E. T. A. Hoffmann—Freud—Lacan," in *Urszenen: Literaturwissenschaft als Diskursanalyse und Diskurskritik*, ed. Friedrich A. Kittler and Horst Turk (Frankfurt am Main: Suhrkamp, 1977), 139; my translation. Hereafter cited in text by page number.

2. Gwen Bergen and Nicole Plette, "Uncanny Women and Anxious Masters: Reading Coppélia against Freud," in *Moving Words: Re-Writing Dance*, ed. Gay Morris (London and New York: Routledge, 1995), 145.

3. Caroline Rooney, *Decolonizing Gender: Literature and the Poetics of the Real* (New York: Routledge, 2007), 87.

4. Helene Cixous points indirectly toward Clara's importance as well when she focuses on her mechanical double in the final section of the story. Cixous highlights how "the beautiful Olympia is effaced by what she represents, for Freud has no eyes for

her" (538). Our reading of Clara seeks to do her justice in a like manner. Helene Cixous, "Fiction and Its Phantom: A Reading of Freud's 'Das Unheimliche,'" *New Literary History* 7, no. 3 (1976): 538.

5. In another formulation, Kittler writes of "Clara's etiology of madness" (142).

6. Samuel Weber is one of the few critics who acknowledge that Clara inserts herself in the dialogue between Lothario and Nathaniel: "this unexpected and unavoidable interference of the other—of the other woman, of woman as the other—can only appear, from a certain perspective, as uncanny: all too familiar and yet irreducibly alien." Samuel Weber, *The Legend of Freud* (Stanford, CA: Stanford University Press, 2000), 19.

7. E. T. A. Hoffmann, "Der Sandmann," in *Werke* (Frankfurt am Main: Insel-Verlag, 1967), 2:22. Translations from Hoffmann are my own, although I have consulted R. J. Hollingdale's translation in *Tales of Hoffmann* (London: Penguin, 1982), 85–126.

8. Andrew Webber notes that the story continually stages its title character on the border line of the figural and actual: "The Sandman himself gravitates between the status of a figure of speech, a figure of legend, and a real identity." Andrew Webber, *Der Doppelgänger: Double Visions in German Literature* (Oxford: Clarendon Press, 1996), 145. Clara helps us bring this insight to the text's self-awareness.

9. Along the same lines, Kittler ultimately sees the narrator of the story as coming in to release the ultimate play of signification that would absorb the reader (162–66). Similarly, in his reading of Hoffmann's first novel *The Devil's Elixirs*, Kittler highlights how in the foreword the fictitious editor promises to fully place the reader into the position of the subject in a bright, alien world of perceptions. Friedrich Kittler, *Optical Media* (Cambridge, UK: Polity, 2010), 113.

10. In "Chemically Pure Consumption: Drugs in Hegel, Heidegger, and Hoffmann," Kittler picks up on a misreading of Hoffmann that sends ghosts (*Geister*) on another unexpected path. Baudelaire remarks upon Hoffmann's note in *Kreisleriana* that a composer should drink champagne to compose good comic operas. In describing this recommendation in terms of a "holy" reverence, Kittler claims that Baudelaire falls from the "heights of German idealism." Hegel's description of the true in the *Phenomenology* as "the Bacchanalian revel in which no member is not drunk" now means that there can be no (heavenly) spirit without (alcoholic) spirits, *Geist* in two senses. Kittler puts forth a scandalous reading that does not take Hegel's description to be a metaphor that reveals the actual interiority of spirit, but instead takes the metaphor to be more accurate than the thing Hegel supposedly uses it to illustrate. Friedrich Kittler, "Der chemisch reine Konsum: Drogen bei Hegel, Hoffmann und Baudelaire," in *Umwege des Lesens: Aus dem Labor philologischer Neugierde*, ed. Christoph Hoffmann and Caroline Welsh (Berlin: Parerga 2006), 111–26. Years after that text, Kittler continued his profound profanation of Hegel in a seminar that I attended on the *Phenomenology of Spirit* in Berlin. There, to take just one example, he translated, or perhaps overwrote, the section on "Religion in the Form of Art" (*Die Kunstreligion*), in terms primarily of artworks themselves as they changed shapes and styles, with the attendant conceptions of the divine as a little more than projected byproducts.

11. David Wellbery, foreword to Friedrich Kittler, *Discourse Networks 1800/1900* (Stanford, CA: Stanford University Press, 1992), xii.

12. Stefani Engelstein, "Sibling Logic; or, Antigone Again," *PMLA* 126, no. 1 (2011): 38. In another article, Engelstein is one of the few critics to note the puzzle of the sibling in "The Sandman." See Engelstein, "Reproductive Machines in E. T. A. Hoffmann," in *Body Dialectics in the Age of Goethe*, ed. Holger Pausch and Marianne Henn (New York: Rodopi Press, 2003), 161–91.

13. This theoretical debate also arises around Levi Strauss's *Elementary Structures of Kinship*, especially in the work of Judith Butler. See Claude Lévi-Strauss, *The Elementary Structures of Kinship* (Boston, MA: Beacon Press, 1969; Judith Butler, *Gender Trouble: Feminism and the Subversion of Identity* (New York: Routledge, 2011).

PART III

LIVE TRANSFERENCE

8

ON THE AUTOBAHN TO LANGUAGE

Mert Bahadır Reisoğlu

> Under the conditions of technology, literature disappears (like
> metaphysics for Heidegger) into the un-death of its endless ending.
> —Kittler, "Dracula's Legacy"

Kittler's 1985 article "Auto Bahnen / Free Ways" published in the same year as *Discourse Networks 1800/1900*, extends his inquiries to transportation and infrastructure. Read in conjunction with "Die Stadt ist ein Medium" ("The City is a Medium"), published three years later, Kittler's underlying preoccupation with the apocalyptic demise of literature in the age of technological media seems to be replaced by a desire to write technological history without the mediation of "nice stories about young German poets" as a "cover-up" of his ideas.[1] The relationship between this history of technology and literature, however, is much more complicated. Literature, whose death is announced, figures in the most unexpected places as undead in Kittler's work. In Kittler's cursory remarks on Heidegger and Lacan, media theory reveals itself as thinking that moves within language by reflecting on what makes it possible.

Kittler's analysis of the autobahn aims to highlight the irruption of the new—a concern that he says he shares with Foucault and Derrida—by way of offering the "forgotten" military history of autobahns against the "feudal and famous" one.[2] The emphasis on the military-technical aspects of this history is more straightforward: While the official narrative centers on the desire to eliminate dust and clamor on the streets by constructing roads just for cars, Kittler turns his attention to the rupture introduced by the division of the roads into two lanes. It is a radical separation of different vehicles and elimination of pedestrians, bicycles and animals from traffic, which announces the institution of something new, a new organization. "It's hard to imagine" Kittler claims, "what people had been willing to put up with."[3] What passes as inconspicuous today as a part of everyday street life (*Straßenalltag*) reveals its militaristic background once the history of this rupture is analyzed. Tracing technological developments to their militaristic origins helps Kittler to emphasize the subterranean function of more "peaceful" practices. "Peace," he claims at the end of the article, "is the continuation of war with the same means of transportation."[4] The joke on Clausewitz not only applies theory of war to infrastructure, but also situates the "means" or the media as the very reason of this continuation by changing difference to sameness. As such "tourist division upon tourist division" riding on the autobahn in postwar Europe can be seen as the continuation of the military use of the same roads and touristic auto-mobility can be construed as a misuse of military equipment.[5] Kittler continues to emphasize this, as is well-known, later in *Gramophone, Film, Typewriter* in the famous analogy between the movie crowds being bombarded by images and soldiers by bullets. In his media-centered archaeology of the present, Kittler continues his series of examples tailing vehicles and media through their uses and abuses.

The autobahn, as Thomas Zeller notes, was not needed by the military due to the "low level of motorization in Germany" at the time.[6] But it was necessary for Hitler's propaganda, for which the autobahn "stood for a drive toward a modern, fast, and visually attractive future."[7] Kittler touches on this political aspect by claiming that "war is wish fulfillment—also and especially for those without a driver's license."[8] The argument that the desire to drive a car is created by the rulers as a component of war, however, does not entail that this "ideology" is embedded within the technology itself. For Kittler, war and technology cannot be disentangled by changes in discourses surrounding it. If the use of the same vehicles on the autobahn during and after the war refers us to the military aspect of tourism, Kittler's juxtaposition of *"Führer"* and *"Führerschein"* (driver's license) goes beyond word play. To the extent that the driver determines his or her own direction, he or she emerges as an automobile subject that is the cause of its own movements. It is only against the background of this technical support of auto-mobility that later elimination of speed limits on the autobahn can be seen as a rejection of totalitarianism in postwar Germany. The concerns of the Nazi architects in Thomas Zeller's historical account showcase this formation of the subject in its relation to what lies outside it.[9] Zeller writes: "The panoramatic experience on the train was replaced by the 'feasibility' of the experience of landscape, as one historian observed with respect to the automobilists of the early twentieth century. They praised the car as a return to a landscape individually appropriated, as a self-guided experience of nature."[10] The subject, as a self-moving agent, is a part of the landscape as a driver, but thanks to his or her auto-motion, the landscape reveals itself as an object for aesthetic visual consumption.

Kittler relates transportation to war by positing two identities. Subjugation of the landscape to aesthetic concerns shows that "autobahn *is* aesthetics," while Hitler's dreams of riding on the autobahn toward Odessa with a camera installed to the car reveals "the identity of aesthetics and blitzkrieg."[11] The identity of technology and war passes through aesthetics, which explains Kittler's incessant return to film and literature in almost all his writings. Transformation and leveling of the landscape into information channels constitute the first aesthetic act while the second one, that of film, which records the first, constitutes the second. An uneasy affiliation with Hegel reveals itself in this succession of the subject acting on dead matter and the following filmic self-recognition. Escaping from Hegel, who might be "[standing] motionless, waiting for us" at the end of the autobahn, as Foucault would say, would necessitate elimination of the subject on both sides of the equation.[12] This is why Kittler returns to the same topic in his later essay "Die Stadt ist ein Medium" to decouple roads and train tracks from any kind of subjective experience. Highways are said to transmit energy in the form of human beings, while trains "format" the passengers by dividing them into "officers," "lower-ranking officers" and "the battalion's infantry."[13] How this reformatting takes place on the highways is not clarified, but in this formulation, "human beings" are strictly conceptualized as one type of information among others. War, as such, does not only enable Kittler to bridge Foucauldian archaeology and genealogy, discourses and institutional practices, as Winthrop-Young points out, but also erases the distinction between subject and object. It is not a war between different subjects but between "different media technologies" that "provoke each other in a fight for supremacy."[14] As the successor of trains, the autobahn seems to wage its war against premodern roads where traffic is not regulated. The implied counterpart to film in this article, I would argue, is literature.

Literature in its alliance with uncontrolled traffic, however, is understood outside the framework of humanism. In his article on Pynchon, Kittler claims that the literature of the discourse network 1800 named the enemies so that their destruction was ordered.[15] Traffic here means not only the traffic of vehicles and persons, but also the traffic of data, of which literature is a part. But this "millenary commerce between literature and strategy" is deemed to be obsolete with the separation of channels into railways (which transport people), telegraph and army postcards (which remain as a remnant of literature).[16] Following the arguments already made in *Discourse Networks*, literature's death is once again announced, this time with regard to channels: "An absolute enemy that would be taken over by machines no longer requires narration, motivation or planning."[17] In World War I, literature either leaves its place to film or imitates it.[18] While the autobahn follows trains in the division of the lanes, it is here in this context, I would argue, that its novelty becomes clear: The channels no longer carry any discourse. Instead, the lanes function as a *"cordon sanitaire"* to separate "the input and output of large-scale modern battles" so that the chance of an encounter between cannon fodders and dead bodies is eliminated.[19] An accident between the two, Kittler claims, would be a "catastrophe," but why it would be so requires further explanation. Separation of the living from the dead, forgetting of death, avoidance from diseases and contamination would certainly be necessary for the "giant snakes of light and steel" to be "our lifelines."[20] Taking living bodies to the future along the path of technological advancement, the autobahn for Kittler is also an escape route that continuously lets people run away from the dead. If the train traveler constantly sees his or her doubles as other commuters, as Kittler famously argues, then the lone driver on the autobahn constantly catches glimpses of ghosts—a trick often used in many horror films. The revenant is coming back from the other direction, the future of the traveler, having already been where the living will eventually be. One of these ghosts could easily be literature, the undead and the contaminant that keeps returning at the moment it is claimed to be dead.

Indeed, it does: What prompts Kittler to write about the autobahn is his muse, Thomas Pynchon, to whose description of the "automotive folly" he devotes a full paragraph at the beginning of the article. Literature's obsolescence does not preclude him from taking his cue from *Gravity's Rainbow*, which deserves praise precisely because of the "exactitude of the research it incorporates."[21] The novel, for Kittler, is "data retrieval from a world war whose classified files are made accessible to this degree only when their strategic goals become reality and no longer require what is called secrecy."[22] Literature as belated espionage allows Kittler to tap into the war of media. But Pynchon's value does not only derive from his engineering background or research. It is because of that non-secrecy, Kittler claims, "paranoia is knowledge itself."[23] In the psychosis of the narrator there is a "confusion of words and things, of designatum and denotatum," he writes. "When the symbolic of signs, numbers and letters determine so-called reality, then gathering the traces becomes the paranoid's primary duty."[24] This will to knowledge—which for Lacan is the tragedy of Oedipus—will have to be analyzed further. But before this, it is important to focus on this "confusion of words and things." In his military narrative on the autobahn, Kittler encounters not only Pynchon, but also Lacan, whom he mentions *in passing* while highlighting the separation of the two lanes on highways. This glimpse of Lacan's ghost in the middle of the autobahn's history is one of Kittler's typical recourses to French theory that serve to ground it in the history of media. The example is taken from Lacan's childhood memory of the boy and the girl who see the restrooms through the train window, which Lacan uses to explain the Saussurean bar between "the primordial position of the signifier and the signified" that are "separated by a barrier resisting signification."[25] Kittler adds: "And because according to Lacan the rails 'materialize the bar in the Saussurean algorithm,' they need not be materially present [*vorhanden*]. As long as they feature two sets of rails, even railway lines destroyed by German shock troops can become the model for automotive segregation."[26] Just as the railway's double tracks become a model (*Vorbild*) for the autobahn, Lacan's example becomes a model for Kittler's story. Its function, however, seems to be ambiguous. Does it ground the structuralist separation of the signifier and the signified in the history of transportation? An unclear link between semantics and transportation is hinted at continuously throughout the article, especially when he claims that the autobahns "delivered traffic (both word and thing) from its obscene double meaning [*Zweideutigkeit*], which already long before Freud was celebrated in countless puns."[27] Both word and thing (*in Wort und Sache*): A parallel is assumed to exist between the traffic of signs and the traffic of vehicles such that the order imposed on the latter is imposed on the former. Judging from the Lacanian example, this would mean that the structuralist division between the signifier and the signified, their "primordial positions," came to be seen that way as a result of the traffic regulation which also restricts possibilities of double entendre.

The passage from one type of traffic to the other is made more difficult by the fact that what is at stake here is not processes of inscription, as in the analyses of *Discourse Networks*, but of movement. Kittler's examples, however, are more playful for a framework that is solely defined by technological determinism. The "confusion of words and things" or the traffic of words and the traffic of things, can be read as a Pynchonesque maneuver that deliberately juxtaposes the two orders. If "we knew nothing about our senses until media provided models and metaphors," then Lacan can write about the "incessant sliding of the signified under the signifier" only thanks to the railway, and as such become a model for Kittler.[28] For Kittler, Lacan—who, as Kittler repeatedly emphasizes, has always derived the titles of his works from the medium in which he expresses himself—becomes a medium through whom the difficulty of speaking about language in language is encountered, if not surpassed, in an essay entitled "Autobahns," as if to imply that Kittler is expressing himself through the medium of the autobahn. The difficulty of relating writing on the autobahn and writing on writing *on* the autobahn hinges on the word *materialize* (*materialisieren*). Do the railroad tracks materialize the Saussurean bar by way of causation, so that the railroad is the origin from which all our discourse on the separation between the signifier and the signified emanates?

In this case, Kittler would be tracing the origin of the separation to uncover the common origin of words and of things, of the two types of traffic, which would cancel the separation doubly both in theory and in method. Or does the railroad materialize the bar by providing a metaphor that will "[flash] between two signifiers, one of which has replaced the other by taking the other's place in the signifying chain, the occulted signifier remaining present by virtue of its (metonymic) connection to the rest of the chain"?[29] The signifier "railroad," then, would reflect "its light into the darkness of incomplete significations," an image that is reminiscent of the traffic on the autobahn, which is frequently described by Kittler as a giant snake of headlights.[30] In his Seminar XX, Lacan refers to this Saussurean bar claiming:

> [There is] nothing you can understand in a bar, even when it is reserved for signifying negation. . . . There is something that is even more certain: adding a bar to the notation S and *s* is already a bit superfluous and even futile, insofar as what it brings out is already indicated by the distance of what is written. The bar, like everything involving what is written, is based only on the following—what is written is not to be understood. That is why you are not obliged to understand my writings. If you don't understand them, so much the better—that will give you the opportunity to explain them. It's the same with the bar. The bar is precisely the point at which, in every use of language, writing may be produced. If, in Saussure's work itself S is above *s*, that is, over the bar, it is because the effects of the unconscious have no basis without this bar. . . . Indeed, were it not for this bar nothing about language could be explained by linguistics. Were it not for this bar above which there are signifiers that pass, you could not see that signifiers are injected into the signified.[31]

The bar's incomprehensibility could be related to its origin—the material that is not materially available, the tracks and median strips—but insofar as it relates to that which makes writing possible, it also refers to the incomprehensibility of Lacan's writings, its inability to become a model. Or rather, the model or metaphor which provides Kittler with the example of the all-encompassing media-technological effect of the separation itself remains incomprehensible. The bar, the mark that marks the separation of signifier and signified, hides behind itself the spacing that makes writing and language possible, to which Kittler alludes to in *Discourse Networks* when he claims: "The readability of signs is a function of their spatiality. The architect's manipulation of space demonstrates that, when the lack is lacking and no empty spaces remain, media disappear, 'naked and obscene', into the chaos from which they were derived."[32] The "obscenity" of the unregulated traffic and its *Zweideutigkeit* is the threat against this separation, which makes media and mediation possible. What is at stake is not only the material—the railroad tracks or the median strips—which are materially not available, but this spacing for which they might also be standing as metaphors. *Zweideutigkeit*, the obscene word play, here derives from the ambiguity that surrounds the identity of what is hidden by the metaphor. What makes the traffic of signs and the traffic of vehicles possible and historically comparable recedes to the background behind the Lacanian example of the bar and Kittler's example of the autobahn. The Pynchonesque maneuver of confusing things and words, taking a glimpse at the chaos of lack of spacing and mediation, is also what enables Kittler to oscillate between two possible readings, one media-historical, the other literary. Auto-mobility and auto-referentiality emerge as the two lanes on the same road, the separation of which is historicized and narrated by Kittler in a way that contributes to but also questions these dichotomies.

For an article that takes a critical stance against the order imposed on traffic and its *Zweideutigkeit* in general, the ambiguity between these two different readings is not unexpected. They point toward two different ways of approaching Kittler's works—an approach that focuses on the materiality of media and traces its archaeology and its entanglements, and one that focuses on its relation to language and literature, questioning the place of poetry in the age of technological media, neither endorsing nor lamenting, but questioning its demise. These two threads are always copresent in Kittler, and they need to be assessed in their complex entanglement. Where metaphors stem from and what they are a symptom of remains ambiguous in Kittler's writings on space as well. While media supply us with metaphors about ourselves—and ones that give rise to *méconnaissance* at their best—in "Die Stadt ist ein Medium" computer terminology is said to "stem nonetheless from the city" with terms such as gates, ports, and circuits.[33] This slippage from one source to the other is noteworthy, for it sends us to a place that only supplies us with metaphors of metaphors. In "Autobahns," the signifier *"Mittelstreifen"* (median strips) wavers between its denotatum, which has a history from the railway to the autobahn, and its designatum, which is not materially available or present-at-hand (*vorhanden*). The bar's emergence as an object is only possible through distantiation and it is here that media theory reflects upon itself. The use of Heideggerian vocabulary is not an accident: The relationship between auto-mobility and Heidegger's thinking on language—from the analysis of the sign structure *Sein und Zeit*, with examples taken from traffic signs, to *Holzwege* and *Unterwegs zur Sprache*—could itself make a book. Heidegger is not only a ghost encountered on the autobahn, but the very figure with whom Kittler starts his trip in the form of an epigraph from "Vom Wesen der Sprache": "The country offers ways only because it is country. It gives way, moves us. We hear the words 'give way' in this sense: to be the original giver and founder of ways."[34] Starting an article on the history of autobahns and their problematic political history with Heidegger's essay on the "fateful source of speech" can be read as a cynical gesture that, as in the example of Lacan, relates language to infrastructure.[35] But this essay by Heidegger is also a reflection on the relationship between technology and language. If "metalanguage and sputnik, metalinguistics and rocketry are the same," as Heidegger claims at the beginning of his piece, then his concerns align with those of Kittler: The possibility of dividing language into signifiers and signifieds, to take the bar as an object, is closely related to technological conditions.[36]

Things and words once again. Underlying Heidegger's rumination on language is the terror caused by the autobahn, its "furious pace" (*steigende Geschwindigkeit*) that comes to signify the domination of calculation and method.[37] The difference between Heidegger and Kittler rather resides in the way freedom is formulated. Where Heidegger speaks of "the freeing and sheltering character of this region" in its "way-making movement" and the way of thinking that counters the speed of the sciences, in Kittler *Be-wëgung* comes to signify political forces that are made visible by the history of the autobahn: "The movement of '33, then, was always already a moving (*Be-wëgung*)."[38] Once again, reading this sentence in both directions, on both lanes, is possible: Either what Heidegger means by *Be-wëgung* in his thinking on language was "always already," without him being aware of it, a symptom or a metaphor of the auto-mobility and the freedom opened up by the "country," which he contrasts to sciences, is "always already" a product of the autobahn, or, insofar as autobahns are aesthetics, the movement of '33 was an instance of this *Be-wëgung* to which poetry and thinking are inextricably bound in the history of Being. The second reading should enable us to go beyond a simple social-ization of Heidegger and to discover the ways in which Heidegger's text acts as a cipher throughout Kittler's piece: When Heidegger speaks of the need to avoid "[forcing] the vibration of the poetic saying into the rigid groove of a univocal statement" through method and calculation, Kittler's side remarks on *Zweideutigkeit* vibrate with Heidegger's concerns.[39] The way, contrary to method which objectifies what it is reaching for and thus annuls the way, "lets us reach what concerns and summons us."[40] This concern, which remains hidden in Kittler's article but comes forth in Heidegger's, is language: "[Language] is always ahead of us. Our speaking merely follows language constantly. [*Wir sprechen ihr ständig nur nach.*] Thus, we are continually lagging behind what we first ought to have overtaken and taken up in order to speak about it."[41] *Nachsprechen* as repetition, as following language without ever attaining or mastering it, continually returning to issues of language and literature even when writing on the autobahn, marks the movement of Kittler's writing as a rewriting of *Unterwegs zur Sprache*. The autobahn leads to language; thinking and writing emerge as movement: "Poetry moves in the element of saying, and so does thinking."[42] Kittler's thinking moves next to poetry in its own rhythm and enters into an ambivalent relationship with the speed of the autobahn. According to Heidegger: "Poetry and thinking are in virtue of their nature held apart by a delicate yet luminous difference, each held in its own darkness: two parallels, in Greek *para allelo*, by one another, against one another, transcending, surpassing one another each in its fashion. Poetry and thinking are not separated if separation is to mean cut off into a relational void. The parallels intersect in the infinite. There they intersect with a section that they themselves do not make."[43] One more separation emerges in addition to that of the median strips and the Saussurean bar, this time separating thinking and poetry that meet at infinity. The origin of the separation resides in language, toward which both the thinker, Kittler or Heidegger, and the poet, Pynchon and others Kittler repeatedly turns to, move at different speeds.

The separation between Kittler's poets and himself, his way of thinking and theirs, are not "cut off into a relational void." Crossovers are always possible, which become visible especially in Kittler's way of writing. Speaking about Gottfried Benn's poetry, he claims that "today's literary critics could only profit from this radar thought, since their constitutive models of writing, book, and library, as they predominate even in poststructuralism, obviously require some modernization."[44] An ambivalence, or *Zweideutigkeit*, puts into play modernization in technology and in literature. If the autobahn—along with all the other media—is that which puts an end to literature, doing literature on the autobahn seems to be a self-destructive act. If literature as an "information technology whose monopoly is now coming to an end . . . registers this very information, that is, the information of its own demise," as "an aesthetics of terror," it remains to be seen how this auto-referentiality figures as auto-mobility and where that terror resides.[45] Driving on the parallel lane, theory (as writing) follows: It "collects, comments upon, and relays passages and texts that show how the novelty of technological media inscribed itself into the old paper of books."[46] In his conversation with Virilio on the "catastrophe" of the "current speeds of transmission and calculation," Kittler says that his real interest lies in seeing the ways in which "culture and politics" will "react to the slow demotion of their power" since "both are predicated upon everyday speech and the normal human nervous system which are both slow."[47] "Modernizing" culture in response to acceleration comes to mean ways of overcoming this slowness. In another interview, Kittler comments on his love for pinball, saying, "It's a way of acquiring quicker reflexes. The discovery made by Helmholtz and Du Bois-Reymond showed that the nerves are the slowest electrical connections on earth. Some ten meters per second, and no faster, which is why a driver's reaction time, 0.1 seconds, is so slow."[48] The writer trains his reflexes in response to both the acceleration and the "catastrophe." It is not an accident that he derives his example from driving: The danger that lies ahead is the possibility of an accident, which, as Wolfgang Schivelbusch reminds us, turns into a catastrophe with the invention of new transportation technologies.[49] Concerns about safety on the autobahn, which become the subject of much public discussion after 1945 in Germany (where the number of accidents exceed all the other countries at the time) run parallel to concerns about aesthetics throughout autobahn's history.[50] If "autobahns are aesthetics," as Kittler says, then deciding between sinuous curves and straight roads reveals different relationships between literature and safety. "Succession surprise and intensification of varied, non-tiring gazes from the moving vehicle" can become distractions that jeopardize the driver or they can ensure that one does not lose control as one would on a straight, monotonous road.[51] An entire new array of narrative inquiries open up once issues of narratology are related to issues of speeds and the gadgets that come with it.

Writing reflects as fast as it can on its own speed and on what makes this speed possible: Kittler's speed in passing from one example to the other, remarks in passing on the most difficult texts of philosophy and psychoanalysis and his way of bringing together different texts can be read as being subservient to this control over speed. Narrative analysis and media analysis converge at a point where narrative time is seen in its relation to technological acceleration. Kittler's sudden cutaways to Lacan or Heidegger could be seen as catalyzers, which "lay out areas of safety, rests, luxuries."[52] As an addition to the nucleus of the main story, it would then enable Kittler to manage the speed, to delay or to accelerate, or to "park" the narrative, and to counter the risks that new technologies bring forth. The official version of autobahn's history, he claims, is "quickly told" (schnell erzählt).[53] In Kittler's early article on "The Sandmann," the plot of which is also "quickly told" as well as in the plots of official stories, this decision to speed up the narrative where summaries of previous stories are concerned allows him to pass quickly over what is already known in order to encounter something that was not uncovered before.[54] Speed for Kittler is a way of getting away from official histories and plots.

An "aesthetics of terror," however, is hard to characterize as one that aims toward security and steering wheel control. Discourse network of 1900 rather seems to embrace the accident both as chance encounter and as shock. Writers appear as "accidental events in a noise that generated accidents and thus can never be overcome by its accidents"; words face the emptiness that "reduces [them] to small amusing accidents"; writing "[assaults] with the power of a shock. Catchphrases emerge from a store of signs to which they return with unimaginable speed, leaving behind in the subject inscriptions without ink or consciousness."[55] With this relationship between writing, chance, shock, and accident, speed reveals its double-sidedness: The desire to maintain control with faster response time can turn itself into desire for more speed, and hence for an accident to occur. The writer's and the theorist's desire to knowledge as such turns into a death drive. "The flight of death across the median strip," one of the biggest threats to autobahn security as Zeller tells us, cancels the separation between the two lanes.[56] Whereas war separates the dead from the living with its *cordon sanitaire*, accident makes the living meet the dead. Within writing that would mean that all the separations that we have seen above are always in danger of being overcome.

In Kittler's writing, what enables the overcoming of the separation between words and things, then, is not only the war, but also the possibility of an accident and as such, the theme of destruction that annuls separations. If "the history of technology is not a history of continuous unfolding but a history of shocks and jumps," writing on the autobahn is a search for that traumatic experience that continues the "series of small and rapid concussions" in train rides.[57] Schivelbusch was already hinting at the "material-mechanical explanation of the causation of trauma" by tracing Freud's inquiries into the trauma experienced by catastrophic train accidents, which he sees as a predecessor to shell shock.[58] The autobahn's relation to shock and trauma is less obvious in Kittler's article. Behind the example taken from Lacan's childhood memory is hidden a childhood memory of the autobahn in Usedom from the 1950s which Kittler associates with the holes that it bore from the bombardments of the Royal Air Force in 1943.[59] One childhood memory replaces the other and becomes its metaphor in order to cover the shell shock present in the former. Using Lacan, Heidegger's way to language is turned into a search for this traumatic kernel and limit experience. "We have built you good roads," says Elfride Heidegger to Lacan after a fast and scary ride to Cerisy according to an anecdote Avital Ronell related to me. While Heidegger hints at the fundamental relationship between death and language, it is Kittler who shows that their togetherness stems from a ride full of horrors.

Insofar as the "real may be represented by the accident, the noise, the small element of reality," this missed "encounter" with the real behind the automaton, or the automobile, calls into question the way danger and death, and particularly the death of literature and death in literature, play a constitutive role in Kittler's writing.[60] While the autobahn and its separation into two lanes are said to render literature obsolete, the article starts with an example in which it is still alive. The example is nothing other than Oedipus whose "chance encounter" or "accident" (*Zufallsbegegnung*) with his father in the unregulated traffic of ancient roads leads to the tragedy. With the construction of autobahns, the "god of chance (whose *herma* once graced every Greek crossroad) has left the stage, runways and their centaurs take over. There is no drama anymore, only the movement of tanks, from Verdun to Volokolamsk and on."[61] Right at the beginning, literature's life is posited as strictly tied to the possibility of chance encounter, accident, and death. Beginning the story with a story about the beginnings of literature warrants more attention. It is interesting that Kittler locates the "jump" in the history from pre-autobahns to autobahns not at the level of technological history, but at the level of literature, from *Oedipus Tyrranus* to *Gravity's Rainbow*. The jump this time is not between 1800 and 1900, but from a mythical past to a contemporary one. Sophocles's work, which Kittler will later define as "the highest poetry, for which we are to thank the Greeks," acts as the mythical origin of the noise and the double meaning that will come to constitute the essence of "drama."[62] If this history of literature is embedded in technological history, it is important to note what the elements of this chance encounter are. The human, who is running away from Delphi and from his fate and whose answer to the question about the definition of humanity "anticipates his own drama," as Lacan would say, encounters a carriage on the famous Diolkos, the railed way across Isythmus of Corinth.[63] This is the very road on which transportation of marbles gave rise to the Temple of Delphi as well as the Naxian Sphinx.[64] The same discussion surrounding autobahn also concern the Greek roads and railways and question whether their use was military or economical.[65] The double-meaning in the story, as well as the drama, already depend on this encounter between two different "vehicles," man on foot versus the Greek railroad system, which "applied high-standard road-construction techniques" with fixed tracks a precursor to the modern railways, as well as to the lanes on the autobahn.[66] It is exactly on these railroads that it becomes clear how "the function of desire," which travels on the "rails of metonymy," "must remain in a fundamental relationship to death," and how every road is bound to end up in death.[67] Tragedy brings this forth by revealing the railway's function in delivering dead bodies. The theaters, such as Eretria in Euboea, utilized these rails to lead the trolleys that would carry the corpses at the end of the play: "A screech would be heard from behind the scenes, the doors in the stage building would open, and onto the stage would trundle a flat trolley carrying the corpse of the murdered king in his bath."[68] Tragic fate sweeps all bodies to death leaving nothing behind and reveals itself to be the catastrophe that results from one lane meeting the other. While Oedipus as a living body stands against Laios, who is always already dead, his fate is marked by death as well. Talking about his death, Lacan says that "it ends so perfectly that he doesn't die like everybody else, that is to say accidentally. He dies from a true death in which he erases his own being."[69] As such, he is "demanding everything, giving up nothing, absolutely unreconciled."[70] Chance encounter and accident are only possible because they are ordained by the tragic fate. The rails of fate make the question "What is man?" the answer given to it, the escape from fate and the tragedy that follows all possible at once.

Writing about the end of literature within the tragic mode traces this traceless death. This "desire to know" the end and to uncover what lies ahead counters military history by endlessly introducing heaps of dead bodies to the scene of writing. Speaking about tragedy, Kittler claims: "As chorus song and Dionysian feast it leads Attica's youth to the threshold of becoming fellow citizens. Girls become brides, ephebes become comrades in arms. By contrast, as plot . . . it tears apart the fabric—be it that of friendship, of trust or more often that of love between man and woman—so terribly, that only death can bring them together again."[71] In a later interview about his earlier works, he also says that "ultimately elements of tragedy may creep in, as in the case of *Discourse Networks*. I myself am not too happy about the fact that everything in that book ends in the noise of machines."[72] Tragedy endlessly introduces separations and differences, tearing apart structures that seem to be given, while death is the ultimate annihilation of all these, the ultimate accident which is not accidental. Emplotment of this tragic fate acts both as a reenactment of the separation and its consolation in death. It is here that Kittler's "writing as drama and only as drama," as he himself defines Derrida's philosophy, reveals its tragic character.[73] Speeding up on the road toward death with the desire to annihilate the separation of the two lanes, Kittler endlessly returns to the supposedly traceless death of literature, without the reenactment of which as an ultimate result of fate, the trauma or the shell shock cannot turn itself into theory. Writing continues to write itself in this drama as trauma, and becomes, like the "motoric" in Rilke, "an exhaustion that endlessly refuses to end."[75] Media theory is the continuation of writing with the same means of inscription.

NOTES

1. Friedrich A. Kittler, "From Discourse Networks to Cultural Mathematics: An Interview with Friedrich A. Kittler," *Theory, Culture and Society* 23, nos. 7–8 (2006): 18.

2. Friedrich A. Kittler, "Technologies of Writing: Interview with Friedrich A. Kittler," *New Literary History* 27, no. 4 (1996): 733; Friedrich A. Kittler, "Auto Bahnen / Free Ways," *Cultural Politics* 11, no. 3 (2015): 376–83.

3. Kittler, "Auto Bahnen," 378.

4. Ibid., 382.

5. Ibid.

6. Thomas Zeller, *Driving Germany: The Landscape of the German Autobahn 1930–1970* (New York: Berghahn Books, 2007), 48.

7. Ibid., 64.

8. Kittler, "Auto Bahnen," 381.

9. Zeller, *Driving Germany*, 27.

10. Ibid., 128.

11. Kittler, "Auto Bahnen," 381–82.

12. Michel Foucault, *The Archaeology of Knowledge*, trans. M. Sheridan (New York: Pantheon Books, 1972), 235.

13. Friedrich A. Kittler, "The City Is a Medium," *New Literary History* 27, no. 4 (1996): 718, 723.

14. Geoffrey Winthrop-Young, "Drill and Distraction in the Yellow Submarine: On the Dominance of War in Friedrich Kittler's Media Theory," *Critical Inquiry* 28, no. 4 (Summer 2002): 843.

15. Friedrich A. Kittler, "Media and Drugs in Pynchon's Second World War," in *Literature, Media, Information Systems*, ed. John Johnston (New York: Routledge, 2012), 103.

16. Friedrich A. Kittler, "Media Wars," in *Literature, Media, Information Systems*, ed. John Johnston (New York: Routledge, 2012), 120.

17. Kittler, "Media and Drugs," 103.

18. Ibid., 104.

19. Kittler, "Auto Bahnen," 379.

20. Ibid., 380.

21. Kittler, "Media and Drugs," 106.

22. Ibid.

23. Ibid.

24. Ibid.

25. Jacques Lacan, "The Instance of the Letter in the Unconscious, or Reason since Freud," in *Écrits: The First Complete Edition in English* (New York: Norton, 2006), 415.

26. Kittler, "Auto Bahnen," 379: "Und weil nach Lacans Einsicht 'die Bahngleise' in dieser Geschichte den Balken des saussureschen Algorithmus materialisieren', muessen sie gar nicht materiell vorhanden sein. Auch eine von deutschen Stoßtrupps gesprengte Eisenbahn, wenn sie nur zweigleisig ist, kann der automotiven Segregation Europas zum Vorbild werden."

27. Ibid., 378.

28. Friedrich A. Kittler, *Optical Media*, trans. A. Enns (Cambridge, UK: Polity, 2010), 34; Lacan, "Instance of the Letter," 419.

29. Lacan, "Instance of the Letter," 422.

30. Ibid., 417; Kittler, "Auto Bahnen," 118.

31. Jacques Lacan, *On Feminine Sexuality: The Limits of Love and Knowledge* (New York: Norton, 1999), 34.

32. Friedrich A. Kittler, *Discourse Networks 1800/1900*, trans. Michael Metteer (Stanford, CA: Stanford University Press, 1990), 257.

33. Kittler, "The City Is a Medium," 720.

34. "Die Gegend ergibt als Gegend erste Wege. Sie be-wëgt. Wir hören das Wort Be-wëgung im Sinne von: Wege allererst vergeben und stiften." Martin Heidegger, *On the Way to Language* (New York: Harper and Row, 1971), 92; *Unterwegs zur Sprache* (Frankfurt am Main: V. Klostermann, 1985), 197.

35. Heidegger, *On the Way to Language*, 67.

36. Ibid., 57.

37. Ibid., 74.

38. Kittler, "Auto Bahnen," 381.

39. Heidegger, *On the Way to Language*, 64.

40. Ibid., 91.

41. Ibid., 75.

42. Ibid., 83.

43. Ibid., 90.

44. Friedrich A. Kittler, "Benn's Poetry: 'A Hit in the Charts': Song under Conditions of Media Technologies," *SubStance*, no. 61 (1990): 11.

45. Friedrich A. Kittler, *Gramophone, Film, Typewriter*, trans. Geoffrey Winthrop-Young and Michael Wutz (Stanford, CA: Stanford University Press, 1999), xl.

46. Ibid.

47. Paul Virilio, Friedrich A. Kittler, and John Armitage, "The Information Bomb: A Conversation," *Angelaki* 4, no. 2 (1999): 83.

48. Kittler, "Technologies of Writing," 739.

49. Wolfgang Schivelbusch, *The Railway Journey: The Industrialization of Time and Space in the 19th Century* (Berkeley: University of California Press, 1986), 131.

50. Zeller, *Driving Germany*, 106.

51. Ibid., 140.

52. Roland Barthes, *Image, Music, Text*, trans. S. Heath (New York: Hill and Wang, 1977), 95.

53. Kittler, "Auto Bahnen," 377.

54. Friedrich A. Kittler, "Das Phantom unsres Ichs und die Literaturpsychologie: Hoffmann—Freud—Lacan," in *Urszenen: Literaturwissenschaft als Diskursanalyse und Diskurskritik*, ed. Friedrich Kittler and Horst Turk (Frankfurt am Main: Suhrkamp, 1977), 140.

55. Kittler, *Discourse Networks*, 184, 204, 223.

56. Zeller, *Driving Germany*, 196.

57. Kittler, "From Discourse Networks to Cultural Mathematics," 28; Schivelbusch, *Railway Journey*, 117.

58. Schivelbusch, *Railway Journey*, 147–48.

59. Friedrich A. Kittler, *Platz der Luftbrücke: Ein Gespräch* (Cologne: Oktagon, 1996), 6.

60. Jacques Lacan, *The Four Fundamental Concepts of Psychoanalysis* (New York: Norton, 1998), 73.

61. Kittler, "Auto Bahnen," 376: "Wo der Zufallsgott (mit seinen Hermen an jeder griechischen Wegekreuzung) ausgespielt hat, beginnen Rollbahnen und ihre Kentauren. Kein Drama mehr, sondern ein Weg der Panzer."

62. Friedrich A. Kittler, *Musik und Mathematik, Bd. 1, Hellas, Tl. 1, Aphrodite* (Munich: Wilhelm Fink Verlag, 2005), 170.

63. Jacques Lacan, *The Other Side of Psychoanalysis* (New York: Norton, 2006), 120.

64. Brian R. MacDonald, "The Diolkos," *Journal of Hellenic Studies*, no. 106 (1986): 193.

65. Jeanette C. Marchand, "Kleonai, the Corinth-Argos Road, and the 'Axis of History,'" *Hesperia: The Journal of the American School of Classical Studies at Athens* 78, no. 1 (January–March 2009): 159; Georges Raepsaet, "Le diolkos de l'Isthme à Corinthe: son tracé, son fonctionnement, avec une annexe. Considérations techniques et mécaniques," *Bulletin de correspondance hellénique* 117, no. 1 (1993): 237.

66. Yanis A. Pikoulas, "Travelling by Land in Ancient Greece," *Travel, Geography and Culture in Ancient Greece, Egypt, and the Near East*, ed. Colin Adams and Jim Roy (Oxford: Oxbow Books, 2007), 80.

67. Lacan, "Instance of the Letter," 431; Jacques Lacan, *The Ethics of Psychoanalysis* (New York: Norton, 1997), 303.

68. M. J. T. Lewis, "Railways in the Greek and Roman World," in *Early Railways: A Selection of Papers from First International Early Railways Conference*, ed. A. Guy and J. Rees (London: Newcomen Society, 2001), 10.

69. Lacan, *Ethics of Psychoanalysis*, 306.

70. Ibid., 310.

71. Kittler, *Musik und Mathematik*, 175.

72. Friedrich A. Kittler, "The Cold Model of Structure," *Cultural Politics* 8, no. 3 (2012): 380.

73. Friedrich A. Kittler, "Derridas Didaktik," in *Jahrbuch der Deutschdidaktik* (Tübingen: Narr, 1989), 35.

9

KITTLER AND HEIDEGGER

The Trouble with Ent-fernung

Dominik Zechner

Young Friedrich had to find a way to avoid being swallowed up by the brilliant force field he had maneuvered himself into when going to Freiburg. Being enthralled by Heidegger could easily morph into an academic death sentence. Not so much politically, but in terms of an all-too-possible absolute surrender facing the master's abyssal brilliance. Kittler could tell you a thing or two about that. Remembering his fellow students back in the day, he clarifies how Heidegger's vicinity posed a profound threat to his admirers. Especially those "who loved Heidegger too much," and thus "never came out of his intellectual shadow in that they simply imitated his language."[1] Kittler himself was perfectly conscious of his own high-end parodist skills when it came to engaging with and appropriating great authors and had to be on his guard so as not to lose traction for his stylistic sensibilities.[2] Kittler rejected the sweet lure of epigonism and found himself on an existential mission not to become crushed by the weight of the Heideggerian lexicon which would have definitely chained Kittler's diction to the untimely dignity of Grimm's dictionary. Such a crush would leave no room for the techno-poetics of which he became an exemplary standard-bearer.

EVOCATIONS OF FREIBURG

Distancing became the key operation. Especially given that Heidegger's primary retirement hobby consisted in mindfucking his students. Says Kittler: "I really knew people who, after an interview with Heidegger of just one hour, never finished their PhD because his questions and answers were so brilliant."[3] It took Professor Heidegger only one hour to devour and destroy an academic baby existence. Shaken by such cruelty—the intentionality of which remains questionable, to be sure—Kittler opted for silence, preferring not to address the master. Encountering Heidegger became a matter of exercising desistance. To avoid getting burned by Heidegger's linguistic and conceptual authority, his blazing closeness that could irrestorably break you, Kittler decided to abstain and watch the spectacle from the auditorium, engaging without engagement. Which meant to desist from occupying the official disciple's position, and refrain from posing any certified claim to succeed the champion of Freiburg (or contest his designated successors).

Commemorating these seemingly negligible events in a late lecture, Kittler found a concise way of framing his life-saving disposition and the strategic ambivalence it sanctioned: "My god, why am I telling you all this? Because I was there without being there. . . . Because the little old man shuffled through the hallways of the Freiburg Philosophical Seminary—but he never had to exchange a word with me, thank heavens!"[4] Heidegger never had to talk to Kittler. Heidegger—who, at a safe remove, forfeits his intimidating edges and simply turns into a little old man who dragged his feet through the university's hallways. And why is it that Kittler can so freely talk about all that? Because he didn't go down with it, he was able to save his own work's investments from the old man's dazzling nearness. Because he, Kittler, becoming medium himself, maintained a Dasein-not-being-there—more or less distanced yet right in the thick of it, part of an ontological broadcast system. Not without reason, as we shall see, is Dasein essentially de-distancing.

In the final analysis, Kittler gives us very little to hang on to when it comes to deciphering his intricate relationship with Martin Heidegger. If anything, he offers no more than a nano-trace of information or insight, astonishingly undignified: "Once I had the privilege of helping Heidegger dispose of his garbage."[5] We thus learn that once Friedrich A. Kittler was compelled to shorten the distance in order to help Martin Heidegger take out the trash. The garbage in question, Kittler explains, consisted in books authored by Heidegger's colleagues, all of which contained "pompous" dedications to the professor. These offshoots of a specific branch of remembrance the philosopher did not care for and wished to relinquish. For young Kittler, the release of books profiled a mark of humility that distinguished a beautiful mind. So, he assisted. Radically at Heidegger's disposal, Kittler disposed of what Heidegger's syntax and system was unwilling to process, leaving us with the question of what it means for a Heidegger to dispose of books, for a Kittler to carry—and carry out—the burden of the unwanted and unsaid? Knowing that he'll never be able to finish disposing of Heidegger.

In his early years, Kittler hardly ever mentioned Heidegger. Nonetheless, Kittler's techno-philosophical edifice never lacked a place, however invisible, for Heidegger. Precisely by dint of the distancing rupture that paralyzed their transmission cablings and disconnected the two, Kittler held dear to his avowed/disavowed *maître* until the very end—to the extent that he was ready violently to refuse merely to address the case of Heidegger, disallowing even the smallest grain of critique. When Peter Weibel went after Heidegger's alleged "metaphysics of language," Kittler immediately pulled the emergency brake, putting a ban on the subject for the rest of the conversation: "You'll never get me to badmouth Heidegger."[6]

Inheritance works out in ways that cannot be predicted nor easily discovered in terms of itineraries and destinations, but may end up in a peculiar scene of carrying out teacher's disposed missions. What is Heidegger's role in Kittler's major works of which his untoward autobiographical memento gives us only a sense? On the surface of things, Kittler barely mentions Heidegger; yet he admits to being under his sway. This relation exceeds any certitude we might have about what constitutes a marginal or, for that matter, central place in the structure of inheritance and anxiety of influence. In strict keeping with the Foucauldian exigency, according to which "it's important to have a small number of authors with whom one thinks, with whom one works, but on whom one doesn't write,"[7] Kittler made a point of avoiding, for the longest time, openly to set foot on Heideggerian paths when conceptualizing and putting together his own work's meticulous architectonics. The primal scene of taking out the trash becomes legible as an allegory for the way in which Kittler affirmed and at the same time disposed of his Heideggerian heritage.

If we follow the unfolding of Kittler's oeuvre closely—of which I can only give a sense in this essay—we can observe a paradoxical development: the more overtly Heidegger is admitted to Kittler's project and integrated, the less he looks like Heidegger. Something odd befalls the master as the rogue heir takes stock and starts assembling a Heidegger for the twenty-first century. To put it candidly, Kittler's endeavor simultaneously relies on the master and is aimed at his destruction. Let me give you some pointers as to how all this goes down: Kittler hardly mentions Heidegger in his coming-out masterpiece, *Discourse Networks 1800/1900*. Only the posthumously published *preface* Kittler appended to clarify some of the discussions that went on around his postdoctoral process (*Habilitationsverfahren*) makes explicit reference to Heidegger.[8] Then there's that ominous moment in *Gramophone, Film, Typewriter*, where an excursus from Heidegger's *Parmenides* seminar is quoted at length. The passage is legendary: Heidegger freaks out about the typewriter's uncanny ability to tear "writing from the essential realm of the hand, i.e. the realm of the word," which causes, in part, "the increasing destruction of the word" ("zunehmende Zerstörung des Wortes").[9] Kittler cites this passage for pages—though not without irony. There's no commentary, argument, not the slightest critical assessment that would accompany or embed Heidegger's worries. *Le maître* is there, he speaks for himself, but Kittler's text disregards him deliberately. We had to wait until the later and latest stages of Kittler's intellectual trajectory, precisely the moment when he turned to Greece, to find a more explicit engagement with Heidegger. In conversation, Kittler called his later works "Heideggerian through and through,"[10] and, indeed, it's the final phase of his oeuvre that made him return to the trash bin once again in order to conclude his reassessment of Martin Heidegger. Let me zone in on several traces we can find in late Kittler.

THE SPACE OF DASEIN

By the late 2000s, Heidegger had become the subject of various lectures and essays, including "Martin Heidegger, Media, and the Gods of Greece." Kittler's later works were determined to curate, in a strikingly explicit fashion, a remastered Heidegger that looked increasingly like Kittler himself.[11] Invocations of Freiburg instantiated some of the numerous projects Kittler left unfinished (and left us with): a very late essay, "Towards an Ontology of Media," formulates the nearly megalomaniacal task of writing up (or "writing on," *anschreiben*, as Kittler would say) a complete ontology of media. The project seeks to develop an analysis of the historical stages of the process according to which philosophy, in its principal manifestation as Western metaphysics, had hitherto mistreated, deliberately disregarded, or simply neglected issues pertaining to essential aspects of technicity and mediality. Placing him at the key position of philosophy's fragile yet eventful overture toward technical media, Kittler declares Heidegger the sole enabler of a nonoblivious relation between thinking and *technology*: "It is only with Heidegger's help that we can hope to develop something like an ontology of technical media."[12] On this matter, let me take one thing and one ontological indicator at a time.

The chosen point of departure for Kittler's plan to carry through ontology's technification is indexed to *Being and Time*. There's a passage in Heidegger's major work to which Kittler obsessively returns wherein the author discusses the technological impact on Dasein's spatiality. I'm talking about paragraph 23, in fact a famous argument, entitled "The Spatiality of Being-in-the-World" ("Die Räumlichkeit des In-der-Welt-seins"). The context is well-known: technical media like spectacles, the street, or telephone, revolutionize the Cartesian understanding of space and transform a geometrical understanding of *Räumlichkeit* into an unstable dynamic of relations. Heidegger's words made Kittler ecstatic: "For someone who, for example, wears spectacles which are distantially so near to him that they are 'sitting on his nose,' this useful thing [*gebrauchte Zeug*] is further away in the surrounding world than the picture on the wall across the room."[13] The technological artifact fundamentally transforms Dasein's sense of space in that it nears the surrounding world while at the same time retreating into a distance that cannot be measured geometrically. The pair of glasses is still there, sitting on my nose, as Heidegger says, but I'm unaware of it. The medial production of nearness coincides with the reduction of distance, resulting in Dasein's essential de-distancing character.[14]

Even though this passage takes up merely a handful of pages in the body of *Being and Time*, for Kittler it represents the essence of Heidegger's assault on metaphysics. In "Towards an Ontology of Media," Kittler holds the following: "At its very end or destruction, ontology turns into an ontology of distances, transmissions, and media."[15] The statement of course refers to Heidegger's set aim to destroy the history of metaphysics, which for Kittler coincides with a new determination of philosophical purpose, namely as ontology of media. In his view, Heidegger completes a process that had been instigated by Aristotle's notion of μεταξύ ("in-between")—the first philosophical term to designate the medial. Yet, what in Aristotle appeared to mark a merely epistemological circumstance, in Heidegger is calibrated as a technological problem with ontological dimensions. According to Kittler's redaction, Heidegger's conceptualization of μεταξύ pathbreakingly assures: "In the middle of absence and presence, farness and nearness, being and soul, there exists no *Nothing* any more, but a mediatic relation. *Es gibt Medien*, we could say, with Heidegger's late lecture on *Time and Being*."[16]

The Heideggerian elevation of Aristotle's elementary media theory from its epistemological grounds to the very summit of ontology for Kittler amounts to a final break with the demands of metaphysics. Until Heidegger's intervention, philosophy had pursued the strangely persistent yet inescapably myopic notion of a metaphysics that stubbornly refused to calibrate nearness in any other way than by identifying Being with "presence, immediacy, and being-here"—thus ontologically covering over, in a categorical fashion, the numerous, if often hidden, systems of transmission to which it remained indebted.[17] With Heidegger—and, according to Kittler, *only* with Heidegger—we observe philosophy reach the techno-nihilist heights of its completion as a millennial claim to presence collapses. This development leaves us in and with a trans-geometric space where the de-distancing ways in which Dasein demolishes its surrounding world undermine the binding laws that structure ontologies of nearness understood as presence.

In addition to introducing the disjunctive series of *Zeug* involving glasses, the street, and telephone, paragraph 23 of *Being and Time* brings into focus a fourth instance of technological redescription by means of the radio. Ushered in under cover of quotation marks, radio appears to share the same putative status as "world," also a quoted quality at this point: "With the 'radio' [*Rundfunk*], for example, Da-sein is bringing about [*vollzieht*] today de-distancing [*Ent-fernung*] of the 'world' which is unforeseeable in its meaning for Da-sein, by way of expanding and destroying the everyday surrounding world [*Umwelt*]."[18] The turning point and surprising moment in this inherently problematic phrasing resides in Heidegger's use of *vollziehen* (to bring about, or, more explicitly, to fulfill, implement, execute, or enforce). Arguably, Heidegger's text after the so-called *Kehre*, an important reorientation of and within Heidegger's thinking, would have little tolerance for such a lexicon that tends to overcapacitate Dasein—as though technology were controllable and less threatening than Heidegger nonetheless asserts it to be. In this passage, the radio becomes a figure for technological destructiveness that falls in the hand, or ear, of Dasein.

Let me stay with the example and the argument that holds Kittler in thrall.[19] By use of radio, Dasein expands and destroys its surrounding world, de-distancing even the greatest remoteness in ways not yet assessable. The dynamic of *Ent-fernung* entails that distance continuously is reduced; spatial remoteness loses empirical significance in light of technological media. Radio functions as a means of achieving such relativity of space—"for example," says Heidegger, *zum Beispiel*. We cannot take for granted that we know what's going on rhetorically when Heidegger introduces this as an example that seems to open up a space of infinite possibilities and substitutions—because technology's arsenal is vast and unpredictable, and an example is never just one. Heidegger himself is aware of the precarity of his utterance, as he endows *Rundfunk* with quotation marks and mobilizes its technological verve by underscoring its exemplarity. The vampiric marks of quotational distancing set up a strange rapport between *Rundfunk* and *Welt*, as though radio's technological intervention in the world dissociated the latter from itself, making world, submitted to the groundless regime of wireless transmission, somewhat less "real," a displaced simulation, henceforth requiring the distorting antennae set up by Heidegger's strategic placement of quote signs. In a Kittlerian sense, quotations are part of Dracula's repertory of sucking substance from any kind of body including a textual one.

The radio, with or without quotation marks, becomes one of the manifold ways for Kittler of nearing the gods and subverting the registers of far and near by which Dasein's ordinary spatiality is marked. Considering the lack of foreseeability and assessability in terms of radio's destructiveness, one is pressed to answer the question prompted by Dasein's alleged agency in this regard, the *Vollzugscharakter* of its actions effecting the destruction of *Umwelt* by way of utilizing a technological *nouveauté*. Is it indeed Dasein that implements *Rund-funk*? Is it not *Rundfunk* that turns Dasein into a broadcast system, stripping it of whatever imagined agency it might claim? For Kittler these questions are decisive. And the way one responds to them will profoundly affect the understanding of Heidegger's historic turn, the *Kehre* famously up- and resetting his off-track routes out of philosophy. Kittler contests the normative reading of Heidegger's turn. What's at stake is the unreadability of inversion—how do we read a theoretical turnaround? What does it mean to reorient oneself in thinking?

Cutting a long story short, we might get to the gist of Kittler's own redirection toward Greece during his final years by paying close attention to the way he reads the overturning upheaval undergone by Heidegger's early work: "Heidegger's turn [*Kehre*] *is* the insight that all modes [*Spielarten*] of transcendental philosophy—whether they take their point of departure in the subject or in Dasein—founder upon the facticity of high-tech media."[20] Heidegger's turn marks the spot where philosophy becomes unable to deny the subjective ungovernability of hardware any longer. That's how Kittler views it. Dasein's agency in coming to grips with the technological infiltration of its surrounding world, or any mere phantasy thereof, collapses under the factual evidence of technology's role in the revelation of Being. Sure enough, this insight of Heidegger's had everything to do with his epochal farewell to humanism, on the grounds of which Kittler found new ways of nearing the mentor: man's relation to technology no longer is that of mastery.

Kittler's narrative runs like this: Almost as though driven by an *ur*-Kittlerian impulse, Heidegger's fateful turnaround has endowed Being with its own history, grounding it in the inescapable material evidentiality of a medial environment rigorously exceeding the powers of man. Even though philosophical practice had ill-fatedly delivered technology over to the conceptual abyss of metaphysical oblivion, τέχνη (often translated as "craft" or "art") had nonetheless continued silently to carry out and execute its propelling force up to the moment of philosophy's inversion, when the eventual acknowledgment of technology's generative relation to Being and its history became unavoidable. And the very place where all this happens is the Heideggerian text: "In other words, Technology itself makes (with Heidegger) the History of Being."[21] Perhaps unknowingly, Kittler's formulation provokes our allegorical ears and invites us to dwell on the conspicuous use of the preposition *mit* (with)—designating a fateful *Mitsein* (Being-with) that entangles the proper name of Heidegger with the historification of Being. If Being's unfolding within and throughout a technologically formatted historical development marks philosophy's turning-away from its subjectivist delusions, why does *Seinsgeschichte* need the *Mithilfe* (assistance) of a parenthesized Heidegger to come about? And why does it seem as though Heidegger can take over precisely where Dasein becomes stripped of its ability to *vollziehen*—transforming the philosopher into something like a philosophical engineer who supervises, if not implements, Being's own being-in-the-making?

THE ESSENCE OF TECHNOLOGY

In order to unravel the problem of Being's historification, we need to understand what happens when Kittler installs *technology* at the generative centers of *Seinsgeschichte*'s manifestation. His lectures on cultural science give us an important hint in this direction. Once again following the lead of *Being and Time*, Kittler tracks the reshaping of Being as set in motion by the machinization of *Zeitmessung* (timekeeping) and arrives at the following assertion: "Clocks are ontic devices, which means that they are subject to fundamental ontology, yet they nonetheless bring about [*zeitigen*] historically differentiated ontologies."[22] Seemingly benign, the almost tautological sentence nevertheless turns out to carry the potential radically to upend the whole Heideggerian enterprise.

A short-cut rendition of what is said here might hold that, according to Kittler, the technical object yields, opens, and multiplies the thinking of Being. A more thoroughgoing and patient approach, however, first would have to take into consideration the pun animating the sentence's rhetorical verve. It's not per accident that Kittler decides on deploying the verb *zeitigen* (to yield, bring forth, result in, or, bring about—setting up a provocative relation to Dasein's alleged ability to "bring about" the destruction of world by broadcasting it) when discussing the technologized quantification of time. What about this enigmatic relation between *Zeit* and *zeitigen*, time and a temporally marked mode of creation? What does the act of bringing-about have to do with temporality and technology? Translated with some audacity, privileging the pun's semantic force, Kittler's sentence reads as follows: *Timekeepers are timing temporally differentiated ontologies.* The semantic horizon circumscribed by the verb *zeitigen* points to the conjunction between ontology and historicity—*Sein* and *Zeit*—that had elicited Kittler's attention. Stemming from the Middle High German word *zītigen* ("to ripen"), *zeitigen*, anything but an aimless buzz, designates the teleological movement of a temporal evolution, indicating a determined focus on effect and outcome, making for a strong, if strange, case of poietic bearing (an apple tree, for instance *zeitigt Früchte*, "it bears fruit").

Kittler's assessment therefore posits the philosophical primacy of the technological artifact over its conceptual frame and holds that ontic machines "bear" historically different ontologies. That, however, is Heidegger turned upside down. If technological devices can generate ontology and its historical differentiation, the ontic outdoes the ontological. The philosophical implications of such a claim could not be more severe as it unambiguously insists on the inescapable submission of thinking to the machine. It's the apparatus, the technological artifact and mere *Zeug*, that *brings about* ontology—the manifoldness of ontologies, their sheer difference at play in the formation and structuring of Being's historical unfolding. Rhetorically tenacious and resolved, Kittler's underscoring of ontology's dependence on the technological artifact poses an important question to which I would like to attempt a response. In view of its revaluation of the ontic, at what point does Kittler's reading become simply unjustifiable if we are to take Heidegger's concept of *technology* seriously? Something quite drastic befalls or passes through Heidegger as his reflection feeds into Kittler's machinery of reappropriating and technologically alienating the "idea" that Being has a history.[23] At what point does the appropriating gesture break off into indefensible violence—all the professed adoration notwithstanding?

A few lines further down, the passage on timekeeping continues: "The clocks of time make it necessary to write a history of presence and absence itself. That's what, ever since Heidegger's turn, we call the History of Being."[24] Yet, is it in fact machines that make the historification of Being a necessity? What Kittler refuses to read, no doubt stubbornly, is the *essentializing* track pursued by Heidegger's post-turn concept of technology. Let me recall the main premise of Heidegger's technology essay: "Technology is not equivalent to the essence of technology. . . . Likewise, the essence of technology is by no means anything technological [*So ist denn auch das Wesen der Technik ganz und gar nichts Technisches*]."[25] By no means: "ganz und gar nicht." Given Kittler's emphasis on media's generative sway over everything nontechnological, a statement like that is impossible to compute under a Kittlerian regime. What is Heidegger saying? There is an important difference between thinking the concept of technology and totalizing technological artifacts; in order to grasp the essence of technology, thinking needs to go beyond the technological object.[26] Technology, in its essential expression, which is to say, in the way it reveals Being, cannot disclose itself to us if our understanding is conditioned solely by technological media.[27] We are therefore required to relinquish the ontic level of technology—a capital fallacy for any good Kittlerian.[28]

According to Kittler's construal of ontology, thinking needs to be technologically configured in order to grasp the concept of media—that is, in order for it to grasp *anything*. Heidegger, however, seeks to isolate a place for thinking, no doubt menaced but not yet permeated by the technological intrusion.[29] The "historial" revelation of Being opens up the space for the technological artifact to arrange and undo our historical manifestation. This is why science— what Heidegger terms "the theory of the real"—remains unable to grasp its own essence, which ultimately coincides with the essence of technology, as it inevitably remains subject to the encroachment of technology. In order to save a possibility for thinking, Heidegger is prompted to isolate what he views as the technologically purified realm of *Besinnung* (reflection), thus positing Being as that which enables the manifestation of technological artifacts without itself having to rely on them. Reflection seeks to open a way of engaging the essence of technology *without* assuming a fundamental *Gegenständigkeit* (objectness) of the material world—that is, without submitting itself to the technological calibration of reality.[30]

Whether *Seinsgeschichte* turns out to be motored by technology or not, what Heidegger's post-turn thinking introduces is the question concerning the possibility of Being's historicality itself. In his 1962 lecture on "Time and Being," Heidegger holds: "What is history-like in the history of Being [*das Geschichtsartige der Geschichte des Seins*] is obviously determined by the way in which Being takes place and by this alone. . . . [T]his means the way in which It gives Being [*die Weise, in der Es Sein gibt*]."[31] Being is determined by an anonymous act of giving. The *Es* of *Es gibt* remains unspecified and ungraspable as it designates a strange *otherwise than Being*, be it Levinasian in nature or not, performing a gesture of bestowal that *precedes* Being and thus technology.[32] Prior to any ontic staging of technology, the *Es gibt* has to enable and ground τέχνη as a poietical mode of bringing forth *Sein*. The gift of *Es gibt* opens the horizon of *Seinsgeschichte* whose current epoch, in turn, can only be understood as technologically constituted. We cannot speak about hardware and its forceful calibration of *Seinsgeschichte* unless Being is already and immemorially bestowed. Technology can appear as the *maker* of Being's history only to the extent that Being, in its *Geschichtsartigkeit* or history-likeness, is *given*. The history of Being may culminate in technology—yet the sheer possibility of such history technology cannot grasp. In other words, technology *makes* history only insofar as it's already *in* history.[33]

What more is there to say? Kittler's legacy remains to be determined for its singular richness and the audacity with which he distorts, often to good purpose, highly invested philosophical traditions. Unlike so many scholars, Kittler has occupied at once the position of renegade and institutional authority. The meaning that his passage gave to the German university, to the literary, philosophical, and military histories with which he must be associated, still needs to be deciphered. There are many metonymies and allegorical scenes of inscription to which Kittler's name will continue to be assigned. But let me return to my impulsively set installation, one signed by him: once Friedrich A. Kittler took out Heidegger's garbage—what a proud trash-bearer he was! Perhaps this moment that he recounts with some cheekiness was for him a necessity, part of a releasement. In a Nietzschean heave, he was no doubt getting rid of something—if only to recycle and refashion a moment in Heidegger's endeavor to sort out technology in regard to Being. Kittler's appropriation has transformed Heidegger into the thinker of hardware—the task of thinking into an exploration of hardware formations that *bring about* the history of Being, making for an interpretation of the *turn* that turns the turner upside down. Despite his protestations and declarations, Kittler, it turns out, never stopped keeping Heidegger at arm's length, maintaining the ironic distance that typically distinguishes the rogue disciple, something he never really wanted or expected to be. Thriving on deliberate misprision, Kittler's technological grounding of Heidegger's post-turn oeuvre is bound up with the strategic effacement of some of Heidegger's core insights and prefers to miss the latter's imperative to de-ontify the concept of technology. In effect, Heidegger's articulated queasiness about the machine landed in the *Abfall* (trash) that marks Kittler's own *Abfall*, the renunciatory falling-away from the mentor's legacy. *You'll never get me to badmouth Heidegger.*

ΠOTES

1. John Armitage, "From Discourse Networks to Cultural Mathematics: An Interview with Friedrich Kittler," *Theory, Culture and Society* 23, nos. 7–8 (2006): 20.

2. Friedrich Kittler and Stefan Banz, *Platz der Luftbrücke: Ein Gespräch mit Stefan Banz* (Nuremberg, Germany: Verlag für moderne Kunst, 2012), 60.

3. Armitage, "From Discourse Networks," 20.

4. Friedrich Kittler, *Eine Kulturgeschichte der Kulturwissenschaft* (Munich: Fink, 2000), 221.

5. E. Khayyat, "The Humility of Thought: An Interview with Friedrich A. Kittler," *boundary 2* 39, no. 3 (2012): 8.

6. Friedrich Kittler, "Meine Theorie ist gar nicht so lebensverbunden, um über alles zu reden: Gespräch mit Peter Weibel," in *Short Cuts* (Frankfurt am Main: Zweitausendeins, 2002), 84.

7. Michel Foucault, "Final Interview," *Raritan* 5, no. 2 (Summer 1985): 8. In 2003, the German publishing house Metzler put together a *Heidegger-Handbuch* containing a short article titled "Heidegger und die Medien- und Technikgeschichte," authored by none other than Friedrich Kittler. The text opens, though without proper allocation or documentation, with the mentioned quote from Foucault, reproduced in French. See Friedrich Kittler, "Heidegger und die Medien- und Technikgeschichte. Oder: Heidegger vor uns," in *Heidegger-Handbuch: Leben—Werk—Wirkung*, ed. Dieter Thomä (Stuttgart: Metzler, 2003), 500.

8. Friedrich Kittler, "Aufschreibesysteme 1800/1900: Vorwort," *Zeitschrift für Medienwissenschaft* 6, no. 1 (2012), 117–26, translated by Geoffrey Winthrop-Young as "Unpublished Preface to *Discourse Networks*," *Grey Room* 63 (Spring 2016): 90–107. This short text, which the author himself never published, represents Kittler's means of intervening

in the now illustrious, yet, back then, quite threatening and tiresome debate about whether his *Habilitationsschrift* formed a ground-breaking achievement that actually accomplished a fundamental reform of German academia in instigating the novel discipline of media history—or merely the unintelligible ramblings of a Schrebrerian basket case. In conversation with John Armitage, he states the following: "So my choice of *Aufschreibesysteme 1800/1900* as the title of my book was considered quite unusual at the time, if not a little provocative, since it was not the done thing to take the title of a tenure track book from the text of a madman" ("From Discourse Networks," 18).

9. Martin Heidegger, *Parmenides*, trans. André Schuwer and Richard Rojcewicz (Bloomington and Indianapolis: Indiana University Press, 1992), 81.

10. Khayyat, "Humility of Thought," 18.

11. Kittler's late pro-Heideggerian campaign knows the potential exception of a witty talk from 1996 in which Kittler launches a sustained critique of the hermeneutic and phenomenological tradition for "its attempt to separate philosophy from calculus and all its applications [*von der mathematischen Analysis samt ihren Anwendungen*]." Friedrich Kittler, "Thinking Colours and/or Machines," *Theory, Culture and Society* 23, nos. 7–8 (2006): 46. Heidegger figures as main culprit throughout the article only to become redeemed by a final recuperative move: "The later Heidegger is more relevant when it comes to understanding universal machines than the Heidegger of *Being and Time*" (49). Kittler feels complicit with Heidegger's later reflections on technology on account of their radical antisubjectivism and the contention that technology is no longer reducible to its tool-character. Nonetheless, he avoids a discussion of Heidegger's disregard for hardware and an ontic construal of technology. In the final analysis, Kittler's endeavor propagates the elimination of ontological difference. "Being," if it is thinkable in Kittler, manifests as machinic process and material fact.

12. Friedrich Kittler, "Towards an Ontology of Media," *Theory, Culture and Society* 26, nos. 2–3 (2009): 23. Kittler's phrase "it's only with Heidegger's help" in this context ironically, if unintentionally, recalls Heidegger's infamous *Spiegel* interview, entitled "Only a God Can Save Us." I'm grateful to Toni Hildebrandt for this hint.

13. Martin Heidegger, *Being and Time*, trans. Joan Stambaugh (Albany: State University of New York Press, 1996), 99.

14. "De-distancing means making distance disappear [*Verschwindenmachen der Ferne*], making the being at a distance of something disappear, bringing it near. Dasein is essentially de-distancing" (ibid., 97).

15. Kittler, "Towards an Ontology of Media," 28.

16. Ibid., 26.

17. Friedrich A. Kittler, "Martin Heidegger, Media, and the Gods of Greece: Deseverance Heralds the Approach of the Gods," in *The Truth of the Technological World: Essays on the Genealogy of Presence*, trans. Erik Butler (Stanford, CA: Stanford University Press, 2013), 291.

18. "Mit dem 'Rundfunk' zum Beispiel vollzieht das Dasein heute eine in ihrem Daseinssinn noch nicht übersehbare Ent-fernung der 'Welt' auf dem Wege einer Erweiterung und Zerstörung der alltäglichen Umwelt." Heidegger, *Being and Time*, 98.

19. The radio, to be sure, is no neutral or innocent *Zeug*. I cannot, at this point, go into the historical implications of radio as the technological figure of a misguided politics, but let us not forget too quickly how the radio addicted an entire *national ear*, alternating between *Hören* and *Gehorsamkeit* the voice of the Führer and Wagner. Ronell emphasizes this when she writes: "The jouissance of the ear was felt by a whole nation, whether it was listening to Wagner or to the constant blare of the radio, which is said to have hypnotized a whole people, a tremendous national ear." Avital Ronell, *The Telephone Book: Technology, Schizophrenia, Electric Speech* (Lincoln and London: University of Nebraska Press, 1989), 21.

20. Kittler, "Martin Heidegger, Media, and the Gods of Greece," 296.

21. See Friedrich Kittler, "Martin Heidegger, Medien und die Götter Griechenlands: Ent-fernen heißt die Götter nähern," in *Die Wahrheit der technischen Welt: Essays zur Genealogie der Gegenwart*, ed. Hans Ulrich Gumbrecht (Berlin: Suhrkamp, 2014), 384. I've cited my own translation since Erik Butler's version doesn't seem to go far enough and chooses to trade in Kittler's creational spin for a rhetorical recuperation. He translates: "In other words (which are Heidegger's, too), technology [*Technik*] itself determines the History of Being." Kittler, "Martin Heidegger, Media, and the Gods of Greece," 297.

22. Kittler, *Kulturgeschichte der Kulturwissenschaft*, 236.

23. See Alessandro Barberi, "Weil das Sein eine Geschichte hat: Ein Gespräch mit Friedrich A. Kittler," *ÖZG* 11, no. 4 (2000): 109.

24. Kittler, *Kulturgeschichte der Kulturwissenschaft*, 236.

25. Heidegger, "Question Concerning Technology," *The Question Concerning Technology and Other Essays*, trans. William Lovitt (New York and London: Garland, 1977), 4.

26. A curious movement in the above-mentioned belated foreword to his *Discourse Networks* shows Kittler turn his back on thinking when he states his conviction that technological thresholds "are not to be thought but only to be described [*nicht zu denken sondern nur zu beschreiben*]." Kittler, "Aufschreibesysteme: Vorwort," 121. Winthrop-Young's recently published translation decides to emphasize Kittler's anti-hermeneutic disposition as he seems to have in mind Hans-Georg Gadamer rather than Heidegger when he formulates: "In order to arrive at empirically more valid results, Foucault's findings have to be applied to these [technological] thresholds (*which need to be described rather than interpreted*)." Kittler, "Unpublished Preface," 97; my emphasis.

27. Ronell sees this very clearly when she holds that, "according to Heidegger, we haven't entered the age of machines or technology; rather, there are machines and technologies because it is the age of technology." *Fighting Theory: Avital Ronell in Conversation with Anne Dufourmantelle*, trans. Catherine Porter (Urbana, Chicago, and Springfield: University of Illinois Press, 2010), 92.

28. In a recent article on Kittler's and Heidegger's relation to mathematics, Stephen Sale develops an argument that differs from my own. His conclusion holds: "Kittler's teasing out of the ambiguity in Heidegger's account of technology does offer the humanities a form of rapprochement with the sciences." Although it could be argued that Kittler is well aware of the "ambiguity in Heidegger's account of technology," it

is the case that Kittler vehemently covers up this very ambiguity because it insists on ontological difference and thus on a concept of technology that goes beyond the material circumstance of hardware. Stephen Sale, "Thinking by Numbers: The Role of Mathematics in Kittler and Heidegger," in *Kittler Now: Current Perspectives in Kittler Studies*, ed. Stephen Sale and Laura Salisbury (Cambridge and Malden, UK: Polity, 2015), 44–70, 66.

29. Avital Ronell's work has expounded this circumstance in detail. Very early in her exploration of Heidegger's intricate relation to technology, Ronell emphasizes his intention to install a nontechnological "protected mode" for his approximation of Being: "The mark to be made here, the incision, indicates the surface of a weakly held limit between technology and Being. Technology, while by no means neutral, but a field of fascination, is viewed as potentially covering an authentic relation to Being. It is from this point onward that claims are made for a relation to Being more original than the technically assumed one." Ronell, *Telephone Book*, 19. It is precisely this limit, however weak, separating technology from Being that makes it possible for Heidegger to posit the possibility of thinking outside the realms of metaphysics and science (both of which realize the claims of *Ge-stell*). Thinking thinks *Ge-stell* without having to rely on a technological grid. Jacques Derrida, commemorating Paul de Man, also critically recalls the Heideggerian chasm between thinking and technology, and points out that there is no way for thinking to engage with technology's essence without both *Denken* and *Wesen* being constituted *technologically*: "[The] maintenance, in a Heideggerian manner, of a heterogeneity between the essence of technology and technology (which is, by the way, one of the most traditional gestures), between thinking memory and science, thinking memory and technicist writing [*l'écriture technicienne*], is precisely a protection against another abyssal risk, that of parasitic contamination, of an an-oppositional difference, etc." Jacques Derrida, *Memoires for Paul de Man*, trans. Cecile Lindsay et al. (New York: Columbia University Press, 1988), 140.

30. See Martin Heidegger, "Science and Reflection," in *The Question Concerning Technology and Other Essays*, trans. William Lovitt (New York and London: Garland, 1977), 155–82.

31. Martin Heidegger, "Time and Being," in *On Time and Being*, trans. Joan Stambaugh (New York, Hagerstown, San Francisco, London: Harper and Row, 1972), 8.

32. See Emanuel Levinas, *Otherwise than Being, or Beyond Essence*, trans. Alphonso Lingis (Pittsburgh, PA: Duquesne University Press, 1998), 4: "The *there is* fills the void left by the negation of Being."

33. "Technology is entrenched *in* our history." Heidegger, *Parmenides*, 86; my emphasis.

10

BONES OF CONTENTION

Friedrich Kittler's Recursive Realism

Chadwick T. Smith

"The sciences are on stage again," writes Friedrich Kittler, delivering the first sentence of "Man as a Drunken Town-Musician." Because his explicit goal in the text entails an attempt to write a revised scientific history of film, subtly cast words and the rhetorical effects of his language may go unnoticed: in this case, the word *again* almost disappears behind science's performance. In addition to restaging film's birth within the nineteenth-century efforts to formulate a science of motion, mathematically modeling the bones in the leg (instead of within the traditions of art or narrative), *again* implies a reformulation in terms of return or homecoming of sorts. We reach this home in the last sentence of Kittler's text, which closes a circuit that is paradigmatic for Kittler's essay, his later oeuvre. Looking forward from film to digital media at the end of his text, he avows: "On computer monitors . . . science steps onto the stage."[1] This text is a staging not only of a science but also of the very form of writing history to which he takes recourse, and is exemplary of a crucial concern—the suggestion that the human is a musician in its essence gestures toward the form of recursion that becomes critical for contemporary German media studies that followed in his "Homeric wake."

Presented in 2000 at the *Stages of Knowledge in the Sciences* conference at the Freie Universität Berlin, the title "Man as a Drunken Town-Musician" is a citation from Emil Du Bois-Reymond's *Natural Science and Fine Art*, the text that— coupled with Wilhelm and Eduard Weber's *Mechanics of the Human Walking Apparatus: An Anatomical-Physiological Investigation*—serves as the foundation of Kittler's essay. Building on these texts, his history of film opens with the equations that underpin the Webers' science of motion and ends with Du Bois-Reymond's commentary on the media technologies that result from them—

the image of a man stumbling in the flickering light of a spinning stroboscope. Yet the bones that initiate this history stubbornly resist complete assimilation into it and resurface in varying modalities throughout this text and in Kittler's larger oeuvre. Initially an object of scientific enquiry into human locomotion at the outset, the bones become raw material as mathematic precision displaces the human drawing hand of illustration and interpretation. In the end, I argue, they become the remains of a human subject dispersed throughout various media, whose body becomes a product of physiology, and whose language is reduced to information technologies. Bones stubbornly remain throughout several texts, the history of media, and a return to Greece, that itself revolves around the reported presence of bones piled up on the shore of the Sirens' island.

The significance of Kittler's recursions, however, extends beyond the confines of film's history and the science of movement—Kittler's recursive technique sets the stage for key developments in German media studies that come in his wake. Since at least 1996, post-Kittlerian German media studies has stressed "how fundamentally the media-theoretical discourse is in need of a media-historical framework of analysis to match media's inherently high physical and mathematical standards."[2] In other words, discursive regimes proper to textual analysis are ill-suited to media studies' objects of investigation. Seeing media and technologies unfolding within the constraints of history, cultural history or cultural studies fits media into normative discursive systems. A media archaeology, on the other hand, reveals that the very conception of history is a "function of cultural (symbolic and signal-based) operations."[3] Thus one may examine the entire cultural and medial ecosystem from the perspective of procedures and processes: cultural techniques (*Kulturtechniken*). While sharing these concerns, Kittler's work at times approaches this framework and lays the ground for it while at others it retreats from it—often in the same text. Yet his work here not only decisively and fundamentally relies on the kind of rigorous mathematical understanding required by it object, "the elementary technique of culture common to all sciences, called mathematical codification," he demonstrates the recursive methodology that remains the core of the contemporary study of these very cultural techniques.[4]

My contribution summarizes the history of film Kittler outlines in "Man as a Drunken Town-Musician" before discussing what can be called the functionality of recursion based in their metaphoric nature. I will follow closely not only the text's deployment of bones, but also its gestures toward musicality—essential for linking contemporary technologies to a Greece that for Kittler held a promising, always already dehumanized trajectory of European culture that was cut short with the rise of Socratic philosophy. "Man as a Drunken Town-Musician" is paradigmatic because it performs a recursive history through an object (bones) that I argue becomes the figure for recursivity's own rhetorical function, that Kittler is writing a type of technical realism that, much its literary analogue, relies disavowing its own metaphoricity. Taken together, the strands of thought in Kittler's essay weave the recursive technique into the larger arc of Kittler's late work and its continuing relevance for the investigation of cultural-technological programs.

I

To explain what recursions enable Kittler to do, we must first consider his larger project. As Geoffrey Winthrop-Young has illustrated, Kittler's earlier work "reinterprets early-nineteenth-century literary culture from a discovery of the imaginary and the consequent depth of the individual as a historical by-product of a certain discourse network."[5] Kittler does this by reinterpreting the Lacanian orders of the imaginary, the symbolic, and the real, and pairs them to different technologies that construct and store different reals, leaving the imaginary to be populated by that technology's uniquely constructed subject. With historical focus then placed on specific medial objects, his later recursions—juxtaposing different instantiations of the same phenomena—may provide a framework for a history of media written from the perspective of media themselves rather than from a dominant human agency.

In "Man as a Drunken Town-Musician" the medium to be examined is film. Kittler does not, however, begin his history in the conventional place, "with diorama painters or magic lantern players, but rather on an elementary threshhold: with the scientific history of moving"—namely with Du Bois-Reymond's book and its remarks on the Weber brothers' project.[6] The Webers had sought to elaborate a general science of motion, but first needed to diagram the individual moving parts—in this case the bones of the legs, of ball-and-socket joints. It is their methodology for generating these diagrams, however that initiates this trek toward film and delights Kittler, who quotes from their book: "The femoral head or so-called sphere was sawn perpendicularly from in front backwards and the section was printed on the paper. The curvature of the two parts here cannot be altered by the drawer. The picture is indeed the imprint of the object itself."[7] To establish a science of movement, the bones needed to present themselves without any mediation of interpretation by human hands, as when anatomy was practiced in "its proud old amphitheaters, where the dissection resulted in findings that made their way to woodcuts only belatedly."[8] This moment of the reported "findings" of dissection is of course code for a hermeneutic process. In its absence, the inscription to which Kittler refers comes from the material trace of the body speaking for itself rather than a sovereign authorial consciousness. It is, to put it in another equally problematic register, self-evident. "Thus," Kittler concludes: "The free will of human drawing-hands in scientific visualization remains just as excluded as it is in the mechanics of human legs. On this worldly scene of all religions and dances of the dead, the skeleton appears on the stage of knowledge and points no longer to allegories of death, but rather to nothing more than its own animation."[9]

No longer *memento mori*, these bones are bereft both of conscious intention and metaphorical meaning and simply indicate, through their materiality, the possibilities and limits of their movement—a movement that can be then described mathematically through partial differential equations. All that remains is for these equations to become visible, and this will be Du Bois-Reymond's prime contribution to the story. What he finds so thrilling in the Weber brothers' text is that they finish their treatise with how-to instructions for the construction of a stroboscope. This enables, as Kittler claims, "for the first time in history of science, the visualization of partial differential equations." The image of these equations "consists of drawing a number of pictures representing the man in his successive positions during two steps."[10] In the end, these equations do not simply recreate the picture of a walking human being, as a painter would. Rather a "peculiar effect presented itself," Du Bois-Reymond writes about the Weber brothers' machine: "The figure portraying the beginning and end of the step, where man rests for a short time on both feet, certainly looks completely as painters have always already portrayed walking people, except that in the middle of the step, where the so-called moving leg swings past the standing leg, the most strange and even ludicrous sight appears: like a drunken town-musician, man seems to trip over his own feet, and no one has ever seen a walking man in such a position."[11] Closing the loop, the final images of a human in motion produced by the equations generated from the direct and unmediated imprint of bones thus become something else than that from which they came. "Science," Kittler can now claim, "becomes the alienation effect which strips quotidian and artistic perception of the fiction of totalization, in order to reveal the naturalistic truth of the drunken town-musician behind the aesthetic appearance of human walking."[12]

The bones that first stood mutely as their own self-evidence, enabling the equations of walking, now return the human to the fully fleshed image of drunken town musician. But with a difference. "Instead of 'word, language and image in the truest sense,'" writes Kittler (citing one of his favorite points of reference, Goethe), "'symbol and number' have taken over the human gait."[13] What Winthrop-Young has characterized as the "hostile takeover of bodies and subjects by text" where this is inherent in the process of reading that results from alphabetization, thus appears in a different vocabulary: the hostile takeover of moving bodies and subjectivity as such by the mathematics that produce film.[14] That is, movement has passed through the equations and appears in scientific visualization and, declares Kittler, "becomes cinematics in the modern sense: it calculates virtual movements in the virtual, that is, visualizable spaces."[15] These spaces then in turn display an altered human form. The "naturalistic truth" Kittler finds here lies in the virtual spaces of the stroboscope or, later, the computer screen, where data visualization now becomes the new anthropology.

II

This return with a difference is the defining characteristic of Kittler's method. Recursion has perhaps been best described as "a prolepsis of the analepsis."[16] It is also the analepsis of the prolepsis—in the vocabulary one can hear a loop—it is a circuit. The process of recursion traces the appearance of a procedure or a phenomenon back to a chosen point in history and then retraces it back to the present. In this way, an altered present is already grounded in and justified by an ordinal beginning itself already changed from the perspective of the present—discourse network 1800 can only be identified from the vantage point of discourse network 1900. Yet the dynamic part of this movement is that 1900 is also changed by this excursion into the past. Recursive histories may thus become ever-expanding loops—with each orbit, the ellipse grows larger, reaching out to encompass more and more territory. Yet by remaining with the iterations of its object and nothing else, it is a closed loop. It is, as Winthrop-Young writes, "a self-enclosed, almost autopoietic process."[17] If this is the case, one must continually ask not only what does this process enable, but also what does it foreclose?

Kittler's recursion allows the drunken town-musician to stumble along somewhere in the middle of a loop and in the process the leg bones—Kittler eagerly picks up du Bois-Reymond's description—become the basis for a new model of the human subject with Kittler's rewriting of a medium's history. Recursion enables this narrative, and these are the stakes of Kittler's history of film. Kittler's recursion now enables an expanding loop of what was already apparent in the famous opening to *Gramophone, Film, Typewriter*—"Media determine our situation"—that a theory of the subject and histories of specific media are intertwined.[18] Kittler's oeuvre has in this way never been about erasing any and all anthropological consideration of the human subject. It has rather aimed at disrupting the naturalization of a specific humanistic tradition. Kittler still tackles the question of the constitution of the subject, yet avoids a vocabulary that pumps up (among others) the romantic, self-sovereign subject. In this way, it is a cultural history that has an alternative anthropology embedded within it.

This alternative history is one that distances itself from traditional narratives, and for Kittler, the specific narrative is the construction of the romantic subject codified in the exemplary case of Goethe, whom he cites. In a famous response to Karl Friedrich Naumann, Goethe stops both his science and his literature short of any numeric make-up when he declares: "I am dependent upon word, language and image in the truest sense, and completely incapable, to act in any way whatsoever through signs and numbers."[19] Here, Goethe ensconces *Dichtung* (poetry) as the true measure of *Wahrheit* (truth) and in Kittler's analyses leads to the founding moment of modern German *Geisteswissenschaften*. When Goethe's professor Faust steps onto the stage and announces a comprehensive skill set bereft of numbers, he drives the wedge between the "two cultures" of the humanities and the sciences. The elevated place granted to Goethe has continued to allow the humanities to disavow their numerical component because Faust, the Magister, has "a passion for the innermost secrets of nature," but it is, as Kittler writes, "a nature which punished loathsome measurings or even numeration of her exterior with contempt."[20] In Kittler's narrative, numbers will remain repressed within and in service to the alphabet throughout the romantic era of literature until a migration of numbers from letters, then comes with the rise of technical images such as photographs and film.

Film, in Kittler's history, makes possible new images that reconfigure the place of the human subject, and film originates with the bones in the Weber brother's laboratory. If recursions are ever more inclusive pairings of like phenomena, we here witness that their potential to rewrite narratives may include Kittler's own. I turn here to the discovery of another bone, one that already had a hand in displacing humankind from its privileged, divine position. When Goethe presented his discovery of the presence of the *Zwischenkieferknochen*, the intermaxillary bone, in humans in 1784 to a crowded Jena salon, its significance was not given its due. The absence of this bone had been accepted scientific doctrine and, as humans were the only creatures thought to lack it, the essential difference between humans and all other animals was brought down to this minimal mark. With its discovery, however, humans were reinserted into other morphologies and put into relation to other creatures. Goethe's discovery was not met with much acceptance, mainly because of the dominance of Petrus Camper's view of human anatomy, which held that the anatomical difference between man and animal was the missing intermaxillary bone in man. Yet, as Nicholas Boyle remarks, another problem faced by Goethe's discovery was that he didn't have a theoretical framework within which to explain the ramification of his findings. Perhaps not until Kittler's own discourse and recursive methods allow for communication between these bones—Goethe's and those in Kittler's own works. If Goethe's discovery can be read as the discovery of an ontological fissure with the potential to recode culture, Goethe then leaps forward and reproduces the work of the later practitioners of cultural techniques that come in Kittler's wide wake.

Crucial at this point is Bernhard Siegert's urging that cultural techniques are procedures that "process ontological distinctions," and primarily the distinction between human and nonhuman. From this perspective, cultural techniques (and the phenomenon to which they attend) "assume the position of a mediating third preceding first and second."[21] Michel Serres's logic of the parasite, as Siegert highlights, is apparent here. The parasite, a third term that could be seen as disrupting a distinction between two terms, may also provide the conditions of possibility for it. Goethe's *Zwischenkieferknochen*—literally a "between" jaw bone—here operates at the very suture between human and animal, a bone that prepares the way for the theoretical framework the discovery itself lacked. With the discovery of the intermaxillary bone, discourse network 1800 was already working to displace the human subject from its privileged position and precisely along the suture lines of a bone. If we follow Kittler's methodology, wherein one examines the reappearance of the same phenomenon again and again at different times and in different contexts without recourse to linear causality, then perhaps Goethe is not the hero of discourse network 1800, the one who escorted the voice of a changing imago of the mother to the whispers of nature in his "Wanderer's Nightsong." If he rather appears as the technician examining the sutures in a bone, then Goethe is enlisted into this alternative cultural history of bones operating along the suture between human and animal, expanding the recursive loop. It is precisely this kind of reimagining and shuffling of historical times, which escape traditional anthropocentric narratives that recursions enable.

In "Man as a Drunken Town-Musician," the recursion reframes the medium of film in terms of a mathematical science of motion based on an examination of bones. The presence of these bones, however, inserts Kittler's drunken musician into another, larger recursion—the return to Greece that occupies his late work. Just as the drunken musician produced by the Webers' science of movement begins with knee joints in their dissection room, the grand historical loop that delivers Europe back to Greece begins for Kittler with both music and a bone—specifically with a "five-hole flute made from the hollow bone of a griffon vulture, discovered 2008 in the Achtal close to Ulm."[22] This musical bone takes its place in year 33,000 of the 35,000 years of history Kittler outlines at the conclusion of *Musik und Mathematik*, volume 1, part 2, *Eros*.

The "naturalistic truth" revealed by the Webers' equations then dovetails into this work. Like Nietzsche and Heidegger, Winthrop-Young has observed, "[Kittler], too is in search of the other, earlier Greece, the Greece of yore before things went wrong, that is, before they became all too abstract, metaphysical, and forgetful of the media in and through which they had evolved."[23] That medium was the Greek vowel alphabet, an upgrade of the Phoenician consonant alphabet that, Kittler argues, allowed for the storage and transmission of Homeric verse. In it, Kittler sees the back-end recursion of the computer's binary code. Digitization is a universal alphabet for the storage and transmission of the real. Like binary code, the Greek vowel alphabet at one time deployed a single system to denote musical ratio and letters through numbers. "The general digitization of channels and information erases the differences between the individual media. Sound and image, voice and text are reduced to surface effects."[24] These effects, which seem to the human user like discreet phenomena, rely, at base, on a common code. The "naturalistic truth" is thus a truth made possible in the digital age—that is, without differentiation between specific media—math and music, are reunited as they were in pre-Socratic Greece, a return to a bone flute.

This loop, however, occludes the fact that recursions, too, produce an archhistorical narrative. In a sense, the juxtaposition of discrete elements from different times and contexts, one that highlights discontinuities rather than linear evolution are unified, knitted together like the seams that run through the skull. He declaws occidental grand narratives by installing a new one that proclaims that there are none. This is recursion, the ever-expanding ellipse of a history that eats its own tail, seals itself off, and resides in its own blind spot. As Claudia Breger has deftly illustrated:

> [German *Kulturwissenshaften* ("cultural studies")] aim to offer an encompassing view of society, history or culture as a "whole," beyond individual power differentials such as class, gender, or race. Within media theory specifically, the preoccupations with hardware are shared by competing approaches like those of Kittler, Norbert Bolz and Hartmut Winkler. Leaning towards grand narratives of media development, they eschew the analysis of concrete representational practices (see Geisler 1999). Toying with Kittler's own polemical gestus, we could say that dominant factions of German media and cultural theory have trouble with cultural as well as textual difference.[25]

In other words, recursions de-differentiate discreet objects, eras, media, and vocabularies. They have trouble with many kinds of difference. Kittler's text, I believe, attempts to occlude this trouble by deploying a metaphor for the work's nonmetaphoricity: bone.

III

The question (What, exactly, do recursions enable and what do they foreclose?) forecloses other, related and significant considerations. These questions prove to be another way of asking: what do recursions *do* and *how* do they do it? To answer these questions, we must again return to the medial objects through which they operate. Media in "Man as a Drunken Town-Musician" operate on the three registers that Winthrop-Young elsewhere identifies in Kittler's use of the term: as a new object of humanistic study, as a new approach to traditional objects, and as a rhetorical device.[26] Film becomes an object worthy of an attention that links it to a theory of the human subject and film itself is then studied not as an artistic medium but as a mathematical science that visualizes partial differential equations. This visualization then leads to another major conclusion to be drawn from Kittler's work: the belief that media enable perception.

That the ability to perceive a given phenomenon must be fabricated before it is experienced, is a point of recursion in *Natural Science and Fine Art*, when du Bois-Reymond writes that "For styles and works of art to even appear, epistemological knowledge must first have established the field of their colors and forms." For Kittler, the scientific "naturalistic truth" seen in the stroboscope is a "peculiar effect" for du Bois-Reymond, but it prepares the sensorium of a different discourse network in which it will no longer be. The alienation effect is the decisive character of "scientific visualization . . . the fact that it is no longer subordinate to the pronounced judgments of traditional art."[27] Movement will have migrated completely into equations. This visualization then does not simply engage a different mode human perception, however; it changes or creates it because "it is decisive that artists, not to mention people in general, cannot perceive the mechanics of the human legs at all." Kittler continues, "Like the vibrations of the violin's string, the phase pictures of walking pass by too quickly to fall into perceptual times. What people can no longer see or hear, however, calls for technical media."[28]

Moving both forward from this history of film to the twentieth century and back to an earlier, phonographic technology, the importance of bones is further calcified in *Gramophone, Film, Typewriter* where a skull fills a similar role. In Kittler's reading of the skull in Rilke's "Ur-Geräusch" ("Primal Sound"), the bone is again not a reassuring *memento mori*, but rather the technical means by which the possible "field of experience" is extended. In this text, Rilke recounts a time from his school years when he ran a primitive record player's needle along the coronal sutures on a skull. Listening to the indecipherable primal sound emanating from it, he asks: "is there any contour that one could not, in a sense, complete in this way and then experience it . . . in another field of sense?"[29] This new sense sits precisely at the outer points of Kittler's recursive loop. For Kittler, Rilke's piece demonstrates writing without a subject: "Before [Rilke], nobody had ever suggested to decode a trace that nobody had encoded and that encoded nothing."[30] This trace thus has no author and signifies no encoded and interpretable meaning. The skull is retroactively altered along with this new thinking of codes, traces, noise, and signal. Putting the figurative needle of Kittler's analyses to the materials of technical media, he opens up new fields of sense, though not "sense-making." The *Ur-Geräusch* simply speaks for itself, speaks through the gramophone and jumps into a real newly created by the techniques of sound reproduction.

While media thus enable changes on the level of the sensorium—rewriting, in other words, extant anthropology—recursions perform an analogous operation at the level of the knowledge that precipitates these technical forms in the first place, establishing the cultural-technological program guiding further development. Yet by what means do they do this? To answer this question, I turn to the third, rhetorical, function of media, because media converge with method in their metaphorical character—the aspect of a medium that is engaged by recursions, themselves metaphors. Particularly instructive for these questions, Larson Powell has demonstrated, through a reading of Kittler's "In the Wake of Odysseus," how recursion is essentially a rhetorical figure—indeed a metaphor—rather than a function.[31] For Powell, this quality distinguishes Kittler's recursions from other recursive theoretical frameworks, such as Niklas Luhmann's, a distinction that will prove critical for my considerations here. Whereas for Luhmann recursivity is a technical, functional operation, "Kittler sees it as lying at the base of 'transcendental knowledge.'[32] Not only is recursion not reflection, or self-knowledge, but also may serve to block off the latter. Already in Luhmann, recursiveness may serve to hide basal paradoxes (with what Luhmann calls 'Invisibilisierung' [invisibilization]), in particular the inability of systems to ground their own legitimacy."[33]

When Kittler, affirming the correspondences between the elements of Nature to the elements of the alphabet, writes: "the basic relation between knowledge and writing has been so deep-seated that it has scarcely reappeared," he practically cites this process of invisibilization.[34] This relationship is the backbone for the "Man as a Drunken Town-Musician." When Kittler calls attention to the way in which this relation can fall out of sight precisely because it is so fundamental, he marks the possibility of an analogous operation within the essay itself. Hidden in plain sight is the fact that the visualization of the data is still a metaphor for the bones that produce the equations that produce the machine and its peculiar effect. This process leads Powell to conclude that:

"Kittler's basal recursions are . . . in opposition to Luhmann, not functional in any technifiable sense (except perhaps rhetorical)."[35] I would suggest that it is precisely within their rhetorical function—that of invisibilization—that recursion finds its technical efficacy.

Though rhetoric and writing have never been far removed from the sphere of *technē*, it must nevertheless be affirmed that he is still *writing* a *history* and, by necessity, utilizing the functions of a traditional linear-alphabetic medium—including the meaning-producing capacities of metaphor. Not a history of media, but their historiography. Because, however, Kittler's aim is to describe the history of a medium from a standpoint outside of the *anthro*-centric tradition—and in such a way that the component of *Geist* in the *Geisteswissenschaften* responsible for the split between the two cultures may be unseated—it is precisely its own written character that must be disavowed. In "Man as a Drunken Town-Musician," metaphoricity must recede to make recursions *real*, that is to say that the bones must be aligned with their own self-evidence in a science of movement in order to produce the alienating effect. Being real may contribute to an altered human sensorium and therefore anthropology. One must remove metaphor from bones so that they may initiate film. The history of film, one that today returns as a "drunken town musician," is itself based on a rewriting and justified through the self-evident—that is, nonmetaphorical—nature of bones. They must become in some way *real* for the "naturalistic truth" to be revealed. Film, in this way, becomes a piece of his larger, Heidegger-inflected and "mediatized version of *Seinsgeschichte* (the history of Being),"[36] and in the process, the bones become the figure for recursions' functionality. The entire operation indeed rests on the metaphor of recursivity itself: the metaphor of nonmetaphoricity.

Kittler's project can in this way be read as a kind of technical or medial realism. Like literary realism's purported aim of describing the world as it is, these genres, armed with the objectivity of their objects' self-evidence, masks creative drives. Recursions' procedural invisibilization is Kittler's analogue to Robert Holub's enduring formulation that realism's primary strategy is to perpetuate a fiction of nonfiction.[27] Thus, "at the very point that realism covers its textual tracks, denying its own status as fiction, it also covers other, ideological traces."[28] Although the term *ideological* perhaps carries, in this case, too strongly negative connotations, Kittler's realism, true to the genre, stages its preferred vision of the world while presenting an idealized configuration of it, purified of that which would contradict its program.

Bones that speak for themselves, without human mediation, are speaking for themselves through human mediation and in the process become a figure for recursion itself, for its invisibilizing function. This is the "functionality" of the virtual space that enables both film and the filmic human subject. If, as Kittler's beloved statement by Nietzsche claims, "our writing tools are working on us,"[29] then the virtual visualization of film is its real functionality in the sphere of its visualization. So, bones precisely don't speak for themselves. The challenge for us may be that bones (and their recursions) can only be real when they aren't. For Kittler's recursion to have any of the "functionality" some find lacking, the bones must make the steps from the "dances of the dead" to a metaphor for the raw material of history and in doing so dance into film's virtuality—a space for united music and mathematics. Kittler's medial realism continues to produce very real effects when the insights gleaned from this method are (recursively) re-expressed in other spheres to produce new technologies, media, or cultural conventions.

Kittler's text is thus not really about a text about a drunken musician; it is a text about bones, but really a text about the equations that those bones produce, and then in the end it is a text about film that produces a different, stumbling man. The recursive history of film presented in "Man as a Drunken Town-Musician" is not only a specific example of the promise and challenges of recursive histories, but also a staging of recursion itself and its metaphoric function and role in Kittler's later works. This text draws together sometimes disparate strands and eras of Kittler's work and thought: chiefly, the return to Greece, the desire to drive the *Geist* out of the *Geisteswissenschaften*, and the technical-medial conditioning of humans' situation. These bones thus form the remainder of the changing human subject bound together in this ball-and-socket joint in a series of disavowed metaphors that make recursion possible.

NOTES

1. Friedrich Kittler, "Man as a Drunken Town-Musician," *MLN* 118, no. 3 (2003): 637.

2. Bernhard Siegert, "Good Vibrations: Faradays Experimente 1830/31," *Kaleidoskopien*, no. 1 (1996): 8.

3. Wolfgang Ernst, "From Media History to Zeitkritik," *Theory, Culture and Society* 30, no. 6 (2013): 134.

4. Kittler, "Town-Musician," 637–38.

5. Geoffrey Winthrop-Young, *Kittler and the Media* (Cambridge, UK: Polity Press, 2011), 85.

6. Kittler, "Town-Musician," 640.

7. Ibid., 643.

8. Ibid., 644.

9. Ibid.

10. Ibid., 649.

11. Emil du Bois-Reymond, "Naturwissenschaft und bildende Kunst," in *Reden* (Leipzig: Veit, 1912), 407. Translation from: Kittler, "Town-Musician," 650.

12. Kittler, "Town-Musician," 650.

13. Ibid., 644.

14. Winthrop-Young, Geoffrey, "Kittler's Siren Recursions," accessed February 16, 2013, www.monoskop.org, 16.

15. Kittler, "Town-Musician," 644.

16. Markus Krajewski, *Der Diener: Mediengeschichte einer Figur zwischen König und Klient* (Frankfurt: Fischer, 2010), 271.

17. Winthrop-Young, "Kittler's Siren," 20.

18. Friedrich Kittler, *Gramophone, Film, Typewriter* (Stanford, CA: Stanford University Press 1999), xxxix.

19. Letter from January 24, 1826, in Goethe, *Briefe und Tagebücher* (Leipzig: Insel-Verlag), 441. Translation from Kittler, "Town-Musician," 638.

20. Kittler, "Town-Musician," 639.

21. Siegert, "Cultural Techniques," 61.

22. Friedrich Kittler, *Musik und Mathematik*, Bd. 1, *Hellas*, Tl. 2, Eros (Munich: Wilhelm Fink, 2009), 293.

23. Geoffrey Winthrop-Young and Nicholas Gane, "Friedrich Kittler: An Introduction," *Theory, Culture and Society* 23, nos. 7–8 (2006): 12.

24. Kittler, *Gramophone*, 1.

25. Claudia Breger, "Gods, German Scholars, and the Gift of Greece: Friedrich Kittler's Philhellenic Fantasies," *Theory, Culture and Society* 23, nos. 7–8 (2006): 113.

26. Geoffrey Winthrop-Young, "Cultural Techniques: Introductory Remarks," *Theory, Culture and Society* 30, no. 6 (2013): 13.

27. Kittler, "Town-Musician," 647.

28. Ibid., 648.

29. Rainer Maria Rilke, "Primal Sound," in *Selected Works*, vol. 1, *Prose* (New York: New Directions, 1961), 51–56. Also quoted in Kittler, *Gramophone*, 41.

30. Kittler, *Gramophone*, 45.

31. Larson Powell, "Excursions and Recursions: Kittler's Homeric Wake," *Cultural Politics* 8, no. 3 (2012): 429–42.

32. Friedrich Kittler, *Eine Kulturgeschichte der Kulturwissenschaften* (Munich: Wilhelm Fink, 2000), 76. Translation from: Powell, "Excursions and Recursions," 436

33. Powell, "Excursions and Recursions," 438.

34. Kittler, "Town-Musician," 637.

35. Powell, "Excursions and Recursions," 437.

36. Ibid., 432.

11

THE ROCKET AND THE AMBIVALENT INTROJECT

Laurence A. Rickels

Robert Bramkamp's 2002 film *Prüfstand 7* (*Test Stand 7*)—part documentary of the V-2 rocket, part adaptation of *Gravity's Rainbow*—relied in both parts on the expertise of Friedrich Kittler, who appears twice in the film. What I learned only in 2012, while reading Bramkamp's book to his film, was that the director's motivation for making the film came out of his reading of *The Case of California*.[1] For the book, Bramkamp conducted an extensive interview with Kittler. At one point the filmmaker raises the question of the technobody as object or objective of the impulse or drive I once respelled psy-fi and recast as the hub where clinical studies of psychosis, the annals of psychological warfare, and bona fide science fictions meet and cross over. "I believe it is true that every cyborg or cyberspace film and all techno fantasy, techno philosophy, including Laurence Rickels, that they all refer to and affirm the conceptual, hoped-for, and feared fusion of human bodies with nonorganic materials—today that would be silicon. I am, I believe, the only skeptic on this score. For the simple reason that I believe that technology is far too good to knock around forever with us humans."[2] When Bramkamp next brings up Pynchon's provenance of the rocket as "won" from the "feminine dark" to associate it with the internal feminine of mourning, which he cites from *The Case of California*, Kittler elides the mourning and identifies Pynchon's "feminine dark" as mother earth, the rocket's point of departure. It was technology that thus left the earth behind at takeoff, Kittler underscores. And he adds that it is incidental to the significance of this rupture whether a rocket is manned or not.[3] The ventriloquist's dispute continues:

> Rickels draws a very strict parallel between technology on the one hand
> and psychoanalysis on the other which he claims is the most formative

science or theorization of the twentieth century. I'm not so sure and would argue instead that Freud was simply mistaken in his analysis of the essence of technology in *Civilization and its Discontents*. According to Freud, all machines are always only prostheses of humans. They are only reading glasses, better eyes, better ears, and so on. As I said before that is a very, very narcissistic view of technology. It could be described in far more inhuman terms, such as the way a coral branch grows. . . . Technology is more likely to accept such inorganic principles than orient itself to lung and muscles. That is precisely the trick of technology—that it can't and really doesn't want to do that.[4]

When this disagreement was current, back in the 1980s during Kittler's two quarters as guest professor at UC Santa Barbara, I offered what I thought was a good boundary. Granted that technology has auto-accelerated beyond corporeal analogues or prostheses, just the same: the Freudian consumerist perspective on media is back when it comes time to bury the dead and the mass media perform the service.[5] In *Gramophone, Film, Typewriter* Kittler had in fact made room, to my mind, for this proviso by identifying the site of every new generation of spooks as the latest new border or outer limit of media extension of the sensorium.[6] That one man's technology is another man's mass psychology isn't a compromise but a trigger.

I offer the interview souvenir I came upon following Friedrich Kittler's death as epigraph to the reading that follows of the rocket in *Gravity's Rainbow* and its science-fiction borderland suspended between projective identification, including identification with lost causes, and integration. I begin again with an exogamous choice.

SIMULATIONS

In her 1963 essay "The Conquest of Space and the Stature of Man," Hannah Arendt also held that man cannot reclaim by outer space transport the Archimedean point of his universal science.[7] She also discounted as special effect of this vanishing point the trust in man's mutation within a large-scale biological process of which technology is a part. But she argued that it is far from incidental that the craft is occupied. For example: "The astronaut, shot into outer space and imprisoned in his instrument-ridden capsule where each actual physical encounter with his surroundings would spell immediate death, might well be taken as the symbolic incarnation of Heisenberg's man—the man who will be less likely ever to meet anything but himself and man-made things the more ardently he wishes to eliminate all anthropocentric considerations from his encounter with the non-human world around him."[8] This external view at close quarters is the import of what's already down to earth. "If we look down from this point upon what is happening on earth and upon the various activities of men, . . . then these activities will indeed appear to ourselves as 'overt behavior.'. . . Under these circumstances, speech and everyday language would indeed be no longer a meaningful utterance that transcends behavior even if it only expresses it, and it would much better be replaced by the extreme and in itself meaningless formalism of mathematical signs."[9]

In his 1988 essay "Media and Drugs in Pynchon's Second World War," Kittler summarized the amalgam that rises up before the rocket POV of *Gravity's Rainbow*: "When technologies take the upper hand over science and aesthetics, information alone counts. And after all, semiotics and the behaviorist techniques Pynchon analyzes as strategies of war share certain roots."[10] Kittler is right that in *Gravity's Rainbow* it takes film and behaviorism to know the time-traveling effects of the rocket. "Imagine a missile one hears approaching only after it explodes. The reversal! A piece of time neatly snipped out . . . a few feet of film run backwards. . . . Pavlov was fascinated with 'ideas of the opposite' . . . you weaken this idea of the opposite, and here all at once is the paranoid patient who would be master yet now feels himself a slave."[11] At the end of what's dubbed a "Pavlovian's Progress,"[12] Slothrop appears as Everyman signaling conditions of paranoia in the meantime as pervasive as information itself, which has "come to be the only real medium of exchange."[13] While information is the plain text of technology it circulates among men shot through with explanation, as Walter Benjamin advised in "The Storyteller,"[14] in other words as opinion, the basis for the behavioral administration of mass psychology.

What Arendt looks down on explicitly and by absence or implication are the two tendencies in the organization and comprehension of mass media society, the behavioral and the psychoanalytic, which in science fiction reign as two orders of simulation. In Aldous Huxley's *Brave New World*, these orders, which can also be characterized as the public relations trajectory of adaptation to information or opinion and the advertising aspect of identification, keep company in one belief system. The future divinity of behavioral and biological adaptation is addressed as Our Ford, although he prefers to be called Our Freud when psychological issues are raised.[15] Otherwise the trend assigned by Huxley to Fordism in 1932 hosts tendencies which have been kept distinct from Freud's name. While it is possible to derive one more paranoid proverb out of Pynchon's reduction of psychoanalysis to occult hobby in *Gravity's Rainbow*, one might also recognize in the foregrounding of the amalgam of Pavlovian behaviorism, film, and rocket another story or allegory of a joint delegation, for example the belief system Ford/Freud. To make the line of separation legible also as adhesive strip, one can turn to science fiction, the genre in which Pynchon initially tested his decision to become a writer.

Philip K. Dick's 1964 novel *The Simulacra* follows out a Freudian understanding of mass-mediatized psychology, but as literally made in Germany and continued in California. In the future, a German-Californian state, the USEA, projects its mass psychology around the mascot status of a ruling couple, consisting of the German chancellor, who is an android, and the first lady, a role played by an actress. It is a corporation/incorporation organized around at least one real identity or missing person with countless cosignatories who are figments of the imagination engaged in keeping a couple of identifications in safe deposit. Untranslated German words in Dick's text attest to this process of encryptment. The *Geheimnis* (secret) of a couple of faux persons is "carried" by the ruling class of so-called *Geheimnisträger* (persons entrusted with confidential information) in order to uphold a state of preservation. But although the USEA state of incorporation fails, in the course of the novel all those trying but inevitably failing to effect a political correction of history through time-traveling intervention have been in reality-training for the ability to mourn.[16] While time travel in Dick's novel, invented at the time of the merger of California and Germany, remains a magnet for fantasies of cure-all reversals of history, the technology itself doesn't deliver change and its alternate histories promote instead acceptance of the irretrievability of loss.

Daniel Galouye's 1964 sci-fi novel *Simulacron 3* follows out the tendency to simulation in public relations. The founder of public relations, Freud's nephew Edward Bernays, recalls in his 1928 study *Propaganda* the example of pianos for sale. Rather than extoll the attractiveness of pianos, for example, which would be mere advertising, the PR strategy was to publicize, via miscellaneous reports, interviews, and editorials, the hottest new accessory of the home or the music room. Once the need for such a space or displacement was instilled it followed that pianos would meet the need to complete the installation as recognizable. The gist of the anecdote is that the PR campaign organizes blanks that advertising and consumerism can proceed to fill.[17] Because the public is ready-made while its adaptation to opinion is ongoing, the PR campaign must be in a position to project or forecast consumerism via sampling of opinions and taking of polls and surveys. In *Simulacron 3*, because the business of polls and surveys has impinged on everyday life, an electronic simulation of consumer society offers the welcome alternative: the changes that pollsters can only ask about can be directly introduced into the simulacron and the reactions of the simulated figures observed in double real time. The world to which we are introduced through the protagonist Hall, who is one of the programmers of "Simulacron 3," turns out to be yet another simulation. And yet this simulated world reacted to stimuli by preparing to launch the very simulacron project that subsumes its own reality.

At one point Hall is dismayed over the grief displayed by Jinx, his deceased employer's daughter; he characterizes the sentiment as: "[A] striking throw-back to the mid-twentieth century . . . before enlightenment had . . . swept away the vicious cruelty of the funeral convention. In those days, proof of death had to be established on a practical plane. Those who attended wakes and funeral services saw and believed. And they went away convinced that the loved one was actually beyond this life and that there would be no complications arising from a supposedly dead person showing up again. That the close ones also went away nursing traumatic wounds made little difference."[18] In the future according to *Simulacron 3*, the news of a loved one's passing means that the body has already been removed. The sci-fi forecast is a 1936 diagnosis in Benjamin's "The Storyteller:" the removal of the dying and the dead from all living quarters circumscribes the encapsulation and internalization of an inoculation we began taking in with the novel. The protagonist's death scene at the end of the novel as reclamation of the whole life as meaningful—rendering that life at every moment the life of one who died thus and then—was what the readership swallowed, an inoculation service that accelerated with the advent of information. At the same time, Benjamin singles out the psychic impact of World War I, traumatic enough to forego a history, as alone responsible for the autoimmune crisis otherwise informed by the novel's happy end in death.[19]

What proves jolting in *Simulacron 3* is to witness the sudden disappearance of your neighbor—simply gone without a trace. This new shock of zero or beyond, which is specific to the electronically simulated nature of its setting, introduces the onset of mourning according to the structure of a PR campaign. "Watching a man disappear isn't something you simply shrug off and forget."[20] PR campaigns must get around the consumer's ability to shrug off even the advertisements of new products. The evidence of electronic erasure simulates a change that remembrance supplies and supports. Utter disappearance of the one you're with in the same instant like a blip from the screen promotes the inside view of reality as infinite regress of simulacra. But each inner world is now a place for absence.

World War I was the setting for the departure of one model of mass media society from the other. While Bernays won the war for his theory of public relations, which found successful application in the propaganda of the entente, his uncle Freud won the postwar period for psychoanalysis over the symptomatizing bodies of war neurotic soldiers. In "Introduction to *Psychoanalysis and the War Neuroses*," Freud's inside view of the shell-shocked soldier as incapacitated by a conflict in his ego between the "peace-ego" and its "parasitic Doppelgänger," the war ego,[21] issued the owner's manual to the psyche's protection and projection. Psychoanalysis was sent to the front of emergency treatment of the war neurotic soldiers during World War I but became in this wartime setting of treatment—and then in time for the second coming of the war under the more aggrandized aegis of psychological warfare—what I prefer to call greater psychoanalysis,[22] the eclecticized and reunified amalgam of all the therapies that took their departure from Freud's science or otherwise shared a border, including behaviorism.

Pynchon conjoins via Pavlov the themes of time modification and paranoia largely in step with the overall comedy routine that begins with the substitution of the infant Slothrop's erections for canine salivation as most elegant binary. The dismissal of psychoanalysis also belongs to this routine. The interpretation of Slothrop's psychokinesis by the "most Freudian of psychical researchers" is dead-pan laughable and yet, seriously, the only instance of interpretative involvement with the outhouse humor rampant in the novel. "He subconsciously needs to abolish all trace of the sexual Other, whom he symbolizes on his map, most significantly, as a star, that anal-sadistic emblem of classroom success which so permeates elementary education in America."[23]

In Gravity's Rainbow the consensus is that nothing will remain of a certain psychoanalytic specialization in the Psi Section, namely, the "search for some measurable basis for the common experience of being haunted by the dead."[24] And yet the search for some measurable basis of this experience aligns the project with Pavlov's own move into the study of psychopathology. The immediate context for this move was a mishap that befell the dogs. Traumatization came into focus as factor in conditioning or deconditioning following a flood that nearly wiped out the entire test population. The surviving dogs were manifestly changed by the ordeal. All their conditioned reflexes were gone, they simply wouldn't eat regardless of stimuli, and the excessive fear they showed no longer fit the grid of response. In the course of reconditioning the animals at considerable effort, Pavlov saw the connection between their aberrancy and traumatized human behavior. The give and take of the stimulus/response model of adaptation didn't bring about profound change. However, once the breakdown of psychic reality was factored in, a working model was secured for opening up the depth of the field of adaptation for far-reaching alteration.

That Pavlov's breaking insight seems delayed or denied in the setting of research dedicated to obtaining through animals a so-called mechanistic explanation of human behavior is the form of tribute paid to the unspoken connection between the hub of human psychic aberration and the wheel of animal fatality or behavior. Pavlov's mother withdrew into psychosomatic illness never to return when he was too young to hate her but old enough to blame the environment rather than internalize the deprivation as his fault line. The influence of this absence, which the test dogs put into Pavlov's scientific perspective, is picked up in *Gravity's Rainbow* as the prospect of deconditioning or extinguishing a reflex to zero or beyond. What computes here is that we are doing the aftermath of early trauma. "Not only must we speak of partial or of complete extinction of a conditioned reflex, but we must also realize that extinction can proceed beyond the point of reducing a reflex to zero. We cannot therefore judge the degree of extinction only by the magnitude of the reflex or its absence, since there can still be a silent extinction beyond the zero."[25]

IDENTIFICATION WITH LOST CAUSES

Pynchon's cultivation of the rocket follows out flight trajectories looping the Cold War through World War II as the mass psychological tendency to carry loss forward unto the prospect of its reversal. Although for the *Pax Americana*, according to Kittler, the rocket and the atom bomb could be combined in nuclear missiles,[26] this functional merger of the effects of Europe's phantom wars could go through only by their uncanny-proofing displacement into a continuous history of innovation. But in real or trauma time the rocket took off as byproduct of the air war, which the Germans had already lost. From the phantasmagoria of the Axis to the extensive psycho-technical research and training (already in the 1920s) that made the German pilot over as "auto pilot" ever in the ready position to merge with the machine in flight, the investment in air power as the ultimate total war front was all along, without knowing it, building up to the crypto fetish of rocket flight. Following the loss of World War I and flying into the loss of World War II, the crypto fetish of rocket flight carried forward the end as "final victory."[27]

The premier lost cause was that of Troy, and the miracle weapon of its overturning the wooden horse. The reversal of Troy's lost cause—skewered upon one weapon, ruse, or fetish—was basic to the poetic historiography of Rome. Shakespeare, our first man on the scene of modernity's spectral transmissions, called the new weapon out in the harbor of world domination Birnam Wood, the immobility of which was the guarantee the witches gave Macbeth that he would remain inviolate—save for the impossible prospect of the woods advancing. When in "Some Character Types Encountered in Psychoanalytic Work" Freud counted the Macbeths among those wrecked by success, he gave the inside view of their other success as among the most identified-with losers in literature. That Lady Macbeth can't "out" the damn spot confirms an internal reservation about the success of her power couple, a success upon which she is wrecked. Since it is clear (*klar*) that Macbeth must realize that he cannot live forever, Freud considers Macduff's outcry that Macbeth has no children the "key" to Macbeth's transformation.[28] Macduff's outcry means, as Freud allows, that only a man without children could order children to be killed. But Freud overhears the curse of infertility upon success and succession. There could be more to hear along this line. Macbeth asks for male offspring in recognition of his wife's inspiring pledge of her own ruthlessness. In passing she makes reference to her having had a child; it's the reason she knows of what she speaks. She declares that if she had vowed to kill her own infant as Macbeth vowed to kill Duncan she would and could commit even that murder.

When Freud speculates that poetic justice pays back the Macbeths for their crimes against generation by granting them childlessness, he overlooks the contradiction he himself mentioned in passing, namely that the infertility fulfills Lady Macbeth's express wish that she be unwomaned to steel her and her husband's resolve to proceed to the first act of murder. That murder was to be "the be-all and the end-all" of consequence, the success that trammeled up succession, allowing the Macbeths to "jump the life to come."[29]

In the season of Lady Macbeth's resolve there is one spot of hesitation: she is unable to murder the man who in his sleep resembles her father, her dead father. To ensure that the patricide is successful, she vows to her husband that she would succeed in killing her dead child. Truth is she would rather be a murdering mother than a mother of substitutes, but can be neither. As in *Hamlet*, murder is tied to the second death of the dead. Getting rid of Duncan amounted for Lady Macbeth to losing the loss of her child and giving a wide berth/birth to the afterlife of successful mourning.[30]

The Macbeths are not psychopaths. Instead they scoop out the spousal medium of mourning, scrub it down, and detonate it. Against their nature, they fill up with the black magic of ruthlessness and destroy forever the very prospect of successful mourning, of succession through substitution. Heroism lies here—in wait for identification that is untenable, undeclared, but ever so strong.

Since Abraham Lincoln identified *Macbeth* as his favorite play, even quoting only days before his assassination Macbeth's despairing envy of dead Duncan's respite from fitful betrayal, *Macbeth* has been the main prop of ambivalence toward the power invested in presidents. After Goethe's *Wilhelm Meister's Apprenticeship*, any future author had to be initiated into the theater of his talent by his mother's gift. Following Lincoln's choice, future presidents have had to memorize lines from *Macbeth* in adolescence.

Gertrude Stein announced that the United States was the most ancient culture of the twentieth century because of the advance preview of techno mass modernity it absorbed through the Civil War.[31] But the Civil War also invested the United States as techno modern by its deposit of the lost war to be carried forward. There is an idealized aspect to this lost cause that's basic to Hollywood films in which the Southern POV holds a majority share in the monumentalization of US history. Off-screen in the 1960s, "reenactment," a new culture industry of the event, specialized in staging battle scenes from the Civil War. The parallel development in science fiction of "alternate history"—which allowed the reversal of losses but only by losing what history shows in the crowd of altered senses of an ending—was soon applied to the Civil War. Ward Moore's 1953 *Bring the Jubilee*, generally considered the first alternate-history sci-fi novel, projects a near future and parallel present in which the South prevailed in the war between the states. For the twentieth century, this victory meant inside the novel's alternate world that the Confederate States and the German Union were the two world powers.[32] With the sudden availability of time travel, the protagonist, who has studied and written on the war's history, interrupts interpretation to be there during the war but then, back in the past, inadvertently sets the recording back on course. But the new recording doesn't simply erase: that the reversal of the lost cause is ongoing in its parallel world is the *Geheimnis* the protagonist carries.

When in the late nineteenth century Julian Green's parents had to choose the site for the European headquarters of his father's export-import firm and their new home, they selected Paris over Berlin because they felt the French, owing to the recent loss of the war with Prussia, would know what it meant to carry a lost war. While Mr. and Mrs. Green "chose" not to bind their lost war to the future of loss in German history, Julian Green would later reflect the pull of the German contest. His 1947 *Si j'étais vous* is a Faust novel in which he quarrels with Nietzsche on religious grounds. Melanie Klein picked it up (in "On Identification") as her main prop for staging what she called projective identification, the secular corollary or corrective to becoming who you are. In Green's fabulation, the Devil's gift of techno prowess and rejuvenation proceeds as body switching, which for Klein's theory illustrates the way in which we project parts of ourselves inside others to circumvent through a kind of outsourcing of functions of contact and defense the anxiety-producing rapport with the other. In clinical practice, projective identification informs the dispute the analyst is suddenly party to without really knowing his part, not even upon deeper reflection, as with countertransference. It is Klein's theorization avant la lettre of the complete Sensurround of crypt deposit and transmission.

Green's corpus switching between the Faustian striving to lose like a winner—the modern German destiny of dissociation—and the Allied determination to win as loser (the redemptive ending of Green's Faust novel) was brought through Klein's reading into proximity to what I prefer to address as the ambivalent introject, which on Klein's turf and terms can be situated between projective identification and integration. Ambivalent introjection is basic to the setting in Pynchon's fabulation of the rocket as reconfigured beyond the former opposition, the index mapping true underworlds. In other terms, the mix or mess of perpetrators and victims is the side effect following upon the onset of integration. Integration—a term and notion that Klein introduced into the lexicon of psychoanalytic theory in her 1940 essay "Mourning and Its Relation to Manic-Depressive States"—is not to be confused with or limited to the positive inclusion of elements of opposition and their adaptation to a greater whole. Integration in Klein's conception pulls up short before the prospect of irretrievable loss and includes this shortfall or incompletion in its structure. Just as the related effort of reparation cannot neutralize or deny the scene of destruction, so integration cannot circumvent or cleanse the untenable comparisons that find juxtaposition in the wake and shakeup of trauma. Out of the resulting chaos and turbulence the impasse of traumatic history shifts toward the onset of the ability to mourn. Among the risks Pynchon takes in entering upon the ambivalent introject is that the story of rocket engineer Pökler begins to read like *Gone with the Wind* set onto modern German history.

COLLECTIVE MOURNING

F. W. Murnau's rendering of the creature of the night as *Doppelgänger* made the jump cut basic to Kittler's genealogy from German romanticism to film and psychoanalysis.[33] It is by the German tradition's focus on the double, to the exclusion of every other figuration of the occult, that the first cinematic science fiction was German. No sooner projected, it was enlisted in the Nazi era of realization of science fantasy—which is why it was the prehistory to be forgotten of a genre now identified as Cold War exclusive. In the documentary portion of Bramkamp's *Test Stand 7*, we learn that Fritz Lang's *Woman in the Moon* was shown in Nazi Germany only in an expurgated version that deleted the camera pans of the rocket designs, because it was felt they already occupied and revealed the planning stage of the V-1 and V-2 rockets. The rockets that then took off bore as mascot insignia reference to Lang's film, on which, as teenager, Wernher von Braun had also worked as assistant to Germany's leading theorist of space travel, Hermann Oberth, the film's technical advisor.

Future worlds made in Germany were left unattended during the Cold War reception of science fiction. Then beginning in the 1980s the *Metropolis* look was in our faces in films, music videos, and the redesign of Disneyland's

Tomorrowland. What also remained largely unaddressed in post–World War II science fiction, as, indeed, in the public sphere at large until the turning point in the 1980s, was the Holocaust. When in his 2003 preface to *Nineteen Eighty-Four* Pynchon commented on its bracketing out of the Holocaust as George Orwell's requirement for thinking his way through in 1948 to the postwar period he was also identifying his 1973 novel as on schedule with this staggering. "There is some felt reticence, as if, with so many other deep issues to worry about, Orwell would have preferred that the world not be presented the added inconvenience of having to think much about the Holocaust. The novel may even have been his way of redefining a world in which the Holocaust did not happen."[34]

That Nazi Germany was the first realized science fiction guaranteed that the long "haul" of *Wiederholung* (repetition) and its compulsions would stagger indefinitely for both the recovering psychopaths and their heirs the onset of the capacity for mourning. Bramkamp reassembles the film history of the rocket by pulling the realized rocket back through *Gravity's Rainbow*. What the streamlining of science faction deferred for German history undergoes ambivalent introjection in the course of Pynchon's rocket novel.

Gravity's Rainbow hitched its status as new *Moby Dick* to the pursuit of the V-2 rocket and its continuity shots, which at or as the end of the *Rainbow*, almost as 9/11 forecast, detonated the movie theater in Los Angeles in which Pynchon assembled his readership. But before the Nazi rocket enters American history through this loop with cinema it is reassembled on the track of its future development as V to the *n*th power in the meeting of otherwise opposed or repressed contingencies. In South-West Africa Germany routed the Herero rebellion and sent the vanquished nation into the desert to perish. In Pynchon's fiction, the surviving heroes, "the Empty Ones," carry out their trauma-enforced suicide-drive in voluntary service to the rocket. Pynchon's *Schwarzkommando*—the mystical blue flower in the no-man's land of technologization and death which guards and guides the super version of the V-2 all the way to its strike against LA—has its recognition value in the racism of the GIs, who may have conquered Germany but are wary of blacks equipped with rockets. The unlikely fiction of the Nazi African-German brigade meets the fact of unlikelihood on the other side: for the World War II effort, African Americans were for the first time accepted for pilot training, but only at the segregated Tuskegee Institute in Alabama. Few were deployed as air men, however. Those in training at the institute called themselves the "Spookwaffe."

It is by the effects of racism that Pynchon conjoins the inscrutable mass murder in the foreground of the Nazi war with the crypto fetishism of the rocket, which must be read as trying to outfly it. The war of political differences, or even that of competition between special interests, was a diversion:

"secretly, it was being dictated instead by the needs of technology. . . . The real crises were crises of allocation and priority, not among firms—it was only staged to look that way—but among the different Technologies, Plastics, Electronics, Aircraft, and their needs."[35] Somewhere over the positivism of machine histories for which the Holocaust does not compute there is the techno war revalorized as continuing beyond both the mass death and the opposition.

A score of pages following the disclosure that the air war "modified, precisely, deliberately, by bombing" sites for conversion "only waiting for the right connections to be set up to be switched on," Katje asks: "Is there room here for the dead?"[36] She has to correct the guilty assumption of a proper response twice over for the shame of it. Those now getting through the recent past and making it to the postwar period at the end of the sentencing recognize "the worst part's the shame."[37] "I meant, would I be allowed to bring my dead in with me. . . . They are my credentials, after all." Nor does she summon her dead ancestors: "I mean the ones who owe their deadness directly to me."[38] But her roundabout way of circumscribing and addressing, as she admits, the genocide—"think of the things you've done. Think of all your 'credentials,' and all mine"—is suddenly recognized by her interlocutor as the medium of postwar Germany's recovery by the industry of repair. "That's the only medium we've got now, . . . our gift for bad faith. We'll have to build everything with it . . . deal it, as the prosecutors deal you your freedom."[39] The closing reference to a shame that cannot be left behind, that hangs on as corporeal connection with dead bodies, connects "building everything" to the advertised and internalized prospect of making good again the object of repair.

Bianca, the woman given in passing in Pynchon's fiction as daughter, love object, and object of mourning searches in Bramkamp's film for her origin in the rocket. That she keeps running up against the so-called oven inside it sparks the eternal flame in a place gone without mention. But the eternal or internal feminine of mourning cannot draw us onward by so direct a hit. And so the film enters the blind alley of the figure of the severed and thrown hand to mediate our identification with Bianca's search for the history internal to the rocket. The severed and thrown hand touches on the mythic significance of Antwerp even or especially in name, one of the targets of the V-2 rocket attacks. But it also joins in the mystery of a photograph of Wernher von Braun's arm in a cast taken at the moment he was crossing the threshold to his postwar assimilation, the mystery Kubrick perhaps revalorized as the reflex salute otherwise so hard to contain (in his 1963 *Dr. Strangelove*). From Ernst Kapp to Freud and McLuhan, the detachable hand waves through the prosthetic understanding of our relationship to technologization. In Pynchon's novel the rocket, as in Kittler's genealogy of media, opens up a technological horizon of auto development, before which the prosthetic or humanist reach of our following falls short. And yet, to the extent that technologization cannot be separated from the European culture of death diagnosed in Pynchon's novel, the prosthetic relation comes to be reinserted in the wake of violence that we cannot but consider as externalized in our technological relation.

In *Test Stand 7* direct hits of the recent past alternate with blind alleys of allegorization, as when the oven is mediated by the hand. By this alternation, the film doubles back to stagger and layer mourning's release within the ongoing work of integration that alone makes history contemporary. By the deregulation and eclecticism it admits, the film proceeds by integration rather than opposition or repression to address problems and processes that are, as we say, bigger than the two of us. Indeed, Bramkamp brings us closer to what he has ever identified as his future goal, collective narration, which must be extended to mourning. Otherwise mourning is the prerogative of individuals or couples and group commemoration solely a forum of denial. We will catch up with deferred individual mourning only if the possibility of collective mourning can be reclaimed from the denial.

NOTES

1. Robert Bramkamp and Olga Fedianina, eds., *Prüfstand 7: Das Buch zum Film* (Berlin: Maas Verlag, 2002), 19.

2. Robert Bramkamp, "Interview mit Friedrich Kittler," in *Prüfstand 7*, 116.

3. Ibid., 122.

4. Ibid., 125.

5. This formulation of the quarrel made it into my *Aberrations of Mourning* (Detroit, MI: Wayne State University Press, 1988), 287: "The Freudian consumerist perspective on the technical media has been exceeded within the genealogy of media; and yet with regard to the corpse this perspective must yet be retained. The development of technical media has turned away from corporeal analogues or prostheses and pursued instead a logic of sheer acceleration or escalation. The functioning of the newest media thus surpasses any sensorium of warfare it nevertheless serves and simulates. And yet at the end of this escalation even the computer retains as its constitutive moment the possibility of total loss of that which has been entrusted to it. The destinal logic of its invention and first application notwithstanding, every technical medium achieves its ultimately only prosthetic range and portrait in the course of disposing of the dead. Thus work on the remainder refastens each new medium to a sensorium which, as Schreber realized, takes cognizance only of corpses."

6. Friedrich Kittler, *Grammophon, Film, Typewriter* (Berlin: Brinkmann und Bose, 1986), 24.

7. Hannah Arendt, "The Conquest of Space and the Stature of Man," in *Between Past and Future: Eight Exercises in Political Thought* (New York: Penguin Books, 1968), 272.

8. Ibid.

9. Ibid., 273–74.

10. Friedrich Kittler, "Medien und Drogen in Pynchons Zweitem Weltkrieg," in Bramkamp and Fedianina, *Prüfstand 7*, 56.

11. Thomas Pynchon, *Gravity's Rainbow* (New York: Viking Press, 1973), 48.

12. Ibid., 169.

13. Ibid., 258.

14. Walter Benjamin, "The Storyteller: Observations on the Works of Nicolai Leskov," trans. Harry Zohn, in *Selected Writings*, vol. 3, ed. Howard Eiland and Michael W. Jennings (Cambridge, MA: Harvard University Press, 2006), 147.

15. Aldous Huxley, *Brave New World* (New York: HarperCollins, 2006), 28.

16. The reading of *The Simulacra* I only touch on here is more fully developed as the first part of my book *Germany: A Science Fiction* (Fort Wayne, IN: Anti-Oedipus Press, 2015).

17. Edward Bernays, *Propaganda* (Brooklyn, NY: Ig Publishing, 2004), 77–78.

18. Daniel Galouye, *Simulacron 3* (New York: Bantam Books, 1964), 41.

19. Benjamin, "The Storyteller," 143–44, 151, and 156.

20. Galouye, *Simulacron*, 9.

21. Sigmund Freud, "Introduction to *Psychoanalysis and the War Neuroses*," in *The Standard Edition of the Complete Psychological Works of Sigmund Freud*, vol. 17, ed. and trans. James Strachey (London: Hogarth Press and the Institute of Psychoanalysis, 1950), 209.

22. The genealogy of „greater psychoanalysis," only briefly sketched here, is the overriding topic of my *Nazi Psychoanalysis*, 3 vols. (Minneapolis: University of Minnesota Press, 2002).

23. Pynchon, *Gravity's Rainbow*, 85.

24. Ibid., 276.

25. Ibid., 84–85.

26. Bramkamp, "Interview mit Friedrich Kittler," in *Prüfstand 7*, 114.

27. This is the focus of *Nazi Psychoanalysis*, vol. 2, *Crypto-Fetishism*.

28. "Some Character-Types Met with in Psychoanalytic Work," *Standard Edition*, 14:299.

29. Act I, scene 7, line 7.

30. See my discussion of *Hamlet* between Melanie Klein and Jacques Lacan via the psychoanalysis of Ian Fleming's Bond with spectrality in *SPECTRE* (Fort Wayne, IN: Anti-Oedipus Press). A more complete reading of the wreckage by success in *Macbeth* can be found in *Germany: A Science Fiction*.

31. Gertrude Stein, *Everybody's Autobiography* (New York: Cooper's Square, 1971), ch. 4.

32. Ward Moore, *Bring the Jubilee* (London: Gollancz, 2000), 76.

33. "Romantik—Psychoanalyse—Film: eine Doppelgängergeschichte," in *Draculas Vermächtnis: Technische Schriften* (Leipzig: Reclam Verlag, 1993).

34. Foreword to George Orwell, *Nineteen Eighty-Four* (Orlando, FL: Harcourt Brace, 2003), xvii.

35. Pynchon, *Gravity's Rainbow*, 521.

36. Ibid., 520, 544.

37. Ibid., 541.

38. Ibid., 545.

39. Ibid., 546.

PART IV

ON THE GENEALOGY OF MEDIA

12

LAMENTING THE VOICE BEHIND THE CHAIR

Nimrod Reitman

> What I fear is not the horrible shape behind my chair but its voice: not
> the words but the frighteningly inarticulate and inhuman tone of that
> shape. If only it could speak as people speak!
> —Nietzsche, Fragment of 1868–69

At a crucial moment in his discussion of voice and technology—which, for him,
amount to much of the same thing—Friedrich Kittler articulates a fracture.
The *Aufschreibesysteme* are oriented toward that crevice constituted by poetry.
Language and poetry—which, for him, amount to much of the same thing—
are created by means, inescapably, of a destructive dishevelment to which each
is destined to measure itself: "[W]hereas in the discourse network of 1800 an
organic continuum extended from the inarticulate minimal signified to the
meaning of factual language, there is now a break. Language (and its plural
suggests) is not the truth and consequently not any truth at all."[1] For Kittler,
the "organic continuum" is a medium given in terms of a maternal mouth that
was circumscribed and opened in his discussion of institutionalized alphabetization and the relinquishing of dialect that the maternal mouth commands.
The continuum—a phantasy of 1800 allowing one to think continuity—is
seen as articulating minimal sounds that are given over to paternal institutions and agencies, only to be broken. Breakage results from the damage that
the poetic word proves capable of tallying as it approaches its zenith in the
discourse network of 1900. At the place of self-assured and institutionalized
relation to language stands now a contoured void, a break. The aporia of language, to the extent that it needs to and may not say something, in kinship
with poetry is manifested in the breakdown and the maiming of the empirical
truth it seemed to carry in the discourse network of 1800 and with which it
must dispense as it approaches the epoch we now recognize as modernity. The

inarticulate minimal sound—a *Seufze* (Goethe), or "sigh," or an *Ur-Geräusch* (Rilke) which instigated a castrating alphabetization and an apostrophization of sexual difference, and that Kittler recognized with the mother's mouth—has been itself apostrophized, called, and broken by the discourse network of 1900. For Kittler, language, at best, is determined by a set of articulations, an inscription that is a result of an undetected noise, a "voice behind the chair."[2]

This muttering and inhuman (*unmenschlich*) sound, a metamorphosis of the monolithic sound emanating from the mother's mouth is what disturbed another Friedrich, Friedrich Nietzsche as he set out to destroy the very German literature and letters that Goethe created. For Kittler, "everything that began with Nietzsche comes to nothing."[3] In itself, this is not bad news, for no one could manipulate "nothing" into narratological and poetological treasure hunts like Nietzsche, who starts his version of modernity on the philosophical fumes of an affirmative nothing—at the same time a source of Nietzschean joy and abyssal scorn. Nietzsche's "nothing" as the beginning moment of literary modernity is what we need to interrogate here, especially in terms of how it relates to the noise that the name—or multiple names—of Nietzsche inescapably carries as it births if only to destroy, according to Kittler, literature.

As philosophical limit or poetic trope, *nothing* can be scanned by the breaths and sighs that bridge the difference between the said and the unsaid. A name for origin and annihilation, *nothing* springs in Friedrich Hölderlin's work between the *nicht mehr* (no longer, no more) and the *noch nicht* (not yet), when poetry emerges in times of destitution out of a difficult span of nothingness. Rainer Maria Rilke, one of Kittler's main protagonists in the *Aufschreibesysteme*, captures this "inner breath around nothing" in the *Sonnets to Orpheus*: "True singing is a different breath, about / nothing. A gust inside the god. A wind" (In Wahrheit singen, ist ein andrer Hauch. / Ein Hauch um nichts. Ein Wehn im Gott. Ein Wind).[4] Rilke opts for another breath, the breath of the other, which surrounds a divine wind-poem, inherited from Hölderlin's poem "Andenken" (Remembrance) and Goethe's resolute diminishment of language, into sighs in his poetic work. Goethe, for his part, avoids the tremors of nothingness that for Hölderlin and Nietzsche, as well as for Rilke and Celan, become essential. For these poets, breath embodies the fragile body of the poet, ever about to expire in the delivery of the poem. Maurice Blanchot reads the secreted space of nothingness as the "most inward" experience "whose pure, silent surging must be preserved."[5] For Blanchot, preservation comes at a price of poetic dissipation, "the breathing intimacy whereby the poet consumes himself in order to augment space and dissipate himself rhythmically."[6] The rhythmical expenditure is given, in the case of Rilke, in terms of Rilke's concept of the Open that Blanchot reads as a transparent and silent intimacy in which "life is sacrificed . . . but for nothing, in the pure relation to which the symbolic name of God is given."[7] Here, "nothing" acquires a different quality, perhaps even denoting a derisory quantity for which life is sacrificed. In a sense, Blanchot draws on Rilke in order to come out of the Hölderlinian impasse where "nothing" is so radical that it constricts the orphic space, on which Blanchot counts for his argument, to the point of foreclosure. In order to requalify the Hölderlinian, and also Nietzschean, experience of nothing, Blanchot, needing space for the expansion of the space of literature, takes recourse to the Rilkean Open that grants some mobility to the poetic act. By the time of *The Step Not Beyond*, Blanchot will shake Rilke to confront abysses without points of exit. There is a reading of the Rilkean Open that is of course far less valorizing than that of the pre-step Blanchot, notably rendered by Heidegger and de Man, when they take up the Open and relieve it of the romantic contours that Blanchot still retains. For Blanchot, the affirmative force of "nothing," despite its destructive capacities yields poetry, at once abundant and impoverishing.

When Kittler calibrates the discourse network of 1900 according to Nietzschean-Rilkean protocols rendering nothing, he opens and at once shatters the organic promise of the discourse network of 1800 for a holistic and all-containing system of writing-speech and, like one of his more famous protagonists, Bettina von Arnim, he too takes a breath and begins to sing—like Rilke's Orpheus—into the wind: "ein andrer Hauch. Ein Hauch um nichts. . . . Ein Wind" (a different breath, about nothing. . . . A wind)." Kittler gives *nothing* a gendered accent, but not in the traditional way to which Lacan has alerted us. The figures that he recruits for feminine interlocution, vigorous and often stubborn, offer episodes of poetic venturesomeness with utmost delicacy and a shared purposive stance. Poetic utterance, sacred missives, and profane emissions, often speak to no one and nothing. Yet the radical nonorientation to which they, through language, are subjected, is shown not to be demeaning, but on the contrary, crucial to any genuine understanding of poetic usages of languages. This is perhaps why Deleuze insists on "the becoming woman" of the true experience of writing. Cases of feminine nonaddress that seek to ventriloquize the inarticulate and aphonic traces share the fragmentary nature and rhetorical vulnerability that *nothing* implies. This instance of nothing can be seen to begin with the Nietzschean metamorphosis of the maternal mouth into a sound production machine whose noise was unendurable for his delicate ears—"*incipit tragoedia.*" Nietzsche's *incipit tragoedia*, whose name is derived from that famous aphorism concluding the fourth book of the *Fröhliche Wissenschaft*, or *La gaya scienza*, kept haunting Nietzsche's friends and scholars beginning with Lou Andreas-Salomé.

Kittler functions as a buffer when it comes to mediating *the event of Nietzsche* in terms of its musical, maternal, and technological implications and the way the singularity of this event relates to the breakage of rhetoric. In order to bring to light Kittler's innovation, as well as his place at the table of scholarly debate, I'll turn provisionally to Paul de Man, if only to underline the rhetorical effects of the substitution of the discourse network of 1800 to that of 1900 and the way it implicates "truth" and the empirical discourse it inscribes. De Man reads the event of Nietzsche in terms of the destruction of the ever-increasing attempt to implement a self-assured metaphorical model of language, that of Romanticism, by metonymically unstable rhetoric of which Nietzsche serves as an exemplary exponent.[8] It is only when Nietzsche puts sexual difference on the table that we can diagnose metonymical instabilities rather than contending with an over-saturated metaphorical language—that of 1800—that sterilizes libidinal aspects of language. Despite appearances, no one will deny that de Man too was concerned with the seductive aspects of rhetoric and, in many instances, may have had the same effect on the student body as Friedrich Kittler.[9]

The shift from the discourse network marked by Kittler as 1800 to that of 1900 has a debunking, or rather, deconstructive, effect in terms of the relation to genre definition, stylistic articulations, common literary tropologies, as well as to gender relations. For de Man, reading Nietzsche's remarks on rhetoric, the break that Kittler too asserts in the movement from the discourse network of 1800 to 1900, namely to a scene of inscription that supersedes the Romantic perception of what consists of a scene of writing, is achieved through a recalibration of three rhetorical tropes: metaphor, metonymy, and synecdoche, along with a conscious veering away from the more traditional rhetorical *loci*, namely, eloquence and persuasion (*Beredsamkeit*).[10] Making eloquence and persuasion dependent on the aforementioned *figures* of speech disturbs the assuredness that governs the discourse network of 1800 in favor of a seductive and unstable model based on reversals and substitutions. Perhaps the most severe example of rhetorical seduction that overwhelms rhetoric occurs in de Man and Kittler, based on Nietzsche's directives, when music intrudes upon the scene of inscription. Nietzsche plays a large role in discerning the infra-rhetorical stakes of the musical incursion. De Man surprisingly sets music aside, even in passages when Nietzsche points in that direction, whereas Kittler is open to the musical score and the complications it introduces into rhetoric and seduction.

The figure of speech that Nietzsche may have feared is not at all rhetorical, but is given beyond the scope of rhetoric, namely, where music and noise warp the ability to figure and open instead a grid of defiguration. It could be that rhetoric may have well found its limit when it reaches the musical score, when a text wants to *become* music, when a philosopher hopes to become a composer, and yet cannot altogether do so. For Nietzsche, and Kittler, this leaves us with an unbearable noise, indeed an *incipit tragoedia*, of the kind that made Zarathustra and metaphysics want to go under: "Like you I must *go under*, as men put it to whom I wish to descend" (*Ich muss, gleich dir, untergehen, wie die Menschen es nennen, zu denen ich hinab will.*)[11]

What are these figures of speech, enticed by musicality, yet not wholly musical? De Man subsumes the musical note under a theory of language that excludes music. He goes so far as to dismiss the musical inclusion as a mere phonocentric gesture—which makes strong sense but does not entirely capture the urgency of Nietzsche's musical titles and reading requirements. For de Man, Nietzsche's rhetoric is given in terms of the figure it seeks to ascertain: "What is here called 'language' is the medium within which the play of reversals and substitutions . . . takes place."[12] Seeing language as a medium for play is revelatory in terms of the relation to the disruptive gesture that Nietzsche's ears would be attuned, though eventually he proved unable to tolerate the play of musical notation. On a more familiar note, language, says de Man, no longer participates in an empirical model of purveying truth but rather becomes a medium of articulation and disarticulation, part of a play of reversals and substitutions. "This medium, or property of language is, therefore, the possibility of substituting binary polarities such as before for after, early for late, outside for inside, cause for effect, without regard for the truth-value of these structures. But this is precisely how Nietzsche also defines the rhetorical figure, the paradigm of all language."[13] Nietzsche's rhetorical utterance is based on the ability to displace a grid of articulations upon which figures of speech appear and disappear from consideration. De Man reads the rhetoric of tropes in terms of a broader relation to a seductive language that Nietzsche deploys, based on metonymical metalepsis, namely, "the exchange or substitution of cause and effect."[14] The Nietzschean *destruction* of the medium's binarity of values as that which determines the nature of the rhetorical figure while forming the basic trope recalls, without coinciding with, Kittler's understanding of Nietzsche's relation to the discourse network of 1900. Kittler's reading confronts the musical zones that de Man's rhetoric tried relentlessly to repress or avoid. The dynamic between these readers—de Man and Kittler—brings about a tension that repeats the stakes of the encounter between rhetoric and music. Rhetoric tensely approaches musical scores and tonalities, provoking perturbation, and perhaps a grudge, born of gender anxiety, at least for de Man, who shows little tolerance for approaching this question, if it is one (or two). The avoidance of gender, even where Nietzsche authorizes its rhetorical download, places de Man's argument in a virile sector that Nietzsche evades. The question emerges of whether a so-called genetic model can have much stability if, unlike Nietzsche's flexible rhetorical ploys and musical embeddedness, it excludes the mark of gender.

The rhetorical fear of music is not free of gender determination. In *Nietzsche contra Wagner*, Nietzsche explicitly states that "music is a woman [*die Musik ist ein Weib*]."[15] Nietzsche places music at crucial rhetorical and metaphysical junctures where it seems to have a double duty. Gendered in the feminine, music serves both as a stabilizer and a destabilizer in the Nietzschean corpus.[16] The fear of music that operates a rhetorical thinking in Nietzsche or a repression of the musical soundtrack in de Man, takes a different turn in Kittler's reading. Just as rhetoric discredited music, turning a blind eye to Nietzsche's insistence on it, rhetoric tends to disconnect the image and shies away from technological forms of projection and image making. While being rhetorically instructed, Kittler brings music into play and achieves something not entirely in tandem with de Man. Conflating Nietzsche with the Lumières brothers, Kittler reads the "enoptical afterimage, or illusion" that the Apollonian ensues in terms of what he recognizes as "the technological medium of film."[17] Nietzsche's attraction to a Wagnerian scenography is not contingent or on the side of undermined narrative, but fundamental and is part of a mechanism of desire for a soundtrack that would be able to carry the technological innovations. "Nietzsche dreams of music," says Kittler, "that would not, like all German music, 'fade away at the sight of the voluptuous blue sea and brightness of the Mediterranean sky.'"[18] The Nietzschean rendering of the *Gesamtkunstwerk* is captured here, as well as his unconscious relation to the all too easy gateway to the south, opened up by Goethe, which makes music fade away and lose sight. For Nietzsche, the optical element, rendered in terms of the Apollonian, is essential to music to the extent that he wants to *see* music. Nietzsche wants music not to recede into the distance, and to be strong enough to resist the orphic gesture of a turned gaze. Following Orpheus, Nietzsche too is going after Eurydice. Here Nietzsche needs music to stay in sight, not to fade away, or fade out—music must be seen. Only when music is seen, can it be heard. Nietzsche's performative utterance of the orphic gesture resists the vanishing point of music (where Eurydice is at once lost and regained), seeking to preserve the unstable musical instance. Alas, as Kittler notes, "Nietzsche was not Wagner. For makers of words, even if they dream of music and movies, there remains only the paradoxical desire to break open the general medium of culture. . . . Therefore, Nietzsche began by countermanding the Faustian revolution."[19] In what way does Nietzsche revoke the Faustian revolution? It seems that Nietzsche, not entirely unlike Faust, wants music to stay put, despite its effervescent nature. Like Faust's attempt to preserve a temporal instance of beauty, Nietzsche wants to sustain the musical moment and stretch it into other spheres of articulation and utterance beyond its acoustic elements and values. At times, music takes the place of philosophy, for we know that the imperative for Nietzsche as early as *The Birth of Tragedy* was: "Socrates, make music!" Countermanding the Faustian revolution may well be pursuing it by being *Faustian, all-too-Faustian*, desiring too much from a medium to the extent that both music and rhetoric can no longer tolerate the tension between them and must collapse into a kind of *Gesamtkunstwerk*, at times uncontrolled. Like de Man, Kittler uses the dream as the basic structure to explain the relationship between the Apollonian and the Dionysian; for both thinkers, the dream hides as it holds, opens itself for meaning in its nonvisibility. However, Kittler's reading prods Nietzsche as he is mobilized to break with the medium of culture, a medium that is given largely in and as rhetorical syntagms, and that de Man's reading opened up in many ways. Indeed, when one is *too* Faustian, one is no longer Faustian. Kittler's all-too-Faustian Nietzsche is set to destroy the Faustian revolution and its promise by replacing Faust on his chair, and opening his ears to the omnipresent noise that disturbed his delicate ears. Sometimes this noise is operatic, most of the times this is the noise of writing, a "white noise" that Kittler reads in terms of its silencing or inhuman, and therefore Dionysian, effect.

For Nietzsche, acutely aware of the voice beyond the chair, the voice would eventually be given over to the lamenting face and voice of Ariadne—identifying opera with its inhuman elements. When Ariadne's lament—hollow and aphonic—reaches Kittler's ears, her plaint would come to signify an attempt to leave the promise of the mother's mouth—romantic poetry—for the sake of a voided nothing, a poetry that functions as an excluded negativity in its very mode of construction.

What are the stakes of the transition from the mother's mouth of 1800, whose poetico-erotic effect is given in the discourse network of 1800 as poetry, to the disintegration of the maternal in 1900?[20] Kittler quotes Meier-Graefe's 1904 assumption regarding German literature as he addresses the nature of the Nietzschean constitution, and at the same time deconstitution, of the discourse network of 1900 in terms of the destructive capacities of the maternal mouth: "Two men determine the German aesthetic of our time: Goethe and Nietzsche. One forms it and the other destroys it." Kittler then adds, "when the one Mother gave way to the plurality of women, when the alphabetization made-flesh gave way to technological media, and when philosophy gave way to the psychological or decomposition of language; poetry also disintegrated."[21] The process of poetry's disintegration should be read in terms of the shift in the truth-value that the mother's mouth must have meant for the discourse network of 1800 and the way mothers were desexualized of their gender in the name of sexual difference. If the mother's mouth of the discourse network of 1800 sought to eradicate dialects and accents in the name of a maternal alphabetization, Nietzsche's idiomatic cast of utterances sets free the metonymical dialect and an array of displacements and substitutions that invite rogue sexual difference, musically charged, back into a perpetually disintegrating grid of inscription. For Nietzsche, music and other sonic signatures are the carriers of truth where rhetoric fails to ascertain its broken promise in terms of the play of gender, genre, and sexual displacement. Kittler persistently recalls the Nietzschean scene of inscription and attempts to read the noise and silence that the seduction system of 1900 brings about in terms of the noise behind the chair—a contour of an unfathomable and uncanny noise that frightened Nietzsche. Unpresentable and obtrusive, this noise is at the same time even more micrological than the minimal sound of the discourse network of 1800 to the extent that Nietzsche finds it difficult to listen to an *ach* within the *Sprach* (language) and is left with a deafening silence, an aphonic sigh (*Ach*), not even a murmur.

The destruction of poetry and language in 1900 leave us with broken tunes and traces of music that can be notated with the help of writing: "The minimal signifies as the murmuring source of language remains merely itself as long as it does not speak; the stylus comes to its aid."[22] Without a stylus, language keeps still. The stylus mediates its articulation and serves as a mouthpiece or metronome—a modern mother's mouth. These rhetorical utterances are related to the mouth even though the identity of the mother remains elusive and engages Kittler's diagnosis of the fissure between Goethe, the Mother of 1800, and Nietzsche, the Mother of 1900. For his part, Nietzsche, ever duplicating and multiplying his signature, traversed even the queasy zone of the maternal. However, even for a philosopher whose predicament has always been *ich bin der und der* (I am such and such [a person]), a maternalized signature comes at a price.[23] At the beginning of *Ecce Homo* Nietzsche stressed the importance of a double provenance—a dead father and a living mother—for any kind of philosophical genealogy and thinking. The invocation of the maternal brings about a cluster of metaphysical and rhetorical problems—autobiographical and symbolical.[24] What does it mean then to rhetorically assume a role of a mother, a scorned mother even? Perhaps a male mother?

In a handwritten inscription inside his *Der Ursprung der Moralischen Empfindungen* (1877), Paul Rée attempted to pay his debt to Nietzsche by mobilizing a rhetoric imbued with a parental metaphor or analogy: "to the father of this essay, most gratefully from its mother." Nietzsche's initial lukewarm response to mother-Rée, inscribed in *Human, All Too Human*, was soon replaced by a vehement break with Rée and his Réealism.[25] It may well be that Nietzsche's break with Rée metonymized his break or, rather, his inability to break with Wagner.[26] Identifying Rée as mother served Nietzsche in his working through, a working through that fails to work, as he was practicing separation from Wagner—at times a good breast, but also bad and harmful. This ever-occurring break with Wagner, experienced through Rée, is one of the variations of the *Eternal Return of the Same.*

Nietzsche's friendship with Rée, notes Kittler, marks and maybe even enables the transition of the discourse network from 1800 to that of 1900. Ill-fated, this shift is premised in breakage—it was Rée who bought Nietzsche his new typewriter from Copenhagen. "[It had] unfortunately been damaged during the trip. A mechanic was able to repair it within a week, but it soon completely ceased functioning."[27] This delivery without deliverance makes one wonder whether Nietzsche's breakup with Rée had not occurred over a broken keyboard, a keyboard that should have helped Nietzsche cope with the noise of the "voice behind the chair."[28] This polyphonic voice intruded upon the philosophe's dark labyrinth and later evolved into the Dionysian dithyramb. Of this voice, says Kittler, what finally begins to speak is "never reached by any word."[29] Nietzsche's wordless speech, nonetheless still a speech, perhaps aphonic, is accompanied and maybe even produced by the noise of the broken typewriter attesting to the broken friendship it ostensibly memorialized.

Lou Andreas-Salomé, Nietzsche's mouthpiece and conduit, sheds some light on the nature of the break with mother-Rée and the way it is laced into his break with mother-Wagner. It appears that Rée served as a transition object in a time when Nietzsche refused to introject a separation from Wagner, who served as a source of a creative nourishment but also provoked the philosopher's destructive drives. Salomé notes that "Nietzsche's concurrence with Rée's intellectual direction is nowhere more completely clear than in the fledging work *Human, All Too Human*; it appeared at a time when he suffered under the break with Wagner and his metaphysics [*zu einer Zeit also, wo er am schwersten unter seiner Trennung von Wagner und dessen Metaphysik litt*]."[30] Nietzsche was transferring unto Rée when his primary object, Wagner, was no longer sufficiently maternal. The German *litt* amounts both to suffering but also implies starvation, lack of nourishment.[31] For Salomé, this was primarily an intellectual transference; however, she connects it to a very particular mode of suffering or starvation; Nietzsche was suffering under (*unter*) a break, not from a break. Placed beneath suffering, this rhetorical locution of a break, where rhetoric itself breaks, may be a way of repeating, or envisioning Nietzsche as Zarathustra in his famous *Untergang*, a theatrical staging of the *incipit tragoedia*. Salomé should know, as Nietzsche identified her as the father of Zarathustra.[32] Despite Salomé resistance to take the paternity test, when she conflates Nietzsche with Zarathustra, Salomé symbolically becomes Nietzsche's father, a man who has been marked by Nietzsche as a very distinct noise maker, at times, even the one behind the chair. For Nietzsche, this father has always been a male mother, whom he called from early age father-womb (*Schoß*) while he was sitting on his lap (*Schoß*) and playing another keyboard—the piano.[33] Salomé pays particular attention to the pain of self-negation that was part of the separation from Rée as she also sketches an interiority or depth of affects that resembles the structure of a Freudian id or unconscious: "An escalation of Nietzsche's *self-negation* always required voluntary pains. . . . He had to put himself again under a foreign spell that would seek to remove his sense of self. Yet neither in terms of his philosophical direction nor in his personal relationship was there reason for this; the causes went much deeper."[34] Nietzsche's pains, seemingly caused by befriending Rée, of whom Salomé states that his personality was "very much his opposite," required self-negation; a negation (*Verneinung*) that both Freud and Lacan would deem crucial for the development of judgment: Freud reminds us that such judgment is premised on a maternal premium, stemming from the syntagm "it's *not* my mother." An erasure of self and signature yields, Nietzsche's self-negation pain, at times voluntary, that is necessary for the development of his sense of self. Salomé traverses here zones that would later stand at the center of the Freudian innovation. She also hints at the *locus* where she thinks one could locate the causes for such pains: not on the surface, certainly not because of Rée, but somewhere deeper and darker, labyrinthine and auditory, much like the talking-cure.[35]

There is a discursive switchover when Salomé sends Nietzsche a poem whose entitling moment and adolescent fervor spells pain—"An den Schmerz." Somehow the poem had its effect and apparently brought Nietzsche to tears while causing him some sort of pain, or did he spill the "tears of Eros?" "It is like a voice for which I have waited since childhood" says Nietzsche in a letter to his assistant Peter Gast on July 13, 1882.[36] Something happens with the mouth of Lou and the way she expresses thought and delivers poetry to Nietzsche's ear. Salomé's poem and the way she mobilizes pain short-circuits the *Aufschreibesysteme* and Kittler's understanding of the mother's mouth as far as paternal agencies are to be interpreted and the way these mouths were meant to voice a romantic cliché of pain. Lou resigns from such romantic distinctions and her painful fervor fails to fit romantic conceptions of pain or the pained utterance. Lou's rogue behavior situates her in a trajectory of women like Bettina von Arnim, perpetually writing "into the wind."

Kittler alerted us to the originating source of the poetic word emanating from the mother's mouth that spoke and brought, in many ways, poetry. Contrasting this maternal figure, Lou still inspires a thinking of the mouth, beautifully contoured by Rilke and tragically meaningful for Freud whose work painfully begins in Irma's mouth and lips, as if from his name to his own mouth: Sig-MUND. Lou serves as a nexus for these eponymous figures as she traverses the mouth-ear circuit and dictates a transition from an obsolescent maternal mouth to a maternal inscription at the hands and ears of Nietzsche—a shuttle system that has been relentlessly related also to spaces of anal inscription.

In her monograph on Nietzsche, Lou recounts a correspondence between Nietzsche and Rée dating to April 24, 1878, when Nietzsche sent a copy of *Human, All Too Human*, a text born of Rée's broken machine: "It belongs to you . . . to the others it is sent as a gift! . . . All my friends are now of one opinion that my book was written by you and originated with you: therefore, I congratulate you on your new paternity! Long live Réealism![37] Unlike the previous correspondence over Ree's book, here Nietzsche lets Rée take the paternity test whereas he assumes, we may think, the role of a mother. This couple, Nietzsche and Rée, a repetition of Nietzsche and Wagner, had eventually to break with each other, and with the faux game of maternal inscription—a breakup documented in *The Gay Science* in the aphorism "Stellar Friendship" that poignantly commences with a lamenting voice: "We were friends but have become estranged."[38]

A writing that writes silence, Nietzsche's broken typewriters, broken keyboards, and broken friendships present what Kittler sees as an "inarticulate tone" defining the "zero point of literature, a tone not only inhuman, but also not animal or demonic. . . . The inhuman tone behind Nietzsche's back is not the speech at the beginning of articulation; it is not speech at all. All discourse is powerless against it because all discourses add to it and fall prey to it, within the realm of sounds and words, all organism, white noise appears."[39] At the "zero point of literature" we are encountering Nietzsche's primal scene, where the philosopher assumes the role of Faust, sitting at the table, submerged in his writing, trying to voice something inarticulable: not speech and not yet writing. This voice marks a *place* where writing begins but also ends, where the dazzling force of speech ceases to manifest itself. This is where the discourse disintegrates itself, becomes a network of inscriptions, a white noise echoed on the white page. In these pained instances, Nietzsche must turn to the musical sphere for articulation. He "sings and sighs." Musically tracked, these instances mark where "the persistent split between the wanderer and his opposing shadow dissolved into a silent inner dialogue [*Zweigesprächs mit sich selbst aufgelöst*]."[40] Of the identity of this wanderer and his shadow one could project Lou and Friedrich, Rée and Nietzsche, Wagner and Nietzsche, singing and sighing.

In a letter to Rée, Nietzsche writes: "I always admire how well armed your arguments are from a point of logic. Indeed, this is something of which I am not capable [*so etwas kann ich nicht machen*]; at most, I can do a bit of sighing or singing [*ein bisschen seufzen oder singen*]."⁴¹ How are we to understand Nietzsche's sudden feelings of debilitation? What is the metaphysical status of his incapacitation? Is this another one of the rhetorical ways in which Nietzsche takes down the house, deciding, or rather preferring, like Bartelby, *not to*? Not to philosophize, not to choose an argumentation through logic. This may also be one of Nietzsche's understated yet missive ironies, for what could be a higher way of philosophizing than singing and sighing for Nietzsche—not a man but dynamite with high-tech ears—whose philosophy is primed both on Goethe's Faustian primal sigh: *habe nun Ach!* (Faust) as well as on the haunting song of the sirens, marking another self-splintering double provenance. For Nietzsche, singing and sighing constitute a philosophy that refuses to suture even loosely what already came apart, destroying all efforts of self-gathering. Similar to the shadow of his wanderer, Nietzsche takes a different route, a more clandestine and inarticulate one that Kittler situates on the level of primary sounds, perhaps not even a sound but a sigh. On these useful expressions Salomé comments that "it was precisely through 'singing and sighing' that the genius of his consciousness forced to the surface his gift for magnificent lamentation and hymns of victory [*Klagegesängen und Siegeshymnen*] over warring ideas [*Gedankenschlacht*]; he had the creative gift for transposing even the most sober or ugly thought into an inner music."⁴² Salomé comments on Nietzsche's ability to transpose the battling thoughts into a musical score made of lamentations, without indicating the measure or marking the tempo for this transposition. Can this be another one of Nietzsche's lessons inscribed in *Human, All Too Human* as the "desire for deep pain" articulated in and as music, in and as the *Passion* for Wagner, the *Passion* for Lou, the *Passion* for a whipping *Peitsche* (now carrying religious tones and overtones)—an instance of *Umnachtung* and forgetfulness that the Nietzschean machine says and unsays at critical moments when it refers to pain as music.

Nietzsche's *Klage der Ariadne* is part of his later oeuvre, an afterword to his philosophical inquiry, written as a singing-sighing poem. Salomé reads these Dionysian dithyrambs in terms of their ascetic and mystical folds, a return, perhaps an *Eternal Return*, to what disturbed Nietzsche in *The Birth of Tragedy*, namely the dissonant aspects of tragedy and music that participate in the origin of the Dionysian and the mystical. Salomé ventriloquizes Nietzsche and asks: "What induces beauty [to] give birth [*dass alle Schönheit zur Zeugung reize*]?" She replies to this Nietzschean question [*was treibt die Schönheit heraus*], a question that traveled from Plato in order to criticize Schopenhauer, by stating that "the artist delivers beauty from the terrifying [*Furchtbaren das Schöne*]."⁴³ Her answer channels another *Umnachtung* and elegiac fall, not the one in Turin but one that will occur in Duino, where "beauty is nothing but the beginning of terror" (*das Schöne ist nichts als des Schrecklichen Anfang*) and commences Rilke's *Duino Elegies*.

Kittler notes, "[The] text that Nietzsche first composed and then transferred into Ariadne's lament came from Lou Salomé. One only has to exchange 'enigna' or 'enigmatic life' for 'Dionysus' in the 'Hymn to Life,' and the woman's verse 'If you have no happiness left to give me, good then, you still have pain!' becomes Nietzsche's Ariadne's 'No! Come back! *With* all your martyring!' The dithyramb (to say nothing of the rest of Nietzsche's relationship to Salomé) thus remains quite close to what suffragettes called 'the language of women.'"[44] Nietzsche's rephrasing of Salomé's text invokes again *The Eternal Return of the Same*. However, the "return" in this case seems to carry a supplementary *demande*, to the extent that the return, though eternal, cannot be of the same (that may be the structure of all *eternal returns*). Nonetheless, Nietzsche wants something from Lou to return as Ariadne, or Dionysus, as he admonishes, in the name of Ariadne: "Come back!" Should this be an enactment of the Eternal Return, as the coming back of Lou, with all, or even despite, her martyring and resistance?

If Dionysus carries feminine proclivities, who is Ariadne, "the mistress of the labyrinth?" Identified by Kittler as the "language of women," can the dithyramb be a dialogue, *Gespräch ohne Gespräch* (a dialogue without a dialogue), between two women? A monologue? Could Ariadne be assuming, even appropriating, the role of the philosopher? Ariadne, notes Kittler, "speaks as the being who has been taught to speak by torture, as the animal whose forgetfulness has been driven out by mnemonic techniques."[45] This logic of forgetfulness—that of unconcealment (*Unverborgenheit*), namely, the forgetfulness of Being in the act of being—unveils something about the character of the torturous sighs and songs that occur at the labyrinth. Nietzsche wrote, indicates Kittler: "Who besides me knows what *Ariadne* is!"[46] Both asking and declaring, or neither asking nor declaring, Nietzsche nonetheless says *what* Ariadne is, not *who*, contesting a Germanic tradition of sexual identity directly attacking Schlegel's address to a feminine beloved as philosophy.[47] Rather than responding to an obsolescent schism between subject and object, Nietzsche's Ariadne attests to a different medium, that which disintegrated the contours of stable sexuality and emits itself in monstrous and unpresentable timber. And indeed, as a disintegrated medium, Ariadne's lament, Kittler notes, "remains unheard."[48] When Dionysus announces, "I am your labyrinth" (*Ich bin dein Labyrinth*), both Dionysus and Ariadne's ears become smaller and smaller: "you have small ears, you have my ears!" It is since *Ecce Homo* that Nietzsche establishes the shuttle system from the anus to the ear, perhaps from his high-tech hears to Lou's work on the anal. Nietzsche was proud of his small ears. Ears like those of Ariadne's and Dionysus's. For Kittler, Nietzsche's Ariadne is not a myth, but rather a presentation of the implacable transgression from the mother's mouth, a phantasmatical construct of fullness, into the emptiness of the system of inscription, devoid of sexuality but seeming to allow women in.[49] The dithyramb as a self-scorn for which Ariadne's figure stands indicates "that there is no mother's mouth at the origin of human speech and masculine writing."[50] It partakes in active forgetfulness; Ariadne, "in contrast to the women of the discourse network of 1800, knows nothing of authorship or love."[51] Kittler may have gone a little too far with his own desire to efface Ariadne's affectivity; he too may be caught in her impossible thread. For forgetfulness may well be the sign of authorship and love. Dionysus asks Ariadne "must one not first hate themselves, if one should love oneself?" (*Muss man sich nicht erst hassen, wenn man sich leben soll?*). Dionysus's language is suffused with textual instability, and is determined by what Nietzsche recognized as a rhetoric of investigative "asking-behind" (*hinterfragen*). Its mode of interpolation misplaces writing as if calling for a different relation to inscription, like a forgotten umbrella, or a stylus, or even a broken typewriter, more in tandem with Freud's Rat-Man or Lou's anal inscriptions. Within this kind of rhetorical inscription, says Kittler, "the phallus is missing or forgotten, or there, where it is not: on women" and writing is "the unmeasured ground without which signs and media would not exist,"[52] though Lacan says women are the phallus. What is the faith and nature of this rhetorical music? Akin to the music Nietzsche composed to Lou's "Hymn to Life" it vacillates—sighing and singing—ever impressing its contours on the tympanic membrane of a disintegrating labyrinth.

NOTES

1. Friedrich A. Kittler, *Discourse Networks 1800/1900*, trans. M. Metteer, C. Cullens (Stanford, CA: Stanford University Press, 1990), 187.

2. Ibid., 192.

3. Ibid., 177.

4. Rainer Maria Rilke, *Sonette an Orpheus*, in *Gesammelte Werke*, Bd. 3, ed. M. Engel, U. Fülleborn, H. Nalewski, and A. Stahl (Frankfurt am Main: Insel Verlag, 2003).

5. Maurice Blanchot, *The Space of Literature*, trans. A. Smock (Lincoln: University of Nebraska Press, 1989), 144.

6. Ibid.

7. Ibid., 145.

8. The problem of implementation and the way it relates to romantic discourse, or rather, the disintegration of a romantic discourse, to the extent that such a discourse exists (de Man as well as Nancy and Lacoue-Labarthe instruct us against a monolithic thinking of such a discourse) is addressed by Rüdiger Campe in his contribution to this

collection, as well as in *The Game of Probability: Literature and Calculation from Pascal to Kleist*, trans. E. H. Wiggins (Stanford, CA: Stanford University Press, 2012).

9. We are still trying to appreciate the richness of the pedagogy of these great teachers but it would be necessary, though no doubt awkward, to look at the traumatic edges and distorted inheritance that happens inevitably, if true learning is to take place under master teachers.

10. Paul de Man, "Rhetoric of Tropes," in *Allegories of Reading: Figural Language in Rousseau, Nietzsche, Rilke, and Proust* (New Haven, CT: Yale University Press, 1979), 105.

11. Friedrich Nietzsche, *The Gay Science*, trans. W. Kaufmann (New York: Vintage Books 1974), 275; *Die fröhliche Wissenschaft*, in *Sämtliche Werke Kritische Studienausgabe in 15 Bänden*, Bd. 3, eds. Giorgio Colli and Mazzino Montinari (Berlin/New York: de Gruyter, 1999), 571.

12. De Man, "Rhetoric of Tropes," 108.

13. Ibid.

14. Ibid.

15. Friedrich Nietzsche, "Eine Musik ohne Zukunft," in *Nietzsche contra Wagner*, in *Sämtliche Werke Kritische Studienausgabe in 15 Bänden*, Bd. 6, ed. Giorgio Colli and Mazzino Montinari (Berlin and New York: de Gruyter, 1999), 424.

16. See Susan Bernstein, "Fear of Music? Nietzsche's Double Vision of the 'Musical-Feminine,'" in *Nietzsche and the Feminine*, ed. Peter Burgard (Charlottesville: University Press of Virginia, 1994), 106.

17. Kittler, *Discourse Networks*, 188. Kittler is not the only one who made this observation. Adorno, punning on Nietzsche's famous book title spoke on "the birth of film out of the spirit of music," as that which already gives forth to what Adorno would conceive in terms of the culture industry.

18. Ibid., 187, with a quote from Nietzsche's *Ecce Homo*, "Why I am so clever."

19. Kittler, *Discourse Networks*, 189.

20. Ibid., 26: "The discourse that the mother in the discourse network of 1800 creates but cannot pronounce is called Poetry."

21. Ibid., 177–78.

22. Ibid., 64–65.

23. This designation concludes the foreword to Nietzsche's autobiographical book *Ecce Homo* (although the concept of autobiography is radically contested here).

24. Derrida demonstrated the rhetorical importance of Nietzsche's double provenance and the aporia it invokes in terms of securing a philosophical system, providing and erasing a signature, and rendering an autobiography given in terms of *Allothanatography*. Jacques Derrida, *The Ear of The Other: Otobiography, Transference, Translation*, trans. A. Ronell (Lincoln: University of Nebraska Press, 1985), 15–19.

25. Of Rée's book Nietzsche ambivalently commented that it "may perhaps in the future serve as the axe which cuts to the root of the 'metaphysical need' of man—whether this be *more* of a blessing than a curse to the general welfare, who can say?" Nietzsche, *Human, All Too Human: A Book for Free Spirits*, trans. R. J. Hollingdale (Cambridge: Cambridge University Press, 1996), §37, 33.

26. See for instance: "Wagner was just one of my sicknesses. Not that I want to be ungrateful to this sickness. I argue that Wagner is *harmful*, but I also argue that there *is* nevertheless someone who can never do without him—the philosopher." Nietzsche, *The Case of Wagner*, in *The Anti-Christ, Ecce Homo, Twilight of the Idols and Other Writings*, ed. A. Ridley, trans. J. Norman (Cambridge: Cambridge University Press, 2005), 233.

27. Kittler, *Discourse Networks*, 193, cited from the biography of Nietzsche written by Kurt Paul Janz.

28. Ibid., 192.

29. Ibid.

30. Lou Salomé, *Nietzsche*, trans. S. Mandel (Urbana and Chicago: University of Illinois Press), 73.

31. Metabolism is a vital part of Nietzsche's rhetoric. Nietzsche was always tracking what nourishes our bodies and phantasms.

32. Laurence A. Rickels, "Friedrich Nichte," in *Looking After Nietzsche* (Albany: State University of New York Press, 1990), 147.

33. See David F. Krell and David Wood, *Exceedingly Nietzsche: Aspects of Contemporary Nietzsche-Interpretation* (London: Routledge, 1988), 59.

34. Salomé, *Nietzsche*, 73; translation modified, my emphasis.

35. By no means does Salomé offer that surface and depth are mere binaries. Like Nietzsche and Freud, Salomé was always aware (at times, even more than her rhetoric) of the dialectical relation between surface and depth that is never mutually exclusive or diametrically opposing.

36. *Nietzsche, A Self-Portrait from His Letters*, ed. P. Fuss and H. Shapiro (Cambridge, MA: Harvard University Press, 1971), 53 (letter 63).

37. Salomé, *Nietzsche*, 73. The German original taken from Lou Andreas Salomé, *Friedrich Nietzsche in Seinen Werken* (Hamburg: Severus Verlag, 2013), 119.

38. Derrida reads this aphorism in the last chapter of *The Politics of Friendship* (London: Verso, 2006).

39. Kittler, *Discourse Networks*, 183.

40. Salomé, *Nietzsche*, 76.

41. Ibid.

42. Ibid., 77.

43. Ibid., 128.

44. Kittler, *Discourse Networks*, 200.

45. Ibid., 196.

46. Ibid., 197, the question is taken from *Ecce Homo*, "Thus spoke Zarathustra," 8.

47. Kittler refers to Schlegel's *On Philosophy* and its address to a passive feminine interlocutor. Ibid., 198.

48. Ibid., 199.

49. Ibid.

50. Ibid., 186.

51. Ibid., 197.

52. Ibid., 204.

13

MEDIA CULTURE

Bildung in the Information Age

Hans-Christian von Herrmann

A short YouTube video entitled "Friedrich Kittler—Abschied von der Sophien-straße" (Friedrich Kittler—Departure from Sophienstraße) shows an impro-vised ten-minute talk given at an event in Berlin in July 2011, which must have been Friedrich Kittler's last public appearance.[1] In spite of the occasion, Kittler is not looking back on the years he spent in the backyard of the building So-phienstraße 22 as professor for the history and aesthetics of media. Instead he is talking about the joy of teaching and the joy of learning, starting with the first line of Sophocles's tragedy *Oedipus the Tyrant*: "Ὦ τέκνα, Κάδμου τοῦ πάλαι νέα τροφή" ("My children, latest generation born from Cadmus").[2] Kittler's mes-sage here is obvious: we as scholars are all children of the Greek alphabet, born from this unique technology which brought together music, mathematics, and poetics in one single coding system. This had been the well-known leitmotif in Kittler's writings since the year 2000 when he made his personal turn, or *Kehre*, to run through the notorious path from Plato to NATO in the opposite direc-tion.[3] But this is not what this essay will address. The issue that I will discuss here is but the simple fact that the pivotal word in Kittler's last public speech is *paideia* (παιδεία), which not only means a transfer of knowledge or a transfer of rules of behavior but also indicates a comprehensive and gathering orientation of all teaching and learning between the generations. No one would argue that what Kittler had in mind was a simple return to the German humanist *Bildung* of the 1800s, although the bias toward ancient Greece is closely related to that concept. What could *paideia* mean in the context of media studies in the sense Kittler had conceived it? In other words, what could *paideia* mean against the backdrop of a digital media culture? Or in what sense is it possible to speak of *Bildung* in the information age?

The following remarks will put Friedrich Kittler in the company of two other scholars: Marshall McLuhan and Jean-François Lyotard. The reason for that is that both of them published books that deal to a large extent with the issue of *paideia* (*Bildung* or education) in response to educational institutions: *Understanding Media: The Extensions of Man* and *La condition postmoderne: Rapport sur le savoir*.[4] As the subtitle indicates, Lyotard presented his essay as a report to the president of the *Conseil de l'université* of the government of Quebec before publishing it. Likewise, McLuhan's study *Understanding Media* is the revised version of a report he wrote for the National Association of Educational Broadcasters in the United States in 1960. In contrast to these two books, Friedrich Kittler's pamphlet and groundbreaking treatise *Discourse Networks 1800/1900*, first published in 1985, was a purely academic project but nevertheless can be read as an examination of the discourse network that constituted the German university since the 1800s and as a polemic proposal for a fundamental reconstruction of this institution.[5]

The issue that McLuhan's *Understanding Media* addressed at the beginning of the 1960s was the painful discrepancy between the everyday culture of electric and electronic media on the one hand and the institutions and routines of a modern educational system totally based on printed knowledge on the other. In his famous 1969 interview in *Playboy* magazine,[6] McLuhan extensively discussed the rupture between the traditional educational system and the new living environment constituted by new media, such as radio and television. For McLuhan, media studies (in the sense of media history and media aesthetics) had the task to make this rupture clearly visible so that new concepts of education could arise. On the one hand, we have the literate culture with its analytical practices of elementary segmentation and visual abstraction, and on the other we have the highly immersive and synesthetic culture of electric and electronic media which is programming and industrializing the human senses. The place where this clash of different media cultures takes place, and becomes so painful, for the first time is in the classrooms of primary schools where children raised in a world of new media are forced by their teachers to enter the Gutenberg galaxy.

PLAYBOY: Might it be possible for the "TV child" to make the adjustment to his educational environment by synthesizing traditional literate-visual forms with the insights of his own electric culture—or must the medium of print be totally unassimilable for him?

MCLUHAN: Such a synthesis is entirely possible, and could create a creative blend of the two cultures—if the educational establishment was aware that there *is* an electric culture. In the absence of such elementary awareness,

I'm afraid that the television child has no future in our schools. You must remember that the TV child has been relentlessly exposed to all the "adult" news of the modern world—war, racial discrimination, rioting, crime, inflation, sexual revolution. The war in Vietnam has written its bloody message on his skin; he has witnessed the assassinations and funerals of the nation's leaders; he's been orbited through the TV screen into the astronaut's dance in space, been inundated by information transmitted via radio, telephone, films, recordings and other people. His parents plopped him down in front of a TV set at the age of two to tranquilize him, and by the time he enters kindergarten, he's clocked as much as 4,000 hours of television. As an IBM executive told me, "My children had lived several lifetimes compared to their grandparents when they began grade one."

PLAYBOY: If you had children young enough to belong to the TV generation, how would you educate them?

MCLUHAN: Certainly not in our current schools, which are intellectual penal institutions. In today's world, to paraphrase Jefferson, the least education is the best education, since very few young minds can survive the intellectual tortures of our educational system. The mosaic image of the TV screen generates a depth-involving *nowness* and simultaneity in the lives of children that makes them scorn the distant visualized goals of traditional education as unreal, irrelevant and puerile. Another basic problem is that in our schools there is simply too much to learn by the traditional analytic methods; this is an age of information overload. The only way to make the schools other than prisons without bars is to start fresh with new techniques and values.[7]

"We don't need no education"—this famous line from Pink Floyd's 1979 album *The Wall* might serve as a short summary of McLuhan's position toward the educational system of his time. It was his ambition as a scholar to generate awareness of the present cultural split, not to abandon literacy but to enable a "creative blend" of the old and the new. The way to get there was the specific form of historic analysis McLuhan developed in his lectures, interviews, and books. It was, as one could say, a transformation of the tools of literary criticism into analytic tools for the aesthetics of new media and the way in which the sensorium of modern man has been shaped by media technologies.

This is exactly the point where Kittler took over when he started to write *Discourse Networks 1800/1900*. Certainly, the theoretical background was different and can be designated by the buzzword "French theory." It was French theory that brought Heidegger and Nietzsche back to Germany after World War II by displacing them in the context of structuralism. But what Kittler found in these texts was also something different. He saw that French theory was at least in part American theory because it had blended linguistic structuralism with game theory, information theory, and cybernetics—all developed in the United States during the 1940s.[8] So the "Austreibung des Geistes aus den Geisteswissenschaften" (the expulsion of spirit from the humanities) that Kittler set on the agenda in 1980 was from the beginning a turn to mathematics and engineering mediated through French structuralism and poststructuralism.[9]

Kittler's writings contain other traces as well that lead back to the history of science and technology of the 1940s. Gottfried Benn, for example, in his story "Der Radardenker" (Radar Thinker) written in 1949 but, similar to the second part of Goethe's *Faust*, published only posthumously, intercepted already the advent of cybernetics as a new science and a new concept of engineering.[10]

> Have you ever realized that virtually everything mankind still thinks today, everything called thought, can already be thought by machines, generated through cybernetics, the new science of creation? And these machines actually outperform human beings, their valves are more precise, their fuses are more robust than in our ruinous wrecks, they rework letters into sound and have memories for eight hours, sick parts are cut out and are replaced by new parts. Thus, thought processes are transferred to robots.[11]

What Benn obviously realizes here in the years after World War II is the emergence of an age where "creation" or *Schöpfung* has become an affair of new sciences and technologies subsumed under the name of cybernetics. This immediately puts an end to Benn's concept of poetry as a spiritual creation by replacing *Geist* with science and machinic processes. In this light, Kittler's *Discourse Networks* is the story of experimental scientists such as Helmholtz and engineers as Edison dethroning poets and philosophers such as Goethe and Hegel at the end of the nineteenth century. One might say the story Kittler is telling leads from literary poetics to technopoetics.

Starting with a reading of Goethe's *Faust* as the tragedy of a new type of scholar devoted not to the Babylonian entanglement of letters but to the unity of a transcendental meaning, part 1 of *Discourse Networks* gives a discourse analysis of the modern German University founded in Berlin by Friedrich Schleiermacher and Wilhelm von Humboldt at the beginning of the nineteenth century. This university had put philosophy with its basic concepts of *Geist* and *Bildung* on top of all academic disciplines. In part 2, the book specifies a new media culture which replaces the academic discourse network of 1800 by a new technical network of data processing. With gramophone, film, and typewriter (which constitute the title of a 1986 book by Kittler[12]) the era of

Geisteswissenschaften comes to an end exactly at that moment in history when their name was coined by Wilhelm Dilthey.[13]

"Media determine our situation, which—in spite or because of it—deserves a description."[14] The first part of this phrase by Kittler is often cited, although only the second part makes the point. "Media determine our situation"—this says more a less the same as "we are living in a technological age"—but the question is, how to describe this fact or destiny. As for McLuhan, for Kittler media studies have never been a simple techno-determinist attitude toward cultural history but an elucidation of a groundbreaking dislocation in the tectonics of knowledge as a whole.

This becomes explicit in a 1993 article Kittler wrote for the journal *Frankfurter Rundschau* entitled "Den Riß zwischen Schreiben und Lesen überwinden" (Overcoming the gap between writing and reading).

> If the humanities arose from an era of perfect literacy, then today they have to react to a situation, which (according to a short formula by Vilém Flusser) is characterized by the exodus of the numbers from the alphabet. So the task is not any more to reduce many books to a homogeneous meaning. First, there are not only books but also technical media, which undermine the traditional concept of *Geist*; second, there are not only natural languages but also formal languages made out of numerical code which repel the traditional concept of understanding. Media cannot be turned into the vehicle of *Geist*, but they can only be used and controlled, and controlling and programming will, despite all rumors, remain a kind of writing for a long time. Mathematical formula can be read and written, but strictly not interpreted. Under these conditions *"Geisteswissenschaften"* which for these reasons should better be called *Kulturwissenschaften* only have the choice to abolish themselves or to change.[15]

It is a fact that the humanities in Germany since then have changed considerably and that Kittler's books and essays were amply used as blueprints for this transformation. *Geisteswissenschaften* have become *Kulturwissenschaften*. And reading does not only mean interpreting of traditional writings anymore but follows the symbolic rules, material practices, and technologies from which different media cultures and cultures of knowledge emerge.

Coming back to McLuhan and his critique of the traditional educational system, it can be said that the Canadian scholar rarely talked about new concepts of education, staying mostly with his historic descriptions in order to make his contemporaries aware of the cultural impact of new technologies. But one of his readers during the 1970s thought he had the right instruments at his disposal to draw the conclusions from McLuhan's media studies and to turn the educational system upside down. I am talking of Alan Kay, the architect of the graphical user interface at Xerox PARC and Apple Incorporated. In a 1984 article published in the *Scientific American* and entitled "Computer Software" he declared: "Any medium powerful enough to extend man's reach is powerful enough to topple his world."[16] The medium Kay was targeting was computer software that, through object-oriented programming, would transform the computer from a calculating machine into a medium or super-medium for all kinds of cultural practices. In a next step, such a concept of software should enable the educational system to pass on from paper-and-pencil literacy to computer literacy. This digital mark-making literacy, according to Kay, "should be attained as early as possible; children should not be made to wait until they can get in a half year of it just before they graduate from high school, as recent reports by educational commissions suggest. Children need informational shoes, bicycles, cars and airplanes from the moment they start to explore the universe of knowledge."[17]

This move from description to designing done by Kay around the year 1980 has obviously proved very successful because we are living today in a world largely built of computer-generated objects or user illusions as Kay says in his article.

In his much-debated 1993 essay "Es gibt keine Software" ("There Is No Software"), Kittler incriminated Kay's strategy as a false abstraction from the concrete hardware of the digital machine and its complexity.[18] What he saw was a misappropriation and economic privatization of a mathematical machine that originally belonged to scientists and not to business companies. His counter-draft can be found in a 2003 essay entitled "Universities: Wet, hard, soft, and harder." It portrays the computer as a new and unifying media system for a university liberated from the submission by the modern national state and returning to its medieval independence.

> Universities have finally succeeded in forming once again a complete media system. Turing's universal machine, vulgo the computer, processes, stores, and transmits whatever data it receives, whether textbooks, measurements, or algebras. Computers, therefore, have come full circle: from the mathematics departments where they once began, making their way through physics, chemistry, and medicine, they have finally arrived in the humanities. For the second time in its eight centuries, the university is technically uniform, simply because all departments share one and the same hardware.[19]

What we find here is the description of a computer or online community which is quite different from the capitalist version of the Internet. It is a social web beyond all commercialized platforms which is used only by scholars, scientists, and engineers—an advanced research project's agency network (or Arpanet) like the one that interconnected American universities and research institutes between 1969 and 1983.

> Actual knowledge needs places to produce, store and transmit itself independently of any company. What better places are there than universities? This applies just as much to digitally processed data as to the digitalized data of history. In the first case, the plans of enormous scientific publishing houses to monopolize academic journals in their hands are probably doomed to failure because Ph.D. advisers, getting at the data much earlier, can publish them digitally. The same holds true for free source code. In the more trivial case of formerly analog data, sounds, and images, their future seems to be up to the gods. Whether or not arts and treasures of bygone cultures can be saved from private digital rights does not seem of primary concern. Whereas in Gutenberg's time the university had to renounce its storage monopoly, its leading role in processing and transmitting now remains as crucial as ever. . . . If envious states succeed in persuading the university in general and cultural studies in particular to think of themselves as a mere compensation and a mere assessment of the consequences of technology, then eight centuries from Bologna to Stanford will have passed in vain. The sciences are too good merely to avert attention from what science does.[20]

"What science does"—this phrase is decisive here and brings us back to the primary question of to what extent Kittler's media studies includes a concept of *Bildung* in the information age. Because science is *doing* something, because it is transforming the world by distinguishing it, because it does not only have a history but *is* "our" history, it can be looked upon as a poetic process. To foster this insight should be the task of media studies which for this reason are the only possible successor on the abandoned throne of philosophy overlooking all departments of the university. Kittler points out that media studies, a field that is but a synonym for the humanities adapted to the information age, can also be called *Wissenswissenschaften*, "knowledge of knowledges."[21]

According to Lyotard's essay *The Postmodern Condition*, two grand narratives legitimized modern knowledge production since the nineteenth century: the French revolutionary narrative of the emancipation of the people by a public educational system and the German ontological narrative of the evolvement of spirit or *Geist* within the history of sciences. The spirit's institutional form is the university, and it is obvious how much Kittler's praise of the digitalized university owes to Humboldt's and Hegel's concept. The retroactive rewriting of the history of knowledge from the vantage point of the information age is a legitimization of the history of science and technology in itself.

But can the university still be this gathering of the entire knowledge? With Lyotard we find a different description of what happens to the university in postmodern times: "The moment knowledge ceases to be an end in itself— the realization of the Idea or the emancipation of men—its transmission is no longer the exclusive responsibility of scholars and students. The notion of 'university franchise' now belongs to a bygone era."[22] What vanishes today, according to Lyotard, is the university as an exclusive community for teaching and learning. It is replaced by a technical system of data processing covering more or less the whole planet.

> The relation to knowledge is not articulated in terms of the realization of the life of the spirit or the emancipation of humanity, but in terms of the users of a complex conceptual and material machinery and those who benefit from its performance capabilities. They have at their disposal no metalanguage or metanarrative in which to formulate the final goal and correct use of that machinery. But they do have brainstorming to improve its performance. . . . [T]he process of delegitimation and the predominance of the performance criterion are sounding the knell of the age of the Professor: a professor is no more competent than memory bank networks in transmitting established knowledge, no more competent than interdisciplinary teams in imagining new moves or new games.[23]

When Kittler spoke about *paideia* in his last public appearance in July 2011, he had only disdain for the new German university with its remodeled programs of study and its default of economic effectiveness when he evoked the community of scholars and students as a mode of existence and as the indispensable core of the humanities. The unfashionable undertone of his concept of media studies could clearly be heard. *Paideia*, or *Bildung*, should not be transferred to the machines, because each scholar, as he said, quoting Nietzsche's *Human, All Too Human*, must become a single regulated engine "heated with illusions, one-sidednesses, passions" and prevented from "overheating" and its "evil and perilous consequences . . . with the aid of the knowledge furnished by science."[24]

When Friedrich Kittler died in October 2011, the headline of his obituary in the newspaper *Die Welt* referred to him as "Der letzte Große aus dem 19. Jahrhundert" (the last great figure from the nineteenth century).[25] It seems it was his commitment to the university of the 1800s that tuned his radar for the end of its legitimacy and for the necessity to reestablish the humanities by referring to the media culture of the twentieth century. Contrary to a widespread criticism, Friedrich Kittler's media studies were not an attempt to proclaim the end of *Bildung* in the information age; they were an attempt to pass it on.

NOTES

1. See "Friedrich Kittler—Abschied von der Sophienstraße," YouTube, www.youtube .com/watch?v=csDCdqU-DGY.

2. Sophocles, *Sophocles*, vol. 1, *Ajax, Electra, Oedipus Tyrannus*, trans. Hugh Lloyd-Jones (Cambridge, MA: Loeb Classical Library, 1994), 326.

3. See Friedrich Kittler, *Musik und Mathematik*, Bd. 1, *Hellas*, Tl. 1, *Aphrodite* (Munich: Wilhelm Fink, 2006), and *Musik und Mathematik*, Bd. 1, *Hellas*, Tl. 2, *Eros* (Munich: Wilhelm Fink, 2009).

4. Marshall McLuhan, *Understanding Media: The Extensions of Man* (New York: McGraw-Hill, 1964); Jean-François Lyotard, *La condition postmoderne: Rapport sur le savoir* (Paris: Minuit, 1979), translated as *The Postmodern Condition: A Report on Knowledge* (Minneapolis: University of Minnesota Press, 1984).

5. Friedrich A. Kittler, *Aufschreibesysteme 1800/1900* (Munich: Wilhelm Fink, 1985), translated as *Discourse Networks 1800/1900* (Stanford, CA: Stanford University Press, 1990).

6. Marshall McLuhan, "Playboy Interview: A Candid Conversation with the High Priest of Popcult and Metaphysician of Media," *Playboy*, March 1969, 53–74, 158.

7. McLuhan, "Playboy Interview," 62–64.

8. See Lydia H. Liu, "The Cybernetic Unconscious: Rethinking Lacan, Poe, and French Theory," *Critical Inquiry*, no. 36 (Winter 2010): 288–320.

9. Friedrich Kittler, ed., *Die Austreibung des Geistes aus den Geisteswissenschaften. Programme des Poststrukturalismus* (Paderborn, Germany: Schöningh, 1980).

10. Gottfried Benn, "Der Radardenker," in *Sämtliche Werke*, vol. 5 (Stuttgart: Klett-Cotta, 1991), 65–79.

11. Benn, "Radardenker," 71; my translation.

12. Friedrich A. Kittler, *Gramophone, Film, Typewriter* (Stanford, CA: Stanford University Press, 1999).

13. See Bernhard Siegert, "Das Leben zählt nicht: Natur- und Geisteswissenschaften bei Wilhem Dilthey aus mediengeschichtlicher Sicht," in *[medien]^i: Dreizehn Vorträge zur Medienkultur*, ed. Claus Pias (Weimar: VDG, 1999): 161–82.

14. Kittler, *Gramophone, Film, Typewriter*, xxxix.

15. Friedrich A. Kittler, "Den Riß zwischen Lesen und Schreiben überwinden: Im Computerzeitalter stehen die Geisteswissenschaften unter Reformdruck," *Frankfurter Rundschau*, January 12, 1993, 16; my translation.

16. Alan Kay, "Computer Software," *Scientific American* 251, no. 3 (1984): 59.

17. Ibid.

18. Friedrich A. Kittler, "There Is No Software," in *The Truth of the Technological World* (Stanford, CA: Stanford University Press, 2014), 219–29.

19. Friedrich Kittler, "Universities: Wet, Hard, Soft, and Harder," *Critical Inquiry* 31, no. 1 (Autumn 2004): 249.

20. Kittler, "Universities," 254.

21. Ibid.

22. Lyotard, *Postmodern Condition*, 50.

23. Ibid., 52–53.

24. Friedrich Nietzsche, *Human, All Too Human: A Book for Free Spirits* (Cambridge: Cambridge University Press, 1996), 119. Cf. Kittler, "Universities," 255.

25. Ulf Poschardt, "Der letzte Große aus dem 19. Jahrhundert: Er lauschte dem Grundrauschen des Geistes: Zum Tode des Berliner Medienwissenschaftlers und Universalgelehrten Friedrich Kittler," *Die Welt*, October 18, 2011, www.welt.de/kultur/literarischewelt/article13667566/Der-letzte-Grosse-aus-dem-19-Jahrhundert.html.

14

RECURSIVE INNOVATION

Geoffrey Winthrop-Young

INCIPIT: STARBURST

The most entertaining of the many recent German introductions to media theory is called *Was mit Medien*.[1] The low-brow title, which literally translates as *Something with media* (a more fitting rendition in slacker argot would be *Like, media and stuff*), is designed to capture the mumbling response of students in media programs when asked what exactly they are studying. In recent years, this sense of bewilderment appears to have progressed from mere confusion to the point at which media and media studies come across as highly questionable, if not downright illusory. To express this state of affairs, some scholars have resorted to the past tense when describing their main discipline object. One of the last lectures by the late Cornelia Vismann was called "Was waren die Staatsmedien?" (What were the state media?), while Claus Pias edited an anthology *Was waren Medien?* (What were media) in which no less than three titles—including his own "Was waren Medien-Wissenschaften?" (What were media studies?)—seem to indicate that media, media studies, and media art are a thing of the past.[2] At the same time there has been an equally revealing sequence of negative propositional statements. First came Friedrich Kittler's "There Is No Software," then Bernhard Siegert's "There Are No Mass Media," and finally Eva Horn's "There Are No Media."[3] For outside observers who view the German media-theoretical scene not without envy, this is strange and scary. In a country in which media studies are more firmly entrenched and enjoy greater financial support than in any other, why this insistence that media and media studies belong to the past? Even worse, why claim they never were?

Leaving aside other, more external reasons the following remarks will focus on the extent to which this erosion of the media concept is rooted in

Kittler's media-theoretical work. We are faced with a quandary: One of the world's leading media theorists wrote about media in such a way that those drawing on his work come to suspect that there are no media, no media theories, and maybe even no media theorists. How are we to make sense of this? Think of Kittler—or rather Kittler's oeuvre—as a star in a strictly astronomical sense: a luminous, energy-rich sphere of fusion and discharge that for a while can maintain a certain stability because its centrifugal forces are opposed by the pull of gravity. As I will outline in the following two sections, the main centrifugal forces are Kittler's refusal to clearly define his key terms and his even more confusing tendency to have the entire theory operate in different registers. The analogue to gravity, in turn, is Kittler's reliance on a certain type of recursive thinking that holds things together because the output of each analytical step is cycled back to act as the input for the next step. Sooner or later, however, this precarious dynamic had to end. Dull satellites last forever, bright stars do not. Yet as in the case of stellar bodies that go supernova, the theory's greatest release of energy came in its demise. As I will argue in the third section, such was the impact of its disintegration that it gave rise to subsequent theories which thrive and shine because they can redeploy the Kittlerian dynamics on a different level. Kittler's algorithms operate long after the programs they were designed for ceased to run.

QUOTED INNOVATION

On a sunny afternoon in early March 2014 the editorial board of Kittler's *Gesammelte Werke: Schriften, Stimmen, Hard- und Software* (Collected works: writings, voices, hard- and software) met a few doors from his former office at Berlin's Humboldt University to discuss the organization of the ten or more volumes dedicated to his over three hundred shorter texts. Kittler himself had requested a thematic arrangement with divisions dedicated to literature, media, philosophy, war, and so on. The board, comprised of several former students and colleagues, agreed to disagree. Many of the papers were too unruly to be confined to one domain; assigning them to any section would violate protocols of editorial neutrality. Instead the papers were to be organized chronologically, a procedure that obeys the rule that the present can and should do no more than provide the future with as impartial an account of the past as possible. Besides, Kittler himself had repeatedly praised the chronological organization of Michel Foucault's *Dits et écrits* because it allowed readers to retrace the twists and turns of Foucault's thinking. One regrettable blemish, however, appeared to be that Kittler's first publication, his printed entry into to the world of academia, was not one of the flamboyant early essays but a five-page review of a minor study of the nineteenth-century writer Wilhelm Raabe—not a very impressive beginning for a multivolume enterprise. Somewhat dispirited, the board looked at the review, only to discover that its first three words, the very first words to be published by Kittler the scholar, amounted to the almost Nietzschean proclamation "incipit nova interpretatio" (A new interpretation begins).[4] For a moment, the ghost of a nicotine-racked Saxon voice trailed through the room: *Warum so überrascht? Das hab' ich doch so geplant*—Why so surprised? I planned it that way.

Interpretatio? There were days when Kittler would have rejected the term. Interpretation was meandering commentary, a nervous hermeneutic tick that compelled readers to discern phantom signifieds behind material signifiers. It was collective domestication, a cultural program designed to discipline reading practices in times when a rapidly growing number of people were threatening to read more and more books in increasingly haphazard ways. Kittler's response was not to throw off the shackles and let readers produce their own reading. Throughout his career he refused to dirty his mind or mouth with talk of reception aesthetics or reader-response theory. Rather, his agenda was to reveal the systematically overlooked extra-textual components that were at work when readers thought they had accessed the innermost meaning of the text. Against interpretation he deployed what he at times called implosion, the act of deciphering the plaintext that underlies, encodes, and regulates the message.[5] This explains why his marked disdain for philosophical and psychological approaches that valorized the self-reflexive capabilities of human consciousness happily coexisted with a preference for texts displaying a high degree of self-reflexivity. His most successful anti-interpretatory implosions— from Hoffmann's *Golden Pot* and Schiller's *Don Carlos* to Pink Floyd's "Brain Damage"—centered on texts and songs that perform their own discursive and medial condition. The medium broadcasts itself, the operation becomes the message.

Kittler's discontent over interpretation was a variant of the rage for relevance also on display in approaches located further to the left. Whether you invoked (Foucauldian) exteriority, (McLuhanesque) mediality, or (Marxist) economics, whether you foregrounded archival regimes that lock in protocols of truth and validity, media-technological infrastructures that inform orders of speech and routines of perception, or dialectical interplays between the conditions of production and the forces of productivity that emit ideological opiates—in each case you were dismissing the customary (bourgeois) blather of interpretation in favor of what is real and counts. Especially in the wild 1980s this attitude could morph into an almost Spenglerian form of engineering worship accompanied by a hearty disdain for all technologically ignorant cultural production. For Kittler—who in *Was mit Medien* is elevated to the lofty status of the "MacGyver of media theory"—matters are clear when technological priorities are clear.[6] The relevance of what you speak is determined by your awareness of the fact that your words are the links of a Lacanian chain of signifiers. The relevance of what you type is determined by your knowledge of what happens between keyboard and screen. The relevance of what you think is determined by your understanding the degree to which you are "subject to gadgets and instruments of mechanical discourse processing."[7] But then again, who knows whether this defiant insight into the mastery imposed on us by exterior systems and hardware did not in fact indicate the real object of desire? Among the most notorious pronouncements of the older Lacan was his rebuke of the student rebels of 1968 that they were looking for a master. One can well imagine the younger Kittler whispering into Lacan's ear: Correction—they are looking for a machine.

And *nova*? How innovative was Kittler? How much of a break does his work represent? In hindsight Kittler's contribution consisted less in providing new critical narratives than in processing old narratives in a new register. Take one major example: One of the most basic structural features of the discourse network 1800, we read, was the exclusion of women. In the new orders of speech, they were either stimulating source or stimulated receiver of aesthetic production, but they were barred from the production itself. The culture of 1800 was a sexually closed circuit in which men as infants, adolescents, writers, civil servants and philosophers processed in ever more complex feedback cycles the "natural" input provided by women. The resulting output was received by girls and women who thereby learned how to be mothers, muses, and occasionally mistresses capable of providing the next round of input. You do not have to be a sociologist to realize that this gender segregation is equally characteristic of the emerging bourgeois nuclear family in which women are confined to the newly fortified private sphere and neither work nor speak in public. Leaving aside the question how historically accurate Kittler's account is, it effectively rewrites middle-class women's exclusion from material production as an exclusion from meaning production.

The refunctionalization of established historiographical narratives does not stop here. For the discourse network 1800 to operate smoothly, language has to undergo a considerable upgrade. For the minimal signifieds emanating from mothers' mouths to make sense to infants' ears—that is, for maternal cooing to successfully inscribe itself into Lacanian *homelettes*—language always already has to be brimming with meaning prior to meaningful articulation. For the content of the message to remain the same regardless of whether it is encoded in air, ink, or lead, language first and foremost has to communicate that its messages remain unaffected by the means of communication. For all of creation to speak meaningfully to sensitized observers, nature must be as subject to verbalization as it is in more contemporary approaches to computation. Among Kittler's most impressive analyses are the inventories of the language acquisition practices, teaching protocols and hermeneutic techniques of the discourse network 1800 that enabled language to function in such a way as to erase the difference between nature and culture, orality and literacy, noise and message. In short, language has to be imbued with divine characteristics of ubiquity and continuity. Divine is the operative word. The plenitude and accessibility of meaning once guaranteed by God is now guaranteed by a spiritualized language. Once nothing in creation was beyond the meaningful intention of the heavenly father; now nothing in communication is beyond the meaningful intention of the almost-as-heavenly mother. The younger Kittler is rewriting in discourse-analytical fashion more conventional historiographies of German literature that depict late eighteenth-century poetry, philosophy, and early psychology as repurposing of religious discourse.[8]

All this is not new, but it is not old either. Nor is it old wine in new bottles, or old bottles filled with new spirits. It is more as if the products of last year's academic harvest were used as this year's fertilizer. Old output is reprocessed as input for a new operation. When Kittler rewrites or recasts established critical narratives, it is not a matter of metaphor, analogy, or transfer but of recursion. And Kittler wouldn't be Kittler if this were not already at work in the initial claim *incipit nova interpretatio*. To begin with, the claim is a quote, complete with inverted commas and page number: "'Incipit nova interpretatio' (7)." Citing an allegedly "disguised" (*verkappt*) claim by Paul Derks, author of the Raabe study under review, of having produced a new interpretation, Kittler goes on to deny that the claim has any validity. This is the earliest instance of Kittler's well-honed bogeyman tactics, for Derks made no such claim. Instead, Derks had used the phrase *incipit nova interpretatio* to defend Raabe scholar Claude David from the claim by yet another scholar that David had said nothing innovative.[9] The young Kittler's first published academic statement amounts to a mise en abyme worthy of seasoned professionals: Scholar A quotes a putative claim by Scholar B only to deny it, though scholar B had in fact applied the quote to Scholar C in order to deny a denial voiced by Scholar D. However, by placing it at the very beginning, Kittler—who as a connoisseur and translator of Derrida was well aware of all the intricacies of citational ambiguity—is both denying and appropriating the quoted claim that was never made. The "disguised" claim of the other turns into a disguised claim for Kittler's own *nova interpretatio*. What is old and new, established and innovative in Kittler must be approached differently: the old has to be disentangled in new ways, the new has to be decoded as a changed return of the old.

AUTOCATALYTIC THEORY CYCLES

Kittler respected his readers enough not to pester them with displays of modesty. On the contrary, he could set the bar of self-comparison pretty high. "When I turned 33, the age of Christ," he recounted a couple of months before his death in an interview with the revealing title "We only have ourselves to draw upon," "I looked at my box of notes and realized how many topics I had assembled that I still wanted to write about. But this life is not long enough."[10] He was an immensely prolific and inquisitive writer, but even if all his projects had come to fruition, even if the entire occidental sweep of *Musik und Mathematik* had been completed, there would still be a skewed relationship between variation and innovation, recursion and rupture. Kittler's work is an intriguing mixture of intimidating breadth of material and a small number of underlying themes. It is both vast and confined; reading it induces a strange mix of agoraphobia and claustrophobia. Or in terms he would have preferred, his oeuvre is composed of an astonishing variety of operations relying on a highly restricted number of algorithms. There is something of Arthur Schopenhauer in him: a precocious child that grew into a conservative rebel very much at odds with his academic surroundings, and who already at a fairly young age hit upon a few grand ideas that he unfolded in ever greater detail over the next decades by drawing on insights and innovations he encountered in domains and disciplines his peers studiously avoided.

Ironically, Kittler's *imitatio Christi* is a case in point, for Jesus at age thirty-three was one of his last objects of investigation. Pink Floyd's *The Final Cut* provided the guiding question: "Tell me true / tell me why / was Jesus crucified?" At first glance Kittler, scion of a Protestant family, provides a distinctly Protestant reading. It wasn't a matter of grace and salvation but of *sola scriptura*. The operative phrase placed under the philological microscope is Matthew 5:18: "For truly, I say to you, until heaven and earth pass away, not an iota, not a dot, will pass from the Law until all is accomplished." "Dot"—also translated as "tittle" or "stroke of the letter"—in Greek is *keraia* ("horns"), which according to Kittler later came to refer to the diacritic signs indicating the vocalic value of words written in the Hebrew consonant alphabet. Jesus, the outsider, is said to be anticipating a reform that was introduced by the Jewish religious establishment generations after his death. In his days, however, he is challenging the monopoly of *hoi grammateis*, the scribes and scholars who were charged with— and made good money from—correctly vocalizing sacred words. This is more than Protestantism, it is Linux. It goes beyond the insistence on *sola scriptura* and raises Jesus above Luther to the level of Thomas Edison, Alan Turing, and Linus Torvalds. Luther, after all, did not introduce a new signifying practice, he merely switched the upper-level vernacular interface. As he was prone to do throughput his career, Kittler evokes and with media-technical expertise reprocesses a basic Lacanian axiom: Jesus is crucified because he threatened to alter established signifying practices and thus modify the moorings that anchor our being. It will be up to St. Paul, the apostle of *pneuma* and vowels, to pick up where Jesus left off. The key Christian doctrine of the eternal resurrection of the flesh after death reprocesses the epochal Greek media-technological innovation that enables us to resurrect the sound of words as they were spoken long after the speakers have died. Only this quasi-eternal stabilization of sound across time allows us to conceive of a Law that does not change letter or stroke even though heaven and earth may pass away.

But how did Kittler get here? The conventional account of his intellectual trajectory is to divide it into three stages: First, the discourse-analytical phase of the 1970s with its Lacanization of Foucault and Foucaultization of Lacan, all of which adds up to a thick layer of poststructuralist topsoil deposited on occasionally revealed Heideggerian base. Then comes the media-theoretical middle phase for which he is most famous. Third, there is the unfinished "Greek" phase with its Innis- or Hegel-sized musings on the recursions into history (including the origins of Christianity) of the alphanumerical Greek vowel alphabet with its self-recursive Holy Trinity of letters, numbers, and tones.[11] The overview is not wrong, but it is of little help unless one adds that these stages recursively feed into another. This is a point as difficult as it is important for understanding Kittler, and it is best approached by taking a closer look at the initially mentioned centripetal and centrifugal forces at the core of his theorizing.

In a recent attempt to initiate Anglophone audiences into the genealogy of so-called German media theory, Bernhard Siegert highlighted the fact that this amorphous body of work had difficulties acquiring a proper name.[12] As in the case of the ominous strangers in Spaghetti Westerns played by Clint Eastwood, no name (and no bullet) ever hit the target. Early candidates such as *Medienanalyse, Literatur- und Medienanalyse* or *Mediendiskursanalyse* did not last long. The preference for *Analyse* (analysis) was a manifest reference to Freud, Foucault, and Lacan; the noticeable absence of *Theorie* (theory) a latent homage to Heidegger. But what was it about this variant of German media theory and its pace-setting Kittlerian current that made it so difficult to grasp—and therefore so easy to dismiss?

The first, obvious response is the vagueness of many of its lead terms. The most notorious example is *war*, but matters are at their most exasperating when we attempt to define the apex term *media*.[13] Kittler, we read, was a media theorist. But what did he mean when he used the word? Was it the same in 1995 as it had been in 1980 or came to be in 2010? It certainly meant more than *mass* media; it appeared to value storage over communication; and it had more to do with inscription than with manipulation. Kittler's dismissal of sociologically and user-oriented inflected definitions of media was never compensated by a satisfactory alternate account of his own. Instead there was a certain McLuhanesque *grandezza*. Regardless of his objections to what he saw as the humanistically entrapped and technologically uninformed anthropocentrism of McLuhan, Kittler was happy to appropriate the latter's generous deployment of the term *media*.[14] He realized that McLuhan possessed in abundance three features indispensable for a new and fruitful engagement with media: a background in philology; a hearty disdain for what most others had accomplished with that background; and an uncanny cultural instinct for what that background should be applied to instead. But like many others who read him with a mixture of admiration and an itch to toss, Kittler concluded that McLuhan lacked the critical depth to fully grasp the importance of what he was hawking. Like James Carey, Mark Poster, Paul Virilio, Vilém Flusser, or Régis Debray, Kittler attempted to return McLuhan's insights back to solid ground by weighing them down with technological, phenomenological, or historical concerns; yet he too was at times overcome by McLuhan's buoyancy and lifted into spheres of apodictic pronouncements teeming with cloudy imprecision.

But the real problem is located on a deeper level. After all, the success of a theory proposal does not depend on the clarity of its key terms. (Critical legend has it that Thomas Kuhn offered no less than twenty-one different definitions of *paradigm* in *The Structure of Scientific Revolutions*, and no Turing machine has yet computed the number of ways *media* is defined in *Understanding Media*.) To draw on Siegert's account, German media theory of the Kittlerian persuasion was engaged in two distinct yet complexly related enterprises. The first was a change of the objects under investigation: "Literature and media analysis replaced the emphasis on authors or styles with a sustained attention to inconspicuous technologies of knowledge (e.g., index cards, writing tools and typewriter), discourse operators (e.g., quotation marks), pedagogical media (e.g., blackboards), unclassifiable media such as phonographs or stamps, musical instruments like the piano, and disciplining techniques (e.g., language acquisition and alphabetization)."[15] This still falls under the McLuhanesque expansion, though with the Foucault-inspired addition of disciplining techniques. However, we must take note of Siegert's emphasis on "inconspicuous" technologies (which include Kittler's ambiguously deployed quotation marks). Ever since McLuhan we know that under our normal narcotic circumstances we realize our media environment as little as a fish realizes the water it swims in. But to pursue this comparison, Siegert is talking less about water than about the small "inconspicuous" elements like individual drops or molecules composed of hydrogen and oxygen that make up water in the first place. And to anticipate the next section, once you have descended to these constituent levels, it makes little sense to go on talking about water.

At the same time the Kittler effect involved addressing how media came to determine cultural constructs such as *Geist, Bildung,* Man, Soul, Truth, Consciousness, and so on. On this level, "the term *media* . . . indicated a change of the frame of reference for the analysis of the phenomena hitherto under the purview of the established humanities."[16] In other words, Kittler pursued a study of media technologies *and* a study of how those media technologies come to determine the guiding concepts behind these studies. Both the objects and the frames of reference for the analysis of the objects change; and the vital crux is that any incisive change of one will lead to a change of the other. Here, then, is the basic algorithm that runs Kittler's theory program: Much like McLuhan, he applied his philological expertise to the study of distinctly nonphilological media objects, yet he also applied the nonphilological expertise he acquired studying these media technologies to the study of imaginary philological discourse constructs. The fabrication of the latter depended on routines of literacy that needed to be viewed from the outside—that is, from the vantage point of a medial other—to be laid bare. This is Kittler's media-theoretical form of *ostranenie* or *Verfremdung,* and it harkens back to McLuhan's fish that only realize their watery medium once they have been thrown ashore.[17] Reduced to its bare skeleton, Kittler's theorizing resembles an autocatalytic loop in which two reactions or operations keep catalyzing each other. Operation 1—the analysis of a hitherto un(der)analyzed media technology—results in media-specific insights which, in turn, serve as a catalyst for operation 2, namely, the analysis of the premises underlying operation 1. The results of operation 2 alter these premises, and these altered premises now guide the next, upgraded installment of operation 1. In short, Kittler's media theory is thus both a theory of media and a theory of mediality, with the two layers constantly feeding back into each other.

While all this makes for ingenuous insights and fascinating reading, it is an analytic procedure with a built-in self-destruct mode. Sooner or later the recursive processes that eroded the surviving phantoms of the discourse network 1800 will start to affect the entities that were instrumentally involved in the erosion—including media. The autocatalytic cycle turns autophagous. The analysis will do unto media what media did unto *Geist, Bildung,* so-called Man, and all the other usual humanist suspects. But how did this work out in the real world of theory?

Every good theorist has a Prospero moment. In Kittler's case it occurs in a frequently quoted passage at the beginning of *Gramophone, Film, Typewriter*: "[O]nce formerly distinct data flows [are turned] into standardized series of digitized numbers, any medium can be translated into any other. With numbers, everything goes. Modulation, transformation, synchronization; delay, storage, transportation; scrambling, scanning, mapping—a total media link on a digital base will erase the very concept of medium. Instead of wiring people and technologies, absolute knowledge will run as an endless loop."[18] Just as the great magician reveals that his audience has been watching an insubstantial pageant, the great media theorist announces that there is no basis for a substantial distinction between media. The next step is close enough to foresee. Future generations will view the erasure of intermedial distinctions as a prelude to the erosion of the distinction between media and environment. "I very much doubt," William Gibson noted, "that our grandchildren will understand the distinction between that which is a computer and that which isn't."[19] Their grandchildren, in turn, may have difficulties understanding the difference between their body and its ubiquitous computing environment. To be clear on this, Kittler is not claiming that there are no media anymore. Rather, their digital demotion renders the concept questionable. Like impoverished aristocrats reduced to work as tourist guides on their former estates, media have been moved to the boundaries of the grand computing machine, where they now function as subaltern interfaces between it and us. Their helpful sounds and images are concessions to our subdigital processing capabilities.

The main difference between Prospero and Kittler, however, is that Prospero had the decency to wait until Act IV before debunking his own show. Kittler, however, published his obituary of analog media in 1986. In terms of the history of technology, that is quite late: It is fifty years after Turing provided the blueprint for a machine to simulate and marginalize all other machines, and forty years after Bell Labs provided the hardware (Shockley) as well as the mathematical theory (Shannon) that helped put Turing's mechanical reverie into wide-spread practice. Paradoxically, the acknowledgment of a medium that terminates all media distinctions stood at the beginning of a theory onslaught that foregrounded these distinctions. Yet once we consider the history of theory rather than that of technology, Kittler's statement becomes a great deal more intriguing because the recognition of the collapse of plural media into a universal *über*-medium preceded the flowering of media-theoretical production that vigorously emphasized media specificities and intermedial differences. But maybe it is less of a paradox than an understandable apotropaic gesture. It is frequently argued that the rise and institutionalization of media theory worldwide was caused by the spread of the personal computer and its colonization of our life world. Maybe theories such as those by Kittler, McLuhan, and Flusser are in part acts of resistance: Just as ideologies of individualism flourish most in times of increasing social standardization, theories of medial distinction thrive in the face of digital standardization.

This somewhat counterintuitive relationship between media theory and practice not only draws attention to the external factors involved in the rise of post-Kittlerian media theory, it also points to an intriguing symmetry between the insistence on intermediality in the face of the erasure "of the very concept of medium" and the intramedial erosion of that concept hinted at in the preceding section. The term *intramediality* refers, first, to the fact that in the course of their historical careers "media" (it is starting to become necessary to place this term in quotation marks) can be used in very different ways. This is old news to media historians as well as to media activists keen on refunctionalizing existing medial infrastructures. Especially in their early phase, the initial trial-and-error period of competing performances, media are characterized by a wide amplitude of functions and contexts. If, for example, you had told Johannes Gutenberg that his printing press heralded a new age of market-driven dissemination of typographic reproduction, he would have protested that its intended function was to ensure calligraphic standardization prompted by increasingly sloppy manuscript production in overworked lay and monastic scriptoria. Before long, however, certain functions and contexts are locked in and subsequently appear to be logical, if not "natural" to the technology. Intramediality, then, stresses the contingencies of media history; it denies hard functionalism, that is, the perception that a given media technology is always already designed and put to use for a specific function, even worse, that it is a priori tied to an equally specific mindset.

In view of the theory loops sketched above, intramediality takes on a second, more deconstructive meaning. For all its emphasis on contingent multifunctionality the first meaning still presupposes the notion of a fully realized, stable media technology that can migrate between established contexts. But in its second meaning, intramediality refers to the acts, events, operations, tools, and protocols from which these media and their corresponding functions and contexts emerge in the first place. In a short paper that should be required reading for students doing "something with media," Joseph Vogl shows how much had to come together for Galileo's telescope to *become* a medium: a particular lens-grinding technology; the combination of two lenses to produce an enlargement effect; the Copernican hypothesis; an improved way of representing results that always involved acts of self-observation; the typographic dissemination of observation results; economic pressures for earthly employments, and so on.[20] Using this scenario as a case in point, Vogl argues that "the history and theory of media must address the singular scenes or situations where media (more strictly: the functions and functioning of media) *come into existence in a coming together of heterogeneous elements*—apparatuses, codes, symbolic systems, forms of knowledge, specific practices, and aesthetic experiences."[21]

In other words, media are an emergent property of the interaction of elements and events that conceptually and chronologically precede media as well as whatever media are said to store, represent, and communicate. Within the German context, the concept that best captures this move toward the intramedial deconstruction of media is cultural techniques. In the days "after Kittler," cultural techniques—a term with a venerable ancestry that reaches back into the late nineteenth century—refer to chains of ontic operations from which ontological domains and constructs arise which are then, in an inevitable exercise of metaphysical retrofitting, said to be the basis of these very operations.[22]

> Every culture begins with the introduction of distinctions: inside/outside, pure/impure, sacred/profane, female/male, human/animal, speech/absence of speech, signal/noise, and so on. The chains that make up these distinctions are recursive, that is, any given distinction may be reentered on either side of the distinction. Thus, the inside/outside distinction can be introduced on the animal side of the human/animal distinction in order to produce the distinction between domestic and wild animals. . . . However, it is crucial to keep in mind that the distinctions in question are processed by media in the broadest sense of the word . . . which therefore cannot be restricted to one or the other side of the distinction. Rather, they assume the position of the mediating third.[23]

We can pinpoint how this approach reacts to Kittler. On the one hand, theorists such as Siegert continue and expand Kittler's point, which was at the core of his antihermeneutic crusade, that media constitute an interim domain, "an abyss of non-meaning that must remain hidden."[24] Media install and operate the noise/signal distinction, but they are neither part of the meaning nor of the meaningless. Instead, their operations allow for this distinction to arise in the first place. On the other hand, Kittler's artifactualism, his polemical deployment of media and penchant for attributing to them an overly determining status in cultural and literary and analyses, served to imbue media with an ontological weight that moved them from their interim or third position into an ontologically weighted counterposition and thus, potentially, into the lofty delusions of imaginary ontologies.

Media was the center from which Kittler had launched his forays against man and meaning, but that center can no longer hold and things of theory fall apart. Therefore, to speak of media in the past tense or to assert that there are no media makes a lot of sense: Media and media theory are so much a thing of the past that it becomes questionable whether they ever really were at all. This is more than readjustment, it is theory admitting the fickle status of its core concept. "Media theory might thus axiomatically claim that no such thing as a medium exists, at least not in a stable generic, disciplinary, substantial, or historical sense."[25] The Deleuzian emphasis on "becoming-media" (Vogl) is at the same time an undoing of media. In the work of those who know his work well there is a discernible tendency to use Kittler's antiontological algorithm against Kittler himself—but this move was programmed by him. If you look under the hood of technologies long enough you will end up under the hood of the concepts tied to these technologies.

EXIT: MAN TO ARCHIVE

What I keep dreaming of and what people don't like to hear . . . is the machines, especially contemporary intelligent machines as conceived by Turing in 1936, are not there for us humans—we are, as it were, built on too large a scale—but that nature, this glowing, cognitive part of nature, is feeding itself back into itself.[26]

The great irony (and epiphany) is that Kittler, the smasher of subjects who discarded humans as outdated carbon platforms in the grand self-processing of silicon nature, produced such an intensely personal work. So personal, in fact, that he, the fervent antihumanist, often sounds all too human, whereas the well-meaning humanists who decry his alleged techno-determinism tend to sound like all-too-predictable trivial machines. In many instances, you need to know the man to understand where his words are coming from and headed to. This applies especially to his later writings: the more rhapsodic sections of *Musik und Mathematik* are probably only intelligible to those familiar with the ups and downs of Kittler's love life. Yet *personal* is a misleading word, *experiential* (though still misleading) comes closer. What ultimately links Kittler to Heidegger is not that he "simply" transferred the latter's theory of technology to media. Nor is it his techno-mathematical "update" of Heideggerian *Seinsgeschichte* or history of being. It is the fact that Kittler's thinking, too, has its roots in *Stimmungen*, in moods or attunements linked to certain—in his case, technologically facilitated—entanglements with being. But while Heidegger favored the revelatory potential of fear and boredom, Kittler went for harder experiential currency: shocks, inscriptions, intoxications, raptures. They provide the first, autobiographical input for the many autocatalytic loops to follow. His intellectual journey—from discourse analysis to media theory and on to his own brand of cultural techniques, from Foucault and Lacan to McLuhan, from Turing and Shannon to Heidegger, who was always already there in the beginning—is a sequence of recursive self-processing in the course of which the self is dispersed in the many archives that condition the ways in which it conducts its self-processing. At the beginning was the left-handed boy who developed a skewed relationship to his own graphic performances because he did not draw and write like others; then came the lyrically active teenager who rediscovered and reprocessed poetry when he started using his parent's typewriter before he graduated to more sophisticated hardware and became the first professor of German to teach computer programming. And to extend the Gibson quote in truly posthumanist fashion: Maybe future generations working through the boxes of papers, tapes, circuit boards, and programs he left to the Marbach Literary Archives will have difficulties distinguishing between Kittler the man and Kittler the archive.

The Kittler I knew was the Wagner junkie and Pink Floyd aficionado who, not without a streak of Puritanism, was prone to grant himself musical (and other) intoxications under the condition that they were subsequently analyzed and reconstructed: "In the case of my generation, whose ears were full of Hendrix crashes and Pink Floyd and who were overwhelmed and completely awed, I tried to move back from these blissful shocks in such a way as at least to be able to build technical apparatuses according to plan that were themselves capable of performing these feats. That, after all, is the only way one can deal with art."[27] In the end that part of Kittler which looked and thought much like Heidegger came back to a different beginning by presenting Odysseus's encounter with the Sirens as the ur-scene of all bewitchment by storage technology. Subsequently, what was once called media history turns into a millennia-spanning set of recursions "where the same issue is taken up and again at regular intervals but with different connotations and results."[28] Each fascination is the input for a new round of analysis on a different level. That, after all, is how you deal with shocks, art and, finally, your own life. By processing your archives, you become an archive for others. No wonder, then, that the inscription surface called Kittler becomes one of the prime exhibits of Kittler's media theory. Ultimately, we only have ourselves to draw upon to trace how things—orders of speech, institutions, media, wars, and gods—have drawn us. This must be done by fixing dates and names and looking under the hood of operations and techniques in a cold, factual way deprived of interpretative reveries of a fixed self. As Winston Churchill, another noted self-processor and auto-archivist, proclaimed, "facts are better than dreams."[29] True enough, but what you learned from Kittler was that it takes a lot of dreaming to reach the point at which facts win out. And once they have scored their victory they program new dreams. Dreams—including those sung by Pink Floyd and analyzed by Kittler—are technical facts' finest hour.

NOTES

1. Nele Heinevetter and Nadine Sanchez, *Was mit Medien: Theorie in 15 Sachgeschichten* (Munich: Fink, 2008).

2. See Claus Pias, "Was waren Medien-Wissenschaften? Stichworte zu einer Standortbestimmung," in *Was waren Medien?*, ed. Claus Pias (Zurich: Diaphanes, 2011), 7–30. See also, in ibid., Dieter Daniels, "Was war die Medienkunst? Ein Resümee und ein Ausblick," 57–80, and Lorenz Engell, "Medien waren: möglich. Eine Polemik," 103–28.

3. Friedrich Kittler, "There Is No Software," in Kittler, *Literature, Media, Information Systems*, ed. John Johnston (Amsterdam: OAP, 1997), 147–55; Bernhard Siegert, "There Are No Mass Media," in *Mapping Benjamin: The Work of Art in the Digital Age*, ed. Hans Ulrich Gumbrecht and Michael Marrinan (Stanford, CA: Stanford University Press, 2003), 30–38; and Eva Horn, "Editor's Introduction: 'There Are No Media,'" *Grey Room*, no. 29 (2007): 7–13.

4. Friedrich Kittler, review of Paul Derks, *Raabe-Studien. Beiträge zur Anwendung psychoanalytischer Interpretationsmodelle: "Stopfkuchen" und "Das Odfeld,"* Jahrbuch der Raabe-Gesellschaft (Bonn, Germany: Bouvier, 1976), 176.

5. On Kittler's use of implosion, see Geoffrey Winthrop-Young, "Implosion and Intoxication: Kittler, a German Classic, and Pink Floyd," *Theory, Culture and Society* 23, nos. 7–8 (2006): 75–91.

6. Heinevetter and Sanchez, *Was mit Medien*, 52.

7. Kittler, *Literature, Media, Information Systems*, 84.

8. See also Geoffrey Winthrop-Young, *Kittler and the Media* (Cambridge, UK: Polity, 2011), 46–51.

9. See Derks, *Raabe-Studien*, 7; Hans-Jürgen Schrader, "Zur Vergegenwärtigung und Interpretation der Geschichte bei Raabe," in *Jahrbuch der Raabe-Gesellschaft* (1973), 49n166 and 51n176; and Claude David, "Über Wilhelm Raabes *Stopfkuchen*," in *Lebendige Form: Interpretationen zur deutschen Literatur*, ed. Jeffrey L. Sammons and Ernst Schürer (Munich: Fink, 1970), 259–75.

10. "We only have ourselves to draw upon. An interview with German media theorist Fredrich Kittler by Andras Rosenfelder," Signandsight.com, October 25, 2011, accessed August 10, 2014, www.signandsight.com/features/2190.html.

11. On Kittler's appraisal of the multifunctional Greek vowel alphabet, see Winthrop-Young, *Kittler and the Media*, 87–96.

12. Bernhard Siegert, "Cultural Techniques: Or the End of the Intellectual Postwar in German Media Theory," *Theory, Culture and Society* 30, no. 6 (2013): 49.

13. On the triple-M approach to Kittler's war (war as motor, model, and motive), see Winthrop-Young, *Kittler and the Media*, 129–42. For Kittler's portrayal of World War II in particular, see Winthrop-Young, *"De Bellis Germanicis*: Kittler, the Third Reich and the German Wars," *Cultural Politics* 11, no, 3 (2015): 361–75.

14. See Friedrich Kittler and Christoph Weinberger, "The Cold Model of Structure," *Cultural Politics* 8, no. 3 (2012): 383: "Initially, I simply took the concept [of media] from McLuhan's *Understanding Media*."

15. Siegert, "Cultural Techniques," 50.

16. Ibid., 49–50.

17. On Kittler and *ostranenie*/defamiliarization, see Geoffrey Winthrop-Young and Annie van den Oever, "Rethinking the Materiality of Technical Media: Friedrich Kittler, *Enfant Terrible* with a Rejuvenating Effect on the Parental Discipline," in *Techné/Technology: Researching Cinema and Media Technologies—Their Development, Use, and Impact*, ed. Annie van den Oever (Amsterdam: Amsterdam University Press, 2014), 234–39.

18. Friedrich Kittler, *Gramophone, Film, Typewriter*, trans. and introduced by Geoffrey Winthrop-Young and Michael Wutz (Stanford, CA: Stanford University Press, 1999), 1–2.

19. William Gibson, *Distrust That Particular Flavor* (New York: G. Putnam, 2012), 215.

20. Joseph Vogl, "Becoming-media: Galileo's Telescope," *Grey Room*, no. 29 (2007): 15–25.

21. Vogl, "Becoming-media," 16; my emphasis.

22. On the evolution of the concept of cultural techniques "after Kittler," see Bernard Dionysius Geoghegan, "After Kittler: On the Cultural Techniques of Recent German Media Theory," *Theory, Culture and Society* 30, no. 6 (2013): 66–82; Geoffrey Winthrop-Young, "Cultural Techniques: Preliminary Observations," *Theory, Culture and Society* 30, no. 6 (2013): 3–19; and Winthrop-Young, "The *Kultur* of Cultural Techniques: Conceptual Inertia and the Parasitic Materialities of Ontologization," *Cultural Politics* 10, no. 3 (2014): 376–88.

23. Siegert, "Cultural Techniques," 61.

24. Ibid., 52.

25. Vogl, "Becoming-media," 15.

26. Friedrich Kittler, *Short Cuts* (Frankfurt am Main: Zweitausendundeins, 2003), 270.

27. Friedrich Kittler and Rudolf Maresch, "Wenn die Freiheit wirklich existiert, dann soll sie doch ausbrechen," in *Am Ende vorbei*, ed. Rudolf Maresch (Vienna: Turia and Kant, 1994), 107.

28. John Armitage, "From Discourse Networks to Cultural Mathematics: An Interview with Friedrich A. Kittler," *Theory, Culture and Society* 23, nos. 7–8 (2006): 33. For a more detailed discussion of Kittler's use of recursion, see Geoffrey Winthrop-Young, "Siren Recursions," in *Kittler Now: Current Perspectives in Kittler Studies*, ed. Stephen Sale and Laura Salisbury (Cambridge, UK: Polity, 2015), 71–94.

29. Winston S. Churchill, *The Second World War*, vol. 1, *The Gathering Storm* (London: Cassell, 1948), 527.

15

KITTLER ON MUSIC

Ute Holl

> But still
> The wave which
> drowned me
> is roaring in my ear and I am dreaming
> of the seabed's magnificent pearl.
> —Friedrich Hölderlin, "Der Rein"[1]

Media theory is characterized by the intimate relationship it entertains to the unknown, the concealed, the unconscious, or, simply, to zero. It is from the operations of blank spaces or intervals that media produce their effects. In many of his studies on sound, Friedrich Kittler had marked this as a ratio of signal and noise. Historically, this differential relationship is unstable, but it is constitutive for the respective production of meaning in music. In his last books on mathematics and music, however, Kittler dissolves this singular and Gestalt-inspired difference of signal and noise into incalculably many relations of sound elements as they are produced with mathematical means. Instead of a clear edge, Kittler discovers iterated and reiterated acoustical transformations, which he describes as an accessible ocean of sound. Thus, these books on music consider the fusion of both, the known and the unknown, the concealed and the unconcealed, as an immersion into Homer's mathesis, thinking in numbers, which concerns music as well as language, or love in the full extension of the term.

Supposing a tiger's leap through the ages, Kittler conceives of a return of Pythagorean universal relations of numbers in the alphanumeric logics of Turing's universal machine—or vice versa: the computer going Aeolian. In a full circle of perceptive modes between digitally configured waveforms and Sappho's lyre songs, between now and antiquity, Kittler, writing on music, simultaneously experiments with poetological and poetic forms of writing himself.

His argument on music is carried, and sometimes carried off, in the musical use of vowels, precisely syncopated by consonants, word wraps, or page breaks. In Kittler's diagnosis of the discourse network of 1900, vowels, which Hermann von Helmholtz had described as effects of physiologically produced overtones, had proved to be permutable, as any typewriter-driven letter. Thus, they could program the reader's speech physiologically, to sound out sense or nonsense, as Christian Morgenstern had demonstrated in *The Great Lalula*, chopping up language into sound and rhythm, composing text beyond hermeneutics.[2] In this, Morgenstern's poetry is contemporary to the operations of a gramophone, film, and a typewriter, performing the real, the imaginary as well as the symbolic aspects of language while largely ignoring any production of sense. Vowels and consonants operate structurally as relays of mutual distinctions. While marking the invention of the Greek vowel alphabet as the beginning of European thinking, Kittler's books on music and mathematics are composed as eulogies of vowels, switching focus from difference to presence, from a consonant's distinctions to a vowel's flow. Against all odds and semiotics of zero, against the drive of counting and the logics of signifiers, here, the vowels *A*, *E*, *I*, *O*, and *U* defy the great old Lalula of nonsense that had characterized the discourse network of 1900. Vowels in the books on music and mathematics operate independently instead of forming structural differences. Thus, these books on music turn into songbooks. They are carried away by a double entendre, strict analysis being superimposed by sounds of language as a musical machine.

What's more, the A and O and the I and U address and produce a secret *Du* of the text, an unknown listener, a lost lover or muse, shifting what is left of a reader between the logics of the visual and the aural, the eyes and the ears. Then again, this *Du* or You or U of the text obviously shares similar memories with the I. Some of these memories can be traced back to bibliographic annotations at the end of the book: haven't we all read the same things? Others again, are evoked by sounds of music and lyrics. Haven't we all listened to the same records and tapes? And some insinuate secrets, that we all are assumed to share. Readers that resist this production of singularity as communal sense perception, will, as any readers of lyrics, turn into observers and simply drop out. While Kittler's books on music and mathematics celebrate the vowel alphabet as the beginning of a European civilization, they simultaneously present it as a prehistory of a coming society which might be called ontologically saturated: the coming of the gods.[3] Therefore, the You of the books might just as well be a goddess or what the love of knowledge holds to be a deity. In shock and awe over those books on music and mathematics, friends and enemies alike diagnosed an ontological turn in Kittler's thinking. But this might just as well have been an ontological turn in understanding Kittler.

However, while obviously enforcing Graecophilia, Kittler's final texts and tapes do not differ from earlier studies on music in that they provoke a constant short-circuiting of sound and signal, technology and physis, effects of technical media and the materiality of speech. Channel noises of academic studies are short-circuited with signals to those readers who are familiar with orders of the discourse. Kittler's writings on music are writings on bodies in the presence of acoustic waves. His texts literally address the same physicalities that they are simultaneously producing with acoustical, harmonic, and rhythmical effects of language and speech. *On music* then, as referred to in the title, can be understood as in *de musica*, contemplating music. Or it can be understood as empowered by music, as in *on drugs*. Kittler's Turing-aged version of ontology is an intentional confusion of media effects.

CONFUSED PERCEPTIONS

In his studies on sound and music, Kittler has examined the histories of tuning, instrumentation and technical recording systems as well as their forms of transmission and distribution. In the context of music, he has reconstructed a history of mathematical reasoning and its implementation into technical devices as well as into physical bodies. Kittler's sound studies examine historical refigurations of senses in changing media systems and sound concepts. In his studies of ancient and modern forms of music, Kittler observes the grades to which *techne* and *episteme*, roughly translatable as art and knowledge, fuse: if both are joined in poetic thinking and technical performance, they will evoke new and unexpected forms of experience.

Probably the most important contribution to musicology and sound studies is Kittler's meticulous reconstruction of the history of calculating, analyzing, and synthesizing frequencies from early modern age to analogue and digital sound systems. In the experiments of Simon Stevin and Marin Mersenne and in the work of Andreas Werckmeister, Kittler has reconstructed an early history of frequency's logics as prehistory of nineteenth-century laboratory experiments. His texts give an account of how the results and achievements of these laboratories eventually shape the sound systems which produce twentieth-century listening cultures. Kittler has repeatedly discussed the works of Joseph Sauveur, who demonstrated that overtones are multiples of the tonic key's vibrations, calling them harmonics, and d'Alembert, who solved the mathematical equation required. Kittler traced the connections of those scientists to Gottfried Wilhelm Leibniz who first conceived of vibrations as waves, as well as to Leonhard Euler who introduced the notion of frequency as waves in time. And he had reminded modern musicology that it was Daniel Bernoulli who had explained all musical vibrations as basically sinus waves, their overtone structures forming what is conceived of as tone colors. Thus Kittler had always linked music and mathematics.

The extended artisan's history of music which Kittler kept reconstructing is not one of inventive geniuses but evidence for the fact that there is no theory of music unless it is actually practiced in producing a sonic world. Playing, composing, and constructing instruments, listening to structures of counterpoint and experimenting with new sounds has been one and the same in all real musical procedures. Musicians according to Kittlerian media theory, have always been scientists and artisans, and implicitly, good scientists need to be at least amateur musicians. In music-making and in listening, as well as in inventing techniques for tuning and tempering, *techne* and *episteme* necessarily fuse. Also, with music-related cultural techniques, new distinctions turn up or conflate. In the face of oscillating membranes, the distinction between inside and outside of literary men needs to be reconsidered, and what has only metaphorically been referred to as the oceanic in psychoanalysis turns into a real art of moving among waves. It is here that Kittler relates to Leibniz, who first connected the sonic experience to the sound of the sea: "It is like what happens when I walk along the seashore: in hearing the roar of the sea, I hear—though without distinguishing them—the individual noises of the waves out of which that total noise is made up. Similarly, our confused perceptions are the outcome of the infinity of impressions that the whole universe makes on us."[4] Noise is the channel that relates us to divinity. And confusion is the precondition of precise and precisely human perception. The oceanic turns into a general theory and practice of confusing boundaries, in Kittler's writings explicitly in the name of love and Aphrodite.[5]

Another protagonist in Kittler's universe of wave-manipulating musicians is Jimi Hendrix, whose piece "1983 (A Merman I Should Turn to Be)" also evokes the idea of immersion into the waves, here including the grading of color, "the arctic stains from silver blue to bloody red, as our feet find the sand, and the sea is straight ahead." This merman's flight is escaping the noise of war into the sounds of the sea. However, Kittler was certainly not up to turning into a merman. And especially around 1983 he would never have traded his two legs or feet for a tail fin. The power of music, poetry, love, and dancing as well as of thinking at large depended, as Kittler has frequently shown with Friedrich Nietzsche, on the incorporation of language as metrical feet, *Versfuss*. Kittler had identified Nietzsche as a contemporary not only of Wagner but also of Helmholtz, of psychophysical laboratories. Nietzsche was the antidote of Helmholtzian *Reichsanstalten*, standardizing psychophysical transferences. Nietzsche's dictum that "aesthetics is nothing more than applied physiology"[6]—a matter of breathing, heartbeat, bloodstream, and eventually of moving, dancing, or marching, whether electrically engendered or not—is exposed as the birth or birthmark of media-theory.[7] Perceiving, *aisthesis*, is a physical matter, as in Greek *physis* or as in nineteenth-century psychophysiology out of the laboratories from Leipzig to Paris. Kittler had explored these laboratories in their technical devices and theoretical formations, hardware and software, in order to study their implementation into humans and humanities, and eventually to drive the "Geist" out of "Geisteswissenschaften." Demonstrating rhythms of speech in stepping up and down Albert-Ludwig's seminar rooms, Kittler's own body turned into a site for musical possessions, materializing the force of media through epochs of literature, from Lohenstein to Morgenstern. In rapping out what was to become the meshes of discourse network's analysis, his lectures on sound and music gathered activists of the local pirate radio stations as well as students of literature, who left their discipline in droves and disbelief to turn into media students, clueless yet of what the new theory was about. They were, however, turned on by some big beat that connected philology to electric sounds—as well as to the darkest sides of German history.

Kittler's studies on music, following Leibniz, Nietzsche, as well as Heidegger and Hendrix, conceived of musically possessed bodies not only as physiological phenomena but also as manifestations of truth. *Soundgeschichte*, "history of sound," in this sense, becomes *Seinsgeschichte*, the discovery of historical moments when poetic speech discloses the factual. In his studies on music in modernity, Kittler had analyzed instrumentation, laboratory gear, or studio technology in order to rematerialize effects that had always been attributed to the divine. Already aesthetically then, polytheism was to be favored over monotheism.

Kittler's investigations on music and mathematics in Greek antiquity reject an approach that simply demands to study the materiality of media. In *Musik und Mathematik* he invokes a basically mathematical toy, the universal model of the *tetraktys*, ten tangible elements, organized in four rows of one, two, three, and four. The order of the *tetraktys* organizes numbers as well as material objects like stones on a beach, it produces a musical order of 1:2 as octave, 2:3 as fifth, and 3:4 as perfect fourth, available as strings on a monochord or lyre. The order of the *tetraktys* describes sounds as well as cosmological harmonies and even gender relations, as Kittler demonstrates in his chapter "Im Liebesspiel," which advocates heterosexual intercourse, even if including divine participants.[8] While the Greek model of *tetraktys* refers to four rows only, the machine is potentially infinite, as Pascal would prove centuries later. It can produce potentially infinite relations. Thus, as an epistemological machine, it can visualize the transition from intervals of integers to the logics of frequencies and harmonics in music, and it demonstrates how a decimal code can construct all sorts of micro-relations and realities. In the *tetraktys*, these relations seem ontologically ordered and simplified—mathematically, musically, gender-wise, and cosmologically. However, it is not the material elements that matter but the relations in between, the intervals, the order of the blanks, which produce the universal order. All relationships are characterized by the intimacy they entertain to the unknown, the concealed, or the unconscious. In pre-Socratic Greece, the gods entered the stage of media thinking exactly through relations imperceptibly implemented in the code.

As generations of philologists before him, Kittler had conceived of gods as events of understanding or—as Roberto Calasso quoting Karl Kerényi—as the "happening of unveiling knowledge."[9] The order of things appears but suddenly: *jäh!* Following system's theory, the presence of a god could be considered as an "Aha!" moment, indecently extended in duration.[10] A scholar of Romance languages, Kittler clearly follows a tradition from Lautréamont to Mallarmé and Baudelaire, who had, as Calasso reminds us, addressed the occurrence of the unlikely as god, particularly on occasions of love. According to Kerényi, *theoria*, "seeing as the gods do", is a feast of truth's occurrence, simultaneously marking the boundaries of human knowledge.[11] Divine *theoria* complements human understanding in referring to the unknown or unconscious implied. In the acoustic realm of music, the unknown had been included in the structure of intervals, of octave, fifth, and fourth. This changed with Leibniz, who conceived of a divine force as analyzing and then synthesizing sounds as infinite summation of sinus waves: a divine Fourier-analyzer, avant la letter, as creator of worlds. Mermaids and mermen, as Hendrix observes, can leave the world polluted by "killing noise" to live and breathe among electric waves. Only humans are bound to perceive the order of things in a constitutive state of confusion—or, on music. Theoretically, it does make a difference whether one considers oneself human, god, or merman. Media theorists however tend to waver here. Nietzsche, in a famous note to Jakob Burckhardt, remarked that he would rather have been a professor in Basel than god in charge of creating a world. Kittler, in claiming that "we are mortal in the realm of time, while immortal in the field of frequency, in the field of Fourier,"[12] can absolutely be suspected of merman-ship, and actually long before the epistemic odyssey of his last books on music and mathematics in Greece.

CONTROL ROOMS

Georg Friedrich Wilhelm Hegel in his lectures on aesthetics conceives of music as elemental power—even force (*Gewalt*)—that seizes the subject involuntarily.[13] In a laudatory speech held in honor of Brian Eno in Berlin in 1998, Kittler, quoting Hegel, refers to music as something that mounts the body, taking possession of the legs, submitting the subject to artificial temporal orders, rather in terms of the Voudoun and its children than in terms of a philosophy of mind.[14] According to Hegel, music is the Self in time, and time is the being of the subject itself: *"die Zeit ist das Sein des Subjekts selber."*[15] Elegantly avoiding to talk on Being and Time, Kittler continues his laudation as a frontal attack on Brian Eno, whose studios were notoriously called control rooms. He politely informs the artist— who was envied for disposing over thirty-one tape-recorders in his studio—that his devices were straight out of the hell of German Intelligence (*Nachrichtendienst*). Connecting Eno to the unconscious of his technical toys, Kittler lets him know that they were designed to survey and intercept secret communication and the movement of submarines—to simulate sounds as if in the presence of bodies, to hide human voices in the noise of transference by scrambling, slicing, and mixing material according to frequency ranges—and that they had been used in Gestapo torture chambers.[16] In this lecture, Kittler's ambivalence over the effects of acoustic electronic media becomes obvious: they promise a liberation of the linear and literal age of Gutenberg, while they are, at the same time, borne out of war zones. Beyond any Hegelian dialectic, Kittler in his laudation draws the full circle of music as mathematics from Pythagoras's secret confederation to ambient music, stating that in the ages between these two events, music had just existed as paper work, an extended arm of some administrators of the ears. Like a meteorite, he claims, Pythagoras's art of sounds had hit the presence of digital composing: "Only the digital computer offers a language for sound which is able to capture all its fractal dimensions, analytically as well as synthetically, elementary and constructive."[17] Still, it is not altogether clear whether that meteorite had actually hit Eno. Black music and Afro-American jazz are credited for having been able to take advantage of the whole range of sounds possible in historical electronic media. They were the first—after Greek antiquity—to rely on the instrumental and technical production of sounds while ignoring the detour of written scores. Apart from a slightly ethnocentric undertone, this might also have offended Brian Peter George St. John Baptiste de la Salle Eno, the pale laureate. In his allegedly laudatory speech, Kittler actually challenges Eno to discover digitally designed sounds that would emancipate physical forces beyond the logics of o and 1, I and U, friend or enemy. Of course he grants Eno the honor of having composed an ultra-short piece of virtually eternal music: the Windows operating system's start-up sound, devised on Eno's Apple Macintosh. Although in light of Kittler's contempt for protected modes of software and iconic desktop design in general, this might have been an insult as well. Eventually, Eno is hailed for being among the few who, with the help of computers, were able to program all the sounds of the world. As some digital revenant of Pythagoras, Eno was justly bestowed with an honorary professorship of Berlin's University of Fine Arts. But popularity of music, as Kittler puts it in his encomium, depends upon the degree to which it dares to immerse into its own technologies.[18] The power of music, in other words, is the effect of circular causalities, connecting historical techniques to historicized bodies. Kittler's speech remains a double bind by every trick in the book: He prompts the laureate to liberate computer music as an aesthetic force in its own right by producing music that takes possession of legs and other limbs, while simultaneously pointing to its origin in military equipment, *Heeresgerät*. The master of ambivalence meets the master of ambience. The satanic twist will not have escaped the audience listening: In music, the real of history seizes its subjects, physically and beyond prospective programs of professors. In an acoustic control room, it is not the sound that is controlled but the subjects.

The laudatory speech for Brian Eno seems symptomatic of Kittler's wrestling with a technical a priori of sonic perception. His own writings on music always reveal the reverse side of his relentless analysis of media's genealogy in war's production. The liberation of bodies cannot be separated from that of the devices they are connected or hooked to. In *Rock Musik—ein Mißbrauch von Heeresgerät*, Kittler systematically traces the audio aesthetics of the Weimar postwar years to experimenting with early radio in the trenches (World War I) and remote-controlled telecommunication to its birth in devices for Blitzkrieg tanks and bombers (Word War II).[19] He also shows that pop music's genealogy in wartime inventions is no secret but openly discussed in the texts of Hendrix, the Beatles, or Roger Waters—the latter born in 1943 and addressed as a war child double of Kittler's, his semblable and brother. With Waters, as with Foucault and Bataille, Kittler always points toward the outlines of a history of madness as constant *sotto voce* not only of pop music but in fact of media theory at large.[20] A form of being off-key marks Kittler's writings on sound and music. And his texts work a bit like pop music themselves, beyond a score, to be understood only in listening to their overtone structure, homonymies, implicit references, hints, and associations in nonsemantic phonetic allusions.

Kittler's pieces on music can be read as compressed versions of his theories on communication procedures. They are acoustic doubles of his philological prose. Some variation for voice, sound, and rhythm, some *canto* seems to accompany each of his works on media history. And they include the emotional enforcement that is missing in the philologically condensed writings. A concise version of the gramophone chapter of *Gramophone, Film, Typewriter*, analyses Pink Floyd's *"Brain Damage"* as a brief history of technical orders of sound. "Der Gott der Ohren" (God of the ears) is dedicated to "Rochus und die Insel," the same Rochus who drove the car to Italy, while tape-man Azzo was "setting the controls for the heart of the sun," with its, as Kittler demonstrates, Phrygian intro and Sala-like exit.[21] The *Insel* (island) refers to both a famous Freiburg *rendez-vous* of friends as well all sorts of islands mentioned in Kittler's sound pieces, and eventually to music itself, an "island in the ocean of noise," as it is called in his studies on music and mathematics.[22] The merman, here, is back at land. In any case, readers need to listen in order to understand. And hearing in technical configurations is attributed to divine perception, notably mediated by the Greek Pan, an order of sound notoriously overstraining human ears and minds. Reconstructing sound cultures from Edison's gramophone to radio- and stereophonics and, as state of the art of the time, Syd Barrett's Azimut Coordinator, which could space out studios or stadiums at will, Kittler argues that pop musicians—experienced in doing calypso-like things and being familiar with their apocalyptic sides—had been media theorists all along in that they reveal the technical condition of all rapping and stepping gods.

Another translation of philological thought into sonic freestyle is the 1979 essay Lullaby of Birdland, dedicated to "Mimi." This prefigures his analysis of the discourse network of 1800 as a making of civil servants (*Beamte*) out of sleepy mother's sons and condenses it into a general analysis of a cultural technique called lullaby. Connecting poetic strategies from Goethe's wanderings and Brentano's Lorelei, Kittler demonstrates how male subjects are submitted to the soft voice of a mother and thus inaugurated into the pleasures of being addressed.[23] The dark side of the matter remains. In music as in poetry, a subject is whoever is addressed but by some nameless other: "Hey you, out there on your own . . . Du, da, on the mountaintop, warte nur, balde!" Beyond *Beamtentum* there is a lot of abyss.

The mothers who are singing, in turn, will have to discover that neither tune nor words on their lips, not even their voices, are properly theirs—they are "multipurpose devices" used to constitute the imaginary of national states.[24] Romantic writers will appropriate this voice and attribute it to hamlets and bushes. Richard Wagner will implement it into the technological real of frequency composing. With the new media and during the nineteenth century, the voice returns as the telephone's, the gramophone's, or the PA system's voice, empowered by the noises of electric circuits. Thus, as media users, we are all summoned to be civil servants. Subjected to his own education, Kittler misses one analytical turn of his quite gender-critical approach. Concluding his text with Charlie "Bird" Parker's "Lullaby of Birdland" in New York's fabled jazz club, he strangely ignores the intentional confusion of sigh and lullaby which Ella Fitzgerald begins with. As in the Schillerian "ach!" it is the same sighing Kittler has German classicism (*Deutsche Dichtung*) start with.[25]

The sound of sighs and music is the masquerade of relentless forces submitting boys to the discipline of civil servants. In spite of his relentless critique, Mimi's Friedrich was one of them. Dismissing academic prose for rhythmic poetic writing then is a serious form of civil disobedience.

Music is expressing the interior perception of historical media standards as martial standardization. Precisely in sound and music, the hallucinogenic effects of mediated data processing connect man to machine, nerves to pulses, libido to power, the real to the imaginary, and war to the bodies of war-born children. Kittler's music studies pay tribute to this vital confusion. It is the midday confusion of the great Pan, whose death, as Greek *logoi* had hit the shores of Italian swamps, he mourns according to Plutarch: "Ὁ μέγας Πὰν τέθνηκε" (The great Pan is dead).[26]

Pan, who rules Kittler's studies on sound, is the god of aural aphrodisian midday pleasures under a vertical sun—the vertical sun Friedrich Nietzsche had postulated as precondition of all clear thinking in *Ecce homo*, and the same vertical sun that hit Kittler in the nude, on the shores of the famous Baggersee near Niederrimsingen, slightly on the edge of civilization and strongly out of service, where he invented a new discipline with eyes squinted against the light. For Kittler, gods are coincidences of the interior perceptive apparatus with the world perceived of as aural presence, privileging the sonic perception of presence over visual logics: "Pan, a concavity of auricular space, has always been closer to the Great Goddess than all of her desperate lovers who kept chasing her but on the field of vision."[27] And Pan according to Kittler is both, lover and epistemologist, in linking aesthetic transformation to knowledge: "Only those who have ears can change and transform, that is: learn."[28] So much for didactics.

GREEKS AGAINST MONOTHEISM

Much of Friedrich Kittler's later writing on music is already present in very early texts, even the menacing turns. Taking his cue from Wagner—as from Hölderlin and Hegel—Kittler has always implemented the force of gods in their plural into his technically informed reasoning. Also, from the beginnings of his studies on media and epistemology, he had emphasized his dislike of those media which he referred to as nomads' mobility devices—Thora, Bible, and Quran—in their rigidity of securing immutable transmissions of texts and of commandments. As systems controlling interpretation and exegeses, the scriptures exclude variations and inventions of events which are the precondition for epiphanies of a variety of gods, men and women in their polymorphic intercourse.[29] In Kittler's theory, cross-traffic between the divine and the human, as mental and physical "Aha!" expressions of truth, is a matter of media situations. It is provided through access and free permutation of signs and signals. The invention of the vowel alphabet then was the initial opening of free access to speech, as well as to musical relations. *Logoi*, as Kittler points out referring to his teacher Johannes Lohmann, are letters, numbers, and swinging strings as operational and operable relations. In free permutation, they produce real worlds.

Poetic thinking, then, requires unlimited access to and disposal over *logoi*, or code and algorithms, plus a bit of courage traditionally denied to professors, in Basel and elsewhere. In taking *techne* and *episteme* for an inseparable practice of art as knowledge, early Greek philosophy could be credited with having launched Europe's culture of sovereign, self-determined and fearless vocalizing of material signs and signals. Speaking, or rather singing as the ancient Greeks did, is to self-responsively pursue and perform knowledge, produce it, as in poetry. *Episteme* as *Wissenschaft*, scientific thinking as free disposal over signs, maintains Kittler, would have been unthinkable in the Testaments or the Quran.[30] From his earliest texts onward, monotheism is scathed not for theological but for aesthetic, epistemic, and political reasons—for demanding allegiance instead of *jouissance* and *fröhliche Wissenschaft*.

In his final work on music and mathematics, Kittler returns to the Pre-Socratics, in a fierce battle against what he perceives of as wars of monotheistic religions which globally endanger free and independent thinking: "wir stehen in offener Feldschlacht."[31] The calling to abuse military equipment against the laws of the letter goes to all media scholars. His warning, that contemporary warriors, who put themselves and others off with promises of afterworldly delights, might eventually destroy the only world we have to live in, sounds much less paranoid today than when Kittler wrote the book.

Kittler's world view of aggressive monotheisms endangering the multitude of ancient or electronically updated Greek gods, invokes a battle between Greek literature and the Old Testament, which James Joyce had sneered at between the World Wars as a very German frontier of languages, "oystrygods gaggin fishygods!," stretching it to Aristophanes's battle of poets and their metrics: "Brékkek Kékkek" against "Ualu! Quàouauh!"[32] This battle of consonant and vowel alphabets had culminated on the eve of German fascism, mostly in exile, prominently with Erich Auerbach's *Mimesis*. And indeed Kittler is implicitly following Auerbach and explicitly Harold Innis in presuming a general "straddle" between "Athens and Jerusalem," between a possible access to language, provided by vowel scripture—the Greek form of full being—as opposed to being exposed to torn forms of existence in a Jewish tradition of thought.[33] In line with this argument, Kittler also resumes a conflict of postwar French philology, most notably between Foucault and Derrida, discussing exclusions and inclusions of speech and scientific formations through writing systems.[34] At this point he keeps criticizing "my friend Jacques" Derrida's work.[35] To Kittler, theorizing the fissure, as Derrida did, is denying the virtues of the Greek vowel alphabet as a means of disclosing a hitherto secret knowledge of language. Arabic and Semitic consonant-based writing systems, he objects, obstruct autonomous operations in language in that the proper pronunciation of words can only be learned from a master. The Greek alphabet in turn can record spoken and sung language, even dialects (*Mundarten*), peripheral forms of speech that operate with all kinds of sounds at will. In distinguishing Greek from monotheistic scriptures, Kittler obviously ignores all modern readings of monotheistic religions, which consider the fissures as symptoms for violence at their core—as Derrida did, in a close reading of Walter Benjamin's "Critique of Violence."[36] When Kittler is linking distinctions of writing systems to theistic models, mono- against polytheistic forms of speech and speaking, he is strategically applying media theory in its fundamental relation to the unknown. In his meticulous study of different Mediterranean writing systems, he shows that vowel alphabets are connected to further cultural techniques, including musical intonations and physical forms of movement, and that they provide access to academia in the Greek sense of studies, underlining that this access was irrespective of class or gender.

Kittler's interpretation of the vowel alphabet has been criticized by historians of writing systems as well as by media theorists.[37] Also, it has been observed that he is here following much of nineteenth century philology in a very Germanic undertaking. Hölderlin's verses of patriotic reversal resonate in Kittler's Greek studies, as well as Nietzsche, arguing against the Titanism of Goethe, who had tried to force the variety of gods into a single Promethean one. Nietzsche's effort was to advance the "renaissance of Hellenic antiquity, . . . in the hope of renewing and purifying German Geist through the fiery magic of music."[38] With respect for fiery magic, Kittler's project was rather to feedback German *Geist* through integrated circuits.

With regard to Martin Heidegger, more Germanic ventures seem to be in stock. *Musik und Mathematik* in its celebration of Pre-Socratic thought could also be read as an exhaustive remembering, repeating, and working-through of Heidegger's severe criticism of Plato's idealistic division of being, as well as his rehabilitation of Aristotelian *energeia* and finally his diagnosis of the loss of reason (*Grund*) in the Latin adaption of Greek philosophy. In his 1955 programmatic Cerisy-la-Salle lecture "Was ist das—die Philosophie?" for instance, Heidegger too has his Pan and postal moment, reminding us to "open our ear, uncovering it for that which speaks to us in the transmission of the *Sein* [be(ing)] *des Seienden* [of being]."[39] But while Heidegger assumes a single philosophical ear only, Kittler conceives of human ears in their stereophonical plural as always linked to technical devices or sound systems. Considering present alphanumerical systems and their potential to construct or—more likely today—to destroy real worlds according to numbers and letters, Kittler is comparing societies who allow for open access to codes with societies who prohibit this or reserve it for a selected few. He parallels the Platonic and later the Roman disclosure of truth to the disclosure of knowledge in the privatization of algorithms as effected by imperialistic copyright laws of the new software empires. In advocating a return to the Pre-Socratic *logos*, he is advocating the appropriation of codes.

As invention of acoustic *theoria*, literally an oxymoron, Kittler's studies of music turn out to be in consistence with the epistemology of media studies at the turn of digital rule. Just as Platonic discourse networks had reduced the great Greek alphabet to a use of words that was forced to speculate on truth as in otherworldly ideas, present copyright and ownership of source codes have reduced us to users of a foreign langue of which we only occasionally feel the effects. Kittler's final books come full circle—from present cultures of numeric data processing, controlled by software industries and national intelligences, to the Greek disclosure of an alphabet accessible to all.

Kittler follows Nietzsche's or Heidegger's Hellenic aspirations, albeit under electronic conditions. The primacy of language is preserved, but today this also means performing or programming formal languages, construing a digitally informed world by numbers. In writing on music and in writing musically, the impact of sounds as forceful operations is again placed over the exclusive hegemony of sense. "Where logos for the first time, pronounces itself as word, it is simultaneously a magic of sound."[40] Hence Kittler's excessive praise of the vowel alphabet—conceived of as both disclosure of *logoi* and access to lingual operations in speech, sound, and living bodies simultaneously. The logics of free algorithms equal an alphabet that, instead of just describing the world, produces one—or many. Hence the ambivalent appreciation of Brian Eno as composer of algorithms who could produce secular sounds and physical relationships simultaneously: a despicable move if in the service of software empires is however welcomed in the fabrication of sex, drugs, and rock and roll, or, as Kittler quotes Jacques Lacan, "jazz, dance, and libido."[41] The Greek seems quite an extendable notion. Kittler celebrates the art of immersion into music in the age of algorithmic processing as a form of recursive thinking beyond concepts of soul or mind, subject or consciousness.

It is this stance, of course, that divides the followers of "the great man himself."[42] Kittler's books on music and mathematics may be understood as a return to an eternal Greece of copulating nymphs, a return to *aletheia* as an island in the sun, with superpotent Pan-men uncovering themselves and others, ready to make love and reproduce, while, as in Parmenides, maidens lead the way. Unhiddenness here is celebrated as a state of pure being, peppered with a bit of Black Forest *Eros*.[43] Welcome to the *Seins*-machine. This is arguably a feasible interpretation. Klaus Theweleit has quickly choked this option in a meticulous recapitulation of Greek mythology as an endless series of rapes, with mother-less children abandoned in caves and on mountaintops. *Warte nur balde*.[44] The recent cult of nymphomania in media studies is probably its most boring as-pect, nevertheless the only field where joint ventures of *techne* and *episteme* have been successful within the cultures of elderly Faustian academic staff. But even to Kittler, nymphs were not merely young girls, maidens, imaginable as an end-less reservoir of young bachelorettes to their professors but also a terrible and scary bunch, "furchtbar."[45] The state of being possessed and drawn into some-thing unknown then, as Calasso describes the threat of the nymphs, resembles the dawning of a new *episteme*, exploring the technical condition of existence.[46] In or on music we can consider escaping the visual primacy of theory, risking the confusion of human perception in a world of frequency machines.

It is not the simple fact of providing sounds for meaning, as in vowels, which distinguishes the Greek alphabet from others. Kittler underlines that Pre-Socratic philosophizing is based on the free permutability of letters, num-bers, and musical notes, thus opening access to *Sein* at large, which makes it unique: "Letters could be translated into numbers, numbers into notes, notes back into letters—a fundamental mobility on which the singularity of Euro-pean culture was based."[47] With digital coding, this culture of Pythagorean philosophy resurfaces. Deciphering *logoi* as simultaneously organizing the ten-sion and tone of strings as well as of bodies, of sounds as well as of waves, of instruments as well as of weapons, Kittler's last project is an exercise in singing the material world electric.

SPEAKING AS THE *LOGOS* DOES

Kittler's program of poetic thinking (*dichterisch denken*) includes poetic transla-tions from the Greek. Translating itself, in Heidegger as in Kittler, is practiced as a procedure of disclosing.[48] In *Discourse Networks*, Kittler had insisted on distinguishing translating according to sense and hermeneutic from transpos-ing, technically transferring signal for signal. In the Greek books, he develops strange combination of both. What seems far out in Kittlerian short hand—musical mimesis as making love of the gods[49]—proves to simply be a Heideg-gerian translation from Heraklit: the conjunction of *philein*, making love, and *omologein*, speaking *as* the *logos* does.[50] No coincidence then that Hendrix uses the same phrasing to introduce his studio work in *Electric Ladyland*.

A supposedly Greek tradition of *poetic thinking* in combining *logoi* as mathematical ratios is, despite Heidegger, not specifically Germanic in the sense of anti-Semitic. As Hannah Arendt brings to mind, the same thought is discernable in Walter Benjamin's poetology. Arendt quotes from his letters, "that each truth has its home, its ancestral palace, in language, that this palace was built with the oldest *logoi*, and that to a truth thus founded the insights of single sciences will remain inferior."[51] Even if this ancestral palace is to be favored over a Todtnau hut, both recover, in speaking according to the *logos*, a messianic force in language, *dits ou écrit*, against the grain of obedience, monotheistic or algorithmic. Kittler on music can be read as a practice of differentiating and multiplying distinctions—even if he contests difference *as such*. Poetic or musical writing on music can be read as an attack on institutionalized forms of thought, speech, and writing, as a commitment to free, responsible, and risky speech, *parrhesia*, as Foucault claimed.[52] This is the liberating aspect of Kittler's texts on music.

In poetic thinking and speech, Kittler's books on music and mathematics analyze the logics of *logoi* while immersing in their technological feedback, eventually following Hegel's command to subject themselves to historical technologies. In listening to music and its vibrations, states Hegel, who is in this case also referring to Pythagoras, human desires can be synchronized, concerted, and harmonized according to different ratios of vibrations.[53] Hegel emphasizes the possible fusion of instrument and human soul: "in virtuous playing, the external instrument will appear as a perfectly formed and appropriated organ of the artistic soul."[54] Programming sounds, tones, and colors on alphanumerically driven machines, as Kittler actually practiced it in resistance against source code politics of an industrial military complex, is to open doors for new forms of perception. "Today's scripture can generate images or sounds precisely because the difference between letters and numbers vanishes in the digital code."[55] At the same time, these experiments risk surrendering the subject to the logics of *logoi*, in that these are operational in themselves. Doing things with *logoi* is today mostly practiced in music: "Few things in the world are more algorithmic than music."[56] While music is the strongest form of rendering speech operational, speech and speaking will only be *omologein* if it opens access to its operational systems. *Omologein* means recursive speech. As the first to actually have practiced this, Kittler discovers Sappho.

In her songs, which Kittler carefully translated, the poet Sappho refers to the sources of her speech, letters as well as numbers and the intervals of the lyre. And she declares female nature to be a letter in which vowels and consonants are distinguished so that language can be transmitted as music.[57] Sappho, then, is a true source-maiden, a nymph, in other words, who reveals the source code while she applies it. In antiquity Kittler traces poetics of circular causal thinking which, in the age of cybernetic machines, could rescue language from being petrified in the laws and orders of symbolic systems. This is not only true for the lyrics but also for the sound of the lyre. In meticulously diversifying, investigating, and, in fact, rebuilding manifold and little-known forms of Greek tuning and scales, Kittler explored and simultaneously aimed at multiplying experience—which is of course, to multiply gods. Quoting Aristotle he states that in different tonalities (*armonai*)—mixolydian, dorian, phrygian, and so on—"we pass through the scales of our attunements: grief/happiness, gentleness/rage, repose/enthusiasm, which musically enfold and emerge, even before '*logos*' intervenes."[58] It is here that Kittler's feedback circuit between Greek gods and the alphanumerical system of the computer generates new creatures that in his ode to sexual ontology he had not really factored: The fact that relations of bodies and instruments are calculable in real numbers, in all combinations of roots and radicals, ratios and irrationalities, would imply that not only sounds can be synthesized ad libitum, but gender too, as Wendy Carlos has aptly shown. While insinuating the effects alphanumerical operations have on social relations, Kittler, hooked to a universe of nymphs, might only grudgingly have accepted that chimeras and syncretic states will form the futures of our love lives. Here, the cosmic merman is back on the position of the sorcerer's apprentice, while "Walle! Walle!" has turned into the tender movements of Wall-e, trying to seduce artificial intelligence in discretely dancing on his chain-tracked feet.

At this point, however, it is probably necessary to distinguish a feminist strand of Kittler's in his historical reconstruction of inevitable links between poetry and knowledge. Beginning with the systematic destruction and banning of Sappho's writing, which Kittler explains with the fact that the great poetess had revealed the source of her art, Kittler continues to observe the exclusion of women from philosophy during the last two thousand years, until, with the advent of the digital age, they, or rather we, have again claimed and gained access to contemporary forms of knowledge. With limitations, quotas and more or less annoying procedures, this is even true for institutions like universities, at least as Basel professors, if not as gods. But a gender line seems to emerge elsewhere: between people who speak or write musically and those who submit to a limited set of prefigured prose, between those who reveal the sources of their writing and those who conceal it. Writing musically himself, Kittler in his books demonstrates the operational effects of language as love's labor recovered. In intimately addressing a muse that is meandering between hallucinated nymph and empirical lover, between Kirke and (anagrammatically) Erika, his last texts on music are lyrical operations in their own right.

But there is also a threat to the operational effects of language. Appropriated by warlords, logics of *logoi* have ever since proved to be effective weapons. These extend from a structural similarity of bow and lyre to Turing machines as devices of destruction. In this respect, then, the volumes of *Musik und Mathematik* can also be read as a search for the last exit off the highway of occidental thinking, an exit from Europe's death drives, which is meanwhile autopiloted by commercial rule on languages and their sources. Read as critique of academic thinking or theory, Kittler on music is first and foremost defying academic fealty as *Gefolgschaft* (following). Poetic thinking is to defy commandments as well as commands, biblical or computer imposed.

RETURN TO MEDIA THEORY

Any text is a test or trap to its readers. Friedrich Kittler's books on music and mathematics may arguably be read as a return to ontology, toward a philosophical discourse of being, in terms of fixed numerical, cosmological, and gender relations. Most probably, Kittler himself would have chosen this reading, and, remembering the acid commentaries he had in stow for Foucault's later books on Greek Antiquity, it might have been a relentless critique. Likewise, Kittler's books on music may be read as a return to ontology in terms of computer science, a description of being in terms of a set of calculable relations. Current codes, then, are traced back to the ontological tetraktys of 1:2, 3:4, 4:5. From there, Kittler could be read as studying the unfolding of sonic spaces or, ontologically speaking, the opening of worlds, in their historical formations of intervals, frequencies, analogue synthesizing, or digital programming. In this reading, his books would eventually discover all those not altogether controllable consequences of signal processing such as interferences, feedback, and space distortion. In fact, all his writings on music follow this trajectory in more or less detailed and technically informed studies, expanding from the tuning of Sappho's lyre to Pink Floyd's Azimuth Coordinator topologically deforming quadrophonic spaces. Sonic devices produce sonic events. However, the interesting twist of Kittler on music is, that this story is neither linear nor technologically deterministic. The surprising discovery of Kittler on music is that feedback occurs already in the field of Pan.

Consequently, cognition in the acoustic field does not rely on diligent studies of blueprints and protocols only, but requires perceptive duration, a bit of hanging out in the midday sun, listening to the sound of crickets, in ruins of Greek theaters or in radio plays of Ingeborg Bachmann: *"nichts Schöneres unter der Sonne, als unter der Sonne zu sein"* (nothing more beautiful under the sun than being under the sun).[59] But Pan is also a relentless god and dozing off in the open at noontime can be a risky project, specifically for Germanic types. Thus, the books on music and their sounds have unsettled some basic assumptions connected to what has institutionally been termed New German Media Theory, even causing a bit of panic in the meanwhile settled community of its scholars.

A first message of Kittler's writings on music is that we are consigned to the acoustic world with our ears as with all skin and bone, membranes and mechanics of transmission. We cannot but live in an ocean of vibrating waves. Kittler's studies on sound and music prove that any notion of a technical a priori is certainly not a matter of technical determinism; rather, it concerns the difficulty of understanding the circular logics of aesthetics as a hitch of all media studies: the fact that any technological environment which we would like to explore includes us in all our physis. Studies of sounds specifically reveal the epistemological difficulty that there is no acoustic equivalent to the blind spot, which, according to Heinz von Foerster, allows for exiting and reentering aesthetic systems. The blind spot in the visual field points toward possible second-order observance—toward an epistemological Off, albeit as blank or negative space. In sonic worlds, there is no second order. Even an epistemology of disturbance and glitch turns into an irritating positivity in the ocean of waves. Signals, disturbed or not, seduce the listener to immerse into the world of constitutively confused perception. Thus, the specific problem of technical media—that they constitutively operate subliminally, below the threshold of conscious perception—turns out to have been a problem of music and listening cultures all along. The structure of soundscapes cannot be analyzed in simply understanding the anatomy of technical media; the concavity of the ear reminds us that architectures of sound include bodies and brains as spaces of resonance.

Secondly, in sound studies specifically, the effects of aesthetical procedures are not altogether calculable. Kittler's mathematical mind conceives of complex sounds as logics of numbers, even condensing a complex phenomenon like modern music on only two basic formulas: "Modern music is based on two contradictory principles, tempering and harmonics, the linear integer multiples and exponential multiples."[60] However, the space of resonance, interferences, and feedbacks—their chain of reaction—is never completely terminable. The sonic world is a world of effects. Practices of playing and composing as well as material qualities of instruments and devices all interfere with nonlinear logics of acoustics, never fully controlling them. The production of possible sounds in an algorithmic combination of numbers is eventually infinite, and thus transcends the symbolic world of the machine. Instead of following Leibniz in attributing this infinity to a singular god, Kittler conceives of a diversified pantheon, transmitting all sorts of mental and physical states. Therefor this pantheon is not conceived of as otherworldly authority but as of presence or at least an oncoming return of this presence: *das Nahen der Götter*. It is here that Kittler is defying deconstructivist criticism of scripture and writing. It is not an inherently metaphysical stance of language itself—written, spoken, or in technically recorded abstractions—which forms a threat to political criticism, but the institutional and commercial inhibition of a free poetic access to language. For Kittler it is first and foremost academic forms of prose, written or spoken, that execute a sort of self-inflicted impotence on the basic power of language. Similarly, digitally composed music has to wrench its algorithmic mixtures from the clenches of industrially concealed source codes and copyrights.

Probably the most important aspect of Kittler on music, then, is the call for intervention. Unfortunately, the term *empowerment* is much too close to *Machtergreifung* to be feasible here. Language is a matter of elegant moves, on tail fins, track chains, or metrical feet. Words, as all sounds, are not representations but productions of new and unprecedented physical spaces. With their help, limits and constraints can be displaced. In a conversation with Peter Weibel, Kittiler outlines the simple task of media theory: "Actually we would have to verify for every historical age what the options were for breaking the circuit."[61] This basically means making differences where none had been before, operating with them to engender sounds, and listen to the effects of the many elements that had not been taken into account before. Then the sea is straight ahead. Well, it's too bad that our friends, mortal in the realm of time, can't be with us today. In the realm of frequency then, they will be.

NOTES

1. "aber noch / Tost die Welle, die mich / Untergetaucht / Im Ohr mir und mir träumt / Von des Meeresgrunds köstlicher Perle." Friedrich Hölderlin, "Der Rhine II," in *Sämtliche Werke und Briefe*, vol. 1, ed. Jochen Schmidt (Frankurt am Main: Deutscher Klassiker Verlag, 1994), 723.

2. Christian Morgenstern, *The Great Lalula and Other Nonsense Rhymes* (New York: Putnam, 1969).

3. Friedrich Kittler, *Das Nahen der Götter vorbereiten*, foreword by Hans Ulrich Gumbrecht (Paderborn, Germany: Wilhelm Fink Verlag, 2011).

4. Gottfried Wilhelm Leibniz, *Principles of Nature and Grace Based on Reason*, implicitly referred to in Friedrich Kittler, *Und der Sinus wird weiterschwingen: Über Musik und Mathematik* (Cologne: Verlag der Kunsthochschule für Medien, 2012), 33.

5. Friedrich Kittler, *Musik und Mathematik*, Bd. 1, *Hellas*, Tl. 1, *Aphrodite* (Paderborn: Wilhelm Fink Verlag, 2006), 337.

6. Friedrich Nietzsche, *Nietzsche contra Wagner: Aktenstücke eines Psychologen*, in *Sämtliche Werke, Kritische Studienausgabe*, vol. 10, ed. Giorgio Colli and Mazzino Montinari (Berlin: de Gruyter, 1980).

7. Friedrich Kittler, "Der Gott der Ohren," in *Das Schwinden der Sinne*, ed. Dietmar Kamper and Christoph Wulf (Frankfurt am Main: Suhrkamp, 1984), 140–55.

8. Kittler, *Musik und Mathematik*, 1.1:283–89.

9. Karl Kerényi, *Antike Religion* (Wiesbaden: Langen Müller Verlag, 1971), 105. Also quoted by Roberto Calasso, *Die Literatur und die Götter* (München: Carl Hanser Verlag, 2003).

10. Dirk Baecker, *Form und Formen der Kommunikation* (Frankfurt am Main: Suhrkamp, 2005), 19.

11. Kerényi, *Antike Religion*, 109.

12. Kittler, *Und der Sinus*, 48: "Gott ist der große Fourier-Analytiker und ich habe ja immer gesagt, im Zeitbereich sind wir sterblich und im Frequenzbereich, im Fourierbereich, sind wir unsterblich. Denn der Sinus ist älter als Jahwes und Elohims Schöpfung. Und der Sinus wird weiterschwingen, wenn dieses Universum in Schutt und Asche gefallen ist, um es mit Horaz zu sagen."

13. G. W. F. Hegel, *The Philosophy of Fine Art* (London: Bell and Sons, 1920), 3:363: "The peculiar power of music is an *elementary* force, that is to say it lies in the element of tone, in which the art here moves. (ßß) The individual is not only carried away . . . but, viewed simply as self-conscious subject, the core and centre of his spiritual existence is interwoven with the work and himself placed in active relations with it."

14. Friedrich Kittler, "Bei Tanzmusik kommt es einem in die Beine." Lecture on the occasion of the 01-Awards 1998 to Brian Eno during the second Multimedia Forum, Berlin November 20, 1998, http://hydra.humanities.uci.edu/kittler/eno.html.

15. Hegel, *Philosophy of Fine Art*, 156.

16. See Kittler, *Musik und Mathematik*, Bd. 1, *Hellas*, Tl. 2, *Eros* (München: Fink Verlag, 2009), 219. Kittler also spared Eno the fact that the tapes for these machines were produced by IG Farben.

17. Kittler, "Tanzmusik."

18. Ibid.: "Die Musik, die wir heute ehren, lehrt andres. Sie lehrt, frei nach Hegel, daß eine Kultur nur so populär ist, wie sie sich in ihre Technologien zu verlieren getraut."

19. Friedrich Kittler, "Rock Musik—ein Mißbrauch von Heeresgerät" [1991], repr. in *Die Wahrheit der technischen Welt*, ed. Hans Ulrich Gumbrecht (Frankfurt am Main: Suhrkamp, 1984), 198–213.

20. Kittler, "Der Gott der Ohren," 146: "Thus the history of the ear in the age of its technical blastability is always already the history of madness."

21. Ibid.

22. Kittler, *Musik und Mathematik*, 1.1:60.

23. Friedrich Kittler, "Lullaby of Birdland" [1979], in *Die Wahrheit der technischen Welt. Essays zur Genealogie der Gegenwart* (Frankfurt am Main: Suhrkamp, 2013), 41–59.

24. Ibid., 48: "The soft voice of the mother is a multifunctional device." "Die sanfte Stimme der Mutter ist ein Vielzweckgerät."

25. Kittler, *Aufschreibesysteme 1800/1900*, 11. Schiller's distich "Sprache," "Spricht die Seele, so spricht, ach! Schon die Seele nicht mehr" is only implicitly quoted, relying on the education of literature students and, to no avail, on those of commissions who judge *Habilitationen* (postdoctoral theses).

26. Plutarch de defectu oraculorum ("Vom Verschwinden der Orakel"), 17 [419C].

27. Kittler, "Der Gott der Ohren," 140: "Pan, eine Wölbung des Ohrraums, war der Großen Göttin immer schon näher als all ihre verzweifelten Liebhaber, die sie nur im Sehfeld jagten."

28. Cf. Kittler, *Musik und Mathematik*, 1.2:187: "Nur die Ohren haben, können anders werden, nämlich lernen."

29. Cf. Kittler, "Rock Musik," 199.

30. Cf. Kittler, *Und der Sinus*, 14.

31. Kittler, *Musik und Mathematik*, 1.1:113.

32. James Joyce, *Finnegans Wake* (New York: Penguin, 1999), 4.

33. Friedrich Kittler, "Schrift und Bild in Bewegung," in *Short Cuts* (Frankfurt am Main: Zweitausendeins, 2002), 89–106, 90.

34. See Ute Holl, *The Moses-Complex* (Chicago: University of Chicago Press, 2017), 56–70.

35. In a summer 2010 lecture, Kittler emphasized the epithet. See Friedrich Kittler, "Götter und Schriften rund ums Mittelmeer. Transskript einer Seminarsitzung im Sommersemester 2010," in Kittler, *Technik oder Kunst? Tumult: Schriften zur Verkehrswissenschaft*, ed. Walter Seitter and Michaela Ott (Wetzlar, Germany: Büchse der Pandora, 2012), 137.

36. See Jacques Derrida, "The Force of Law: The Mystical Foundation of Authority," in *Acts of Religion* (New York: Routledge, 2002), 230–98.

37. A concise overview is given in Michaela Ott, "Philebos Erbe," in Kittler, *Technik oder Kunst?*, 91–99.

38. Friedrich Nietzsche, "Die Geburt der Tragödie aus dem Geist der Musik," in *Sämtliche Werke: Kritische Studienausgabe in 15 Bänden*, ed. Giorgio Colli and Mazzino Montinari (Berlin: de Gruyter, 1999), 1:131.

39. Martin Heidegger, *Was ist das—die Philosophie?* (Pfullingen, Germany: Neske, 1952), 34: "unser Ohr, öffnen, freimachen für das, was sich uns in der Überlieferung als Sein des Seienden zuspricht." On the difficulty of translating Heidegger, see Miles Groth, *Translating Heidegger* (New York: Humanity Books, 2004). Concerning translations of and in Heidegger, see Parvis Emad, "Heidegger and the Question of Translation. A Closer Look," in *Studia Phaenomenologica, Romanian Journal for Phenomenology*, vol. 10 (2010), 293–312. Emad is specifically discussing Heidegger's Cerisy-la-Salle seminar which accompanied the lecture mentioned.

40. Kittler, *Musik und Mathematik*, 1.2:65.

41. Cf. Friedrich Kittler, "Die Welt des Symbolischen—eine Welt der Maschine," in *Draculas Vermächtnis. Technische Schriften* (Leipzig: Reclam, 1993), 59. Mai Wegener has shown that Kittler here is in fact twisting a Hegelian argument of Lacan's. See Mai Wegener, "Radikalisch entkoppelt," in Kittler, *Technik oder Kunst?*, 79–82.

42. Cf. Tom McCarthy, "Kittler and the Sirens," *London Review of Books* (blog), November 9, 2001, www.lrb.co.uk/blog/author/tom-mccarthy/.

43. Cf. *"Mein liebes Seelchen!" Briefe Martin Heideggers an seine Frau Elfride 1915–1970*, ed. Gertrud Heidegger (Munich: Deutsche Verlagsanstalt, 2007), 264.

44. Cf. Klaus Theweleit, *Buch der Königstöchter. Von Göttermännern und Menschenfrauen. Mythenbildung, vorhomerisch, amerikanisch* (Frankfurt am Main: Stroemfeld/Roter Stern, 2013).

45. Friedrich Kittler, *Isolde als Sirene, Tristans Narrheit als Wahrheitsereignis* (München: Fink, 2012), 25.

46. Calasso, *Die Literatur und die Götter*, 34.

47. Kittler, "Schrift und Bild in Bewegung," 92: "Buchstaben ließen sich mithin in Zahlen, Zahlen in Noten und Noten wieder in Buchstaben übersetzen—eine fundamentale Beweglichkeit, auf der die Einmaligkeit der europäischen Kultur wahrhaft beruht hat."

48. Cf. Hans Ulrich Gumbrecht on Kittler's translations of "Folie Tristan," in Hans Ulrich Gumbrecht, "Tristans Narrheit als Wahrheitsereignis: Über zwei späte Texte von Friedrich Kittler, die Seinsgeschichte freilegen wollen," in Hans Ulrich Gumbrecht and Friedrich Kittler, *Isolde als Sirene* (Munich: Fink Verlag, 2012), 17. Translation in chapter 2 of the present volume.

49. Kittler, *Musik und Mathematik*, 1.2:127: "Götter machen Liebe vor, wir Sterblichen sie nach. Und das heist Mimesis, nichts sonst."

50. Cf. Martin Heidegger, *Der Ursprung des Kunstwerks*, 21.

51. Cf. Hannah Arendt, quoting from Walter Benjamin's letters, in Hannah Arendt, *Men in Dark Times* (San Diego, New York, London: Harcourt Brace Jovanovich, 1955), 201.

52. Michel Foucault, *Fearless Speech*, ed. by Joseph Pearson (Los Angeles: Semiotext(e), 2001).

53. Hegel, *Philosophy of Fine Art*, 385–86.

54. Ibid., 429: ". . . so erscheint in dieser Virtuosität das fremde Instrument als ein vollendet durchgebildetes eigenstes Organ der künstlerischen Seele."

55. Friedrich Kittler, "Meine Theorie ist gar nicht so lebensverbunden, um über alles zu reden. Gespräch mit Peter Weibel" [1992], in *Short Cuts*, 81: "Die Schrift von heute dagegen kann Bilder oder Töne generieren, eben weil der Unterschied zwischen Buchstaben und Zahlen im digitalen Code verschwindet."

56. Kittler, *Musik und Mathematik*, 1.2:213: "Kaum etwas auf der Welt ist algorithmischer als die Musik."

57. Kittler, *Musik und Mathematik*, 1.1:163. See also Jacques Derrida, *La carte postale: de Socrate à Freud et au-delà* (Paris: Flammarion 1980). I thank Erhard Schüttpelz for making me aware of the fact that Derrida here is also referring to and processing James Joyce's *Finnegans Wake*.

58. Kittler, *Musik und Mathematik*, 1.2:188

59. Ingeborg Bachmann, "To the Sun," in *Encounter* 22, no.4 (April 1964): 32.

60. Kittler, "Und der Sinus," 37: "Neuzeitliche Musik beruht auf den zwei widerprüchlichen Prinzipien der Temperierung und der Obertönigkeit, auf den Prinzipien der linear ganzzahligen Vielfachen und der exponentiellen Vielfachen, und spielt das alles, im Unterschied zu der griechischen Musik, zusammen."

61. Friedrich Kittler, "Gespräch mit Peter Weibel," 85: "Eigentlich müsste man zu jeder gegeben historischen Zeit prüfen, wie ihre Umschaltmöglichkeiten funktioniert haben."

16

THE TRACK OF THE FLY

On Hearing and Animality in the Age of Technical Media

Bernhard Siegert

> BRAIN SAYS STRANGE THINGS NOW
> —André, on a typewriter in *The Fly*

The histories of media Friedrich Kittler was interested in had never been pre-histories or early histories of media; neither was he interested in the development, distribution, and blackboxing of media. He was not interested in the history of *media* but in the *history* of media. In the terms of David Wills: It is the question whether we face the media and bring them in front of us as represented objects of the world and our analysis, or whether we have them in our back, as something that moves and mobilizes us as if from behind and so technologizes ourselves.[1] Asked about his attitude toward interpretation or understanding, Kittler once said, a good interpretation for him consisted of finding the "manual" (*Handbuch*) or the algorithm that was behind or in the back of literary texts or other artworks of Western culture that officially had been ascribed to the Spirit, Nature, or the Muses. Whether he was writing on literature, music, media, or the cultural history of numbers—Kittler always had been a codebreaker. Hence, there is a basic assumption in the background of many of his writings, that the fictionality of literary characters or the ideality and generality of philosophical concepts is only a trick that intends to conceal a factual singular individual, a factual historical event, or a factual contingent desire. This had nothing to do with narrow-minded positivism. It had to do with the Nietzschean project to replace the masks of ideality, humanity, truth, or the Spirit with the historical facticity of discourses, desires, and technology.

In this sense, what follows is a history of dorsal media. There are some undisputed facts about Kittler—for example, that he preferred manipulating hardware over manipulating software, or that he preferred acoustics over optics. This essay is tuned in to some of the leitmotifs that accompanied Kittler throughout his life starting in the 1980s, such as the history of stereo sound, the history of frequency knowledge, Mucho Maas (Pynchon's DJ in *The Crying of Lot No. 49*), the military technology behind acoustics and media of entertainment, and the band that knew it all: Pink Floyd. Especially dear to him was the song "Grantchester Meadows" of which he believed that it was a secret homage to Alan Turing. Be this as it may. My ears were tuned more into the mad spatial modeling of a buzzing fly in the final bars of that song. This is its story.

An Allegory of Film Sound

One of Berlin's cinemas is called Zoo-Palast (zoo palace), which takes its name from its proximity to the zoological garden. There is also a 1958 film by the German-born director Kurt Neumann entitled "The Fly," which ends with a Freudian slip that lets the name of the Berlin cinema appear as the generic title of the cinema as a medium.

The slip occurs in the form of a misremembrance within a sequence of two scenes. There is the one scene in which François Delambre (Vincent Price) tries to lure his nephew, little Philippe, away from the site where his mother is just taken to the madhouse. For this purpose, François is advertising the medium which defines our situation as we watch the film: "I take you to the movies." And there is the other scene, three minutes later, which is the final scene of the film after the boy's dad has been smashed for the second time, in which the boy comes back to his uncle's proposal, but now recalling it in a slightly different way: "You taking me to the zoo like you promised?"[2] Whether that was a subversive idea of the director or simply a continuity error doesn't matter. What matters is what you hear and what you see, the factual enactment of discourses as Kittler would had said. What is uttered is a desire for the zoo as a shifted object of a "desired desire" of the movies, that was insinuated by the uncle and ideal father of the child. That is not an innocent ending of a film that is about a father and husband who is transformed into an animal, the subject of the film's title, a fly. In zoos flies are a *tertium datur*. The zoo is a representational space in which a special organization of seeing and showing—which consists of tags, bars and ditches—serves the purpose that certain counted living beings appear as objects of perception and certain counted living beings appear as subjects of perception while innumerable uncounted living beings form background noise. Not that there are no flies in the zoo. Swarms of them sit on the mucous membranes of elephants or zebras. But nobody visits a zoo because of the flies. In the zoo, flies are just noise, parasites in the double meaning of the French word *parasite*.[3] The reestablishment of this order therefore can properly be called a happy end at the end of a movie, the horror of which consists in a becoming-animal which, on the one hand, is directly connected to the media which this film deals with and on the other, which it is itself.

The film is structured by the simple architectonic system of a house that has two parts: an aboveground nuclear family idyll and a belowground celibatarian machine world. Aboveground rules the oedipal triangle: André, Helène, and their son Philippe. Belowground, in the laboratory, André is writing, calculating, and constructing his dream machine in weeklong solitude: a teleporter called disintegrator/integrator. This machine dissolves ashtrays, champagne bottles, guinea pigs, and eventually its inventor into atoms which it transmits wirelessly and reintegrates in the receiver booth. The unhappy outcome of these experiments is well known: By chance a fly gets into the teleporter during the self-experiment and causes the fact that André, mixed with something absolutely different, is propelled out of his family idyll on an irreversible line of flight.[4] In *Mille Plateaux*, Gilles Deleuze and Félix Guattari used the concept of "becoming-animal" to describe a deterritorializing option of the cultural organization of social bodies, which they oppose to those bodies that are organized by institutions such as the state or the family.[5] Deleuze and Guattari distinguish three kinds of animals,[6] and all three of them appear in *The Fly*. First, the oedipal animal, which is the animal of childhood; the pet, animals such as cats and dogs behind which psychoanalysis is able to detect the image of mom and dad or the little brother. Second, animals of classification or animals of state that are animals with an attribute or a quality. I count among them also the animals of philosophers such as the Aristotelian *zoon logon echon*, the animal which possesses language.[7] Third, the demonic animal, which confronts this anthropology of a single attribute which defines the difference between human and animal. This *enchaînement* has nothing to do with the technics of a stable identity but with metamorphosis. The demonic animal pertains not to the state apparatus like the animals of the zoo or philosophy but to the war machine.

If Deleuze and Guattari describe becoming-animal as a "becoming-molecular,"[8] they literally describe the technical principle underlying André's disintegrator. After his accident, André deterritorializes along the line of a becoming-fly, which becomes possible by means of a split that belongs to the materiality of the sound film itself: the split between sound and image track. Indeed, the fly as an object of filmic perception is nothing but the permanent suspension or infringement of a basic rule of sound editing, which says: "To convince the spectator of the authenticity of the dialogue and/or the sound effects, the editor has to procure synchronization between sound and image

FIGURE 1. Helène detects the sound of a buzzing fly.

FIGURE 2. Close-up of the fly.

as quick as possible within a scene."[9] The fly, however, is positively the embod-
iment of an asynchronicity between the visible and locatable on the one hand,
and the invisible audible and unlocatable on the other. Either you can see it in
close-up, but then you don't hear it, or you hear it (when it buzzes around),
but then you don't see it. It is an allegory of film sound itself. In one of the first
scenes of the film we see Helène (Patricia Owens) while she is interrogated
by the police inspector (Herbert Marshall). Helène has killed her husband by
bringing down an industrial press on him and is now simulating insanity. Her
head moves around while we hear the sound of a buzzing fly (Figure 1). Then
she gets up, obviously because her eyes have spotted the flying sound source.
After a cut, we see the fly in close-up sitting on a lamp shade—but we don't
hear it anymore (Figure 2). In another sequence—which belongs to the long
flashback which tells Helène's story—André lives already as fly man in the
basement, and mother and son are hunting the fly that has his head. Again
and again the alternation between hearing the fly without seeing it and seeing
it (in close-up) without hearing it is staged. Finally, Helène disperses several
handfuls of sugar on a table to lure the André-fly into visibility and soundless-

ness; the sugar marks not only a landing spot for the André-fly but also for our gazes.

SYNCHRONIZATION

It is well known that since Edison the story of film sound was a story of solving problems of synchronization. To help solve the synchronization problems, three German inventors came up with an optical sound solution known as the Tri-Ergon process and the technicians at Warner Bros. advanced the playback system in 1929 which allowed synchronization of background music and dialogue.[10] But the playback system couldn't solve the problem of synchronization of dialogue during outdoor takes, because it was a problem of the unselective early microphones. Therefore, it enhanced the development of the back-projection method.[11]

The asynchronicity between visibility and audibility or the asynchronicity of the fly thematizes "the sound film's fundamental lie: the implication that the sound is produced by the image when in fact it remains independent from it."[12] But without analog media which do not only register oscillations but also reproduce and mix them (mechanically, optoelectrically, or electromagnetically), there is no theory of autonomous sound. The discourse which not only commanded the subordination of sound under the image but inscribed it literally into the bodies is an opto-logocentric discourse which can be traced back media historically to the order of senses that was implemented by the alphabetization campaign of the late eighteenth century, which Kittler has so elaborately described in *Discourse Networks 1800/1900*. Western Europe owes to this campaign spelling books that start with the image of a cat which is subtitled "meow." Hence, the origins of the oedipal animal lie in the discourse of pedagogy, for instance, in Johann Heinrich Pestalozzi's essay "On the sense of hearing with respect to the education of the human being [*Menschenbildung*] by sound and language" from 1804. If we do not relate them to concrete practices of power, even the animals of Deleuze and Guattari will remain animals of philosophy. Pestalozzi writes: "O Mother! You to whom I am talking—as soon as your child recognizes your voice as being your voice the circle of such insights is extended further and further, it will gradually realize the connection between the bird song and the bird, the barking and the dog [and the meowing and the cat]."[13] Only since pedagogy has introduced the identification of the mother voice with the mother as a model for identifying the sounds of dogs and cats, have psychoanalysts been able to rediscover behind all animal sounds the image of mom. In the laboratories of experimental psychology this connection between sound and image was developed in a more general way during the nineteenth century. Wilhelm Wundt claimed that a pure sound is unimaginable: "In general sounds remain on the level of accompanying sensations, which can give a characteristic relation to other imaginations, especially visual imaginations, but sounds cannot gain an autonomous meaning."[14] This wisdom was repeated by film theorist Christian Metz decades later. Only if sounds are metonymically connected to visual ideas—if they are, as Wundt writes, "most intimately associated to visual imaginations like the thunder of the thunderstorm, the murmuring of the wind, the crackling of the fire"[15]— can they become part of an imagination at all. Until today specialists for sound effects in radio or film studios work according to this principle. But for the same reason soundmen are professional psychotics: As sound effects specialist Robert Mott wrote, "To use the components of a sound for the creation of other sounds one has first of all to dissociate the names of the sounds from the sounds."[16] People who are unable to synchronize immediately sounds with imaginations are either suffering from aphasia or soundmen.

Therefore, it is especially amusing that *The Fly* contains an often-criticized sequence that demonstrates the dissociation of image and sound by means of the cat Dandelo, which André misuses as a laboratory animal. He thus practices the deconstruction of the Pestalozzian oedipal animal. While the script of James Clavell only planned to have the cat disappear, Neumann and his sound directors Eugene Grossman and Harry Leonard designed its fate to become a fade-out on the sound track.[17] For a short moment Dandelo turns into a stealth cat which seems to be everywhere—like Alberich in Wagner's *Rheingold*; Kittler always admired the stereophonic staging of that scene (in which Alberich becomes invisible under the "Tarnhelm") by John Culshaw, the producer of Sir Georg Solti's "Century Ring."[18] As a being of the soundtrack it blows up the image space and becomes a "stream of cat-atoms" which are impossible to localize.

FROM SPATIAL SOUND DETECTION IN WAR TO MEDIA COMPETITION IN POSTWAR

However, my reading does not yet answer the question why Danedelo is able to meow "from all parts of the room,"[19] as one film critic put it, nor does it answer the question of what enables Helène to localize the sound of a fly within a room. The answer is not that difficult. It involves the development of military sound technologies during two world wars. During World War I gestalt psychologists Erich Moritz von Hornbostel and Max Wertheimer designed acoustic locators for the artillery's direction detection of camouflaged emplacements of batteries and acoustic direction detectors for submarines.[20]

The first part of the answer relates to Hornbostel's and Wertheimer's theory of sound localization (which proved the theory, that sound location depends on the time difference between the two ears of an individual): Helène is able to locate a moving sound in space, because sound localization had become a weapon and a media technology and thereby a positive fact of knowledge. The second part of the answer relates to an invention by Fred Waller, the former director of special effects at Paramount who, in the service of the US Air Force, developed a method that made it possible to simulate aerial warfare as a virtual reality. He used five film projectors to project five attacking enemy airplanes on a curved screen which approximated in size and form the human visual field.[21] After World War II, Waller would convert his military device into a medium of entertainment and call it Cinerama. The Twentieth Century Fox equivalent of Cinerama was called CinemaScope, the widescreen format in which *The Fly* was shot. CinemaScope was a technique that used an anamorphic lens system which had been developed by the Swiss optometrist Henri Chrétien in 1928. In 1952, Spyros Skouras, the president of Twentieth Century Fox, bought the rights for the advancement of Chrétien's "anamorphoscope," which he presented to the public in 1953, one year after the introduction of Cinerama.[22] But the mono sound systems were unable to provide the sound for a technique that approximated with 146 degrees in width and 55 degrees in height the limits of the field of human vision. Such a wide visual field required a correspondingly widened sound perspective which is the reason why Cinerama and Cinema-Scope enforced the introduction of stereo sound into film sound technology.[23] Helène can only locate the sound of a fly because the fly is an effect of stereo and multiple track technology. In CinemaScope, the sound is distributed from four separate magnetic audio tracks to three speakers behind the screen and one "surround-sound" loudspeaker. Beginning with the biblical epic *The Robe* (1953), Fox produced only films with four-track stereo magnetic sound. But many cinema owners refused to install stereo sound systems in their cinemas, which, in 1956, caused Fox to switch over to a compatible system called MagOptical Stereophonic Sound, which was compatible with the old optical sound standard.[24] However, it is not by chance that the buzz of the fly in Helène's head or in the room is a self-reference of CinemaScope stereo sound. It is the result of a staff memo of Fox's almighty director of production Daryl Zanuck in which he ordered, "that every picture that goes into production in CinemaScope should contain subject matter which utilizes to the fullest extent the full possibilities of this medium."[25] What could be a better response to this order than a film in which the main character is an invisible flying sound source?

Thus, Helène's sound hallucination relates to the state of the art of film sound technology in 1958. The symptom of her madness to locate the sound of an invisible source is nothing but a military weapon which the film industry now forged into a weapon against the new medium of television. After all, it is on principle nothing but television, which André has tinkered with in his subterranean laboratory, and from which he has emerged as an asynchronic schizoid subject. The story of George Langelaan was inspired by genetics,[26] but Clavell's screenplay replaced genetics with television. While Langelaan rather emphasized the difference between teleportation of matter and television,[27] André in Clavell's screenplay and in Neumann's film insisted that both technologies are based on the same principle.

Helène: "It is impossible."

André: "Take television. What happens? A stream of electrons, sound and picture impulses, is transmitted through wires or in the air. The TV camera is the desintegrator. Your set unscrambles or integrates the electrons back into pictures and sound! . . . This is the same principle exactly!"

Helène becomes a victim of CinemaScope (or MagOptical Stereophonic Sound), because her husband has deserted to television. This is, very simple, the message of the film, its *Klartext* as Kittler would have said. And the irony of history has it, that Al Hedison, who played the role of André, in fact soon after *The Fly* shared the fate of André and Dandelo. As Bill Warren put it: "He soon faded into television."[28]

TO BEE IS TO BUZZ

World War II and its media produced the insight that the human being is no longer the subject of the symbolic, but the subject of the deterritorializing real and its technologies. Especially conservative apocalypticists of the West were quite disenchanted with this situation. In 1947 Carl Schmitt revoked the Cartesian logic of the subject: "Cogito ergo sum," Schmitt repeatedly wrote into his *Glossarium*, "sum, sum, sum, Bienchen summ herum"[29]—an onomatopoetic pun which is based on a children's poem that roughly translates to "buzz, buzz, buzz, o bee, buzz around." *Buzz* in German is *summ* which sounds exactly like the Latin word *sum* (I am). Thus, Schmitt's pun merges Descartes's famous phrase with the sound a bee makes with the outcome of something that amounts in its English translation to "cogito ergo buzz." In Carl Schmitt's slightly infantile joke, the "I am" (*sum*) no longer designates the fixed and point-shaped Cartesian *res cogitans*, which is opposed to the *res extensa*, but a sound source that moves around in space. Schmitt is not just comparing the cogito with an insect, he turns it into an insect. Someone who does not hear a signified in the word *sum*, but the real acoustic signal of a flying object, has left the spaces of the Text and the Law, and has transformed himself into a soundman.

With André-fly, Carl Schmitt's buzzing bee cogito becomes a reality that is produced by the stereo sound of CinemaScope. The decline of the West is technically implemented by stereo surround sound. No wonder that Carl Schmitt judged cinema as being "neither presence nor representation," but "gruesome, ghastly, soul, eye, and ear destroying."[30]

MEDIA ARCHAEOLOGY OF THE FLY

Animals such as flies that are cosubstantial with their "buzz buzz buzz" (or *sum sum sum*) are not just self-referential effects of media. They are epistemic and technical objects by which the human being and its boundaries are known (this is a kind of reflection that is missing in Parikka's *Insect Media*). Therefore, it is necessary to implement in media studies the perspective of an archaeology of the sciences. This enables us to ask: how and by what is the fly given?

The image of the monstrous fly from the Neumann movie refers to an image that within the memory of Western scientific culture is forever connected to the invention of the microscope. Robert Hooke's *Micrographia*, published in 1665, brought to the attention of a large public monstrously enlarged images of insects (and other objects) which became famous especially because of their precision of details. Here we find the prototype of the monstrous fly head in *The Fly* (Figure 3). Hooke's *Micrographia* also anticipated the famous "fly's view" from the Neumann film (Figures 4 and 5).[31]

But Hooke is not only interested in the anatomy of the fly as it appears within the order of things established by the microscope but also in the physiology of its wing movements, which transcend human perception. "What the vibrative motion of the wing is, and after what manner they are moved, I have endeavored by many trials to find out."[32] These trials concern the number of up and down movements of the wing per minute. These movements are, as Hooke tells us, "one of the quickest vibrating spontaneous motions of any in the world." How Hooke was able to measure the speed of this motion in the first place was something Samuel Pepys learned in August 1666. According to his diary, "[I] discoursed with Mr. Hooke a little, whom we met in the streete, about the nature of sounds, and he did make me understand the nature of musicall sounds made by strings, mighty prettily; and told me that having come to a certain number of vibrations proper to make any tone, he is able to tell how many strokes a fly makes with her wings (those flies that hum in their flying) by the note that it answers to in musique during their flying."[33] According to the *Micrographia*, Hooke compared the "sounds" of the flies

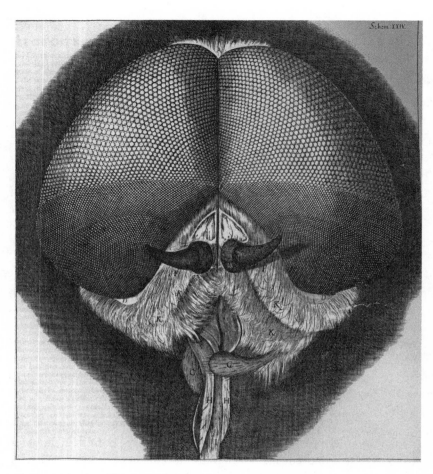

FIGURE 3. Fly's head from Robert Hooke, *Micrographia*, scheme XXIV.

with the "vibration of a musical string, tun'd unison to it" and thus concluded that the wings make "many hundreds, if not some thousands of vibrations in a second minute of time."[34] What carries the fly from the regions of emblematic meaning to the level of scientific discourse is thus the revolution of acoustic knowledge in the modern period: the identification of the pitch with frequency.[35] Marin Mersenne had established a rule for the determination of absolute frequency in 1636, and applied it to determine the frequency of strings that could not be measured any longer visually.[36] Thereby Mersenne replaced the millennium-old Pythagorean order of intervals or *logoi* by irrational proportions of numbers.[37] Since then language and sound are no longer written

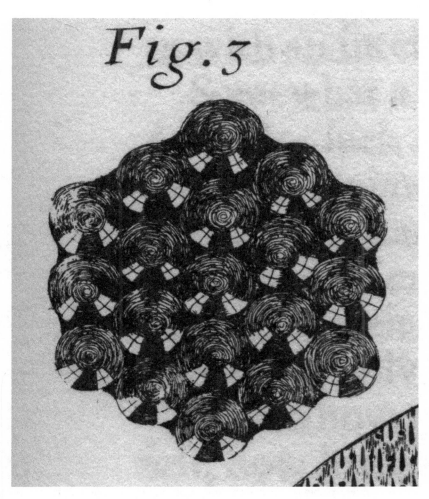

FIGURE 4. Fly's view from Robert Hooke, *Micrographia*, scheme XXIII.

in the same code. The vibrating string which revolutionized the concept of analysis in the eighteenth century (or the buzzing fly) designates in Mersenne and in Hooke the transition from the microscopic order of vision to the frequency based order of hearing. "But then when the Eye is unable to assist us any further in distinguishing the swiftness of Vibrations, there the Ear comes in with its assistance, and carries us much further."[38] Whereas the capability of the eye to distinguish movements is limited at a certain frequency by the afterimage effect, mathematical theory can turn the ear into a measuring device for movements way beyond the resolution limit of the human eye. We don't know

whether Hooke knew about Mersenne's results. However, what distinguishes flies from strings is that strings obey Newton's laws of motion whereas flies follow a spontaneous motion of their souls. In the *Micrographia* Hooke wrote with amazement about "the exceeding quickness of these Animal spirits that must cause these motions" and the "exceeding vividness of the governing faculty or Anima of the Insect, which is able to dispose and regulate so the motive faculties, as to cause every peculiar organ, not onely to move or act so quick, but to do it also so regularly."[39] While Hooke explained the regulation of the flies in 1665 with the help of a "certain pendulum," which he thought he had discovered underneath the wings of the flies (and thus declared that flies on principle are clocks), he turned in his *Lectures of Light* of 1682 to a general theory of frequency based on the microscope. According to that theory, the sense perception of all living beings depends on "sensible moments," the frequency of which is directly proportional to the size of the body. The smaller a living being the more sensible moments it experiences per minute. A fly's soul is thus able, according to Hooke, to distinguish at least three moments during the period which it takes to cause one of its wing beats. Therefore, the fly's soul is perfectly able to control the sound of its wings.[40] The length of time is not an absolute constant given by an astronomical clock, but is a variable that depends on the specific frequency of the soul. Since there are flies that one cannot hear, the conclusion is close at hand that there are also frequencies and fields of perception that go beyond humans. Hence Hooke conceived, that there are "beyond the reach of our ears . . . infinite shriller and shriller Notes," which can be heard by ears which like those of the flies are fit to perceive such high frequencies. These "lesser Creatures" dispose of a bandwidth in the very high frequency range which is comparable to ours in the low frequency range.[41]

What we can observe here is the opening up of the empty space of the unconscious in the history of knowledge. This space is opened up by the drifting apart of a theory according to which animals are machines (clocks for instance) and a theory according to which animals are beings of an augmented consciousness. The animal in the late seventeenth century appears as the alternative between machine and angel. Machine and angel (or spirit) define the borders which demarcate the human by separating it from the realms of the nonhuman. The fly is a nonhuman actor within the actor network that created a new discourse on the borders of the human being which points to a new beyond of the Human. Just think of the problems of Kant in his *Critique of Aesthetic Judgment* to believe in the plausibility of the theory that the mind executes during the perception of sounds as many acts of thought as there are vibrations per second which correspond to a certain pitch.[42] Thus you can fathom what was at stake with the entrance of the fly into the actor network that defines the Human: a subject that would have to be equipped with the soul of a fly to be able to hear and see. This is still uncharted ground for animal studies, a ground that lies beyond ethics: to conceive of the circumstances, first, that man appeared in the history of knowledge (in terms of Foucault) by occupying a space which was opened up by the animal in its dual being of machine and spirit, and, second, that the possibility to think media and to think the unconscious appears historically as a theory of the animal. What the animal for Hooke meant was the possibility to conceive of a nonhuman by which the human is defined and which is at the same time of a technological and a spiritual nature. Nineteenth-century experimental physiology, which in the meantime would have replaced the fly by the frog, identified the dual nature of this nonhuman as the physiological unconscious.

The fly not only helped to replace the humanistic order of *logoi* with the nonhumanistic code of real numbers within the being of the human being, it also initiated a becoming posthuman long before the genetic experiments and the cybernetic hybridizations of man and animal in the 1950s. The question, which media studies should share in the spirit of Kittler with those who survey the field of "posthumanities," contrasts with the agenda of those who still think in categories of the post- or transhuman—not *how did we become posthuman?*, but *how was the human always already mixed with and dependent on the nonhuman?*

THE REAL BEYOND THE SYMBOLIC: STOP READING AND START LISTENING

In 1965 three English students of architecture plus one art student named Syd Barrett founded the band Pink Floyd. When Kittler was asked in 1982 by Klaus Lindemann to contribute to a volume of interpretations of poems from 1775 until the present he submitted a marvelous interpretation of Pink Floyd's "Brain Damage." Here he pointed out how Syd Barrett's invention of the so-called Azimuth Coordinator helped the band to achieve its notorious fame of a technological avant-garde and provided it with a sound that surpassed quite a bit MagOptical Stereophonic Sound. The Azimuth Coordinator made it possible to vary continuously in all three dimensions the spatial location of arbitrary sound elements. As a result, the audience of Pink Floyd concerts never needed to simulate, like Helène, a brain damage, because they experienced it.[43] In 1969 Pink Floyd released their presumably most experimental record: *Ummagumma*. At the end of "Grantchester Meadows" the fly from the Neumann's 1958 movie returns one more time as a self-reference of stereo sound and a becoming-animal on the border of the Human. And here ends the track of the fly.[44]

NOTES

1. David Wills, *Dorsality: Thinking Back through Technology and Politics* (Minneapolis and London: University of Minnesota Press, 2008).

2. *The Fly*, directed and produced by Kurt Neumann (USA 1958); screenplay by James Clavell after a story by George Langelaan; camera: Karl Struss; sound directors: Eugene Grossman and Harry M. Leonard.

3. See Michel Serres, *Der Parasit*, trans. Michael Bischoff (Frankfurt am Main: Suhrkamp, 1981), 83 and passim.

4. See Adam Knee, "The Metamorphosis of *The Fly*," *Wide Angle* 14, no. 1 (1992): 20–23. Knee concentrates on the gender relation and interprets André's metamorphosis—in analogy to Kafkas "Metamorphosis"—as the fulfilment of a wish to flee. But then, in a turn typical for gender studies, he values this wish negatively, that is as a manifestation of the alleged male incapability to cope with the family and female desires.

5. See Gilles Deleuze and Félix Guattari, *A Thousand Plateaus: Capitalism and Schizophrenia*, trans. by Brian Massumi (London: Continuum, 2005).

6. Ibid., 240–41.

7. See Aristotle, *Politics*, 2.1.

8. Deleuze and Guattari, *A Thousand Plateaus*, 272.

9. John Belton, "Technology and Aesthetics of Film Sound," in *Film Sound: Theory and Practice*, ed. Elisabeth Weis and John Belton (New York: Columbia University Press, 1985), 64.

10. See Friedrich Kittler, "Das Werk der Drei: Vom Stummfilm zum Tonfilm," in *Zwischen Offenbarung und Rauschen: Zur Kultur- und Mediengeschichte der Stimme*, ed. Friedrich Kittler, Thomas Macho, Sigrid Weigel (Berlin: De Gruyter, 2002), 357–76. Direct sound and direct mixing of dialogue and background music is impossible because speech requires a very short reverberation time while orchestra music requires usually a very long reverberation time.

11. See Rick Altman, "Evolution of Sound Technology," in Weis and Belton, *Film Sound*, 46.

12. Ibid.

13. Johann Heinrich Pestalozzi, "Über den Sinn des Gehörs in Hinsicht auf Menschenbildung durch Ton und Sprache," in *Ausgewählte Schriften*, ed. Wilhelm Flitner (Frankfurt am Main: Cotta, 1983), 248.

14. Wilhelm Wundt, *Grundzüge der physiologischen Psychologie*, 4th ed. (Leipzig: Wilhelm Engelmann, 1893), 2:47.

15. Ibid.

16. Robert L. Mott, *Sound Effects: Radio, TV, and Film* (Boston, MA: Focal Press, 1990), 67.

17. Information about Kurt Neumann is scarce. Mel Schuster's *Motion Picture Directors* lists Kurt Neumann among those directors, "on whom no material was found." Born 1908 in Nuremberg, he studied music in the 1920s (presumably in Berlin—he possibly knew Hornbostel). Carl Laemmle brought him to Hollywood in the early 1930s, where he initially produced German versions of American movies, but soon he was a director of B-movies, too. Immediately after the war he directed several Tarzan films—*Tarzan and the Amazons* (1945), *Tarzan and the Leopard Woman* (1946), *Tarzan and the Huntress* (1947), and *Tarzan and the She-Devil* (1953). At the end of 1952, Neumann returned to Germany where he shot the unsuccessful *Rummelplatz der Liebe* (1953). He died in 1958 in Hollywood, only one week after the premiere of *The Fly*. See *Cineforum* 31, no. 306 (1991): 33. For the filmography of Neumann and the other crew members of *The Fly*, see the article "Neumann, Kurt" in the All-Movie Guide at www.allmovie.com/index.html.

18. See Friedrich Kittler, "Der Gott der Ohren," in *Draculas Vermächtnis: Technische Schriften* (Leipzig: Reclam, 1993), 136.

19. Bill Warren, *Keep Watching the Skies: American Science Fiction Movies of the Fifties* (Jefferson, NC, and London: McFarland, 1986), 2:82.

20. See Christoph Hoffmann, "Wissenschaft und Militär: Das Berliner Psychologische Institut und der I. Weltkrieg," in *Psychologie und Geschichte* 5, nos. 3–4 (1994): 261–85.

21. See David Hauptmann, "Stereo Variable Area: Eine (Kurz-)Geschichte des Mehrkanaltons im Film," *Theatralität, Performance, Medialität*, no. 2 (1997): 60.

22. See Aubrey Solomon, *Twentieth Century-Fox: A Corporate and Financial History*. (Metuchen, NJ, and London: McFarland, 1988), 83.

23. See Belton, "Technology and Aesthetics," 68. For the purpose of the clear preparation of the media historical cut of the 1950s, which represents the condition of *The Fly*, I ignore the anachronistic predecessor—the mother—of all multiple track spatial sound cinema events: Disney's *Fantasia* of 1941, based on Bell Labs technology, produced in four-channel optical sound by the Disney Studios in cooperation with radio engineers from the Radio Corporation of America and the first conductor who preferred standing behind a mixing console rather than on the rostrum, Leopold Stokowski. See Bojan Budisavljevic, Stokowskis Klangumlaufbahn, "Technobiographisches zwischen Dirigenten- und Mischpult," *Kaleidoskopien*, no. 2 (1997): 55.

24. See Solomon, *Twentieth Century-Fox*, 89.

25. Daryl Zanuck, memo to staff, March 12, 1953. Quoted in Solomon, *Twentieth Century-Fox*, 86.

26. The dedication reads: "For Jean Rostand, who once talked with me extensively on mutation."

27. "Whereas only sound and pictures had been, so far, transmitted through space by radio and television, Andre claimed to have discovered a way of transmitting matter. Matter, any solid object, placed in his 'transmitter' was instantly disintegrated and reintegrated in a special receiving set." George Langelaan, *Die Fliege: Eine phantastische Erzählung* (Frankfurt am Main: Fischer, 1988), 40.

28. Warren, *Keep Watching the Skies*, 83.

29. Carl Schmitt, *Glossarium: Aufzeichnungen der Jahre 1947–1951*, ed. Eberhard Freiherr von Medem (Berlin: Duncker and Humblot, 1991), 58; see also 28.

30. Schmitt, *Glossarium*, 16.

31. See Marielene Putscher, *Geschichte der medizinischen Abbildung: Von 1600 bis zur Gegenwart* (Munich: Moos, 1972), 35.

32. Robert Hooke, *Micrographia, or Some Physiological Descriptions of Minute Bodies Made by Magnifying Glasses with Observations and Inquiries Thereupon* (London: Jo. Martyn and Ja. Allestry, 1665), 172.

33. *The Diary of Samuel Pepys*, vol. 7, 239 (August 8, 1666). See also Sigalia Dostrovsky and John T. Cannon, "Entstehung der musikalischen Akustik (1600–1750)," in *Geschichte der Musiktheorie*, Bd. 6, *Hören, Messen und Rechnen in der frühen Neuzeit*, ed. Frieder Zaminer (Darmstadt: Wissenschaftliche Buchgesellschaft, 1987), 32.

34. Hooke, *Micrographia*, 173.

35. See Steven Connor, *Fly* (London: Reaktion Books, 2006).

36. See Dostrovsky and Cannon, "Entstehung der musikalischen Akustik," 30.

37. See Friedrich Kittler, "Vernehmen, was du wähnst," *Kaleidoskopien*, no. 2 (1997): 11.

38. Robert Hooke, "Lectures of Light, explicating its Nature, Properties, and Effects &c.," in *The Posthumous Works* (London: Samuel Smith and Benjamin Walford, 1705), 135.

39. Hooke, *Micrographia*, 173.

40. Hooke, "Lectures of Light," 134.

41. Ibid., 135.

42. Immanuel Kant, *Kritik der Urteilskraft. Werkausgabe*, Bd. 10, ed. by Wilhelm Weischedel (Frankfurt am Main: Suhrkamp, 1974), B 212.

43. See Kittler, "Der Gott der Ohren," 137 and 140.

44. Pink Floyd, "Grantchester Meadows," on *Ummagumma* (EMI 1969; digitally remastered 1994).

EPILOGUE

Sigh!—*A Lecture Performance*

Avital Ronell

Avital Ronell: Well, you may not like it.

Susan Bernstein: We're not here to "like it;" this is not a matter of ice cream flavors or other contingent desires.

AR: I was down and out, casting about for some sort of holding pattern. It's true that I was saved by a few people: I befriended Friedrich, started working under Derrida's supervision, and a stipendium came through at the time for study in Berlin.

SB: Please continue. Set up the notational systems so that we can evaluate your case. *media*

AR: Alright, then. Here goes. I ask for immunity for the duration of my recitation. Ahem. It's harsh, but then life is harsh and I am the carrier of so many phantoms. I am remote-controlled by those agitating within me, and I am responsible to them. There are calls that I must answer, as if I were driven by restitutional anxiety, a true mania constituting an interminable *Trauerarbeit*. My signature wittiness provides the laugh track to inassimilable horror. The burst of laughter tunnels through to where understanding no longer obtains.

[*Recording of spooky laughter; interim, Avital looks more professorial after a one-minute interval; she stands up and goes to the podium.*]

AR: After Goethe, I went into a bit of a slump, a Kleinian depressive disposition. That's when you're supposed to gain some ground and lucidity. I don't know. I had lost my job and was kicked out of Germanistik. I had dug up too much dirt on my main man, [Eckermann,] going so far as to locate his crypt and call him "Dreckermann," which for me was loving but no one believed me, and I was shot down for scoping the abjected, concealed dimension of

Goethe's monumentality. Thought the news would be greeted with gratitude—boy, was I off target! Lost my job in Germanistik as a result. "Ashes,
ashes, we all fall down." Anyway, I was down and out, unsheltered. The
Humboldt stipendium came through for study in Berlin. After Goethe, I
devoted myself to the analysis of the technologically inflected state.

SB: Let's stay with that, we'll isolate and dive in. Just stay focused. Can you do
that for me?

AR: Ok, here goes. I studied, if that's the word—no, it's not the word. I was
hounded, nightly, by the persecutions of the Third Reich. I tried to turn
this family disaster—

SB: A "family" drama?

AR: Well . . . I've heard it had historical dimensions as well. I tried to turn
an aspect of the historical trauma and memory blitzes into an object of
study—maybe to tame it or get a controlling handle on it, or something.
Um, OK, here goes. Stutter, stutter. Tick, tick, tick . . . That's when technology was dealt into my thinking of the mythological inscriptions of state.
In this weighty context, I proceeded to isolate the technological takeover.
I couldn't get too close, so I slipped into the space of my investigations rhetorically, by means of synecdoche and metonymy. I could get only as far as
the telephone. Friedrich handled the rest.

This fragment of dialogue is taken from a play I wrote and performed in
at Hau3 in Berlin, *What Was I Thinking? Autothanatography and Spectral Colloquy.*[1] Remembering its performance—when Laurence Rickels nearly stole the
show as head nurse in the asylum where I was thematically parked, with me in
coercive custody of an icy version of Susan Bernstein, whose relentless prods
required the production of autobiographemes—helps me return to the time
when I last saw Friedrich Kittler. Though he was weakened by illness, we
managed to share meals that summer, and to fill in the blanks of a sizeable
store of unsolved mysteries: we took the time it took, hours upon hours and
repeated encounters, to review our reciprocal history—the adventures and
outrageous feints that bound us, to each other as to our sprawling network.
Those sessions were in some measure soberly reflective, for we scaled back
on ego-led narratives, recalling and commenting the near misses, invoking
those we had failed, those whom we foolishly had repelled or overlooked,
those who became too close for comfort—or had abandoned us remorselessly
in a fit of parricidal rage. We took inventory of injustices that had been meted
out to us, separately or as part of an imaginary contingent, and I, for my part,
felt very mature about how we handled our private docudrama, the way we
were able to tell each other things without noticeable inhibition or narrative

rerouting—without too much shame or duplicity. We resisted putting up for view repressive counter-memories or outright falsifications, my more typical contribution to intimate recounting. .

We had our issues. Several students or friends had booked out on us; some stuck around. Soon after my Friedrich had passed on, Thomas Pepper called me to share his grief. The call, plush and soothing, helped steady my hand. It is probably entirely unnecessary to aver that I had been quaking with sorrow for many days and solar nights by then. Usually, huddled with a loss of this magnitude—incalculably undermining of my ability to stand with life or others—I go into voluntary lockdown until I have shed the look of psychotic dishevelment and can come out with an intention to appear, to behave minimally resocialized. It seems wrong to say "usually" and "this magnitude," as if there were some measure or norm to account for loss and throw its weight into comparativity with "similar" episodes of severe deprivation, life drainage, and utter haplessness. Tom Pepper had a story to tell me. It seems wrong as well to rebroadcast the sensitive communication, wikileaking all over the place, but I tell myself that, in this volume at least, I am among friends and need not tighten the rhetorical strings or redirect a lifelong habit of compulsive disclosure. Here, too, I may be wrong. After Derrida's politics of friendship that sort of observation admittedly doesn't serve as a good excuse—that we are among friends, or whatever—but I will declassify the attestation nonetheless, taking the risk of sounding coyly self-destructive. I am not so constituted. Tom's story of consoling tonalities consisted in divulging the time when Friedrich and he had defected from a conference in Norway, choosing to go on an excursion together. Tom was precise on details—the ferry ride, the walk, the rock on which they sat to take a breather (maybe in the form of a cigarette break for Friedrich, I can't recall). They came around to talking about a common friend ("O, my friends!"). Friedrich asked which of my works Tom had preferred. On the telephone, I was afraid to hear the answer, and now I've repressed it. Tom may have said, *"The Telephone Book?"*—adding a question mark, because it resembled a quiz, or maybe he wasn't sure what or if he preferred. Friedrich said, categorically, "No!" It was *Dictations* that had destroyed Germanistik. For that service rendered, it would remain on the top of his greatest hits list, crediting the book with having caused manifest damage in his precincts. The story, as you see, has stayed with me. Later on, when teaching for his last rounds, Friedrich put *The Test Drive* on his minimalist bibliography—possibly because it openly dealt with some of his more or less copyrighted themes and contained a scene of our drinking and smoking together in California, revving up our engines as allied troubleshooters. That cameo was meant to bolster my treatment of the Turing test. But it also appears to have stood for our primal scene to the extent, I think, that it shadowed us getting high together and establishing all sorts of dossiers that proved to serve as blueprints for future works. I was worried that he might go off on me—it wouldn't be the first time—but that didn't happen, and, instead, he reprieved me. Friedrich Kittler seemed willing to affirm my portraiture of drunken haze from which our share of urgency and pressing tropologies emerged, our stash of *tropium*, our alerted sense of the techno-scientific imposition, with its epochal and addictive edges. In the meantime, I have cleaned up. (Why do I find it necessary to make such a statement, I wonder to myself?) We both had set our Heideggerian itineraries, and he declared a lifelong love affair with the after-last philosopher, Nietzsche being the last and having a lasting effect on both of us. Friedrich was stirred but not shaken by Derrida, and preferred to hang back with Foucault. That was one of our partitions, an unavoidable *différend*, but Friedrich did not appear to mind so much and anyway he continued to shine his light on me, finding me cute and destructive, impishly deconstructive in my scholars-gone-wild tendencies. I considered myself a painfully earnest baby scholar, sacrificial and basically chaste. But that's another story.

Among the many things that I could tell you, I thought I might isolate one or two aspects of ongoing disruption within the seemingly secured spaces of thought that we shared. For instance, I might indicate the sheer stamina of Friedrich's arrival on the scene—I could say "intellectual scene," but that would be limiting, throwing me into a paleoynimic rut. To make it stick, I would have to go first to Lyotard and Blanchot's grappling with this word, *intellectual*, in order to give a sense of its depleted coverage. At one point, we had signed on with the project of *inventing disorders*; yet we were always menaced with losing the greater part of optimism about sustaining a worthy rebellion. Still, the turn toward media technology, already signaled in Plato but refitted to our needs, phantasms, and pathologies, was a way of undermining the ruling legitimacies with which we were faced. Friedrich's innovations allowed us to scramble the master codes, attack, with nearly Derridean precision, the sovereignty of the book and desecrate, where necessary, pernicious grammars of authority. It was our way, no doubt, of hacking in full view of disbelieving witnesses into the institution and reconfiguring the future of the archive. Despite our reticence on this point, we conducted guerilla raids, some of us, on the cognitive regimens that oppressed us, particularly those that threatened, we feared, to dumb us down—by the day, by the lecture, by the conference minutes. And so, led by Kittler, we entered a danger zone, eroding files, interrupting complacencies, immunizing the world from oppressive traditions involving knowledge storage and diffusion, and somehow even shaking up the prerogatives of sexual difference, though, undeniably, studies in the neighborhood of technology still, in some cases, brandish masculinist idols—by which I mean to indicate the survival of figures and habits of gender assignments, including what happens with the Turing test, even as the advent of genderless or rather gender-free, like caffeine-free, configurations had begun to assert themselves. In one of my reflections I wondered why there are so many cowboys in cyburbia—but that's another story, requiring another access code.[2] Let us continue with the present conversation, scanning my Kittlerian files.

The technomania of recent decades is perhaps drawing to a close as we are called upon to offer a sober reflection of where we have been, riding the inexorable wave of the technological incursion, what we've missed or miscalculated, our history of hyperbolic hopes and overextended tropes—but also the story of tremendous creativity, insight and political insistence. My own relation to media technological reflections has changed along with Friedrich's, perhaps improved, possibly switched into something else, barely recognizable in terms of those heady days when Kittler, as well as Nancy, Derrida, Lacoue-Labarthe, S. Weber, and so many others started up our idiomatic search engines, initialized, in my case, by a fateful conjunction of philosophy and psychoanalysis. A younger generation was waiting at the gate, including German cohorts such as Siegert, Dotzler, von Hermann, and Wetzel—mostly guys, if I am not mistaken, and not much gender-bending going on, with only some exceptions. They were luminous and continue to hit it out of the park. I had a visitor's pass with the many groups that Kittler generated and it is an injustice to refrain from enumerating them here, they are each so compelling, so I must offer apologies for the all too hasty rundown that cannot turn into an exhaustive or just history. I think of those who deserve to be registered in the remembrance of Kittler's circles, and I become unavoidably frustrated by my sense of limitation and paucity. I bring to mind those who counted for Friedrich, including Elisabeth Weber, who created a bridge between Derrida and Friedrich in her work, after study time with Lévinas. My home ground, *wie gesagt*, was *Germanistik*, which propelled me to the French side of things or, more appropriately, to the French appropriation of German thought. Forming gangs, though not so often tight as thieves, we drew up new maps and claimed territories that to some extent still hold today, though often disavowed or partially effaced. We do not sail under our own flag in the chronicles of the lingering culture wars and their residual static, but must forge alliances among incompatible if porous entities.

Nonetheless, the media technological territories that "we" farmed but also forced onto academic itineraries and new curricula were hospitable to and nurtured dissident energies, fugitive economies, and the beginnings of that monstrous aggregate that never quite works: interdisciplinary studies. Despite its inbuilt flaws, media technology, owing to its distinct mappings, has allowed for a durable if often secluded powwow among the transdisciplines of science, medicine, literature, economics, philosophy, legal studies, cinema and film studies, architecture, psychoanalysis—if only too rarely, psychoanalysis.

Media technology was the off ramp that many of us took to get a breather from the monumental monotony of the main highway of university transmission systems, and for some of us this detour was an existential necessity as well as a matter of "intellectual" probity—or let us take a cue from Benjamin and Kraus and call this a matter for "the rights of nerves." Entire nervous systems were at stake! Who could tolerate another recap of Goethe's dependency on Charlotte von Stein or the real story behind Werther's *Leiden* or Emilia's wrong turn and how she landed on Werther's suicide desktop—the positivist details for which normal, straight, and boring *Wissenschaft* was responsible, though it never went there, preferring instead to clean up Goethe's act and Lessing's deviancy. We couldn't take it any more, some of us, so we split. Still, there were custody battles. We were, some of us, not about to renounce Werther or any of the children soaked with tears, blood-drenched, gender-fragile: our children of German literature. They had to come along for the ride if they were to be sprung from the aura-sapping, deadly zones of regulated scholarship. So we thought, some of us. Poetically tuned, Kittler had led us to jam on the "ach!" of Sprache, to maternal pedagogies and lyrical breathalyzers. He broke down our resistance with the breathtaking repertory that he built, and won hearts with the tender acuity he showed literary history. The hard-edged grappling with musical theory still awaits its resonant and matching reception, though the upbeat has begun with Peter McMurray and others.

My only complaint about the splintered-off area of the culture wars that Friedrich in many ways initiated is that, in his aftermath, too often the ghosts were crowded out and left behind. Along with the growing population of ghosts left to their invisible stalks in the backrooms of the new technological emergence, a vital aspect of *theory*—the undecidable limit between literature and philosophy—was left more or less in the dust, tossed out, more or less abandoned. By this I mean that in my view (and don't forget that I wear night goggles so I take the insomniac view and stay up at night waiting for my ghosts: "There it goes, Horatio, thou art a scholar, speak to it"), in my unblinking view, media technology has in part wanted to demagnetize its field of vision or inquiry, clear the static, obliterate the parasite, mute the phantom—acts or aggressive passivities that amount to a betrayal and forgetting of its own history, which cannot be dissociated from any history of phantoms, no matter how improbable or difficult it remains to call up such an immaterial group of stalkers, whether they belong to the dead or rather undead colleagues of medial invention. Media technology to a significant degree has turned away from the very "obliterature" in which it originated. There would be no media technology without the invisible channel of ghostly visitations by which it is to this day tuned. The phantomal submission is not necessarily thematizable but a history of the spectral invasion that belongs, since Kittler, to any presentation of technological pervasiveness. . . . Excuse me. I don't know why I'm getting so worked up over this possible lacuna in contemporary studies, invoking nearly moralistic tonalities, which is not my style—*wait, correction.* It *is* my style. I have an awful tendency to *dozier* about and disturb the politer protocols to whose *justesse* I aspire when reflecting on general trends and tendencies in our shared fields of study. I apologize.

This hammering, this relentless making of a point, is not only a characteristic infirmity of scholarly speech but, in this case, comes, I imagine, from the habits of the detective agency for which I work. We track down the truth, that is, indissociably, *the crime* that started it all—we hunt down Oedipal tracks, genealogical purges, exclusionary operations, falsifications, metaphysical incidents, hermeneutic façades, and weak horizons in the most remote regions of thought. Not so long ago we had a specific case at hand. Friedrich and I called the dossier "The Test Drive" and had it published—admittedly, in my name, so that I could take the blame for some of the shenanigans, still unaccounted for—as a pretend-book (in my other job I get credit for the publication of our cases after I dress it up as scholarship, put it out there in earnest). In that investigation, we tracked down and interrogated the main culprits behind the age of experimentation. We outsourced some of our work to Husserl, Popper, Carnap, Derrida, Rheinberger—fellows who in some cases didn't even know that they were recruited to play a significant role in our team's findings. They may not know that they belong to an affiliate squad, but they each have a registration number. The search was prompted by Nietzsche, who nailed our technological age in terms of the "experimental disposition" that his work uncovered. We needed to build a dossier on Nietzsche's purported discovery by exposing what he was up to in the *Gay Science*—he confronted us with some very suspicious moves. We were looking into the "scientificity of science" in the Nietzschean vocabulary and in terms of the ends of man. Speaking of the ends of man—no, I'll get to that later.

Anyway, in an intellectually run detective agency, friendship is a hard nut to crack. It's as if everyone just sits in solitary, conferring with Nietzschean shadows in the aftermath of what Derrida has said that everyone else has said about the constitutive glitches in having or being a friend. How much dependency gets uploaded into the zones of friendship?

After Goethe, I went into a bit of a slump, feeling friendless, pulled into a Kleinian depressive disposition. I had lost my job and was kicked out of *Germanistik*. I had dug up too much dirt on my main man, Eckermann—wait a minute, I've already gone over this psychically dented material: *am I on repetition compulsion, traumatically stuck, or what!?!* I apologize for veering off like this. Let me take a breath, returning to the origin of another program.

(Ok. I'm back, sort of. *Sigh:* SighSignSing. Ahem.)

For Friedrich Kittler, the encounter with German letters, softened by a *Seufzer,* commences in a sigh. Even though he turned out in long stretches of his legacy to be a man's man—he fires up the technological libido and shows ballistic drivenness, delving into forbidden war cathexes, sleuthing in the cut-off narratives of our time, revisiting shrouded theaters of battle and the persistent glare of computer terminals—Kittler started up his own engines with feminine accents, as if to match his long flowing hair and sweet-toned accent. He brought to the podium the spritely, forgotten, but crucial Bettina von Arnim with his unforgettable paper, "Into the Wind, Bettina," a now legendary intervention first offered at the colloquium on the genre organized by Nancy and Lacoue-Labarthe, where Derrida presented "Law of Genre/Gender." Hamacher, too, was on-site, as were Weber, Paul de Man, and so many other A-listers in this Woodstock-at-Strasbourg of German philosophy and literature. Kittler's voice, though commanding, was softly supported by his lilting inflection and tender intonations. A soft-spoken advocate for any number of lost causes and genders in those days, he summoned up women's reading habits in the eighteenth century, Nietzsche's initializing stock of girl students, the flooding of the secretarial pool that changed the fate of letters and love stories (men started writing up the collective transference onto the secretary and gal Friday figures, the sudden population boom of Della Streets and Lois Lanes), the first time "Ladies" was added in the form of a public address: *"Ladies* and Gentlemen! Meine *Damen* und Herren!" And Kittler famously zoomed in on the *ach!* of Sprache—the ache of whatever thus spake, the indwelling "alas!" that he drew from language (*Sprache*). He observed in fact that German literature commenced in the *sigh:* "Die deutsche Literatur hebt an mit einem Seufzer."[3] Let me return to this cluster of concerns shortly. Right now, I need a time-out, a breather. I will switch off and regroup.

Even though the normative time for mourning has elapsed, I am still in considerable agony over this loss that I cannot settle with. When it washes over me, I want to cut out. Instead, I will be content to abide with a compromise formation. The multigenres that inform my own discursive run in this volume are meant to reflect, if possible, the different modalities and genders/genres that his oeuvre evokes and stimulates into play. Philosophizing with a stammer, I divert my course. It is now two years since the commemorative event at New York University. *Two years*: the normative time, says Freud, for a successful mourning. I am messing up.

I am committed to reading my friends, dead or alive, dead and alive, to reading them in the largest possible sense of translating and probing and wondering about their remote interiorities, even reading their signals to gauge whether they are mad, with or without me in certain instances. Yet, I also need to read *to* them. There's a sense in which I was always performing for Friedrich as a way of addressing his singularity and calling down our friendship. I will read to you, Friedrich, perform for you.

We are standing together breathing in and out.
Kaum ein Hauch

Kaum ein Hauch

Barely a breath,
 barely a whisper:
  respiration-aspiration-inspiration,

barely a breath . . .

 Kaum einen Hauch spürest du

Friedrich, the breathtaking, often-traveled zones where, or perhaps *when*, following his tempo, breath was at issue, sometimes heaving, but oftentimes barely trackable, still other times strongly in your face ("mein ganzes Lebenswerk: Atem" [my entire life's work: breath]). In a different way than we could grasp through Hölderlin's wind poems, the nor'easterly language carrier of greeting, there was the matter of Bettina. She wrote *into* the wind following very special velocities of saying to which Friedrich attuned us. Friedrich breathed life into the most moribund zones of scholarship— yes, scholarship for which he was considered, at times, the kiss of death—but he delivered his kiss more like the prince prodding Snow White out of toxic slumber.

If we are moved to reopen the scene of commemorative writing with the accent on music, and perhaps even with somewhat of a French accent—*mais oui, mais oui*—these accent marks come from Friedrich himself. Friedrich Kittler delivered dents and static and noise and scratches—accent marks and foreign phantoms—that he planted in the soil of Germanicity, ever practicing a politics of contamination. [*Noise! One minute.*] We understand how Friedrich became Greek and crashed against the walls of the incorporated intrusion. {{{{{{}}}}}} [*Something romantic and schmaltzy, one minute.*]

The first time I heard Friedrich—live, up close and personal—was that summer in Strasbourg. The gathering from all around in the heat of the summer became my Woodstock, offering up a private screening and life-spanning sneak preview, my very own Bayreuth, remastered—or, to be more truthful, my own Sonnenstein [*put up image of the* Schreber *asylum?*] or, even more precisely, my own asylum at Endenich [*image of the Schumann asylum?*], where I had accompanied Robert Schumann. Here, in Strasbourg, my year of teen passion, we assembled for the first time: Paul de Man, Werner Hamacher, Chris Fynsk, Wolfgang Iser, the foreboding Robert Jauss, and, of course, Derrida, as well as dozens upon dozens of figures and proper names that would become part of a kinship network, maybe a community without community—certainly without communion. I had already hooked up with Larry [*a musical or sound boost*], my primal community, but what happened at Bayreuth-Sonnenstein-Endenich-Strasbourg was destinal in another way, if not, to speak with Derrida, *destinerring*. Ever since the first encounter with Friedrich's voice I was put on the Hölderlinian ex-centric path, modulating mediations and vibing off techno-media. Let us meditate and remember. I call upon your assist, Mother of the Muses. [*Musical accompaniment: video, muted, of Friedrich teaching.*]

Friedrich was young, beautiful, streaming his long hair and sing-songing through the paper on Bettina, into the wind. I had never heard such a voice before, quietly—pianissimo, pianissimo—assertive. He broke through the armor of my ambivalence: the German language, stubbornly resisting transferability, nonetheless joined its musical counterpart, establishing a relation of affinity between music, pianissimo, pianissimo, *leise,* and the language that had sprung from Friedrich's mouth. [*Music.*]

His mouth. *Friedrich's mouth,* I tell you: This mouth that spoke to us through covert and wide-ranging broadcast systems, often patching into unconscious registers, typing up unprecedented links: the office space planting love, the new secretary. takes her post—*Ladies, Ladies,* [*explosive sound*] the catastrophic date when someone began his lecture with "Meine Damen," yes, with "Meine Damen und Herren"—"*Ladies,* Ladies and Gentlemen." Fr. Kittler pinpointed the event, the advent of a new syntagm: "*Ladies and Gentlemen!*"—the feminine flooding of office spaces *type type type, hello, this is your operator, tap, tap, tap* and classrooms filled with girl students reading in the mother tongue. Friedrich, the other, Nietzsche, taught girls in his classroom "*Meine Damen u. Herren! Tja, meine Damen!*" A philologizing mouth connected to note-taking fingers, nimble fingers, *tap tap tap this is your operator.* [*Sound effects to mark transition. To accompany the next segment could I possibly have some will-to-power sound, like the opening of R. Strauss, Zarathustra?*]

"Friedrich Kittler" as concept and powerhouse ("Nur was schaltbar ist, ist überhaupt") switched on the power but was also responsible for a number of telling power outages in the domains under which we routinely come alive or are crushed, eviscerated. He downsized the so-called humanities while driving and rerouting the very possibility of a cognitive circuitry. He squatted in the university system over which he shrewdly ruled: subversive and commanding at once, our Friedrich.

On the ground, Mr. Kittler cut deals among different territorial bosses, some of whose marks are represented in this volume.

> *Welche Sprache sprachen wir?*
>
> *Quelle langue parlions nous?*
>
> *What language did we speak?*

Friedrich, I am calling you in our languages, in the codes you taught, according to the tracks of reading that you laid down for us . . .

He was, at the time, they say, a wunderkind. He knew, they say, *Faust* by heart. "Aber Faust ist allein." That was my signal, the Goethe track, to sign up with Kittler's network. Years later, after a disastrous translation-for-hire fizzled out, he himself translated my Goethe book, and then left the only copy on the bus. [*Swoosh! Bang!*] We kept on giving each other gifts that seemed destined to dissolve or blow up in our faces. Once on the phone, he, impatient, *raised his voice to me*: "Give up your narcissism. A book is like a Molotov cocktail. Just throw it, already. The pin, Avi, has been pulled. Let it go." I stood my ground, refusing to let a piece-of-shit-joke-of-a-translation be published. *He yelled; I dug in.* Then he said, suddenly breathless: "OK, I'll translate it myself." *Page for page*; breathlessly.

> Kaum einen Hauch.
> Kaum einen Hauch
> **Barely a breath**
> Spürest du.

[*Fadeout music*]

Listening to Friedrich, I liked to travel beneath the sonic layers. Friedrich, your mouth, the way language sourced in you, the craving for cigarettes, a bottle of gin: count me in, what else have you got? Santa Barbara, Berkeley, New York City, Bochum, Paris, Berlin, count me in, Freiburg: your *bedingungslose Liebeserklärung für Heidegger* (your profession of "unconditional love for Heidegger"): count me in, kind of, stilling me in the radically ambivalent stance I hold.

Your love for love, the way we spoke about love that last time, all day in your apartment, and then during the taxi ride and in the restaurant. You said that Lacan said that *all love is requited*. You were shattered by the girl in your class who repelled, you thought, your love: the beginning of the end, you said, on the transferential turnkey *Repelled?* How could that have happened, the shudder, the aversion? You said Lacan said love was *always* requited. You were shattered by the girl in your class. "Always requited." I saw this phrase quoted in *Dracula's Legacy*. Maybe you tripped over the translation: I'm thinking, did you fall into a calamitous error in translation, Friedrich? And as Heidegger (on whom you bestowed your unconditional love) had said, Heidegger said, Friedrich, that an error in translation could trip us up for two hundred, maybe two thousand years, Friedrich—really scarring and digging into the body, Friedrich, I am talking *Leib* with Husserl, not mere *Körper* or exteriority. Heidegger said, remember, "Wir leben indem wir leiben," we body in, we body forth, we body live, intimately. All love: *requited*, Friedrich. I thought, what if Lacan meant—or wrote, rather—something like "all love is returned?" *Returned*, Friedrich. Turning the dials, maybe returned to sender, Friedrich. Or, sent off as in one of metaphysics' great turnovers. Or, the way the envelope in *La lettre volée* [*The Purloined Letter*] is turned inside out like a glove. We turned ourselves inside out, Friedrich, like the discarded *g-love*.

I want to return your love, and, if the time had been granted us, we would replay the stakes, jamming the transferential networks, keying into the worlds that you convoked in the absence of world, in the decline of *Menschen*—you always said *Leute*, calling up your peeps to unload the metaphysical skin of *Menschen*. And when *Menschen* showed up on your scanners, you tended to say "so-called *Menschen*."

While close to you I started studying strategies for making so-called friends—sizing the performativity of asserting friendship, however ill-fated among colleagues, the student body, within and without the vampirizing bureaus of our university (I remember your genealogy of the *Gymnasium*: when and where and why *um Himmelswillen* did the university append a gym, and, by the way, thank goodness they did, because I had to build muscle, stress manage, man up, pump irony nearly every day when I got my recess pass and they let me off the leash for a short spell. You, you metabolized anguish differently. Puff, puff, rock 'n' roll, sip, gulp, sip gulp, puff, puff. [*Sound effects.*] I tried to make and keep friends on my way, and you, Friedrich, you derailed the kinship network by bravely making enemies, by your often rapid turnover of friends; not all were disposed of, there were lifers, but you oddly drummed people out, I'm not sure how one does that—others are so overcrowded and alone at once, standing room only in the spectral section. Still others go from zero to dick in under thirty seconds and mash up the most sensitive creatures that come to work and be with them. You, Friedrich, brought love and gratitude from all

around; yet, you also turned many away, in your way, creating a whole economy class of those who went sour, as we say in English and German, but differently. So the range of transferential adhesion became wide and large—from
the class of psychotic "fusionals," those from whom you could not unstick, no
matter what, to the avenger types ready to come out *just about now* from cold
storage. That square footage of transference in itself is a *Leistung*, my friend,
quite a feat, and somehow, I feel honor-bound to mention, if tremulously, that
some of us here disconnected a while ago; others stayed on for the long haul;
still others are poised as Nietzschean friends of the future, yet to come around.
I want to express my admiration for the trove of ambivalence you managed to
build—a historically necessary turn, no doubt, given the shadows and abysses
that you dropped into, implacably.

[*Sonic intrusion and/or fadeout.*]

AUDIENCE: Kaum . . .

Kaum . . .

Kaum . . .

SINGLY, WHISPERING YET DRAMATICALLY: ein Hauch!

[*Sonic accompaniment/choreography.*]

I want to return to a moment that others may not underscore and I place under
the heading of your "becoming Greek." I am on repetition compulsion. Let me
resume, rewind. For I will not have said this enough times: You were—despite
all the drab land- and soundscapes, and the hollow clanging of the technological death-drive, some strange pronouncements and stranger levels of ballistic
excitation—you were, despite it all, attached to the idea of *beauty*. You turned
your gaze to the precincts of Grecian beauty. Sound byte: The way he oriented
himself toward beauty was part of a deeply felt philosophical move.

*Your beauty had preceded you. And when you exclaimed "into the wind, Bettina,"
your hair streamed.*

One of the projects on my to-do list: Not only in the sense of the "Tyranny of Greece over Germany" and other angles of Winckelmania, and not
only in terms of the Kittler *Odyssey*, your visit with the sirens in an extravagant burst of geo-empirical resolve your famous convoy to the Greek isles,
but also, I would like to unfold one day the Dionysian starts and fits with
which we associate some of your insights, even the most scientific, the way you
pushed off from the shores of norms and their inherited knowledge systems.
[*Sound.*]

Friedrich could easily become ensnared by his material and empirical pursuits. Sometimes he confounded his friends by his literal-mindedness, his stubborn attempts to pin things down without theoretical bulwarking. When he turned his gaze on Greece, however, and set the GPS to locate the call of the sirens, Friedrich was still, inescapably, philosophically engaged: he was trying to find something more originary, a lost ground, the origin of language and music. He traveled the labyrinth of the ear understanding only too well the dangers of tracing the call to a locatable source. The calamitous encounter with beauty in some ways pushed him overboard. [*Sound*.]

But Friedrich, intensely aware of the snares of dangerous merger, had also auditioned opera, knowing full well that opera continually remixes Babel, always introducing the trauma of separation—a traumatic fissuring that Wagner sought to mute. Friedrich, for the most part, disabled the totalitarian merger. "Warte nur, bald rauschest du auch" (riffing off Goethe: soon you, too, will sound/noise). [*Sound*.]

How Friedrich became Greek

Not everyone could stomach certain aspects of the Kittler phenomenon. His locutions were in many ways uncompromising, bereft of sentimental adornment, and hard-nosed in the style of apodictic assertion. He did not apologize for his country's Nazi past, took no recourse to mollifying tonalities. Friedrich was spare in the cautionary framing of his work; maybe he didn't feel it was his place to apologize for the unthinkable; maybe he thought it wasn't "unthinkable" and kept the pose of an implacable scientific glare, the critical glacialization for which he in some circles was known, even disparaged. Scoping the metaphysical buildup, he followed theoretical consequences to their dismal endpoint, culminating in his nation's history with deluded genocidal prerogative. He tallied the destructions of world for which the techno-scientific mind-cast was responsible. I valued the way he went about his work, undeterred, obstinately on point. I will not hide from you the part or parts of his work that still make me shudder. For, when all is said and done, I am not on a recovery mission or part of a cleanup crew commissioned by mourning, writing through an idealizing haze—well, maybe, a little; but I have not removed my critical sensors or totally lost my mind.

Friedrich had his tendencies. He prompted and prodded, he provoked and pushed; he could kick you over considerable edges. I follow him to the limit of unsayables, dumbly watching the curls of his cigarette smoke spiral upward. He pushed and provoked. He huffed and puffed. Puff, puff. He hacked. He stopped taking transatlantic flights, because he needed to smoke and they wouldn't let him.

A couple of times he pushed some of us too far. This "too far" awaits reflection, its particular articulation and measure. I do not deny that sometimes the startling prod—the Heideggerian "Stoss" a hesitation between violation and caress—evokes precisely what one needs at times of critical slumber: to be pushed too far. In terms of historical recklessness, we have gone too far, and Friedrich can provide the gauge for the hubristic lunge.

Friedrich stayed close to the ground of our shared Greek heritage, sometimes frayed, sometimes forgotten, often mismanaged. More often distorted—though, what memory endowment is not given to such torsions? Friedrich dazzled with Greekness, bravely walked into ancient rifts and the claims they continued to have on his work. Let us move forward by tuning Plato, by seeing the way at very least that Friedrich was tuned by Plato.

Whether configured in the feminine, or as music, or as language, or routed all along the Goethe ramp, beauty entranced Friedrich in ways that we want to account for, at least, partially, at this time. In the way he embraced beauty, the way he conducted Eros, Friedrich was Greek. Friedrich went after the sirens in the end; he wanted to encounter the extreme limit of possible encounter, traveling the destructive edges of desire, tapping an account drawn out by the writings of Kafka and Blanchot. Following the call, both piercing and aphonic, our Friedrich wanted to know the place—if it was even a matter of place—where the sirens had broken eardrums, wept, seduced, turned silent. Friedrich Kittler thought he could go there. And, once again, he went very far.

Let us be clear. Besides Plato, most philosophers have not dropped anchor in the deep waters of Eros (apart from St. Bernard and Lévinas). Friedrich was keyed into the beauty, exaltation, the blossoming out of Eros—the way it was in excess with regard to its very concept, if "concept" there was. Beauty proffers the only form that bursts out, raying resplendently—justice and wisdom, as Jean-Luc Nancy tells us, do not blow up beyond their appearances. But beauty—beauty is in the first place splendid to see, though it takes us beyond sight: it comes at us as the excess of phenomenality even as it remains the form itself of the visible, underlying the possibility of vision.

Beauty, as extreme flush of brilliance, evokes transport, ecstatically divine vision, skimming off phronesis, as form that one cannot see. At once a stroke of divine vision and that which exceeds the visible, beauty makes us crazy beyond words, which is why Aristotle swoops in at the seductive shimmer of beauty to caution <u>prudence</u>. The nonvisible, the sheer dazzle of beauty is important for Plato, delivering an excess over and above the appearance on which it depends: the desirable is not visible—a quality, or nonquality, of key importance for Freud and Lacan, who read off the <u>Glanz</u> and shimmer—but orients itself toward the extreme limit of this dazzle. Beauty means that we are bedazzled, not moving toward the intelligible but held at the portal of the sensible, breath-taken. The excitation of what happens at first sight, when one is struck or already blinded, at first sight, meaning also off or out of sight, occurs in art and Eros, when the body, according to Nancy, is thrown outside itself, ex-cited, reminding us of the Latin <u>exciter</u>: to be called outside of oneself, to be called out, outside oneself to one's greatest, most intimate interiority: <u>ex-citer</u>.

This excursus may help to explain why I indulged the imprudence of making something of Friedrich's beauty at first sight, his beauty in all senses, in the sense of <u>übersinnlich</u> or as what jumps the senses, and I wonder if it's a girlie thing to have done so, even though it's an age-old guy thing, starting with the ancients, so tensed up were they by the iridescence of beauty. In enraptured excitement the body, rising up, gets lost. [<u>Clang.</u>]

The time for acute grief, they say, has come to an end, and the moment has come to offer reflection. I do not customarily separate grief from reflection, but I understand the imperative to get over oneself somehow, for the purposes of assuming the stances and responsibility of thinking, of offering hospitality to the work and person of our friend and teacher yet to come, one whom I will not cease to address, receive, contemplate. It's not only his work or how he "worked it" that compels our attention, but also the way he suspended working through, precisely *refusing* to "work through" the more lacerating motifs and disastrous commitments of our time which, since Heidegger, whom Kittler loved "unconditionally," involves the university, its peculiar language and housing projects. Friedrich studied and commanded the university in unprecedented ways, much like Derrida, who boldly reviewed the university in the eyes of its pupils. He gave me the means by which to imagine self-constitution—or even a *Selbstbehauptung* (self-affirmation), Heidegger's freighted term—in and *despite* a hostile university environment.

Let me resume my narration, the story of a faltering *selbst-Behauptung* that led me to Friedrich in the first place. For the most part, I was at a loss. These

r paneled by sheer driveness, when one didn't always
w to become a genuine scholar without losing one's
break it down by stating that I come from a blended
lagged by shared custody of mostly lost and forgotten
ist, utterly forlorn, I was largely on my so-called own,
"we are family" stride. This was not easy, nor always
with Kittler gave me a techno-theoretical zip code, a
uote the coded phrasing of the other guardian. Still,
led our sectors differently, according to different flags
of urgency. One could say that we practiced distinct modalities of *complaining*,
differently cutting up our shares of the *schreiben/Schrei* assigned by our reciprocal and overlapping heritages, unleashing the plaintive cry.

For Friedrich Kittler, the encounter with German letters, softened by a
Seufzer, a sigh, lies somewhere between a moan and lament. *Seufzer* rings out
at the starting gate of the literary adventure, tilting toward the eternal feminine of language utterance—one is tempted to say, *mutterances*, in a trans-
linguistic sweep that involves the maternal marker, *Mutter*, and the English
drone of muttering, something that gets said under the breath, just below the
sonic level of sense-making. Perhaps the mutter is a way of revving up the
complaint, as well as the inventory of German literature: is one addressing
oneself, as split-off part, or simply falling chronically short of a proper address
when muttering "to oneself" following the covert boomerang trajectory of
the whimpered shortfall? Yet this is how Goethe has Faust start up when he
opens the scene of the modern German language, the start-up fund of German literature: "Habe nun ach! Philosophie," and so forth, mutters Faust. The
scene opens on a complaint, just as *Werther* enfolded the right to complain
as one of the principal themes of the Sturm und Drang suicide novel. Faust
groans that he's at a dead-end: he has done all the work, knows everything, yet
knows not enough of what really counts, that is, the incalculable, and cannot
be satisfied by mere knowledge—the cognitive levers available to him, lock-
ing him only into the realm of the possible. Nor can he be expected to keep
himself in a restricted Kantian zone of knowability. This is a loose translation,
but on point and battle ready. (With Kittlerian bravado, I'd defend it against
any philological busybody.) *Faust*, breakthrough work of German modernity,
comes online with a hysteric's wish for *more*, wanting the *impossible*. Many of
us remember the Freudian joke that asks, "What's the difference between a
hysteric and an obsessional neurotic?" The hysteric says, "Is that all there is?"
The neurotic, stalling, stopped short by the overwhelmed sense of encroach-
ing things, says, "This is too much." Faust opens up the hysteric's *demande*
for more and better, but with *"ach!"* interceding the matter of an initiating

surrender comes up, a ready resignation—the place where the complaint strikes out *demande*. I will unpack this elsewhere, to show how the complaint serves notice to the analyst, functions as the psychoanalyst's defeat, erasing the *demande*—an intrigue for which analysis must pay back all sorts of psychic loans: *"Ach!"*

The sigh that initiates German literature grew up in the neighborhood of the swoon, the eclipse of meaning that populated so many texts of the eighteenth century, where the experience of *Ohnmacht* has said something about textuality and its diminishing capture, its suspension of consciousness at moments of decision. In Kleist's *Marquise von O* the protagonist famously faints and the text follows her down by instituting a dash at the nonrendered core of events. The narrative ceases to be, it cannot say what has happened. The evental pivot of the story disappears into a voided syncope. We are given to understand, by the insertion of a diacritical mark and her bloating "figure," that the text concedes failure on this point, unable to control or tell a rape scene. For Kleist, the origin of inscriptive saying, here and elsewhere, is smeared by an initial violation. Everything subsequently grows around the textual gash, a traumatic seizure that marks the dilemma of all texts: tenacious silencing and embedded disturbance, an origin that cannot testify for itself, knowing no witness or advocate to haul in a lost causality, some generative principle to call up hospitable ground. The text, left to fend for itself, ducks into corners, substituting for storytelling with a stock of trip ups, descents, and blushes. The blush, in particular, serves to carry an entire phrasal regime in Kleist that vies with muted language. The red splotch, or *read* splotch, registers a level of affect or meaning that remains at a loss for words, uncontrolled, unreadably lodged between shame and excitement, confession and disavowal—it indicates the bleeding qualities of a text that swarms over its boundaries into shock areas that cannot be subdued by meaning or even, for that matter, perceived.

In the case of the Marquise one wonders if the blush speaks for her, at moments when she cannot stand up for herself, or does it rather betray her with a sudden spread of skin mapping, releasing a secret or indexing a moral blemish, a pigmentation in concourse with the scarlet letter and birthmark of Hawthorne's brandishing. In some instances, the blush manages to register a complaint for the reticent Marquise, and it signs off on an unspoken accusation. As blossoming of sense, blushing betokens involuntary emergence, though it has been layered with cultural significance: who is capable of blushing, of evincing moral indignation or decency's outrage? The ability to blush, to show a purported inner life of morality, has delivered some troubling racialist output that no one wants to overlook. *Ach!*

CODA: WHAT I SAID WHEN I WAS INVITED TO SPEAK AT THE FUNERAL
"Laß das Heulen!"

*. . . schon eine erste Kontrollinstanz, die einigermaßen universal ist.
Sie befiehlt Menschen, menschliche Sprache, tierisches Heulen und
unmenschliches Blabla voneinander zu scheiden.*

Aufschreibesysteme, 22

He writes and cites the injunction: "'Stop crying!' A first more or less universal control point. It commands that humans distinguish human speech from animal howling from inhuman blah blah blah." *Yet, I weep, I howl. I must suppress my weeping; I halt my howling. I move tentatively toward what he understood better than any other as Spr-ach-e.*

My dear Friends, essential colleagues, copilots and instigators of trouble, my brothers and sisters, Doktor children of Friedrich! (And so the question immediately arises of how we relate to one another, what kind of disruptive kinship we establish or network of signifiers we find ourselves enmeshed in, and how we might detect crucial or even contingent bonds.) I shall do my utmost to simplify. I reset.

Dear fellow and sister mourners:

On the face of it, I have only one thing to say, barely eliciting language, barely able to float, a mere sonic stutter that Kittler taught us to read: *Ach!* Vibing off *Faust*, he gave us a sense of dispossession and the affirmative stance of letting go: "Habe nun ach . . ." I will cut off the utterance and leave it be, waving at the distance, remembering only and evermore what he wrote about the **"Zerlegung Spr/ach/e"** when he threw us a first Molotov cocktail in the guise of a book, the still arriving *Aufschreibesysteme*.

Deeply moved, I am considerably appeased to have found the stamina to share this moment of impossible transition with you, to say with you, in all our languages, good-bye to the great teacher and friend, Friedrich Kittler, who was my spirit partner, the soul mate, according to all sorts of imponderable grids and **scores**—what the French call *partition*, indicating musical notations as well as divisions, those of self-divisions and rhythmic intimacies, involving the phrasing of cadences. (**Cadences**: Nietzsche saw the cadence as essential to the understanding of humankind and what was said—when the time came to separate from him—that Wagner lacked. I want to take back and own that very sense of cadence; can I have it please?) Friedrich: he had an acute sense of cadence and reminded me constantly that we are not immortal. E-mails and phone calls saying that we are not immortals, but *sterblich*: Finite and *zerbrechlich* (fragile).

He urged, with stern conviction, that I come to see him in Berlin. Time and again, he set the metronome and reminded me of our mortal torsions and fateful reductions. He called, wrote, and commanded me in keenly felt ways.

I am in acute grief, truly bereft, yet in my capacity, however weakened, of carrier of a poetic word I am bound to say this much: I did not come here to bring you down or strike the peculiar atonalities of a *Klagelied* (lamentation). I have to imagine that, among us, there are widely varied transferential programs running, some in the background, some subtle, half-intelligible, or noisily foregrounding, and some frank pitches of confusion and irresolution with this being, Friedrich—A. or no A.—Kittler. Our Friedrich bristled with abundant being, so he inescapably provoked capacious and even, at times, I suppose, extreme forms of reactivity to his vigorous dazzle.

I have perhaps another history with him, with its unique and precious facets, in some ways less programmable than other intense relations may be, with their internal combustions and danger zones, their relatable narrations. I am open to telling you something about this incomparable cut of relatedness, its ecstatic breaches, and the nearness to Friedrich and his families of students and friends that brace and honor me to this day. But I stand here not only in the astonishing light of a strong and stellar friendship. I have the sense that, somewhat like a person of indecipherable, if provisional impact, I also nonetheless belong to several districts and fields; I hold and speak for deliberations that have been made among different territorial bases, only some of which I represent. I come here to sign on the American adherents, on both coasts—the algorithms of our encounter having involved the West and the East Coasts, principally California and New York City—and I also bring greetings from those in Paris who mourn with us. In terms of those who have already have left their mortal bodies I know that Jacques Derrida was attached to Friedrich, as were Lacoue-Labarthe and so many friends, most recently at the Louvre, where Friedrich had presented a part of his work.

For some reason I lucked out, for I am the beneficiary of the powerful and cloudless friendship that Friedrich showed me, granting me something like unconditional approbation. I don't know how it came about, the generosity of friendship, yet it installed itself with a kind of traumatic implacability—a spontaneous and absolute gift that I could not feel I deserved. Let me tell you a couple of things about us in abbreviated form so that you can at least have a snapshot or flavor of an inexhaustible tremor of reciprocation, openheartedness, the warmth and confidence that sealed our earthly deal from day one. *Ach!*

I met, or rather experienced Friedrich at what I would call the Woodstock of my intellectual history, the Bayreuth ("bereits bereut" says Nietzsche deciphering the ur-Woodstock, the very opposite of my euphorically pitched Woodstock).

It was 1978 or 1979—I have to check. It is inscribed in Derrida's *Postkarte*, so it has been officially postmarked and part of the technology that Derrida sets in motion in that book of encounters and telecommunicational outreach. I am too lost and bereft to historicize the first encounter with exactitude: I apologize. 1978 or 1979, therefore. *Ach! Ach!* Why this stutter? I will pull myself together and tell the story, part of it at least. Our version of Woodstock/Bayreuth (or Woodstock the sequel as anti-Bayreuth, in any case the originary sequel, but let me continue and release the stall) took place in Strasbourg: the famous colloquium on the genre/*Gattung*. At that occasion, I met nearly everyone who was to become important to me. My cannibalistic libido was in full throttle.

I introjected and incorporated and ate up most of the Daseins and lectures that came to perform there: nearly everyone who was anyone in German and French letters—or in what was ambivalently to be tagged and retagged as "theory," "Continental philosophy," "literary theory," "media technology," and so forth. We were sailing out under inappropriable flags. Then one very sunny afternoon, I had **my own Weltatem experience**: young Friedrich on Bettina. I cannot begin to describe the thrall, the rich and jolting discovery, the voice and sing-song German and English pronunciations, the sheer audacity and heart-stopping brilliance of the delivery. The tender tone and beautiful face, at once pretty and handsome, boygirlboygirl. It was love at first bite! We were all stalled, really halted, by the thrill of his language, the very sound of his voice. Soft but deliberate. The wavy hair.

Believe it or not, beyond the rich mappings he was to produce, the off-ramp to media technology and the other neighborhoods of thought that he owned—beyond the fact that he was **the good breast of Germanistik** (how else was I to approach *Germanistik* if not by means of his special deviancy?), Friedrich Kittler introduced a way to think about women that had not been seen before. He created his very own branch affiliate of wayward feminism that still needs to be explored and savored (admitting here what Sigrid Weigel and Antje Pfannkuchen have begun to do). At the same time, he was, in the literary and technological fields that he ruled, unquestionably butch. This may seem contradictory, but it's not. He made it necessary to sing in the wind, Bettina. He nurtured us newly. Derrida, de Man, Lacoue-Labarthe, Nancy—all the big guns were stunned. I remain frozen in that moment of discovery and commitment to the incomparable intervention, audacious and singular, calibrated on intensely intelligent triggers of awareness.

Of course, parts of Friedrich were reputed to be difficult and recalcitrant. He could repel certain offers or situations mercilessly. Nonetheless we spent endless, immortal days in the sun, talking, planning, rock 'n' rolling in the timespan of a frankly Nietzschean Great Health that was allotted to us. We were strong in our sense of fragility—defiant, "throned on the highest bliss" (Milton), grateful to be able to break down the clichés that blunted our friends in the university; we were well enough, in those days, to stay up all night and talk about Jimmy Hendrix and Johnny Goethe, making them our organic buddies and support group. We didn't do hard drugs together, *bereits bereut*, but we were manifestly high on each other and lectured together in Berkeley and Santa Barbara and New York and Bochum. And once, in Bochum, after we had said good night—it was very late—a group of us led by Bernhard (Siegert) realized that we were suffering from an unacceptable load of separation anxiety. So we turned the car around and walked up the stairs to Friedrich's apartment—it was way past 2:00 am—and rang his doorbell. Again. Friedrich gave a sigh of relief upon seeing us return, saying something like: "You've understood. Thank God." He said he was glad that we had come back to him, and he welcomed us inside. Again.

Here, today, on this afflicting occasion, I must walk away empty-handed, as Benjamin says of the *Trauerspiel*'s allegory. I must break off my narration. My words do not even amount to a reflection. They're an effect of a mere reflex, a stagger and the hold-out sigh. Basically, I remain *Spr/ach/los*. Honestly, I just wanted to show up for you and him, for my adopted families and Wolf, Alma, Susanne, Erika Kittler, and those who visit me in New York and Paris, and who talk to me about Friedrich Kittler. I stop myself. Hier das Ach, Minimalsignifikat poetischer Liebe. . . . "Die Tränen wären ihr beinahe aus den Augen gestürzt, und sie sprach laut: 'Ach es ist ja wahr, er liebt mich nicht, und ich werde nimmermehr Frau Hofrätin!'": (Here, the "ach," as minimal signification of poetic love. . . . The tears nearly cascaded from her eyes and she cried out loudly, "Ach! It is true, he does not love me, and I will never ever become Mrs. CEO.")

Thank you, my Friedrich.[4]

NOTES

1. Avital Ronell, *What Was I Thinking? A Critical Autobiography and Spectral Colloquy: The History of My Unthought*, ed. Sladja Blazan (Berlin: Druckerei Elsholz, 2011).

2. Avital Ronell, *Finitude's Score: Essay Toward the End of the Millennium* (Lincoln and London: University of Nebraska Press, 1994)

3. "Die deutsche Dichtung hebt an mit einem Seufzer" is the opening sentence and salvo of Kittler's *Aufschreibesysteme 1800/1900* (Munich: Wilhelm Fink Verlag, 2003), 11.

4. As I was putting together this contribution, I received an unexpected message from his literary executor and, I believe, official wife, Susanne Holl. Preparing the digital *Nachlass* files for the Literaturarchiv Marbach, she found a note regarding or possibly addressed to me, in any case about someone bearing my name. It's as if he were speaking

from the beyond, showing me with characteristic irony how we are given to warp and distortion as we set about to mirror and reminisce about each another. With the exception maybe of "The Ballad of John and Yoko," "Here Comes the Sun," and possibly "Get Back," I am not a Beatles' girl, but he had me on an idiomatic playlist. Thank you, my Friedrich, for these instabilities, too. Susanne e/writes:

Dearest Avital,

this is just ein kleiner Gruß, though a bittersweet one. Currently I am preparing a working session in the Literaturarchiv Marbach. . . . In looking through his text files I found one bearing your name: avital.lat. It is very short and seems to be the beginning of an Aufsatz (he always started with his name, and then he typed the title in capital letters). I can't help but sending it to you without hesitation, take it as a token of Friedrich—and of my admiration. Yours, Susanne (Hope you are well!!!)

Friedrich Kittler

WAS ZU TUN IST

Was Avital uns alles schon geschrieben hat.

Imagine, unsere Wissenschaft von gestern: Sie fing bei einem Beatles-Song an, fand imagination auch bei Locke und kehrte endlich, wenn noch Zeit blieb, bei Aristoteles und dem phantasma heim. Am liebsten aber schwelgte sie in Konstruktionen, unbegrenzten Möglichkeiten, denen in der Seinsgeschichte nichts entsprach.

Denn wir sind die Sterblichen, lauter Grenzen ausgesetzt.

Imagine, unsere Wissenschaft von heute: Wir fangen bei Homeros an, weil mit Homeros alles anfing und schreiben uns nach vorn, immer aber rekursiv. Es gibt gar keinen Fortschritt, geschweige denn zum MIT; Denken bleibt der Dank für Allerältestes.

CONTRIBUTORS

RÜDIGER CAMPE is professor and chair of German and professor of comparative literature at Yale University. His books include *Affekt und Ausdruck* [Passion and Expression] (1990), *The Game of Probability: Literature and Calculation between Pascal and Kleist* (2012), and *Rethinking Emotion: Interiority and Exteriority in Premodern, Modern and Contemporary Thought* (2014), which he coedited with Julia Weber. He has widely published on aesthetics and rhetoric; literature, philosophy and the history of science; baroque theater; and the modern novel since the eighteenth century. He focuses on fundamental topics of the humanities from antiquity to modernity: intuition and visualization, advocacy and agency (*Fürsprache*), and the scene of writing.

JEFFREY CHAMPLIN teaches literature at the Barenboim-Said Academy in Berlin and is associate fellow at the Hannah Arendt Center at Bard College. He is the author of *The Making of a Terrorist: On Classic German Rogues* (2015) and the editor of *Terror and the Roots of Poetics* (2013). Champlin has also published articles on authors including Sophocles, Goethe, Kleist, Hegel, Arendt, and Sarah Kane.

BERNHARD J. DOTZLER is professor of media studies at the University of Regensburg. He is the author of *Papiermaschinen: Versuch über Communication and Control in Literatur und Technik* (1996), *L'Inconnue de l'art: Über Medien-Kunst* (2003), *Diskurs und Medium: Zur Archäologie der Computerkultur* (2006), *Diskurs und Medium II: Das Argument der Literatur* (2010), *Diskurs und Medium III: Philologische Untersuchungen: Medien und Wissen in literaturgeschichtlichen Beispielen* (2011), coeditor, with Henning Schmidgen, of *Parasiten und Sirenen: Zwischenräume als Orte der materiellen Wissensproduktion* (2008), and editor of *Bild/Kritik* (2010).

HANS ULRICH GUMBRECHT is the Albert Guérard Professor in Literature at Stanford University. His books on literary theory and literary and cultural history include *Eine Geschichte der spanischen Literatur* (1990); *Making Sense in Life and Literature* (1992); *In 1926—Living at the Edge of Time* (1998); *Vom Leben und Sterben der grossen Romanisten* (2002); *The Powers of Philology* (2003); *Production of Presence* (2004); *In Praise of Athletic Beauty* (2006); *California Graffiti—Bilder vom westlichen Ende der Welt* (2010); *Unsere breite Gegenwart*; and *Stimmungen lesen: After 1945— Latency as Origin of the Present* (2013). Gumbrecht is a regular contributor to the *Frankfurter Allgemeine Zeitung, Neue Zürcher Zeitung*, and *Estado de São Paulo*. He is a member of the American Academy of Arts and Sciences, Professeur attaché at Collège de France, and a Professor Catedratico Visitante Permanente at the Universidade de Lisboa.

HANS-CHRISTIAN VON HERRMANN is professor of literature and science at Technische Universität Berlin. He published books on Brecht's media aesthetics and on the media history of the European Theater. In 2015, he coedited *Lesen—ein Handapparat* (with Jeannie Moser), a book on reading as a cultural technique in transition.

UTE HOLL is professor for media aesthetics at Basel University. Her main fields of research are the history and aesthetics of audiovisual media—specifically of acoustics, electro-acoustics, and radiophonic cultures—filmic forms and cinematic perception, and aesthetic theories of technical media. Her publications include *Kino, Trance und Kybernetik* (2012), *Cinema, Trance and Cybernetics* (2017); *Der Moses Komplex: Politik der Töne, Politik der Bilder* (2014), translated as *The Moses Complex: Schoenberg, Freud, Straub/Huillet* (2016). She also coedited, with Matthias Wittmann, *Memoryscapes: Filmische Formen der Erinnerung* (2014).

ALEXANDER LAMBROW is a Ph.D. candidate in the Department of Germanic Languages and Literatures at Harvard University. His research interests include modernist literature, film studies, and critical theory.

ANTJE PFANNKUCHEN teaches at Dickinson College in Pennsylvania. Her research is concerned with the relationships of media technology, science, literature, and art, especially in the late eighteenth and early nineteenth centuries. She has published articles on Georg Christoph Lichtenberg, Johann Kaspar Lavater, and Ezra Pound. Her book *Printing the Invisible* (forthcoming) investigates the connections between the prehistory of photography and German romantic poetry and science.

LAURENCE A. RICKELS: After thirty years teaching German and comparative literature at the University of California, Santa Barbara, in 2011 Laurence A. Rickels accepted the professorship in art and theory at the Staatliche Akademie der Bildenden Künste Karlsruhe as successor to Klaus Theweleit. Twice an Emeritus in 2017, he still holds the Sigmund Freud Chair in Media and Philosophy at the European Graduate School and, in spring semester 2018, joins the German faculty of New York University as Eberhard Berent Visiting Professor and Distinguished Writer in Residence. Rickels is the author of *Aberrations of Mourning* (1988), *The Case of California* (1991), *Nazi Psychoanalysis* (2002), *The Vampire Lectures* (1999), *The Devil Notebooks* (2008), *Ulrike Ottinger. The Autobiography of Art Cinema* (2008), *I Think I Am. Philip K. Dick* (2010), *SPECTRE* (2013), *Germany. A Science Fiction* (2014), and *The Psycho Records* (2016).

MERT BAHADIR REISOĞLU is a doctoral candidate in comparative literature at New York University. After having earned his BA in philosophy and literature at Yale University, he has written his master's thesis on the role of sacrifice in Bataille's work. His dissertation concerns the relationship between Turkish-German literature and transnational media. His research interests are Turkish-German literature, contemporary German literature, modernism, media theory, film history, and contemporary Turkish literature.

NIMROD REITMAN received his PhD from the Department of German at New York University in June 2015 and is currently the 2016 Albert Einstein Fellow at the Einstein Forum, Potsdam. The historical and philosophical frameworks of his research aim at marking disjunctions in figuration as seen both in the philosophy and the history of thought in romantic and modernist poetry. His dissertation—entitled "On the Serious Motherhood of Men: Dissonance in Music, Rhetoric, and Poetry"—describes covert maternal tropologies and disruptions effected by femininity in theories of subjectivity and the history and rhetoric of lamentation in German, Italian, and Hebrew literature. He has also curated several exhibitions in Israel and Germany.

AVITAL RONELL has relentlessly enfolded *Germanistik* in deconstructive reading practices, frequently taking the off-ramp into media theory, of which she is one of the founders. She has taught an annual course with Derrida at New York University. Most recently she offered a lecture performance at the Théâtre de l'Odéon with Pierre Alferi on the disappearance of authority. Her recent works include *The Test Drive* (2007), *The ÜberReader* (2007), *Fighting Theory : In Conversation with Anne Dufourmantelle* (2010), and *Loser Sons: Politics and Authority* (2013). A forthcoming book, *Complaint: Grievance among Friends*, is on the runway.

BERNHARD SIEGERT, Dr. phil. habil., is the Gerd Bucerius Professor for Theory and History of Cultural Techniques at the Media Faculty at Bauhaus University Weimar. Since 2008, he has also been a director of the International Research Center for Cultural Techniques and Media Philosophy at Weimar and since 2013, he has been the speaker of the DFG Research Network "Media and Mimesis" (Weimar, Bochum, Munich, Zurich, Basel, Frankfurt am Main) funded by the Deutsche Forschungsgemeinschaft (DFG). His recent books include *Passage des Digitalen: Zeichenpraktiken der neuzeitlichen Wissenschaften 1500–1900* (2003); *Passagiere und Papiere: Schreibakte auf der Schwelle zwischen Spanien und Amerika* (2006), and *Cultural Techniques: Grids, Filters, Doors, and Other Articulations of the Real* (2015). He is also the coeditor of the journal *Zeitschrift für Medien- und Kulturforschung* and of the yearbook *Archiv für Mediengeschichte*.

CHADWICK T. SMITH teaches in the German Department at New York University. His research focuses on nineteenth- and twentieth-century German literature and contemporary media studies and the points of contact between literature, science, and society, and in particular the channels through which these are mediated in inaction with one another. He has published and presented widely on the media and cultural studies of Vilém Flusser, exile and technology, and the ethics of design. He is also the translator of Sigrid Weigel's *Walter Benjamin: Images, the Creaturely, and the Holy* (2013) and the *The Science of Literature* by Helmut Müller-Sievers (2015).

ELISABETH WEBER received her PhD in philosophy at the Albert-Ludwigs-Universität Freiburg. She teaches German and comparative literature at the University of California, Santa Barbara and is an affiliate professor of religious studies. She is the author of *Verfolgung und Trauma: Zu Emmanuel Levinas' Autrement qu'être ou au-delà de l'essence* (1990). Her recent books include *Speaking about Torture*, coedited with Julie Carlson (2012), and *Living Together: Jacques Derrida's Communities of Violence and Peace* (2013).

SAMUEL WEBER is Avalon Foundation Professor of Humanities at Northwestern University and codirector of its Paris Program in Critical Theory. Together with Shierry Weber Nicholsen, he translated Adorno's *Prisms* (1982) into English. His other publications include *Theatricality as Medium* (2004); *Targets of Opportunity: On the Militarization of Thinking* (2005); and *Benjamin's -abilities* (2008).

GEOFFREY WINTHROP-YOUNG teaches at the University of British Columbia in Vancouver, Canada. Among his recent publications are *Kittler and the Media*, a coedited volume on cultural techniques, and various papers on German media theory and media archaeology.

DOMINIK ZECHNER studied media studies and philosophy in Vienna and New York. After receiving his master's degree for a thesis on Jacques Derrida's *Mal d'archive* in 2013, Dominik joined the doctoral program at the Department of German at New York University on a mission to explore figures of survival and finitude in twentieth-century thought and literature. He also briefly studied at Princeton University and the New School for Social Research; he has been a visiting scholar at the European Graduate School in Saas-Fee, and has held summer fellowships at the universities of Basel, Bern, and Zürich. He has published on Derrida's *Carte postale* and Kafka's *Sorge des Hausvaters*.

INDEX

MEANING SYSTEMS

The Beginning of Heaven and Earth Has No Name: Seven Days with Second-Order Cybernetics. Edited by Albert Müller and Karl H. Müller. Translated by Elinor Rooks and Michael Kasenbacher.
HEINZ VON FOERSTER

Cultural Techniques: Grids, Filters, Doors, and Other Articulations of the Real. Translated by Geoffrey Winthrop-Young.
BERNHARD SIEGERT

Interdependence: Biology and Beyond.
KRITI SHARMA

Earth, Life, and System: Evolution and Ecology on a Gaian Planet.
BRUCE CLARKE (ED.)

Upside-Down Gods and Gregory Bateson's World of Difference.
PETER HARRIES-JONES

The Technological Introject: Friedrich Kittler between Implementation and the Incalcuable.
JEFFREY CHAMPLIN AND ANTJE PFANNKUCHEN (EDS.)

Google Me: One-Click Democracy. Translated by Michael Syrotinski.
BARBARA CASSIN